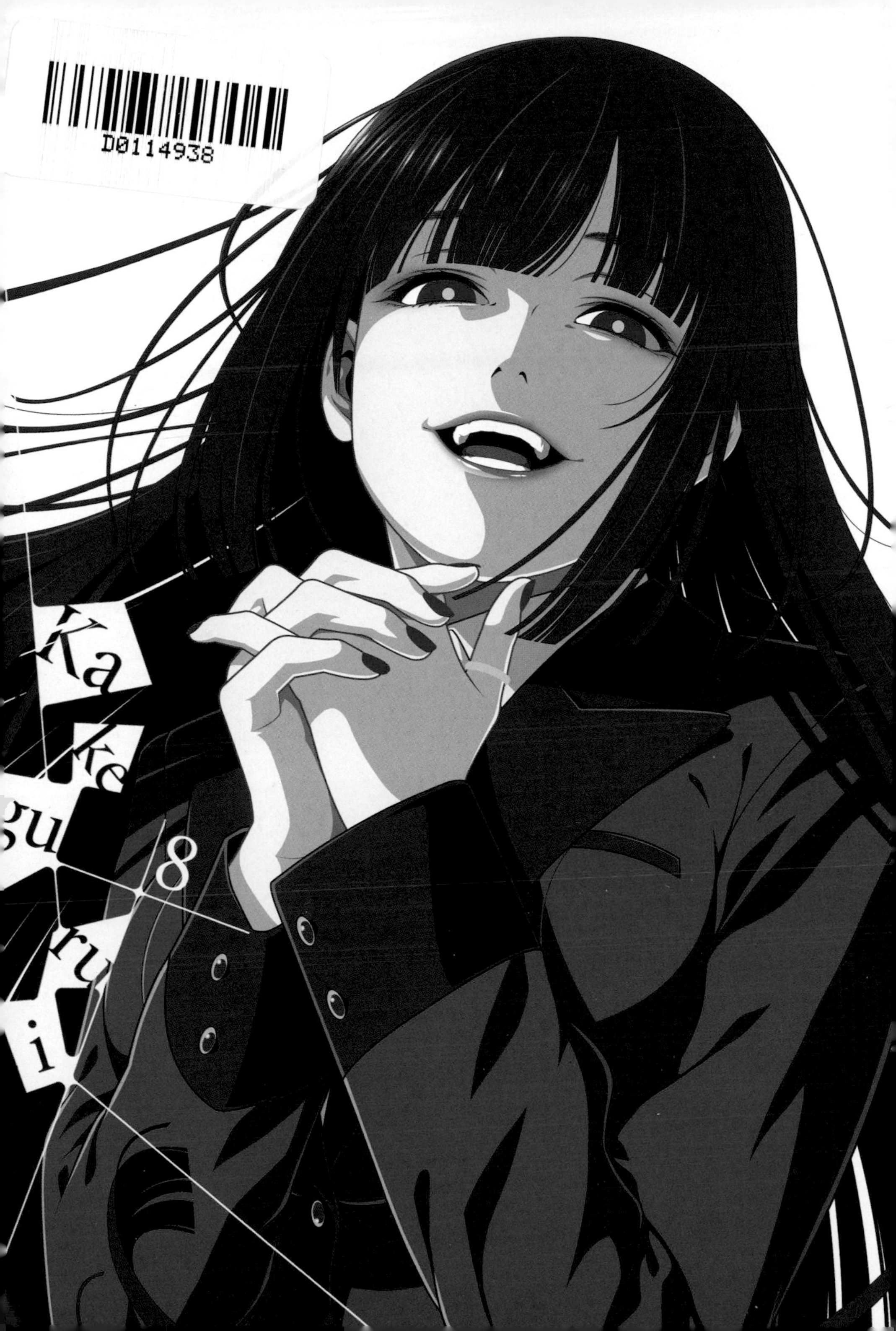
Kakegurui
8

⑧

**K
A
K
E
G
U
R
U
I**

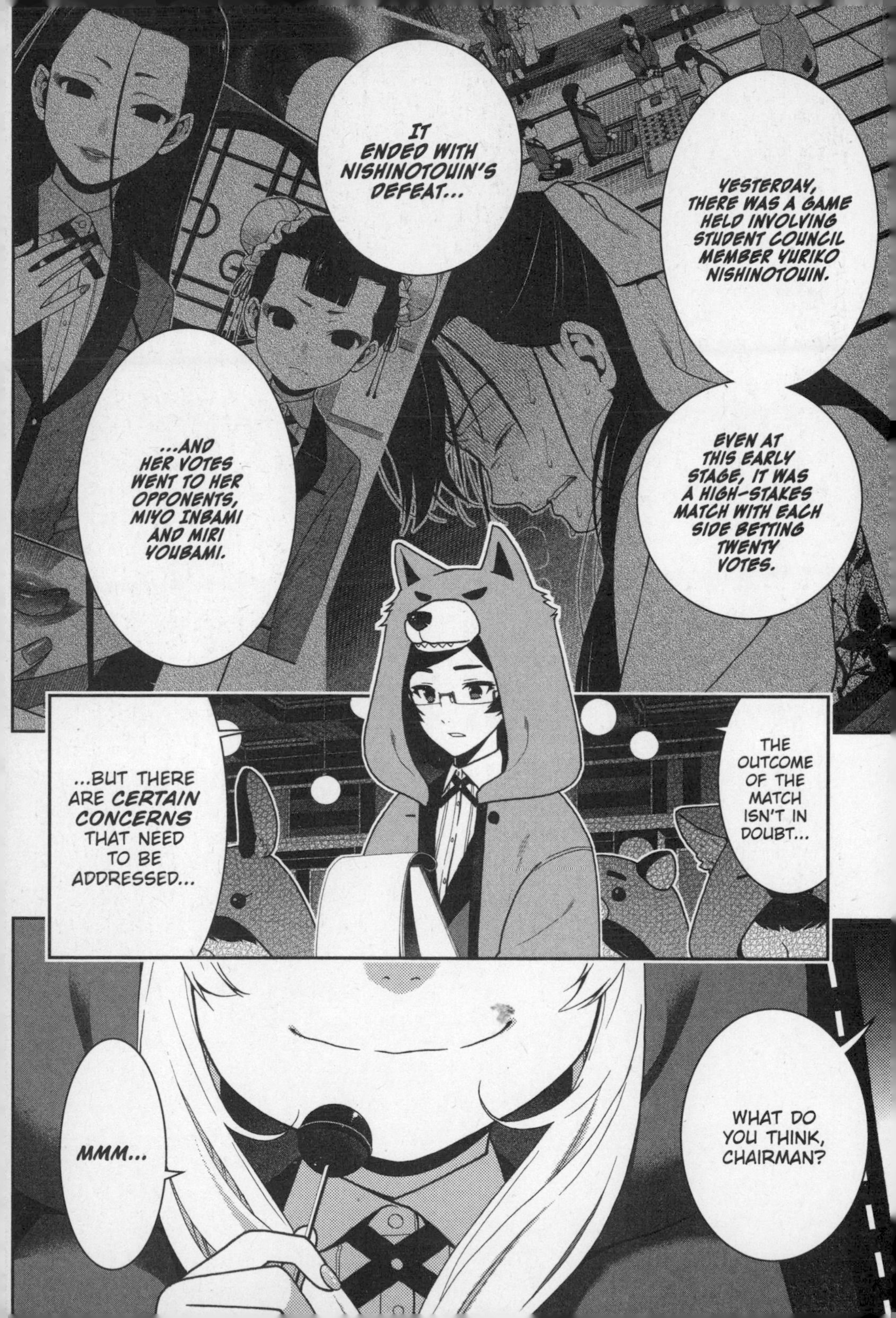
Yesterday, there was a game held involving student council member Yuriko Nishinotouin.
Even at this early stage, it was a high-stakes match with each side betting twenty votes.
It ended with Nishinotouin's defeat...
...and her votes went to her opponents, Miyo Inbami and Miri Youbami.
The outcome of the match isn't in doubt...
...but there are *certain concerns* that need to be addressed...
What do you think, Chairman?
Mmm...

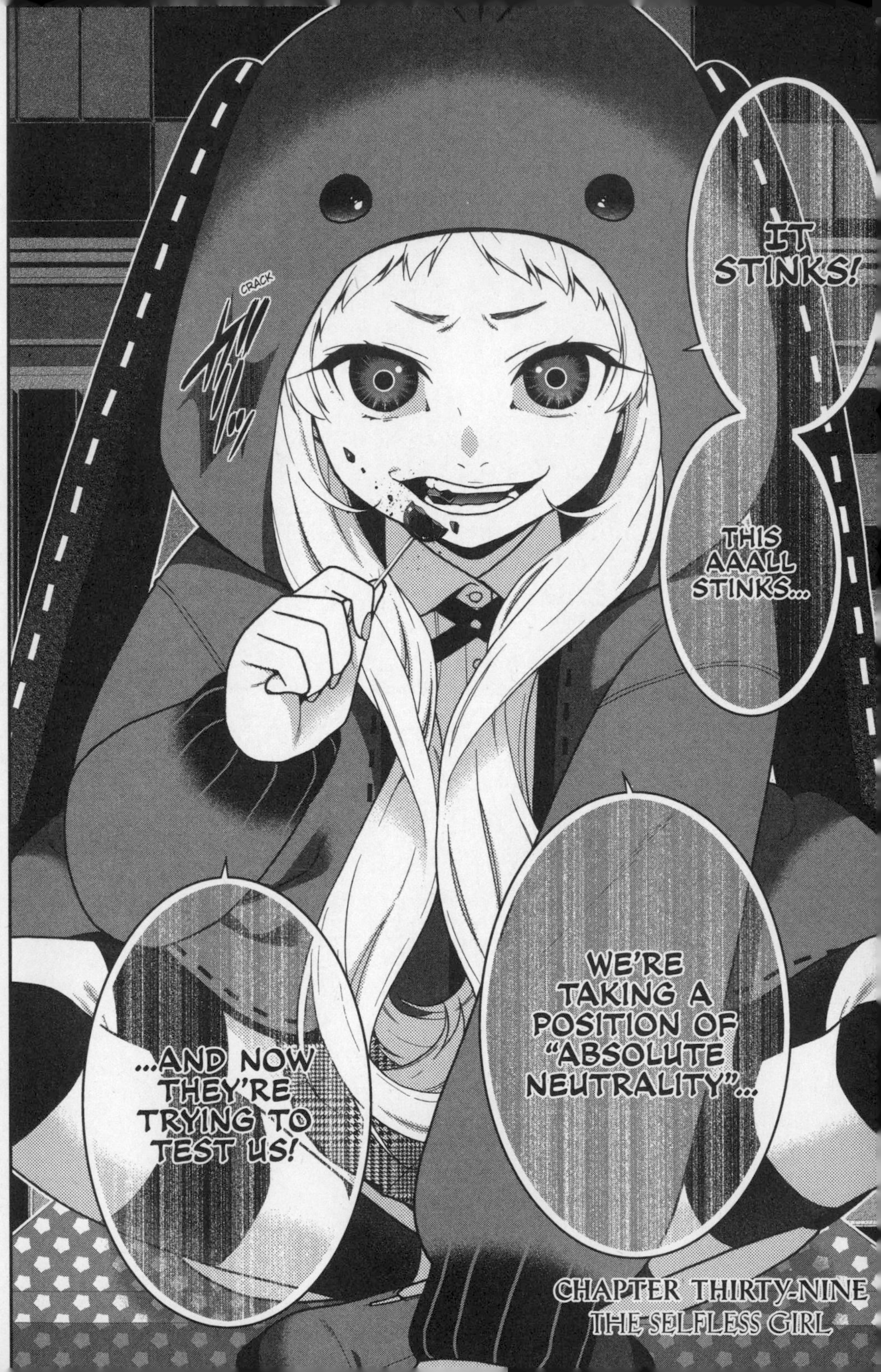
IT STINKS!
THIS AAALL STINKS...
CRACK
WE'RE TAKING A POSITION OF "ABSOLUTE NEUTRALITY"...
...AND NOW THEY'RE TRYING TO TEST US!

CHAPTER THIRTY-NINE
THE SELFLESS GIRL

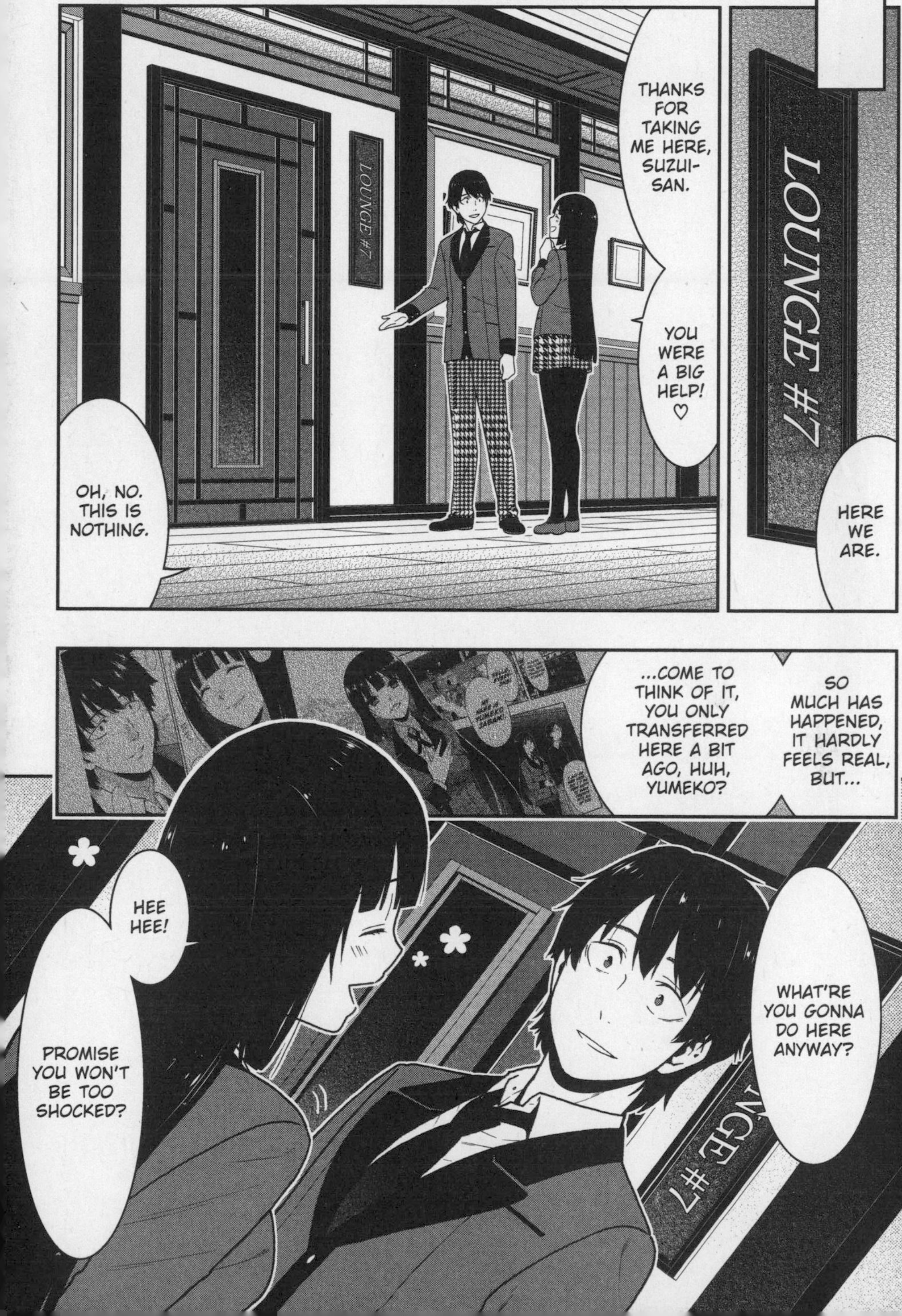
LOUNGE #7
HERE WE ARE.
THANKS FOR TAKING ME HERE, SUZUI-SAN.
YOU WERE A BIG HELP! ♡
LOUNGE #7
OH, NO. THIS IS NOTHING.
SO MUCH HAS HAPPENED, IT HARDLY FEELS REAL, BUT...
...COME TO THINK OF IT, YOU ONLY TRANSFERRED HERE A BIT AGO, HUH, YUMEKO?
WHAT'RE YOU GONNA DO HERE ANYWAY?
HEE HEE!
PROMISE YOU WON'T BE TOO SHOCKED?

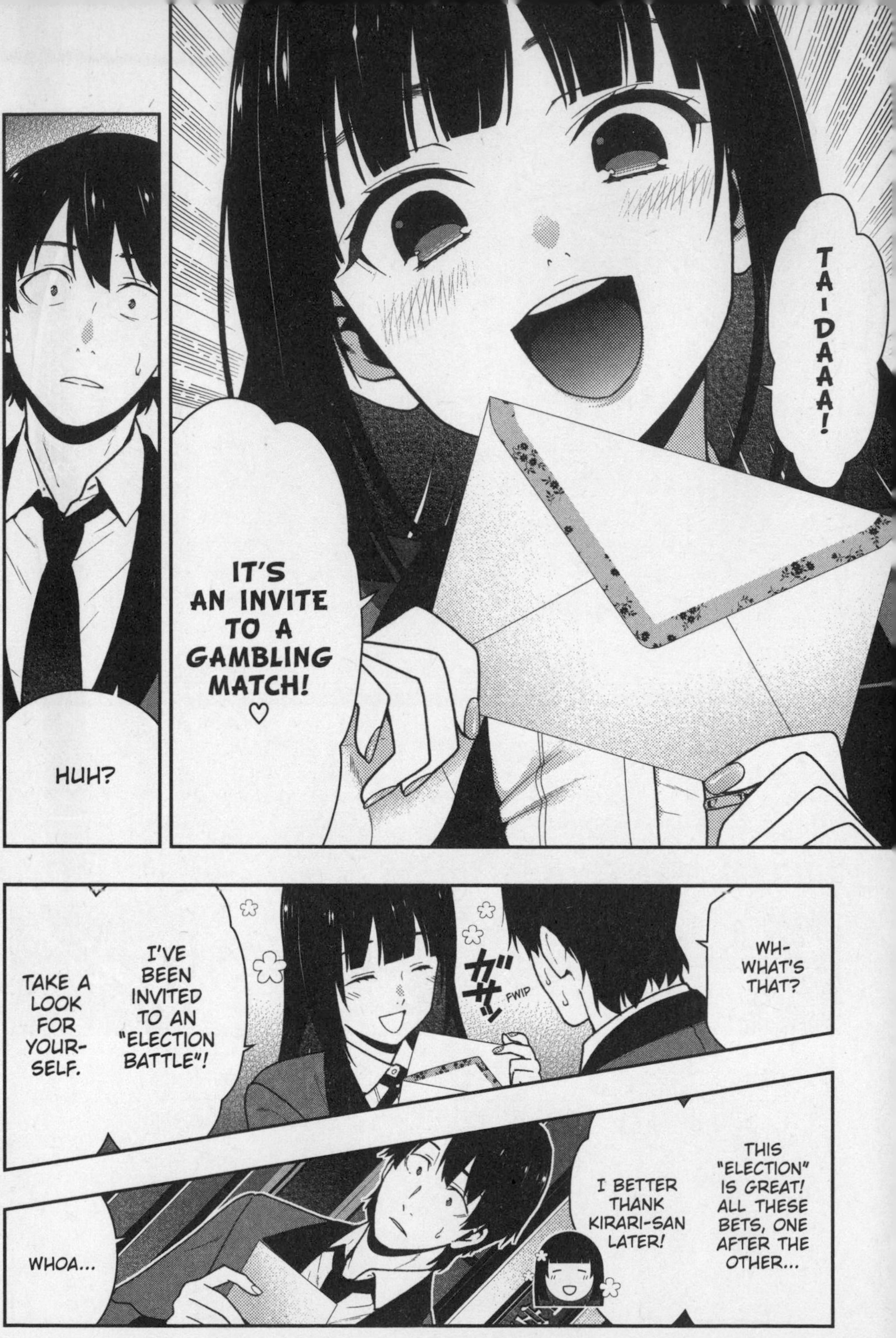
TA-DAAAA!
IT'S AN INVITE TO A GAMBLING MATCH! ♡
HUH?
WH-WHAT'S THAT?
FWIP
I'VE BEEN INVITED TO AN "ELECTION BATTLE"!
TAKE A LOOK FOR YOUR-SELF.
THIS "ELECTION" IS GREAT! ALL THESE BETS, ONE AFTER THE OTHER...
I BETTER THANK KIRARI-SAN LATER!
WHOA...

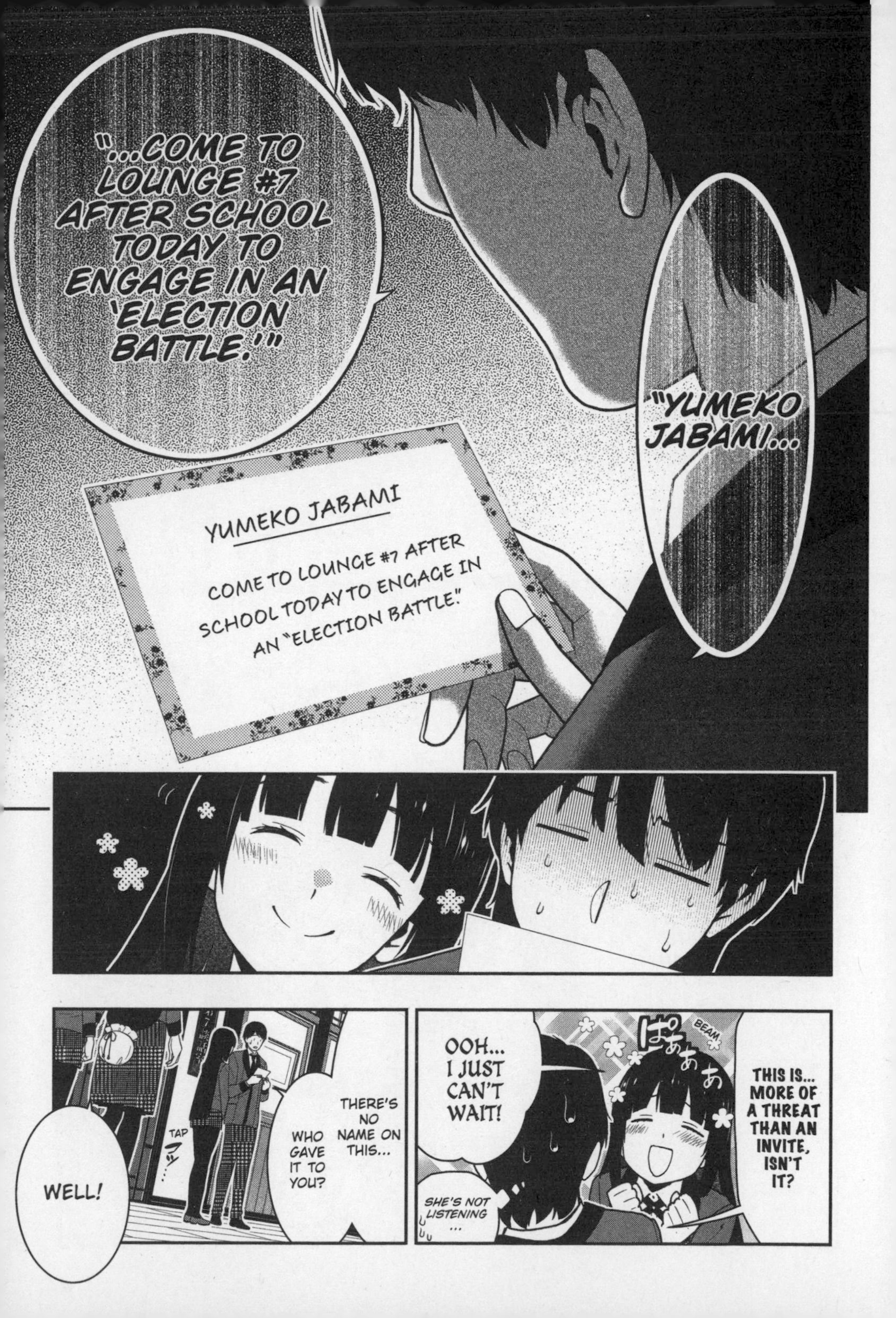
"YUMEKO JABAMI...
"...COME TO LOUNGE #7 AFTER SCHOOL TODAY TO ENGAGE IN AN 'ELECTION BATTLE.'"
YUMEKO JABAMI
COME TO LOUNGE #7 AFTER SCHOOL TODAY TO ENGAGE IN AN "ELECTION BATTLE."
THIS IS... MORE OF A THREAT THAN AN INVITE, ISN'T IT?
ぱあああ
BEAM
OOH... I JUST CAN'T WAIT!
SHE'S NOT LISTENING ...
THERE'S NO NAME ON THIS...
WHO GAVE IT TO YOU?
TAP
WELL!

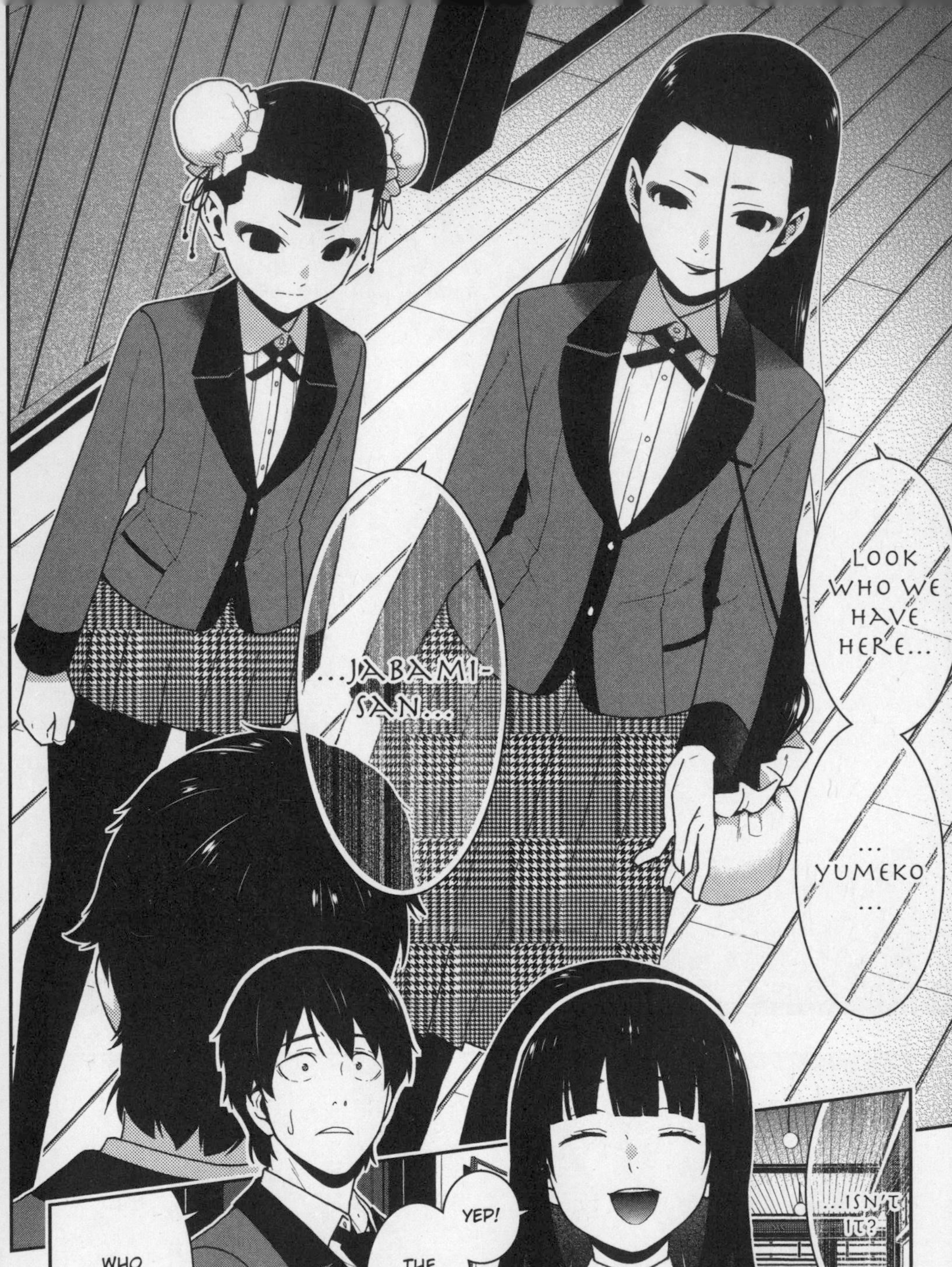
LOOK WHO WE HAVE HERE...
... YUMEKO ...
...JABAMI-SAN...
...ISN'T IT?
YEP!
THE ONE AND ONLY.
WHO ARE YOU GUYS...?

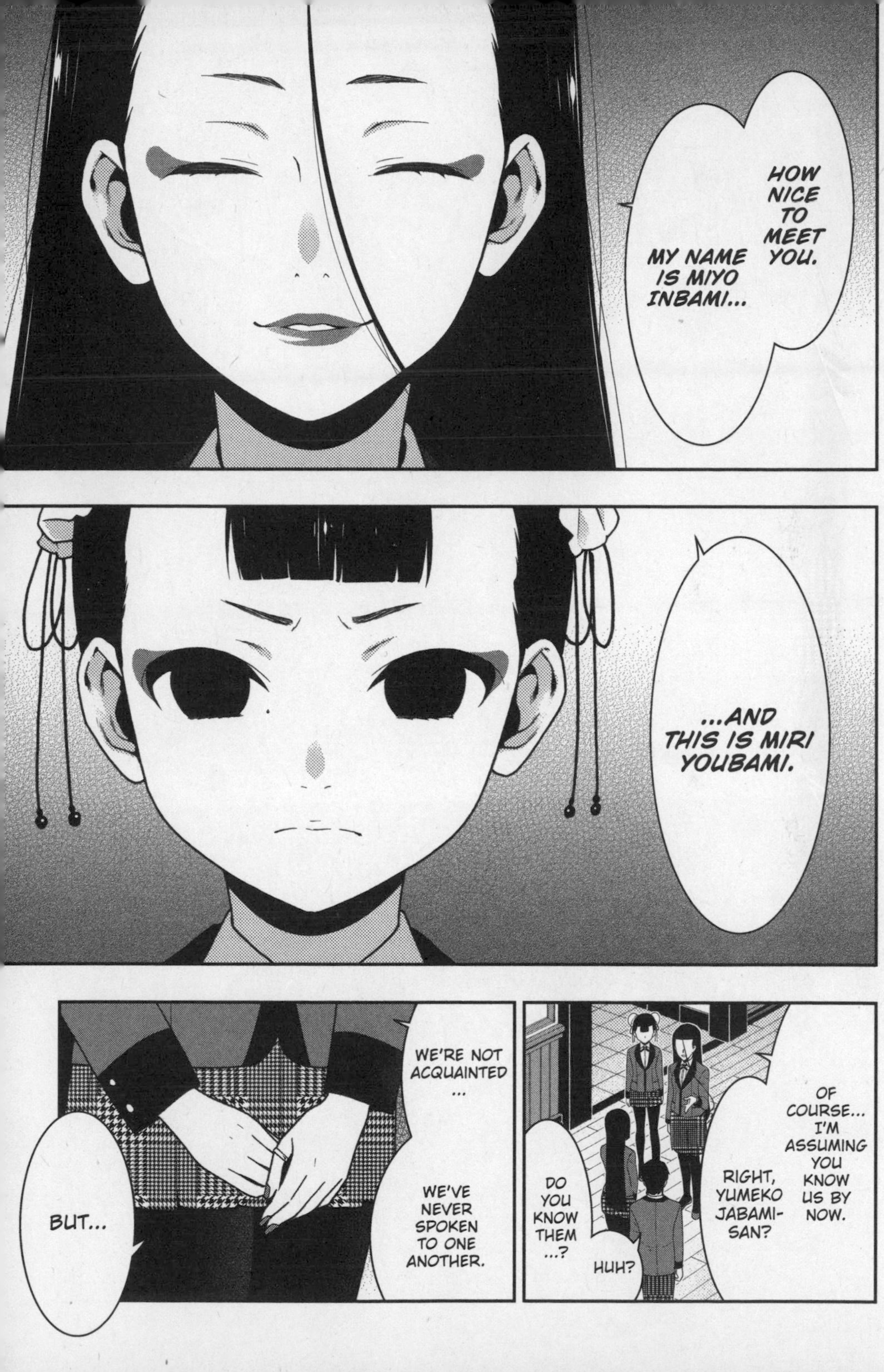
HOW NICE TO MEET YOU.
MY NAME IS MIYO INBAMI...
...AND THIS IS MIRI YOUBAMI.
OF COURSE... I'M ASSUMING YOU KNOW US BY NOW.
RIGHT, YUMEKO JABAMI-SAN?
DO YOU KNOW THEM ...?
HUH?
WE'RE NOT ACQUAINTED ...
WE'VE NEVER SPOKEN TO ONE ANOTHER.
BUT...

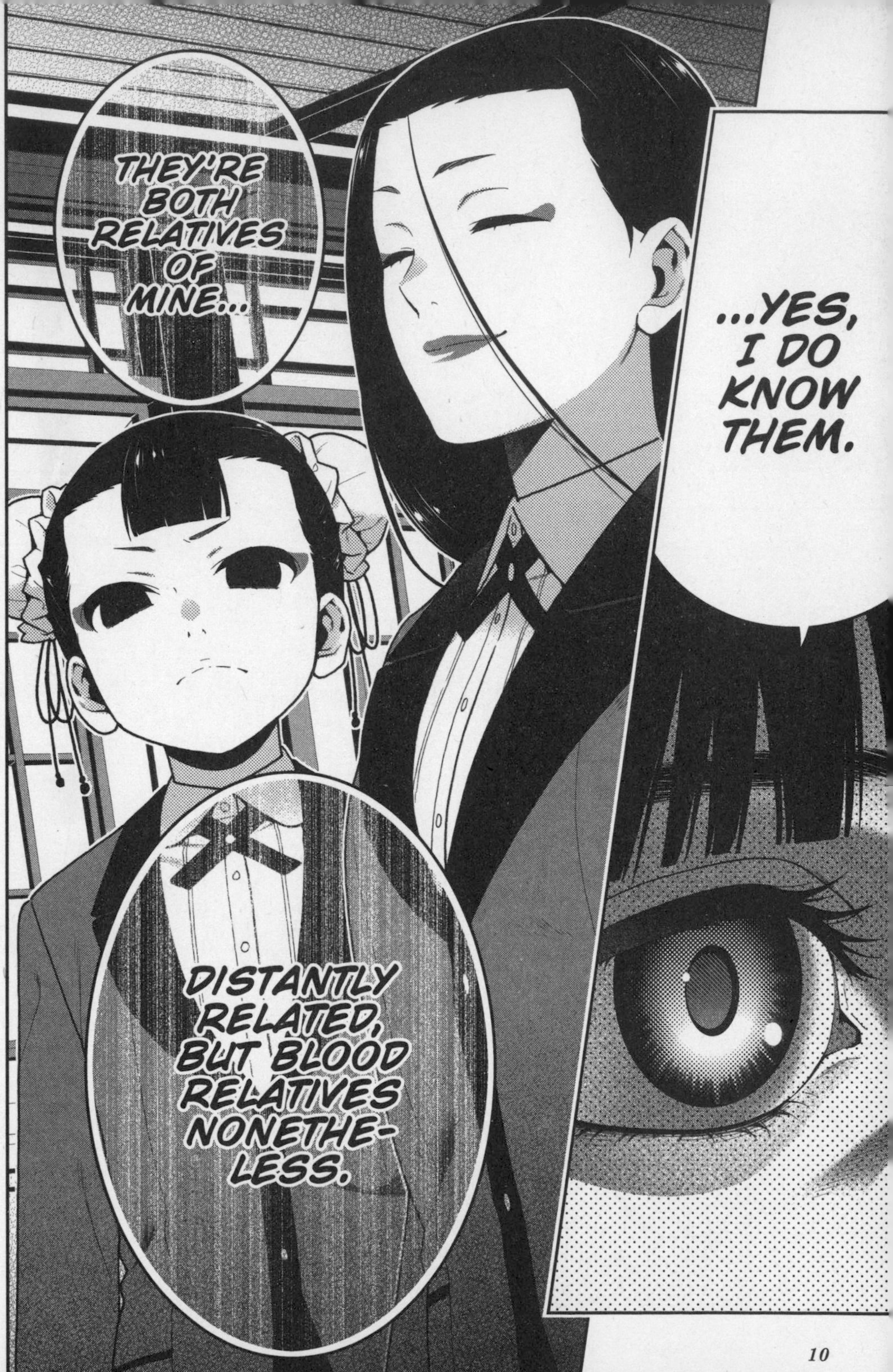
...YES, I DO KNOW THEM.
THEY'RE BOTH RELATIVES OF MINE...
DISTANTLY RELATED, BUT BLOOD RELATIVES NONETHE-LESS.

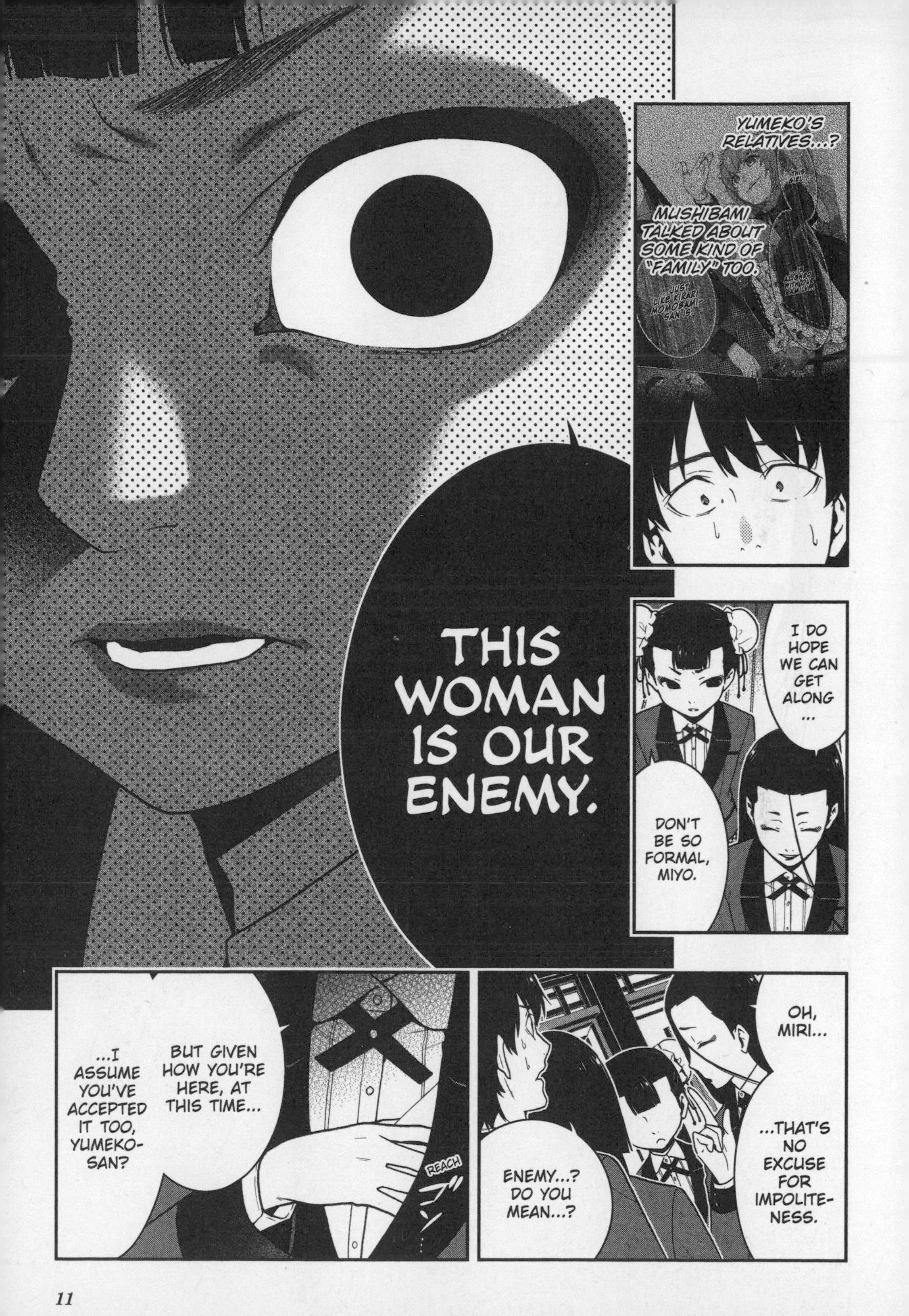
YUMEKO'S RELATIVES...?
THIS GIRL...
...IS ALIGNED WITH OUR FAMILY...
MUSHIBAMI TALKED ABOUT SOME KIND OF "FAMILY" TOO.
...JUST LIKE KIRARI MOMOBAMI-SAN IS.
I DO HOPE WE CAN GET ALONG...
DON'T BE SO FORMAL, MIYO.
THIS WOMAN IS OUR ENEMY.
OH, MIRI...
...THAT'S NO EXCUSE FOR IMPOLITENESS.
ENEMY...? DO YOU MEAN...?
BUT GIVEN HOW YOU'RE HERE, AT THIS TIME...
...I ASSUME YOU'VE ACCEPTED IT TOO, YUMEKO-SAN?
REACH

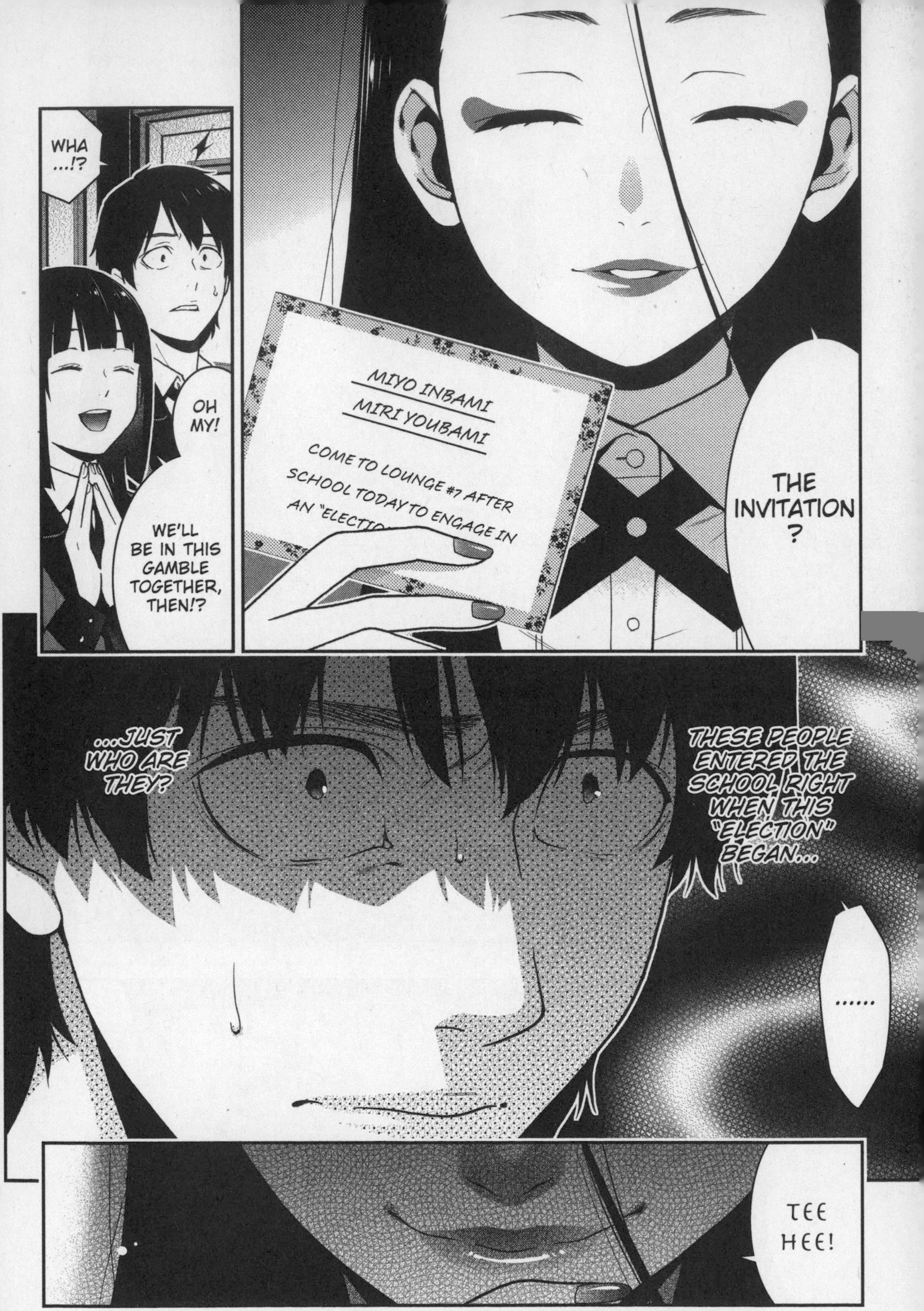
MIYO INBAMI
MIRI YOUBAMI
COME TO LOUNGE #7 AFTER SCHOOL TODAY TO ENGAGE IN
THE INVITATION ?
WHA ...!?
OH MY!
WE'LL BE IN THIS GAMBLE TOGETHER, THEN!?
THESE PEOPLE ENTERED THE SCHOOL RIGHT WHEN THIS "ELECTION" BEGAN...
...JUST WHO ARE THEY?
......
TEE HEE!

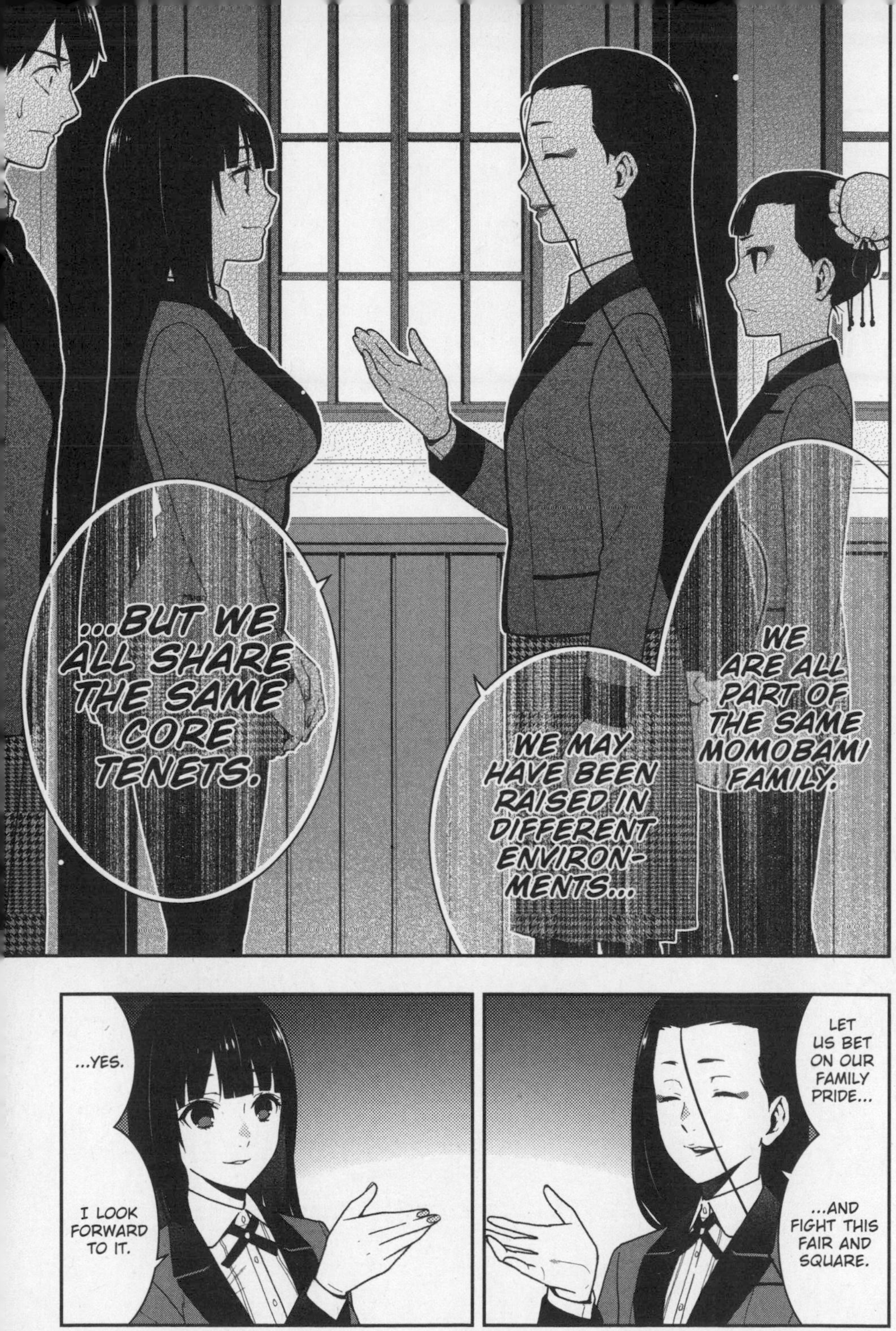
WE ARE ALL PART OF THE SAME MOMOBAMI FAMILY.
WE MAY HAVE BEEN RAISED IN DIFFERENT ENVIRON-MENTS...
...BUT WE ALL SHARE THE SAME CORE TENETS.
LET US BET ON OUR FAMILY PRIDE...
...AND FIGHT THIS FAIR AND SQUARE.
...YES.
I LOOK FORWARD TO IT.

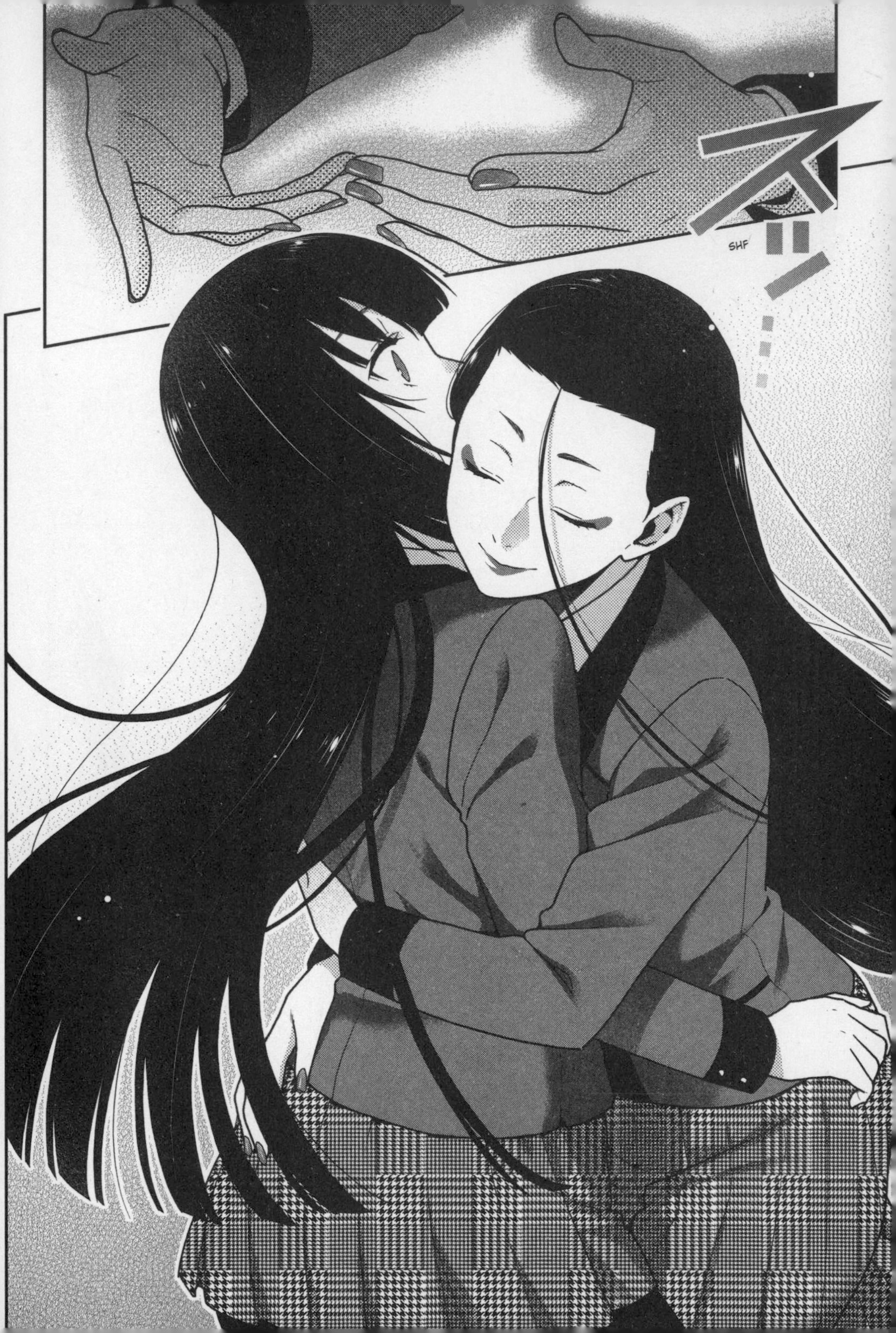
SHF

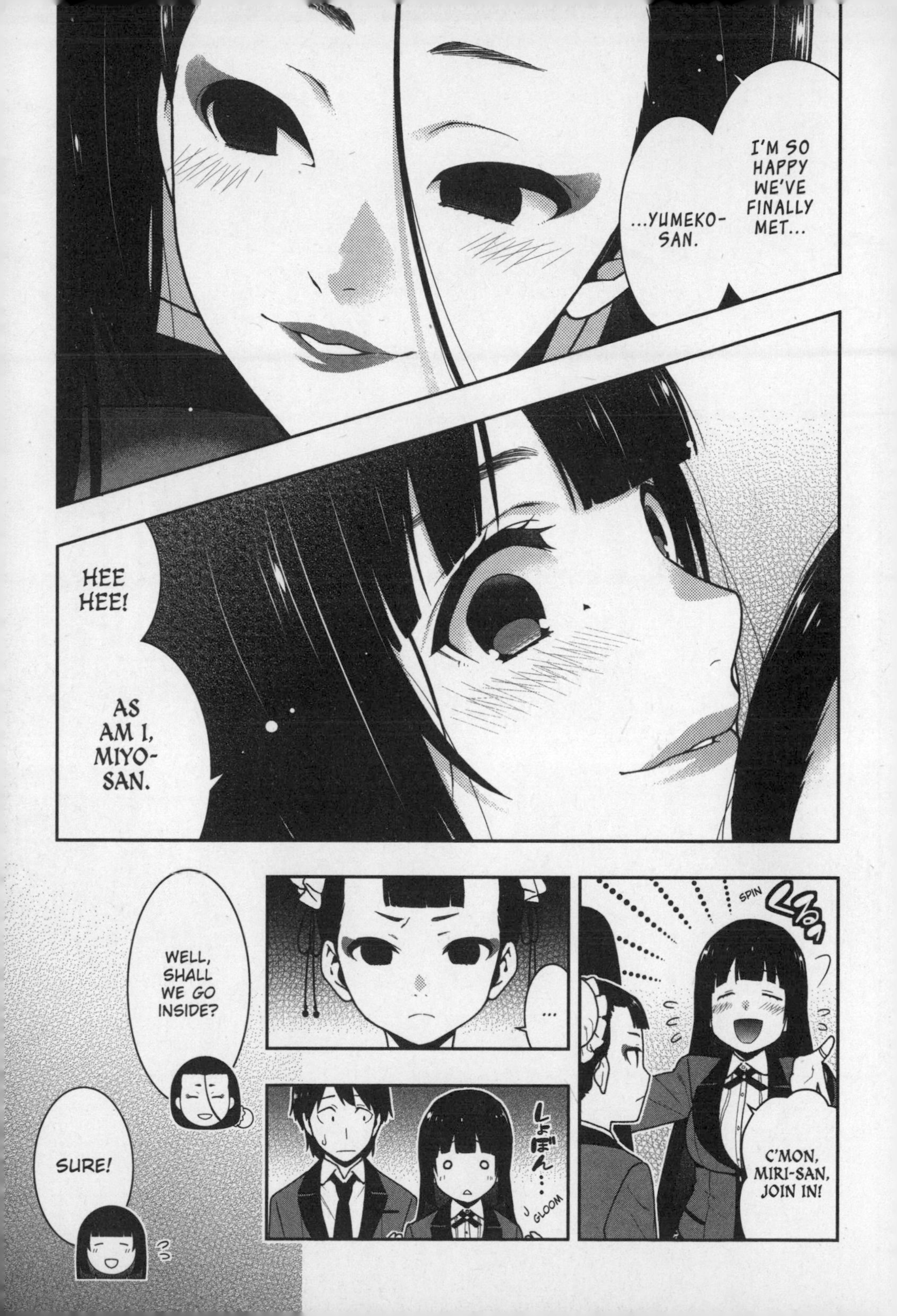
I'M SO HAPPY WE'VE FINALLY MET...
...YUMEKO-SAN.
HEE HEE!
AS AM I, MIYO-SAN.
SPIN
C'MON, MIRI-SAN, JOIN IN!
...
しょぼん…
GLOOM
WELL, SHALL WE GO INSIDE?
SURE!

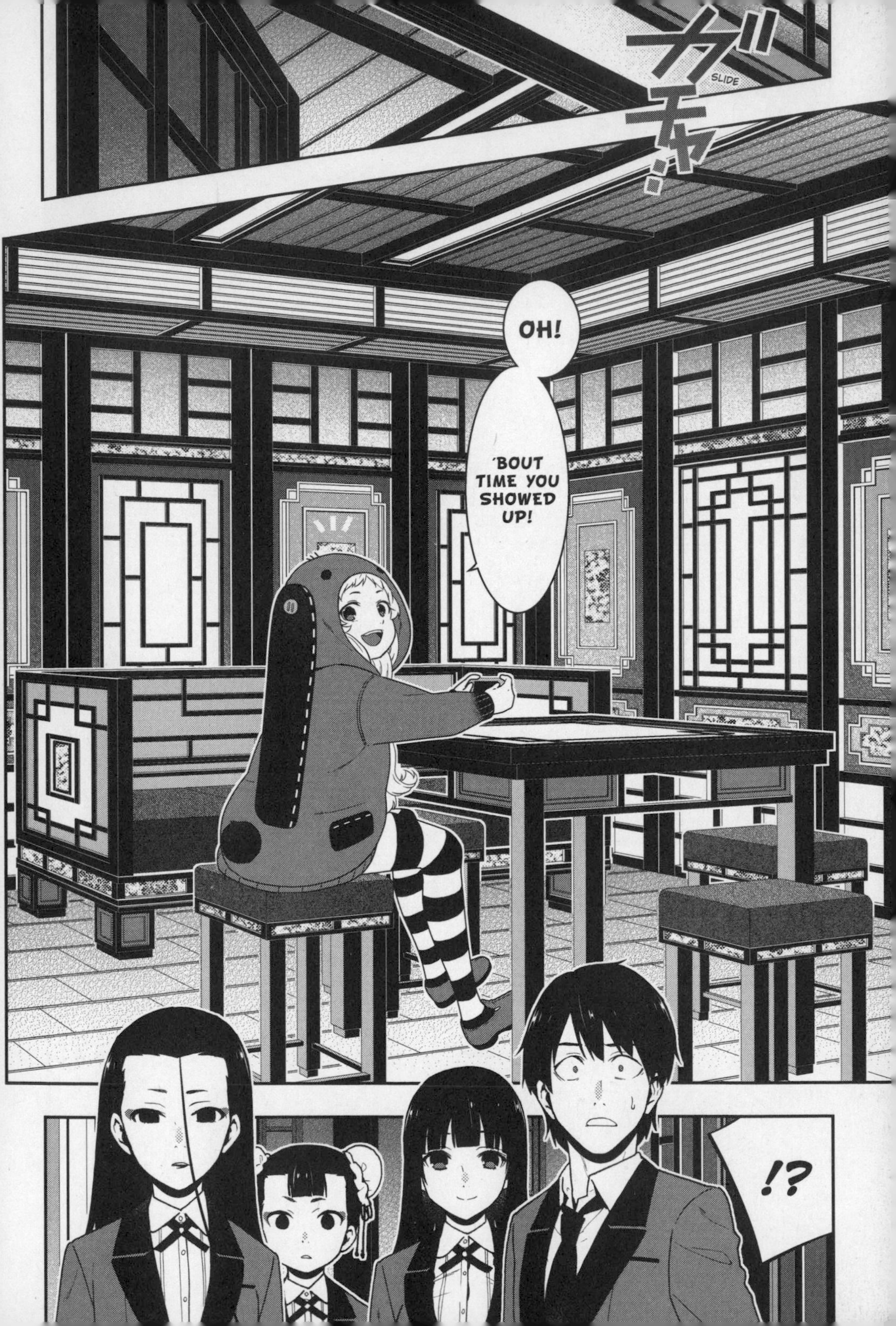
ガチャ
SLIDE
OH!
'BOUT TIME YOU SHOWED UP!
!?

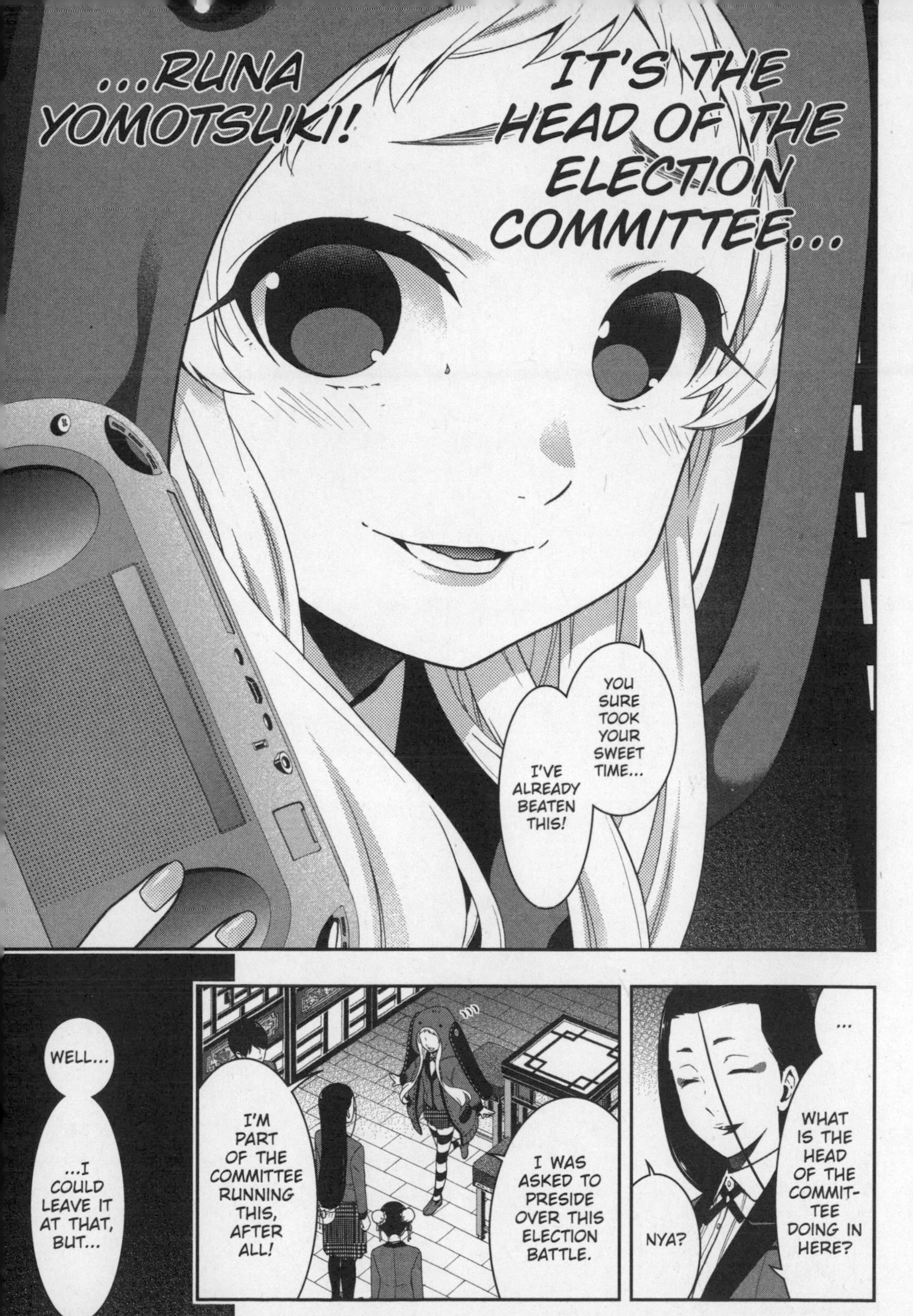
IT'S THE HEAD OF THE ELECTION COMMITTEE...
...RUNA YOMOTSUKI!
YOU SURE TOOK YOUR SWEET TIME...
I'VE ALREADY BEATEN THIS!
...
WHAT IS THE HEAD OF THE COMMIT-TEE DOING IN HERE?
NYA?
I WAS ASKED TO PRESIDE OVER THIS ELECTION BATTLE.
I'M PART OF THE COMMITTEE RUNNING THIS, AFTER ALL!
WELL...
...I COULD LEAVE IT AT THAT, BUT...

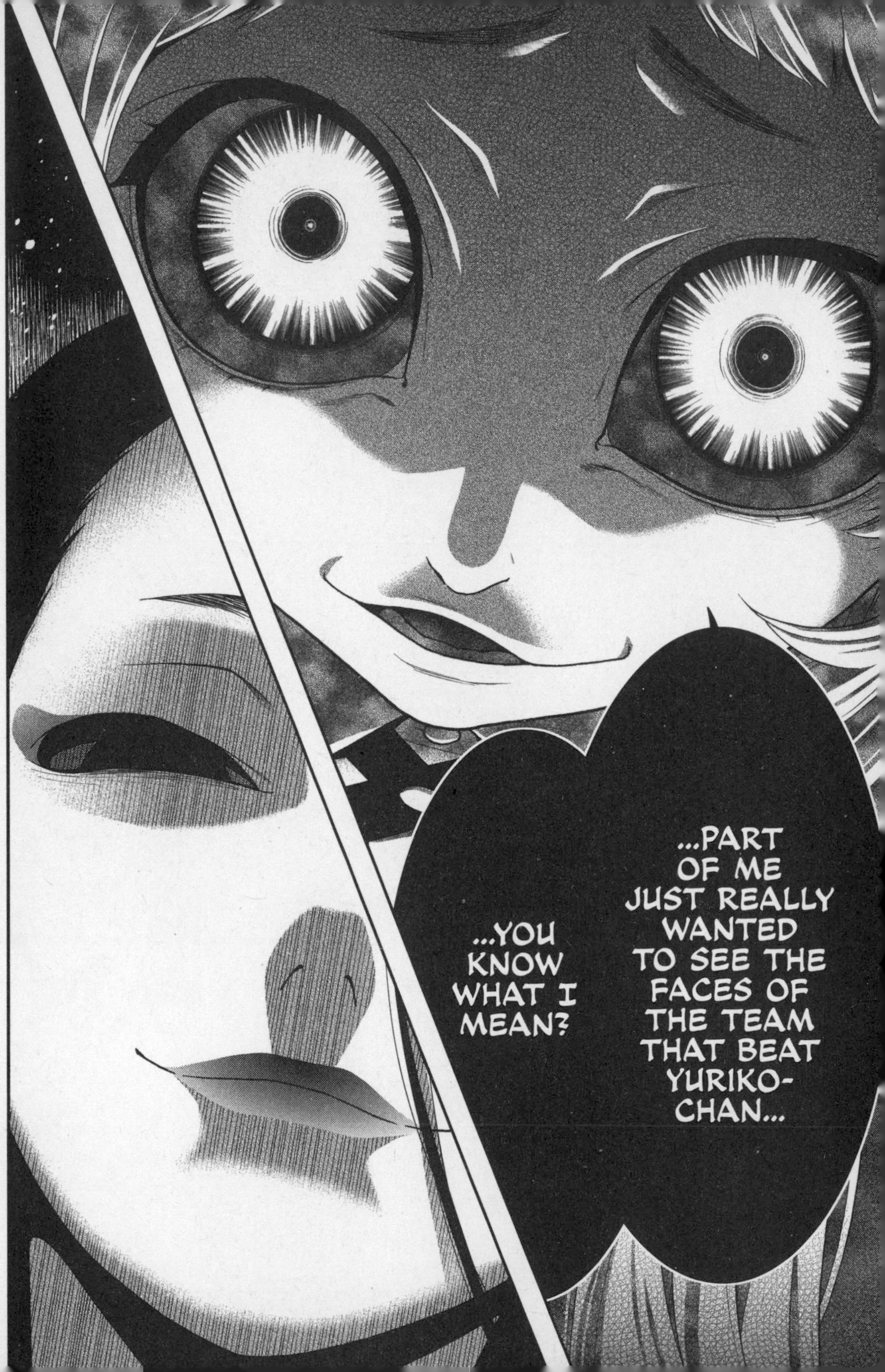
...PART OF ME JUST REALLY WANTED TO SEE THE FACES OF THE TEAM THAT BEAT YURIKO-CHAN...
...YOU KNOW WHAT I MEAN?

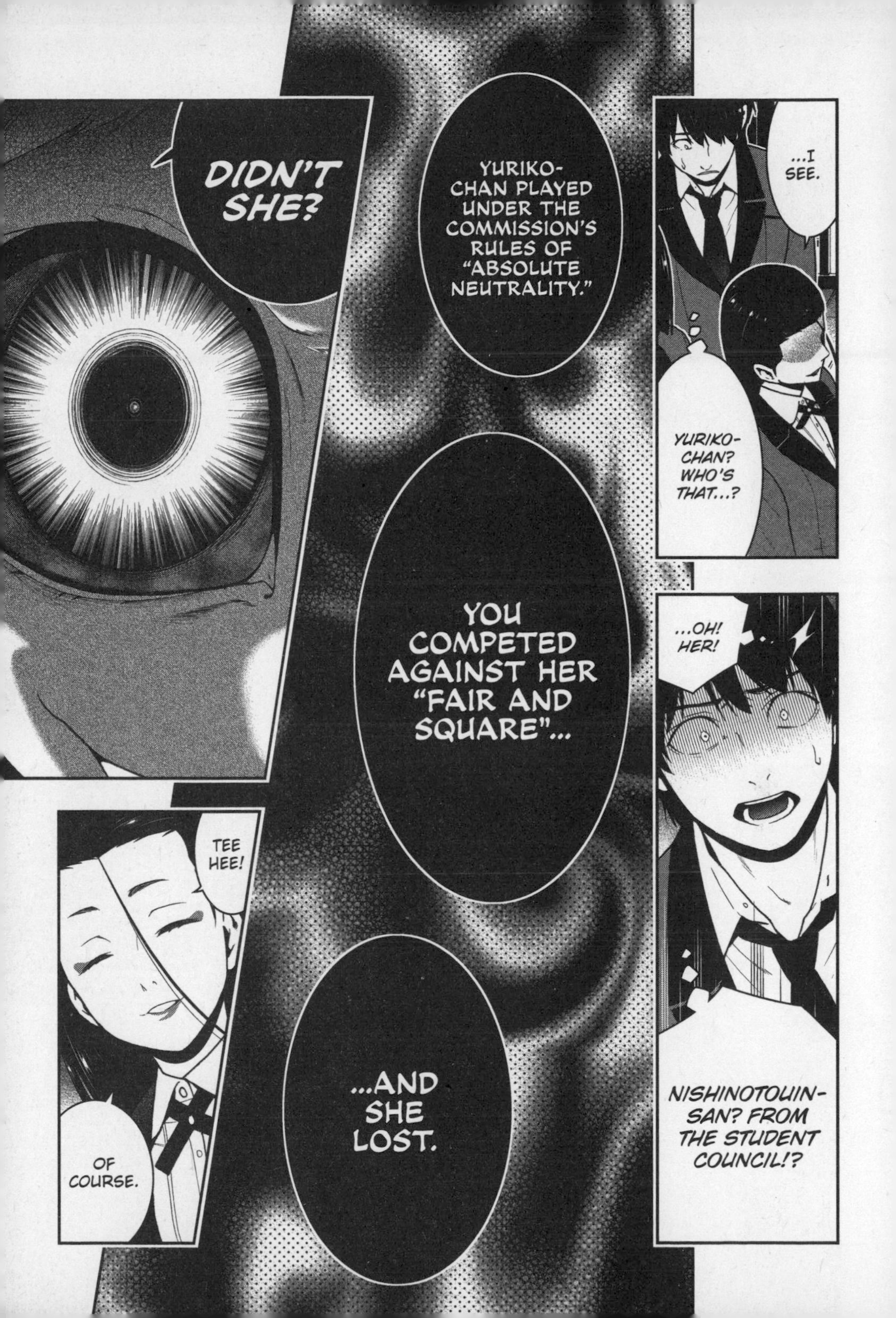

...I SEE.
YURIKO-CHAN? WHO'S THAT...?
...OH! HER!
NISHINOTOUIN-SAN? FROM THE STUDENT COUNCIL!?
YURIKO-CHAN PLAYED UNDER THE COMMISSION'S RULES OF "ABSOLUTE NEUTRALITY."
YOU COMPETED AGAINST HER "FAIR AND SQUARE"...
...AND SHE LOST.
DIDN'T SHE?
TEE HEE!
OF COURSE.

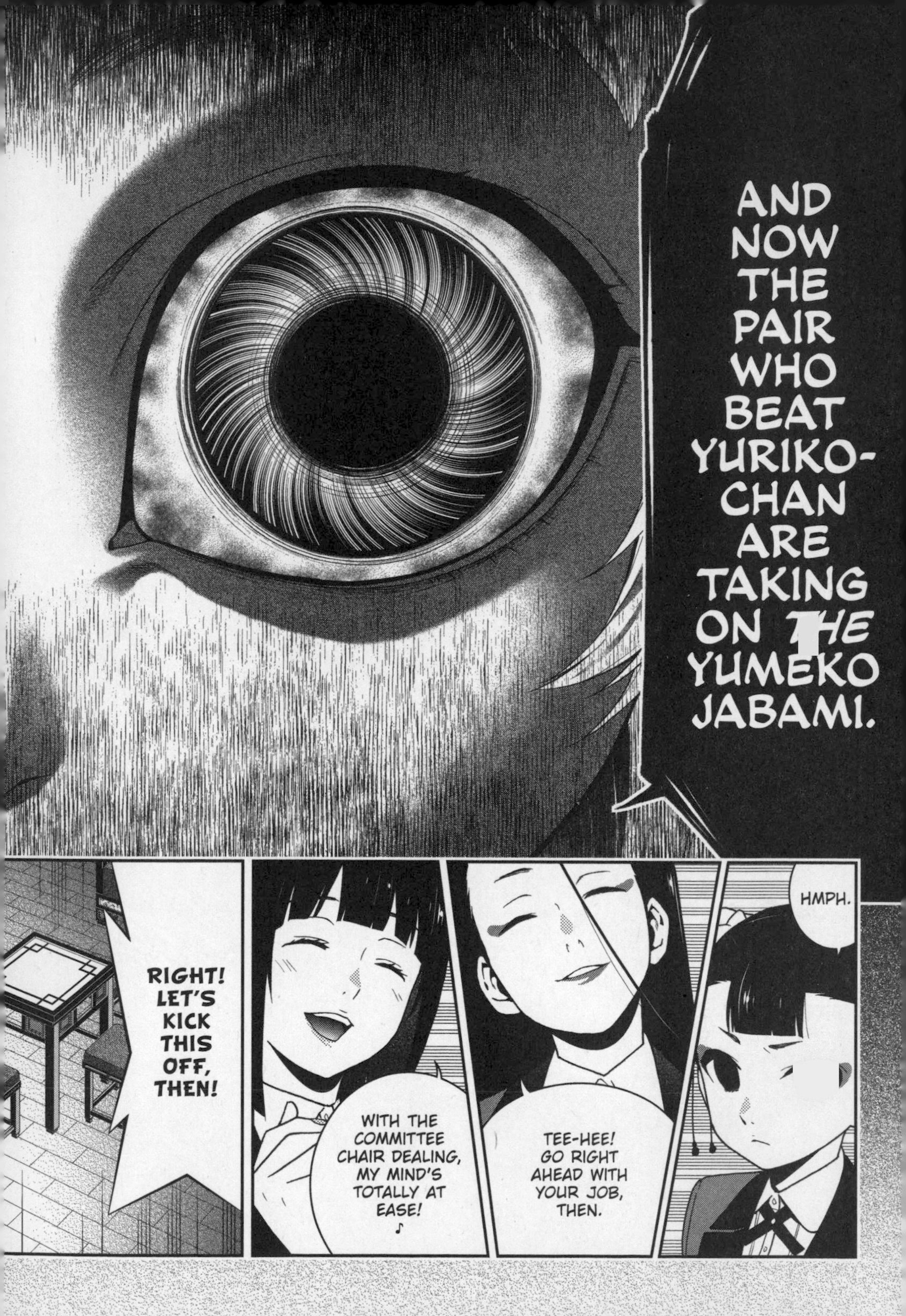
AND NOW THE PAIR WHO BEAT YURIKO-CHAN ARE TAKING ON THE YUMEKO JABAMI.
HMPH.
TEE-HEE! GO RIGHT AHEAD WITH YOUR JOB, THEN.
WITH THE COMMITTEE CHAIR DEALING, MY MIND'S TOTALLY AT EASE! ♪
RIGHT! LET'S KICK THIS OFF, THEN!

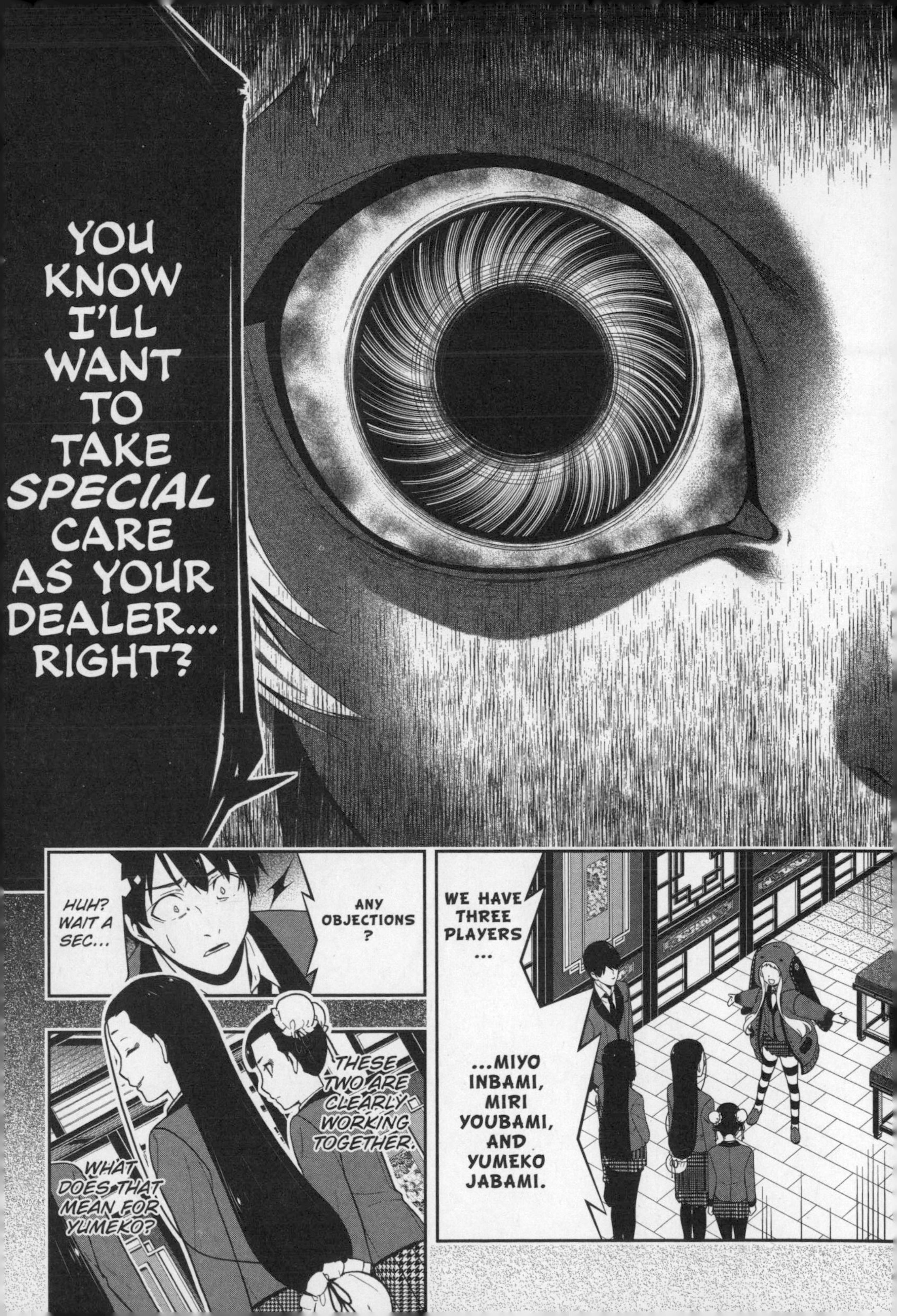
YOU KNOW I'LL WANT TO TAKE SPECIAL CARE AS YOUR DEALER... RIGHT?
WE HAVE THREE PLAYERS...
...MIYO INBAMI, MIRI YOUBAMI, AND YUMEKO JABAMI.
ANY OBJECTIONS?
HUH? WAIT A SEC...
THESE TWO ARE CLEARLY WORKING TOGETHER.
WHAT DOES THAT MEAN FOR YUMEKO?

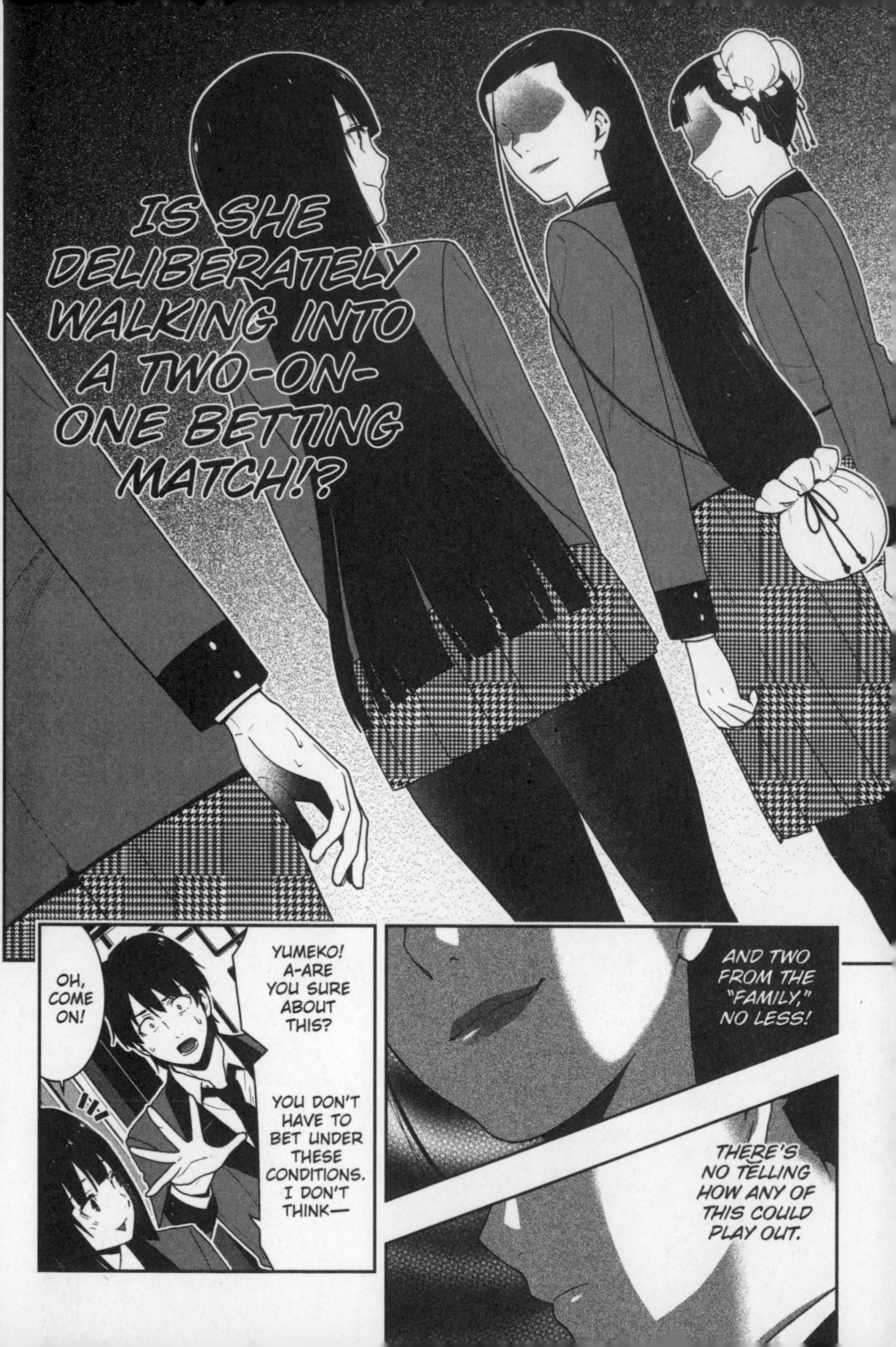
IS SHE DELIBERATELY WALKING INTO A TWO-ON-ONE BETTING MATCH!?
AND TWO FROM THE "FAMILY," NO LESS!
THERE'S NO TELLING HOW ANY OF THIS COULD PLAY OUT.
YUMEKO! A-ARE YOU SURE ABOUT THIS?
YOU DON'T HAVE TO BET UNDER THESE CONDITIONS. I DON'T THINK—
OH, COME ON!

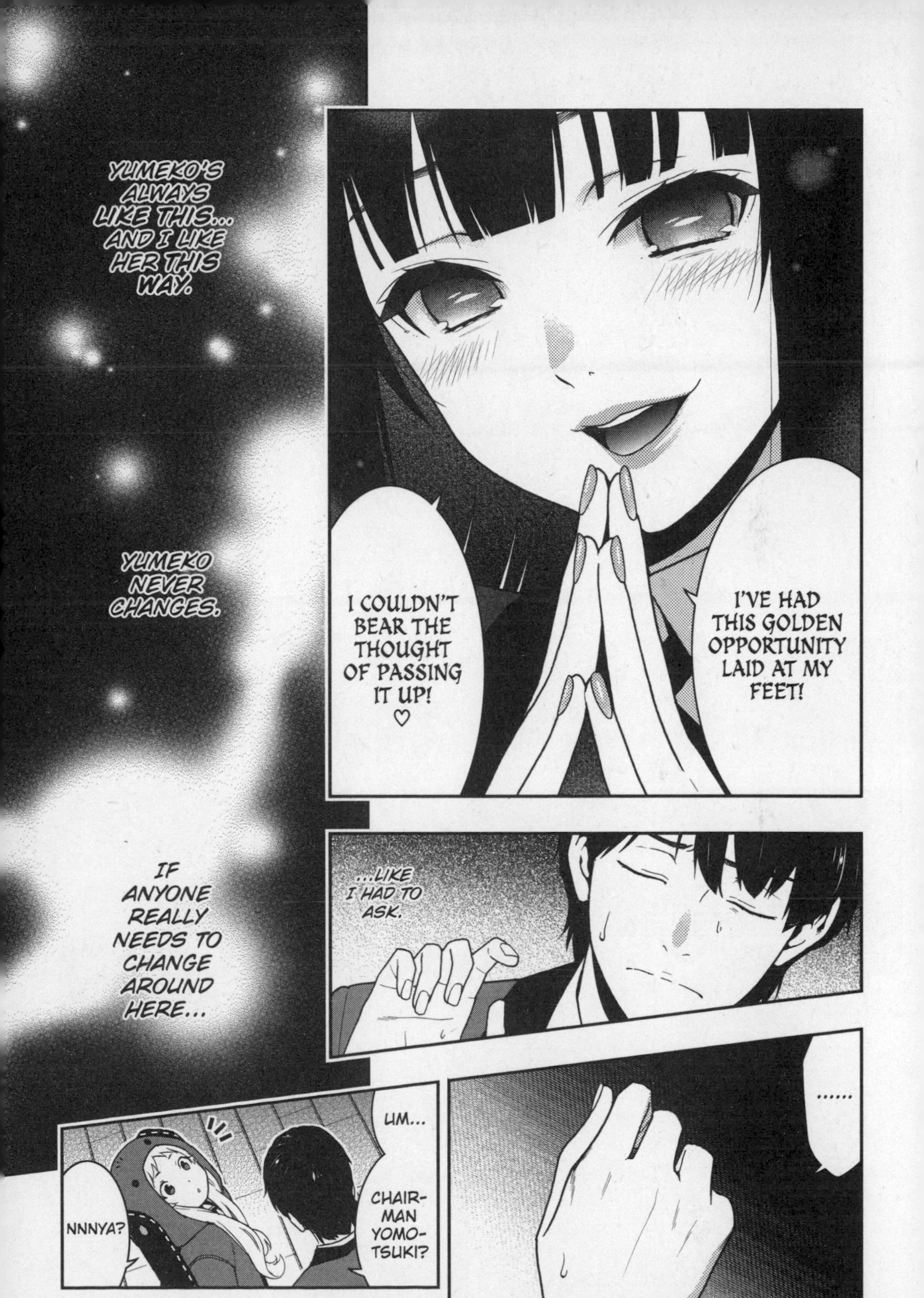
I'VE HAD THIS GOLDEN OPPORTUNITY LAID AT MY FEET!
I COULDN'T BEAR THE THOUGHT OF PASSING IT UP! ♡
...LIKE I HAD TO ASK.
YUMEKO'S ALWAYS LIKE THIS... AND I LIKE HER THIS WAY.
YUMEKO NEVER CHANGES.
IF ANYONE REALLY NEEDS TO CHANGE AROUND HERE...
......
UM...
CHAIRMAN YOMOTSUKI?
NNNYA?

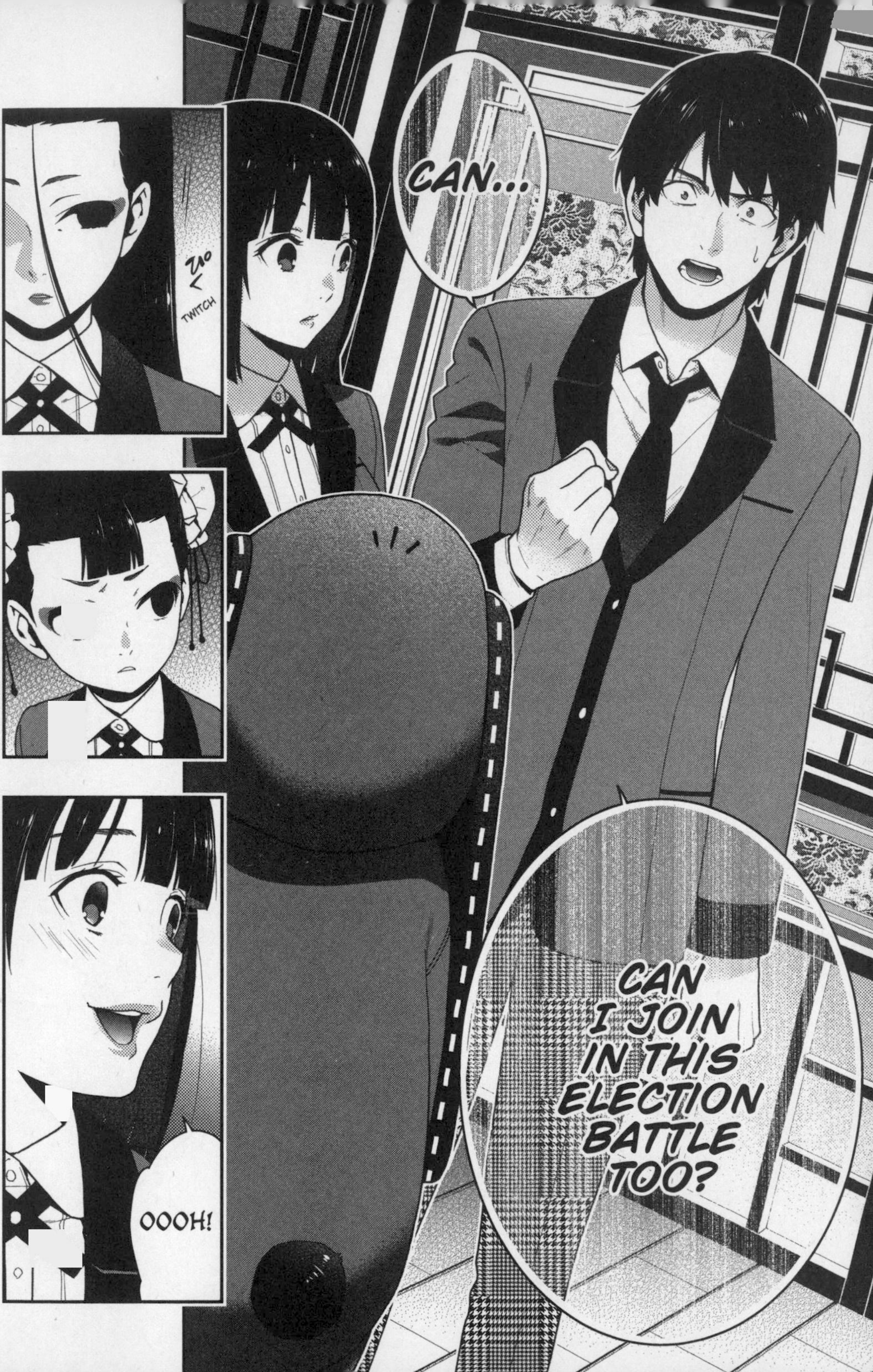
CAN...
CAN I JOIN IN THIS ELECTION BATTLE TOO?
TWITCH
OOOH!

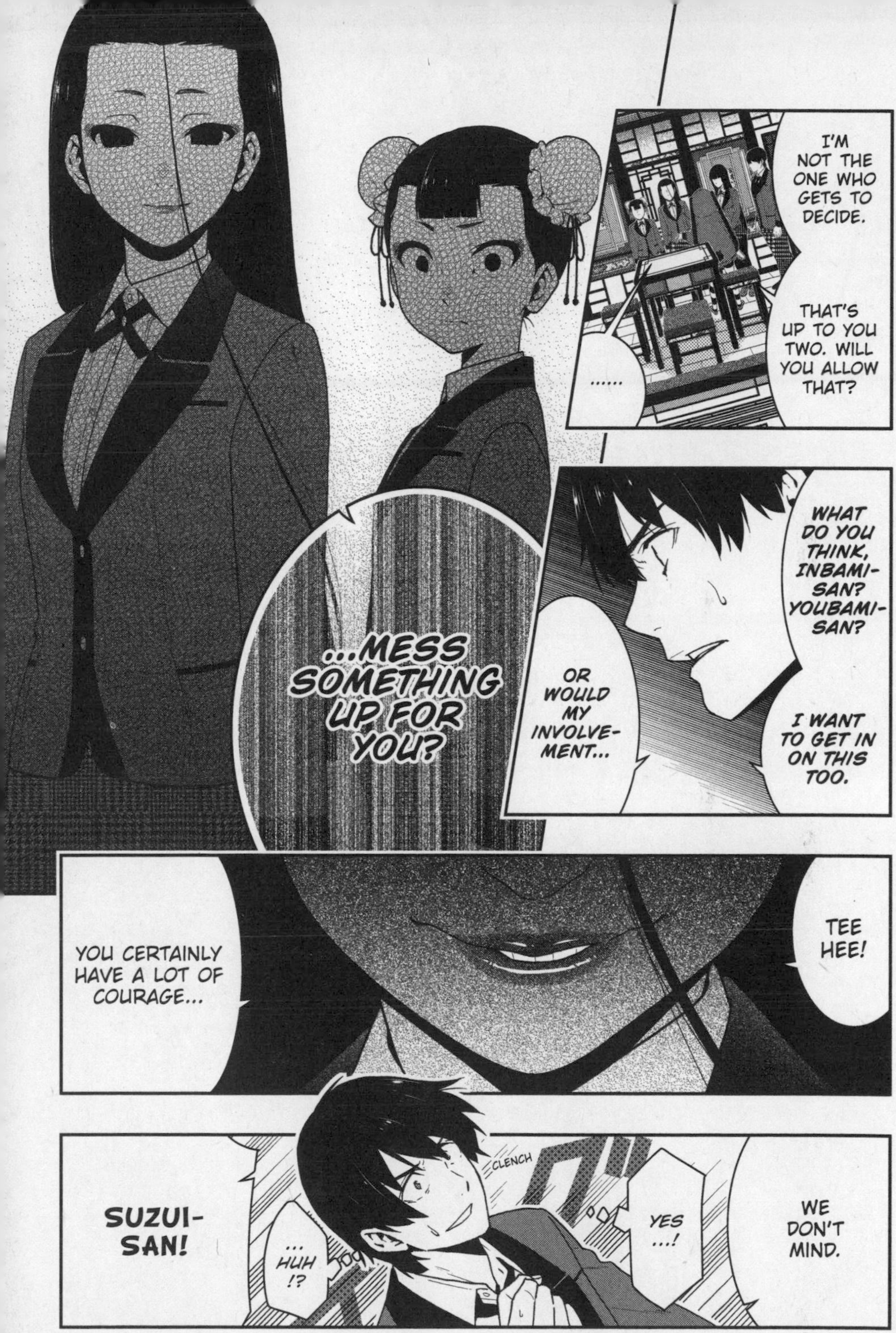
I'M NOT THE ONE WHO GETS TO DECIDE.
THAT'S UP TO YOU TWO. WILL YOU ALLOW THAT?
......
WHAT DO YOU THINK, INBAMI-SAN? YOUBAMI-SAN?
I WANT TO GET IN ON THIS TOO.
OR WOULD MY INVOLVEMENT...
...MESS SOMETHING UP FOR YOU?
TEE HEE!
YOU CERTAINLY HAVE A LOT OF COURAGE...
WE DON'T MIND.
YES ...!
CLENCH
... HUH !?
SUZUI-SAN!

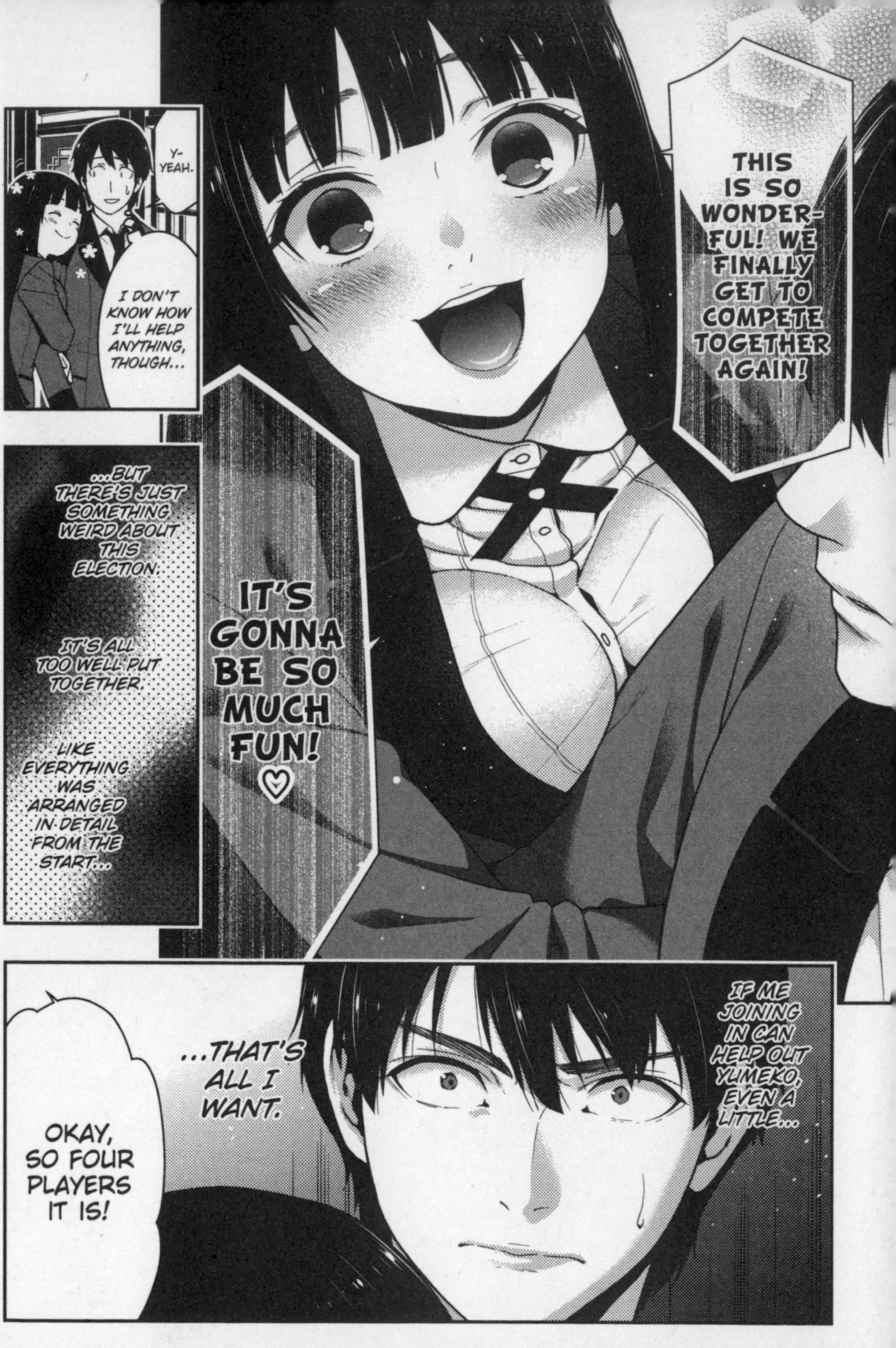
THIS IS SO WONDERFUL! WE FINALLY GET TO COMPETE TOGETHER AGAIN!
IT'S GONNA BE SO MUCH FUN! ♡
Y-YEAH.
I DON'T KNOW HOW I'LL HELP ANYTHING, THOUGH...
...BUT THERE'S JUST SOMETHING WEIRD ABOUT THIS ELECTION.
IT'S ALL TOO WELL PUT TOGETHER.
LIKE EVERYTHING WAS ARRANGED IN DETAIL FROM THE START...
IF ME JOINING IN CAN HELP OUT YUMEKO, EVEN A LITTLE...
...THAT'S ALL I WANT.
OKAY, SO FOUR PLAYERS IT IS!

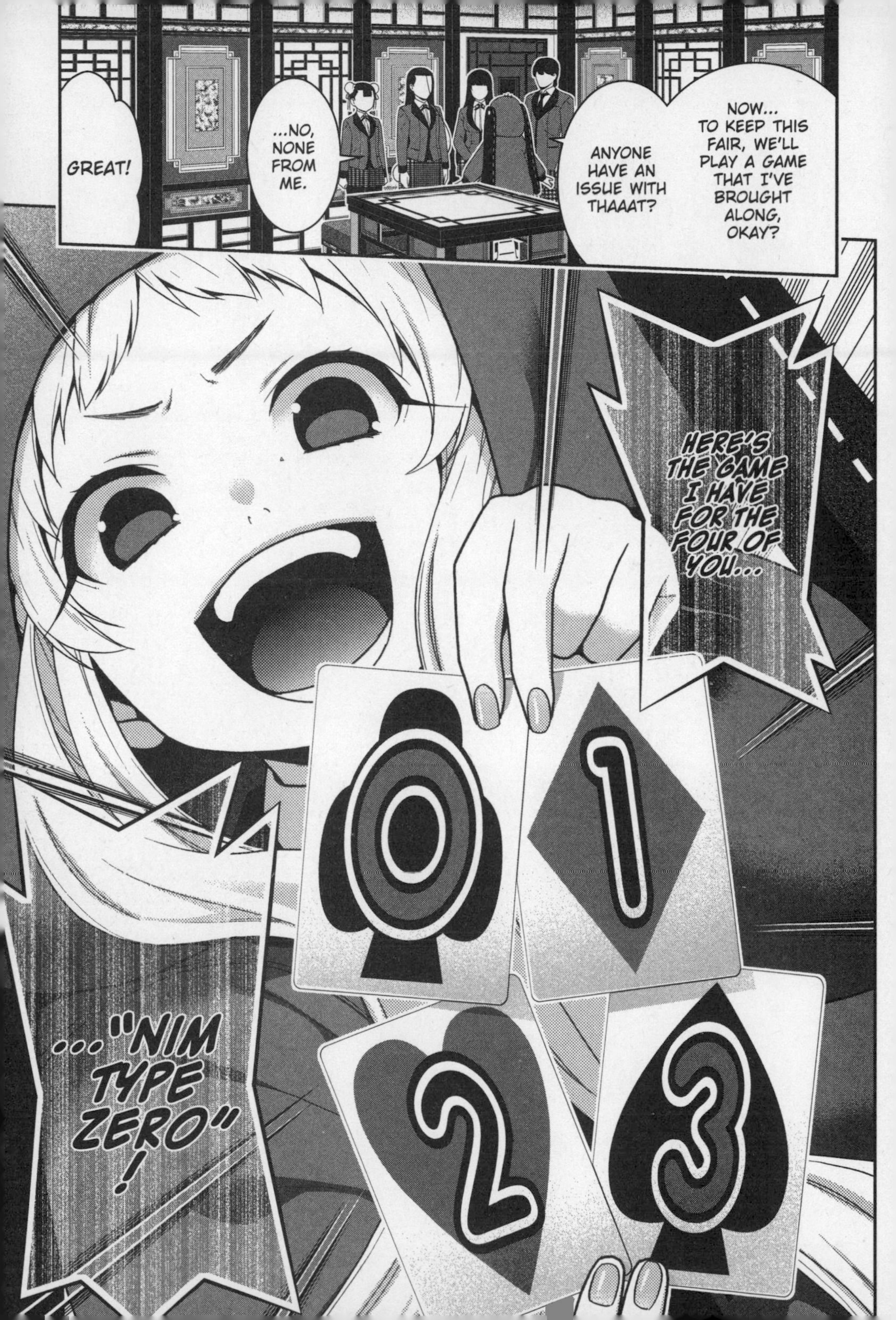
NOW... TO KEEP THIS FAIR, WE'LL PLAY A GAME THAT I'VE BROUGHT ALONG, OKAY?
ANYONE HAVE AN ISSUE WITH THAAAT?
...NO, NONE FROM ME.
GREAT!
HERE'S THE GAME I HAVE FOR THE FOUR OF YOU...
..."NIM TYPE ZERO"!

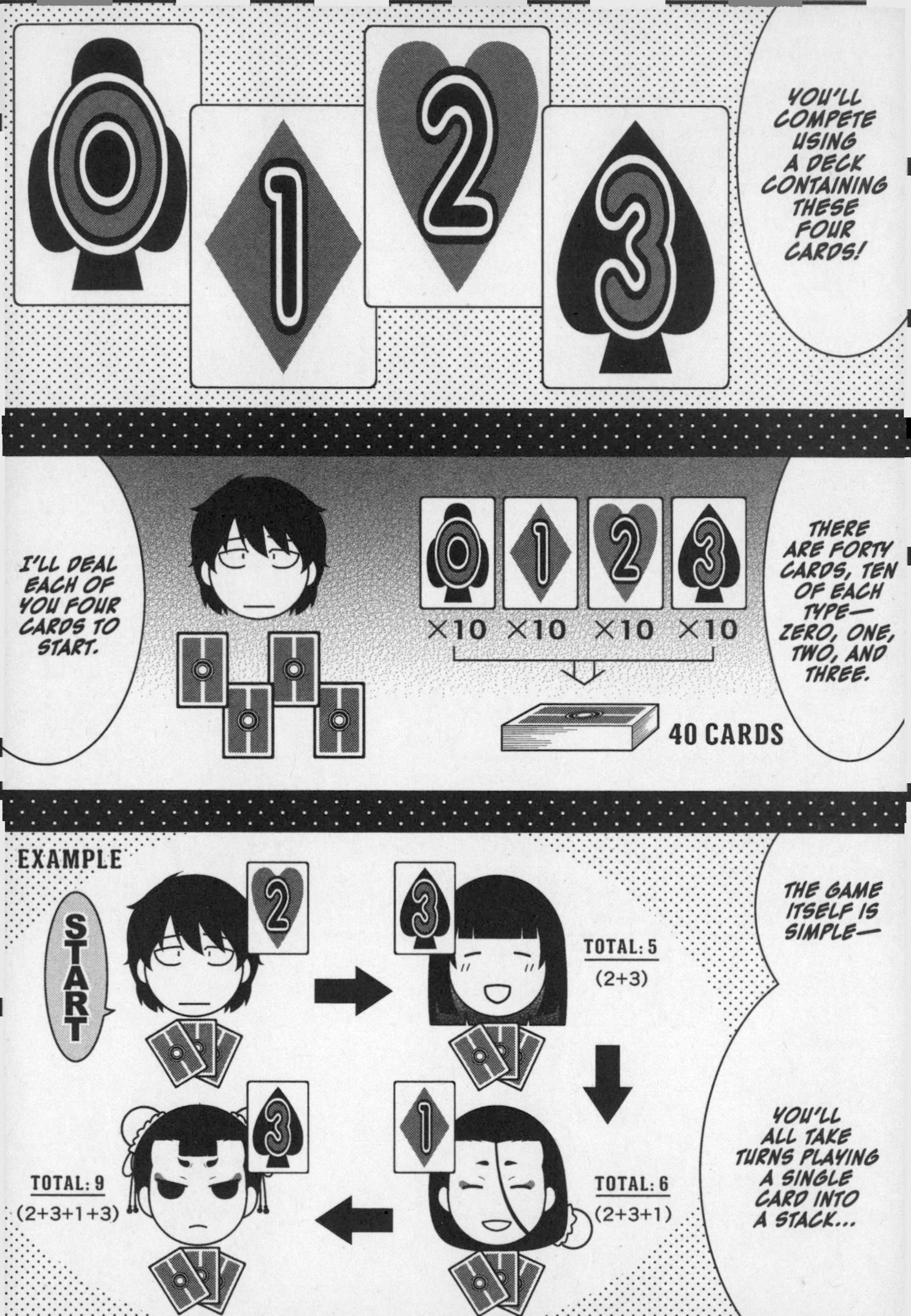

YOU'LL COMPETE USING A DECK CONTAINING THESE FOUR CARDS!
0
1
2
3
THERE ARE FORTY CARDS, TEN OF EACH TYPE—ZERO, ONE, TWO, AND THREE.
×10 ×10 ×10 ×10
40 CARDS
I'LL DEAL EACH OF YOU FOUR CARDS TO START.
THE GAME ITSELF IS SIMPLE—
YOU'LL ALL TAKE TURNS PLAYING A SINGLE CARD INTO A STACK...
EXAMPLE
START
TOTAL: 5
(2+3)
TOTAL: 6
(2+3+1)
TOTAL: 9
(2+3+1+3)

TOTAL: 11
(2+3+1+3+2)

LOSE

IF YOU PLAY A CARD THAT BRINGS THE STACK'S TOTAL VALUE OVER NINE, YOU'RE OUT.

WE'LL PLAY A TOTAL OF THREE ROUNDS.

THAT'S THE GIST OF IT. SIMPLE, RIGHT?

BET	...BET MONEY
CALL	...MATCH A PREVIOUS BET
RAISE	...BET ADDITIONAL MONEY
FOLD	...EXIT THE HAND

THAT WAY, YOU'RE FREE TO LEAVE A HAND IF YOUR CARDS SUCK, OR TRY AND BLUFF YOUR OPPONENTS INTO FOLDING!

...SO WE'LL ALSO PLACE BETS, LIKE IN POKER.

THAT ALONE WOULD MAKE IT A TOTAL GAME OF CHANCE...

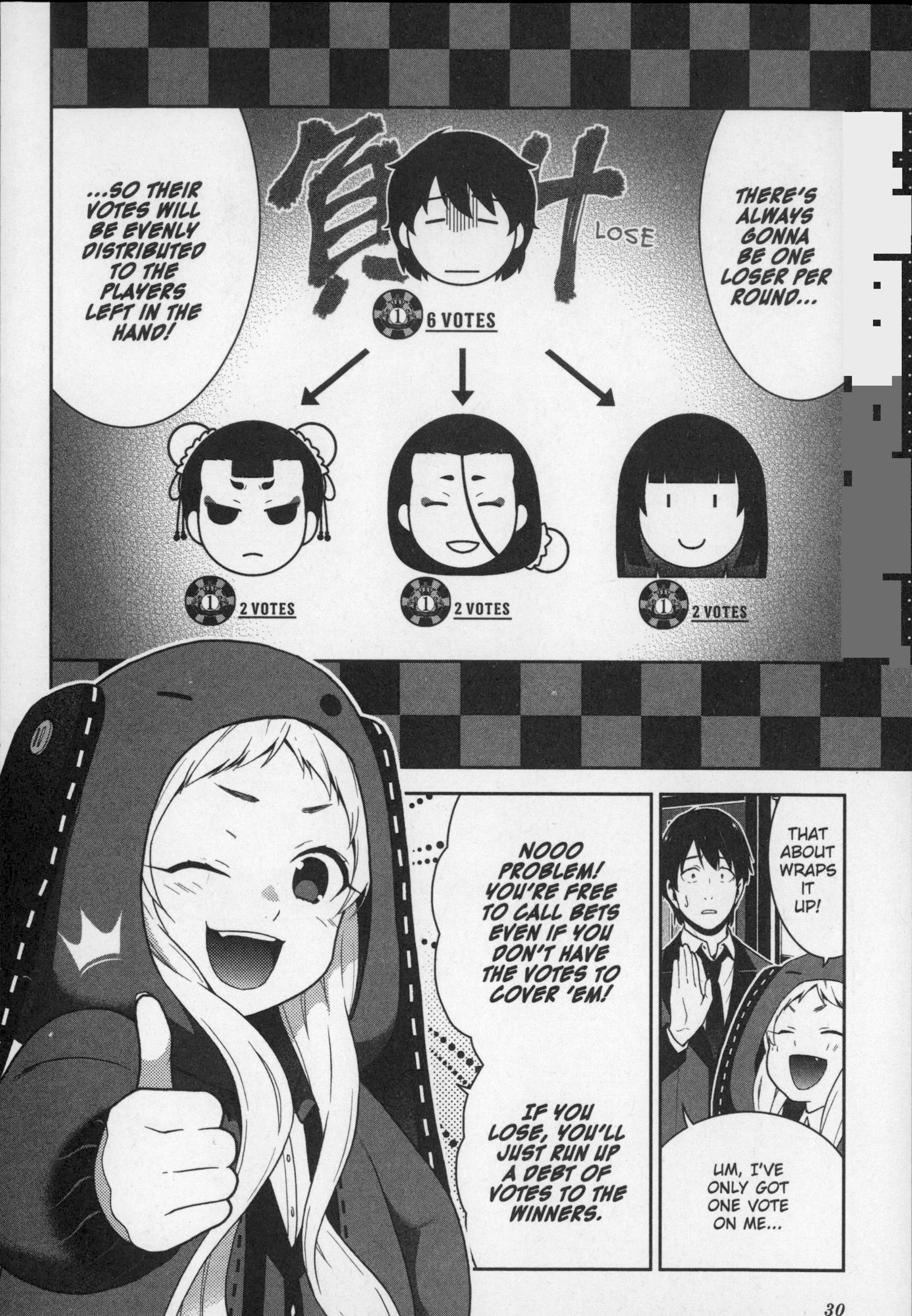
THERE'S ALWAYS GONNA BE ONE LOSER PER ROUND...
...SO THEIR VOTES WILL BE EVENLY DISTRIBUTED TO THE PLAYERS LEFT IN THE HAND!
負け
LOSE
6 VOTES
2 VOTES
2 VOTES
2 VOTES
THAT ABOUT WRAPS IT UP!
UM, I'VE ONLY GOT ONE VOTE ON ME...
NOOO PROBLEM! YOU'RE FREE TO CALL BETS EVEN IF YOU DON'T HAVE THE VOTES TO COVER 'EM!
IF YOU LOSE, YOU'LL JUST RUN UP A DEBT OF VOTES TO THE WINNERS.

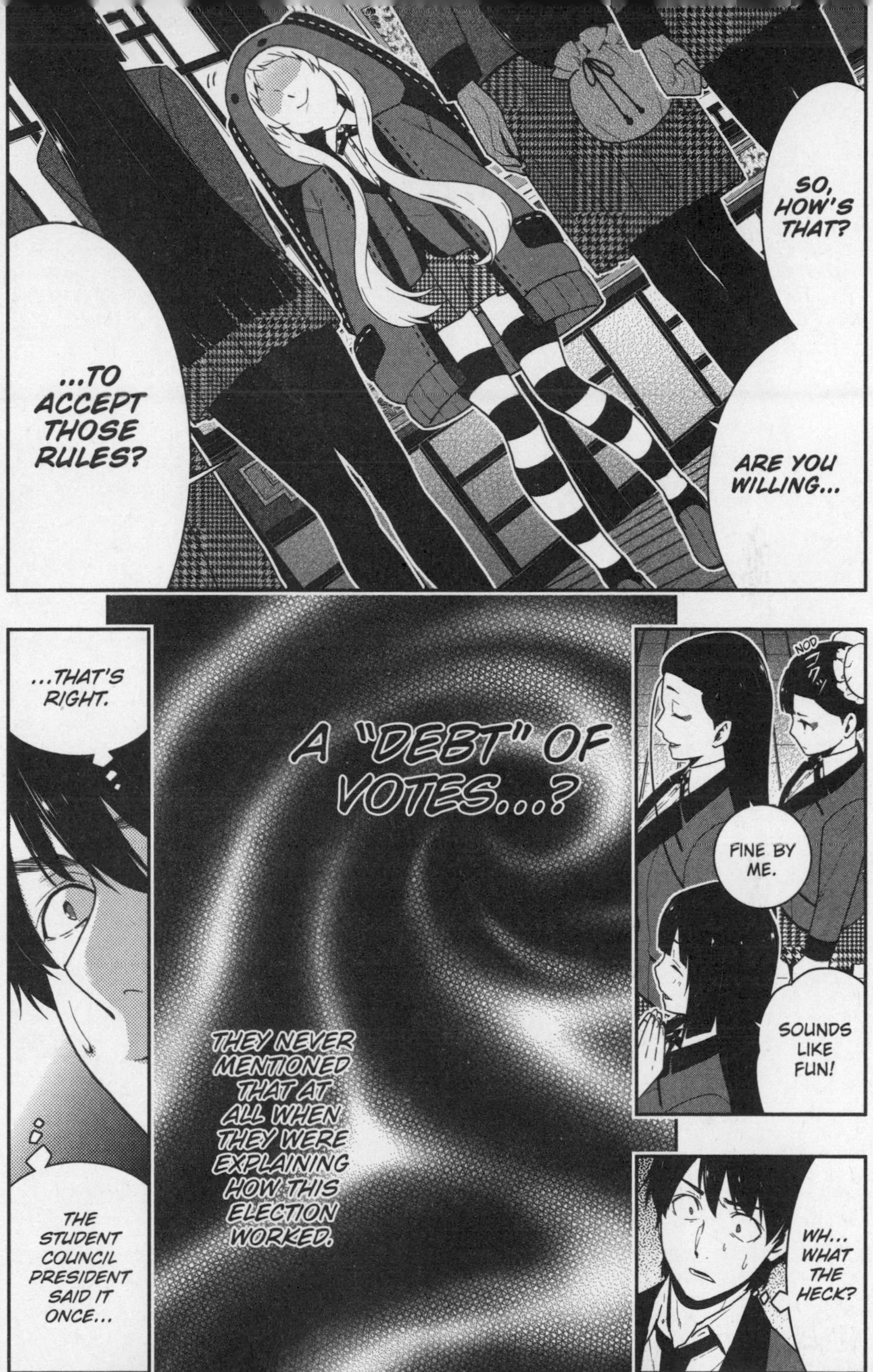
SO, HOW'S THAT?
ARE YOU WILLING...
...TO ACCEPT THOSE RULES?
NOD
FINE BY ME.
SOUNDS LIKE FUN!
WH... WHAT THE HECK?
A "DEBT" OF VOTES...?
THEY NEVER MENTIONED THAT AT ALL WHEN THEY WERE EXPLAINING HOW THIS ELECTION WORKED.
...THAT'S RIGHT.
THE STUDENT COUNCIL PRESIDENT SAID IT ONCE...

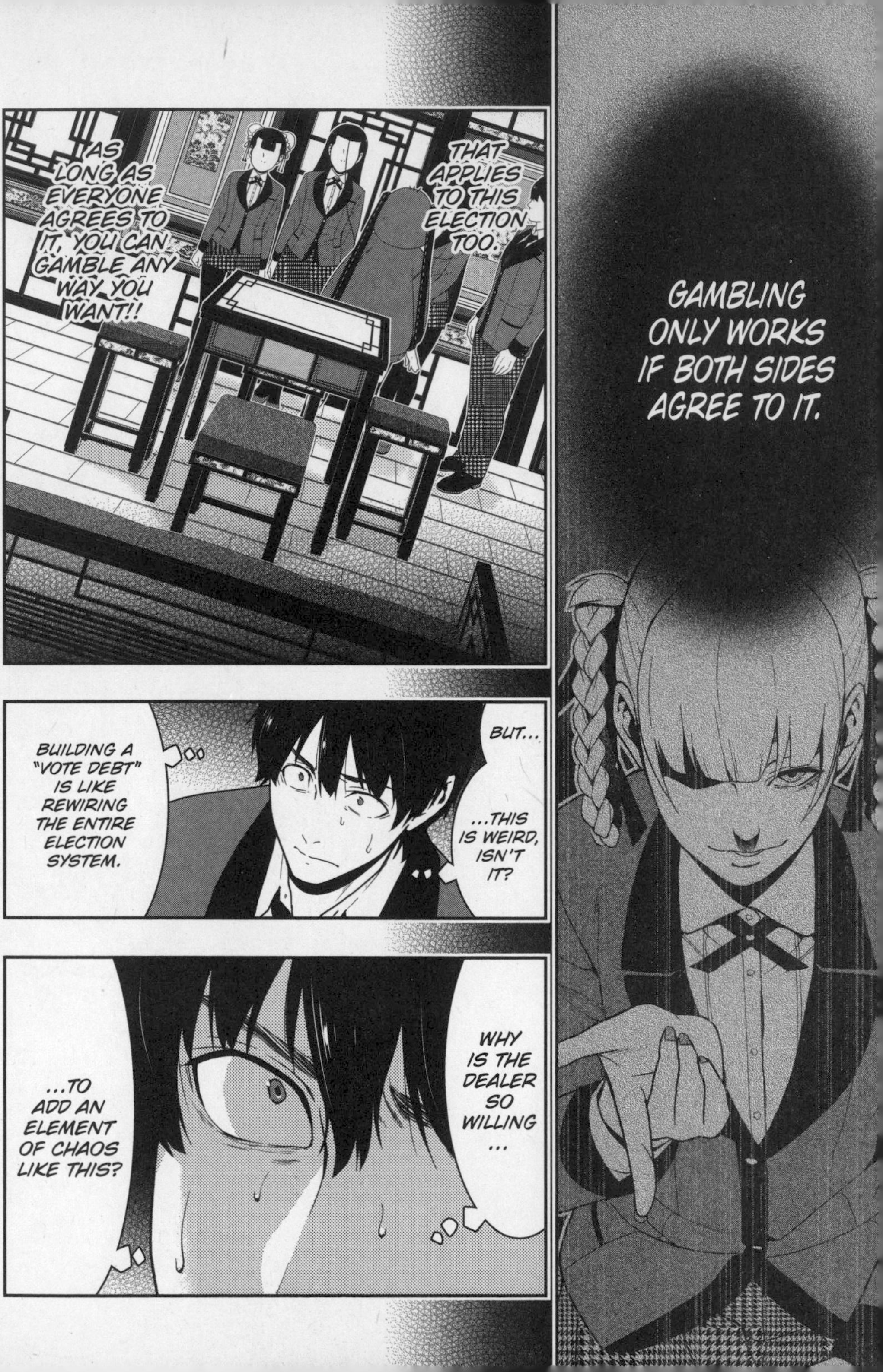
GAMBLING ONLY WORKS IF BOTH SIDES AGREE TO IT.
AS LONG AS EVERYONE AGREES TO IT, YOU CAN GAMBLE ANY WAY YOU WANT!!
THAT APPLIES TO THIS ELECTION TOO.
BUT...
...THIS IS WEIRD, ISN'T IT?
BUILDING A "VOTE DEBT" IS LIKE REWIRING THE ENTIRE ELECTION SYSTEM.
WHY IS THE DEALER SO WILLING...
...TO ADD AN ELEMENT OF CHAOS LIKE THIS?

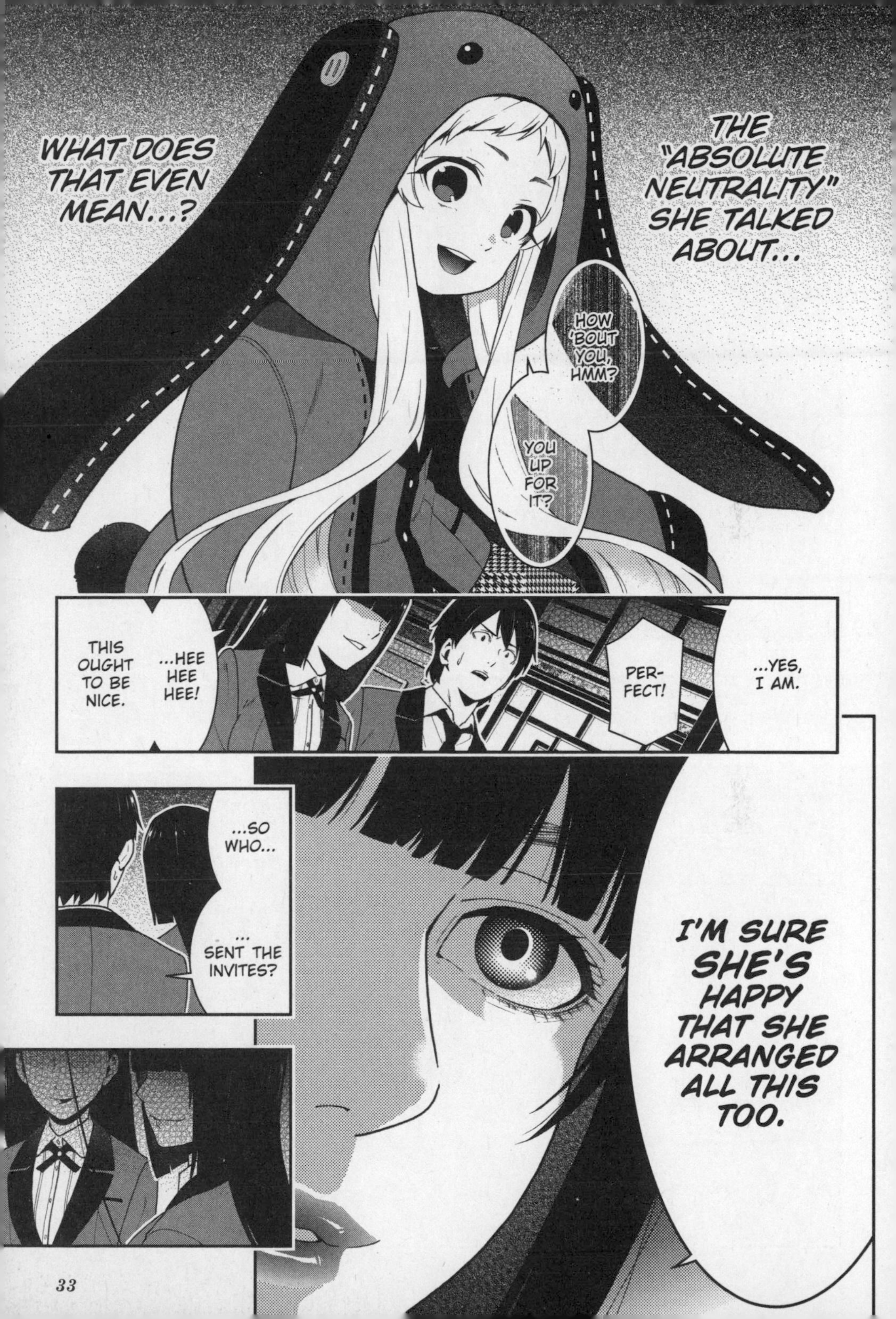
THE "ABSOLUTE NEUTRALITY" SHE TALKED ABOUT...
HOW 'BOUT YOU, HMM?
YOU UP FOR IT?
WHAT DOES THAT EVEN MEAN...?
...YES, I AM.
PER-FECT!
...HEE HEE HEE!
THIS OUGHT TO BE NICE.
I'M SURE SHE'S HAPPY THAT SHE ARRANGED ALL THIS TOO.
...SO WHO...
... SENT THE INVITES?

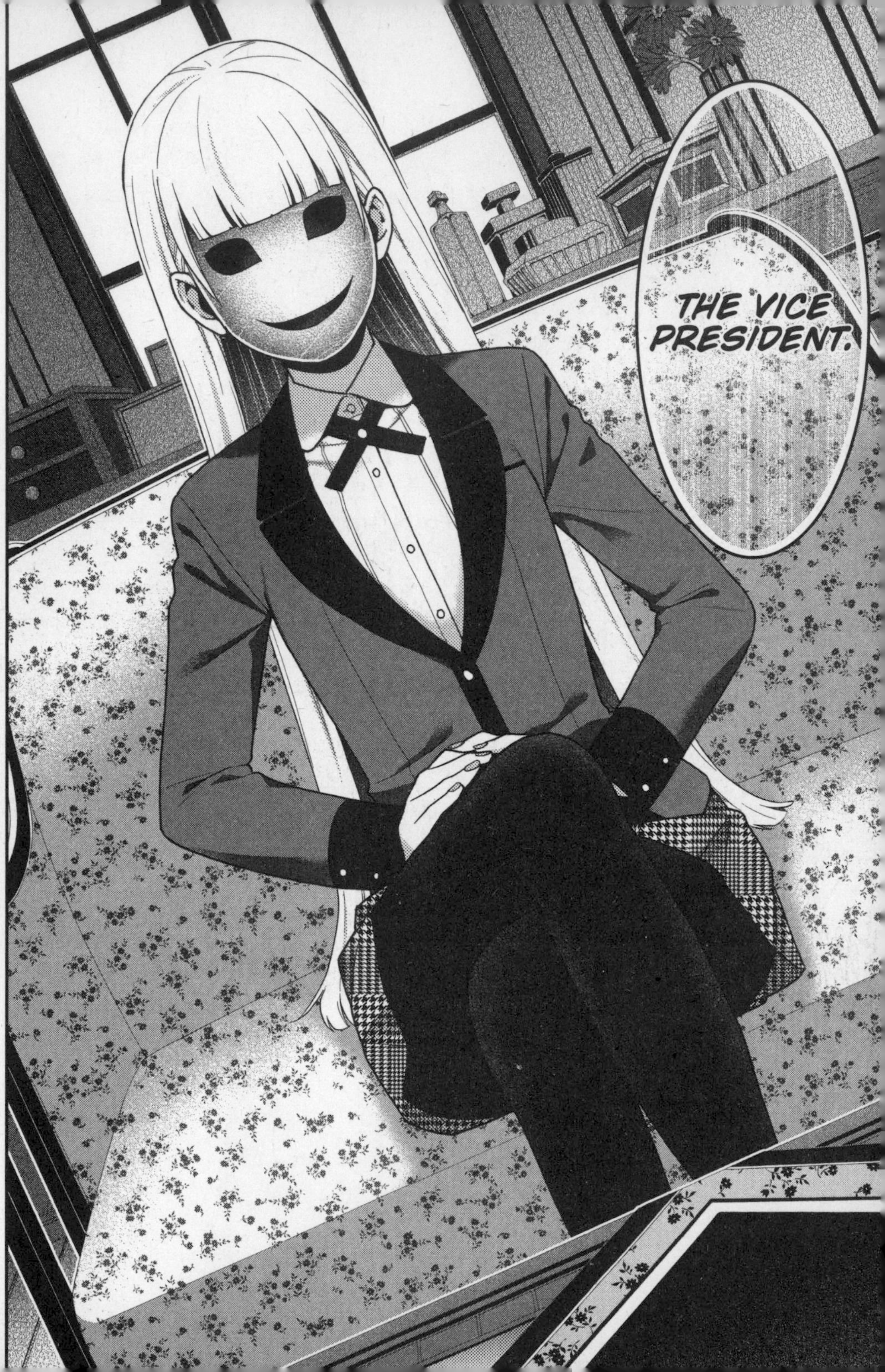
THE VICE PRESIDENT.

KAKEGURUI

— Compulsive Gambler —

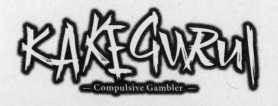

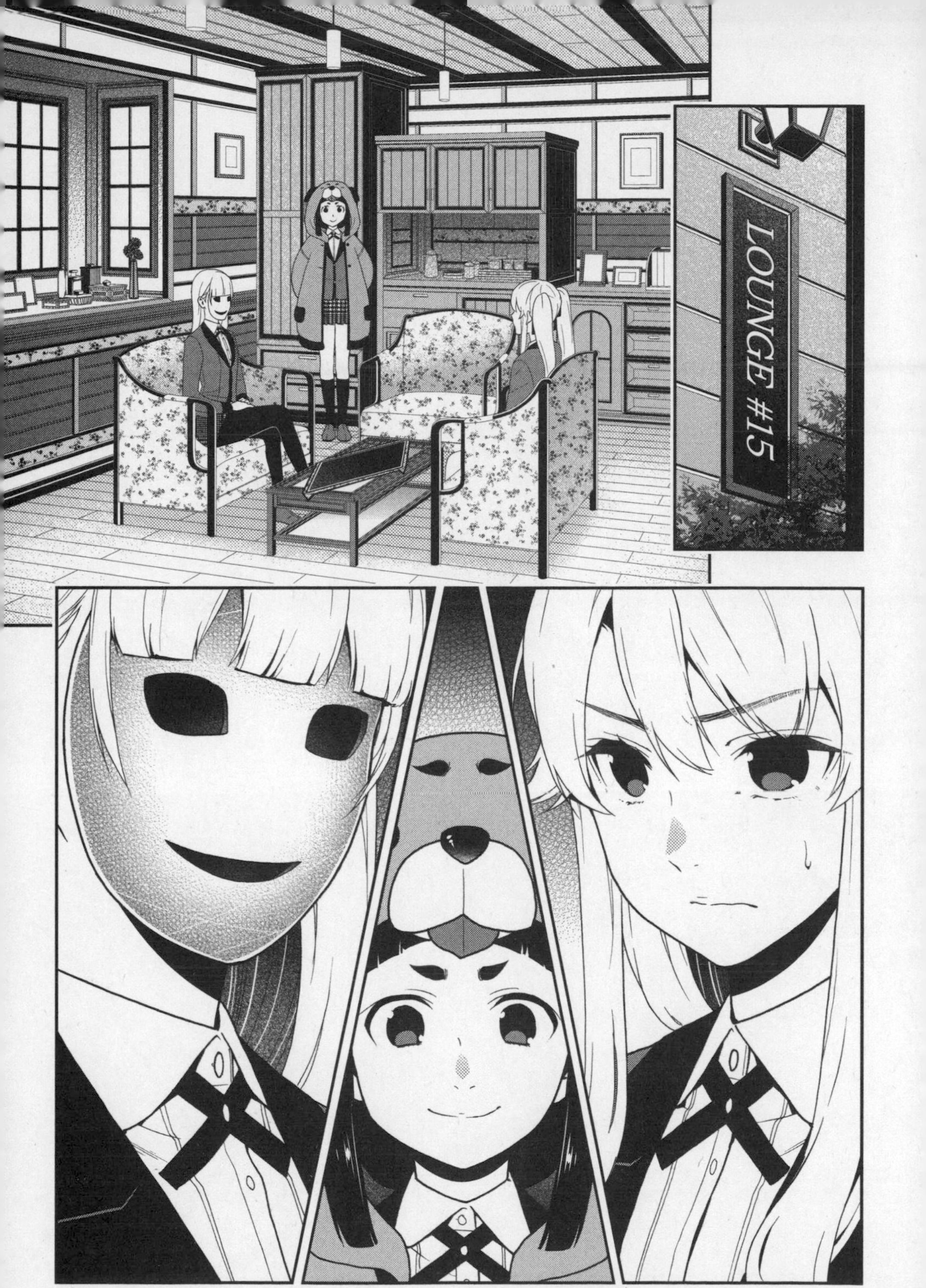
LOUNGE #15

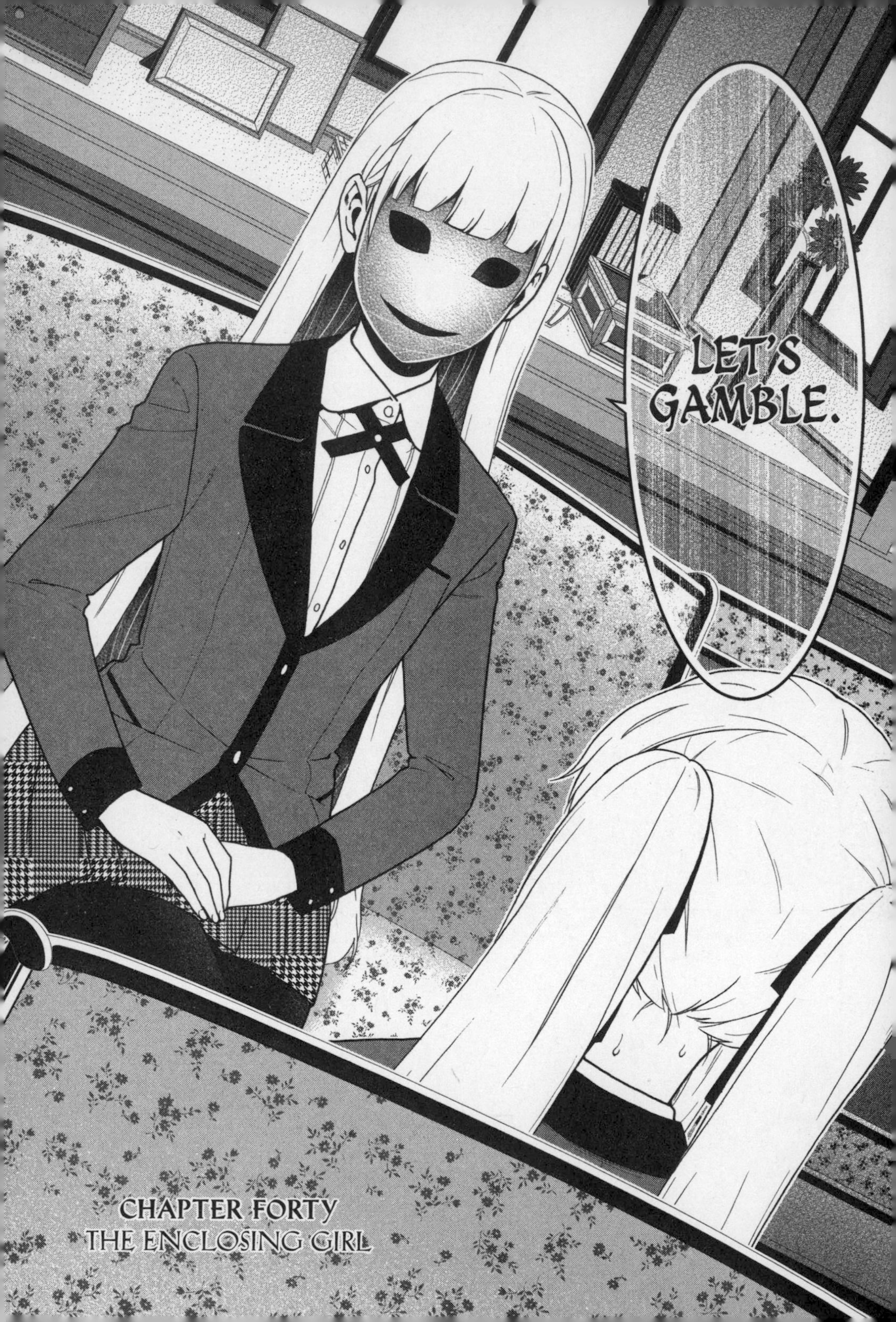
LET'S GAMBLE.

CHAPTER FORTY
THE ENCLOSING GIRL

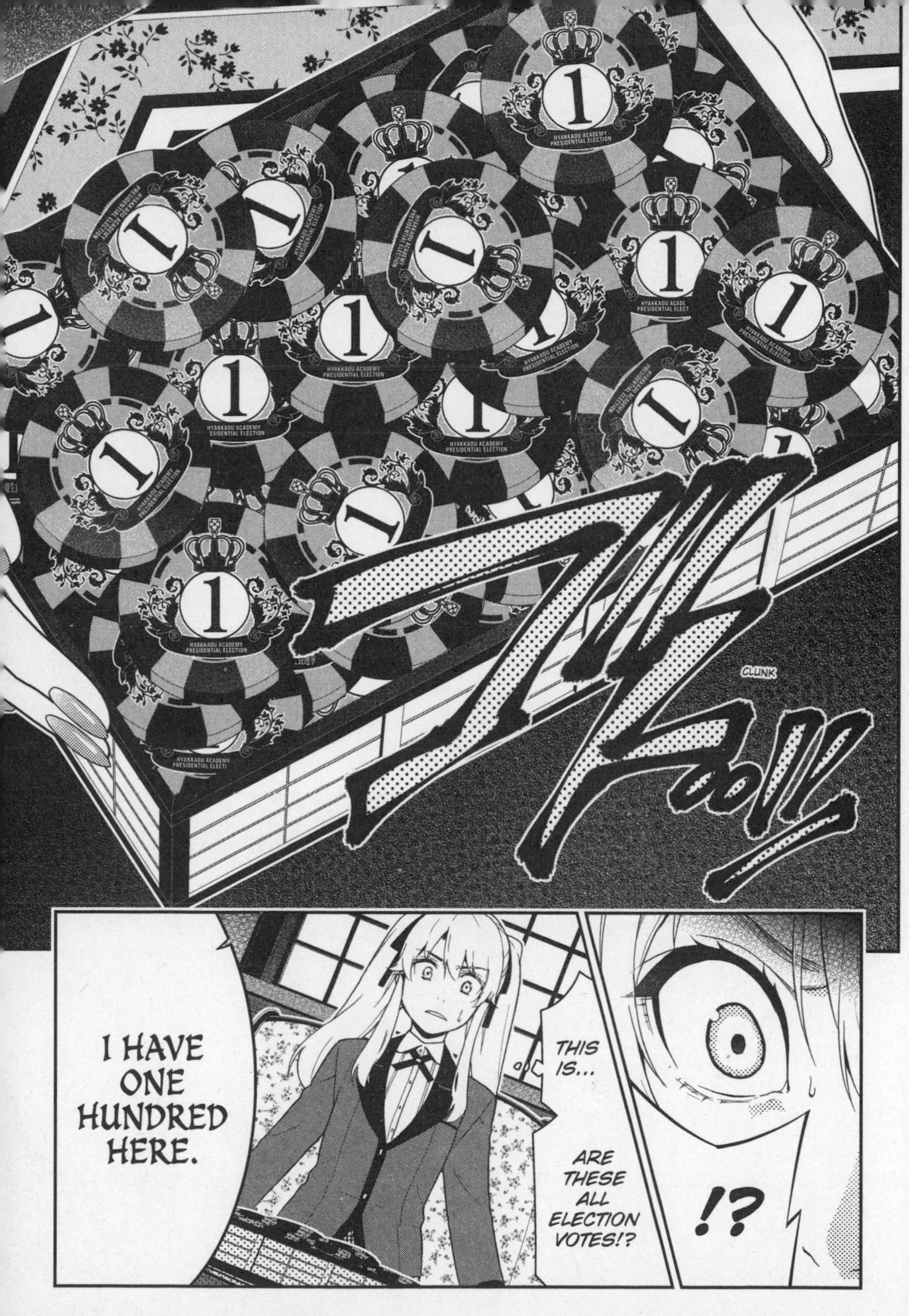
HYAKKAOU ACADEMY PRESIDENTIAL ELECTION
CLUNK
!?
THIS IS...
ARE THESE ALL ELECTION VOTES!?
I HAVE ONE HUNDRED HERE.

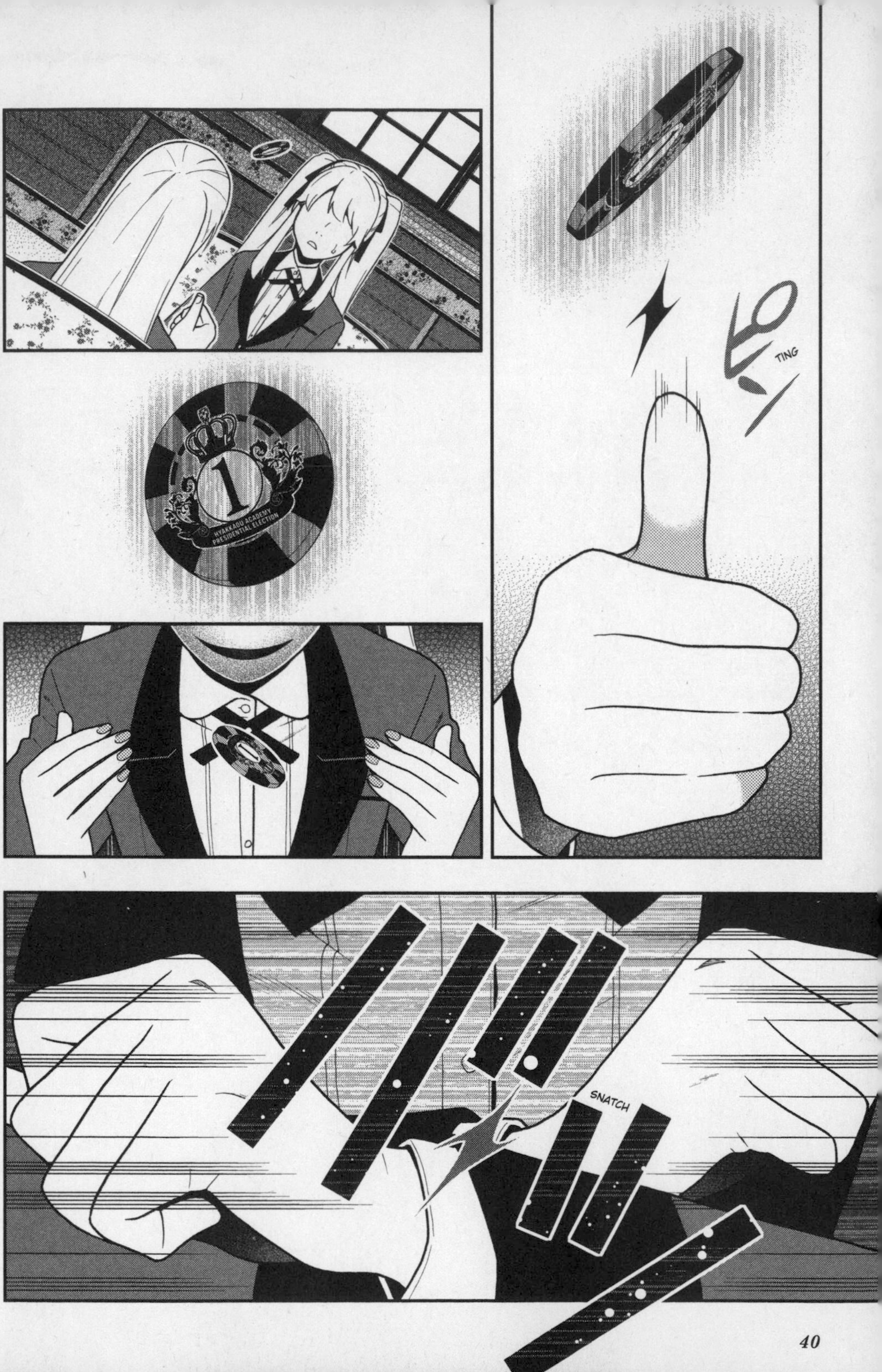
TING
HYAKKAOU ACADEMY
PRESIDENTIAL ELECTION
SNATCH

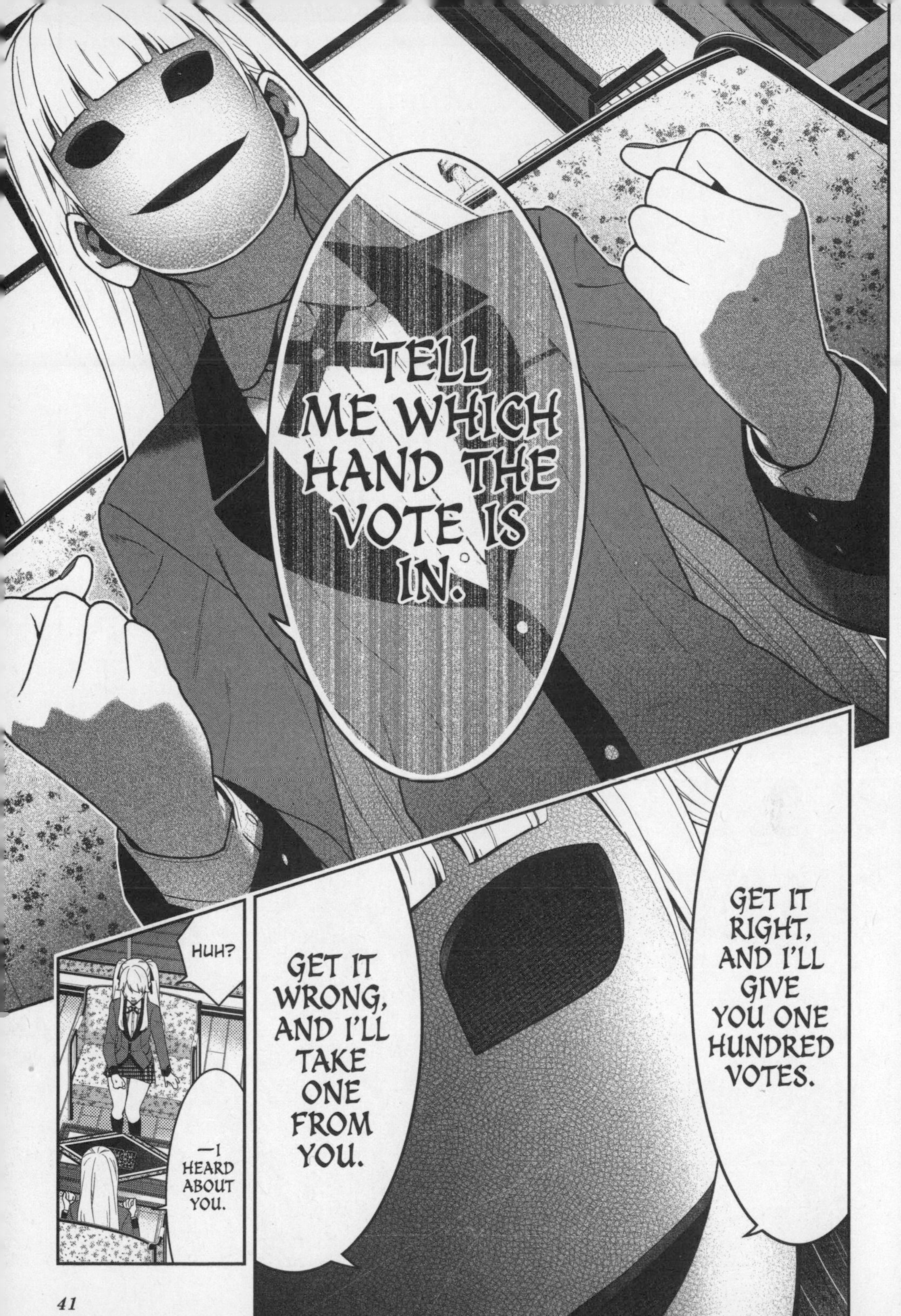
TELL ME WHICH HAND THE VOTE IS IN.
GET IT RIGHT, AND I'LL GIVE YOU ONE HUNDRED VOTES.
GET IT WRONG, AND I'LL TAKE ONE FROM YOU.
HUH?
—I HEARD ABOUT YOU.

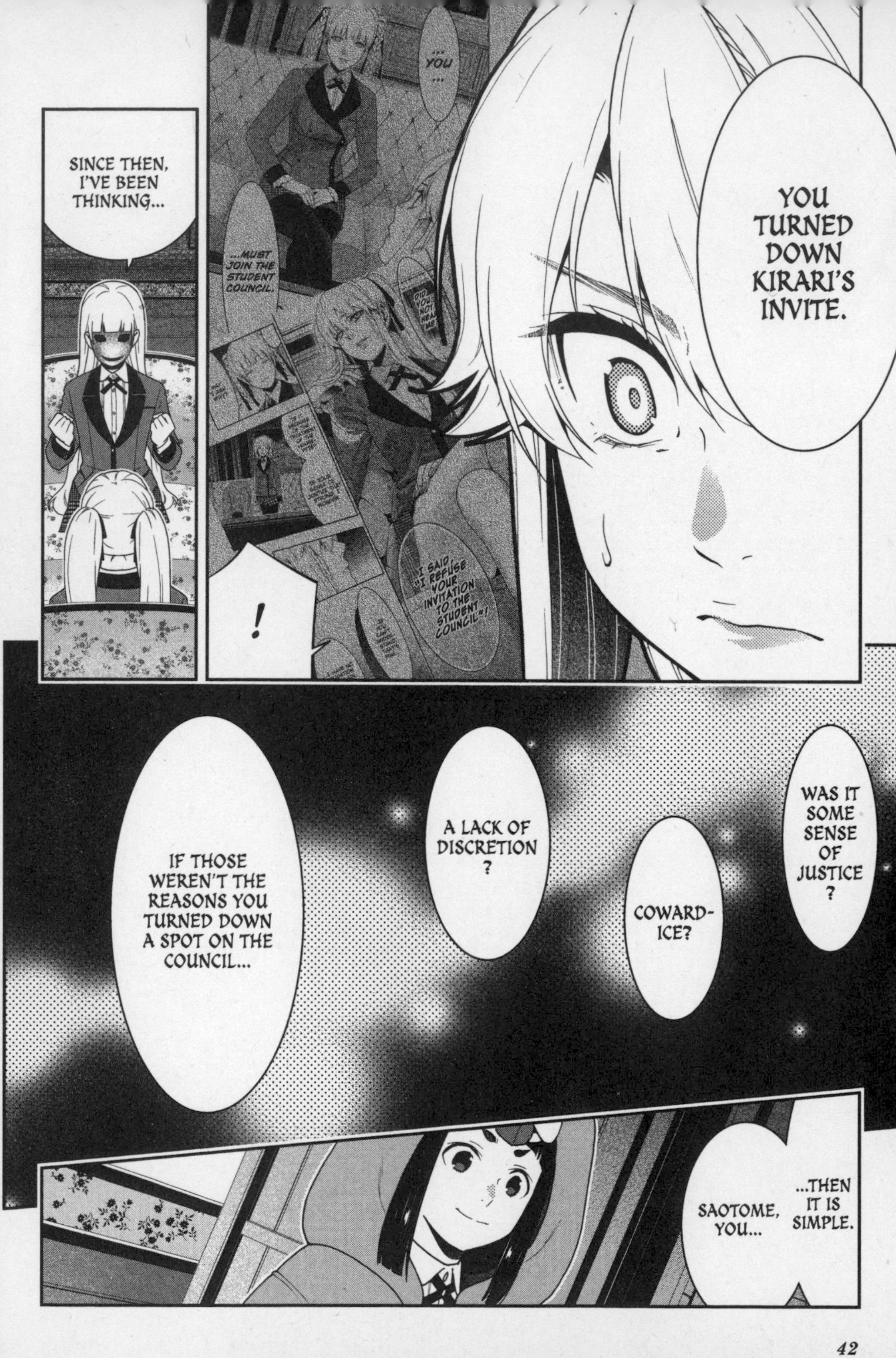
YOU TURNED DOWN KIRARI'S INVITE.
...YOU ...
...MUST JOIN THE STUDENT COUNCIL.
"I SAID, "I REFUSE YOUR INVITATION TO THE STUDENT COUNCIL"!
!
SINCE THEN, I'VE BEEN THINKING...
WAS IT SOME SENSE OF JUSTICE ?
COWARD-ICE?
A LACK OF DISCRETION ?
IF THOSE WEREN'T THE REASONS YOU TURNED DOWN A SPOT ON THE COUNCIL...
...THEN IT IS SIMPLE.
SAOTOME, YOU...

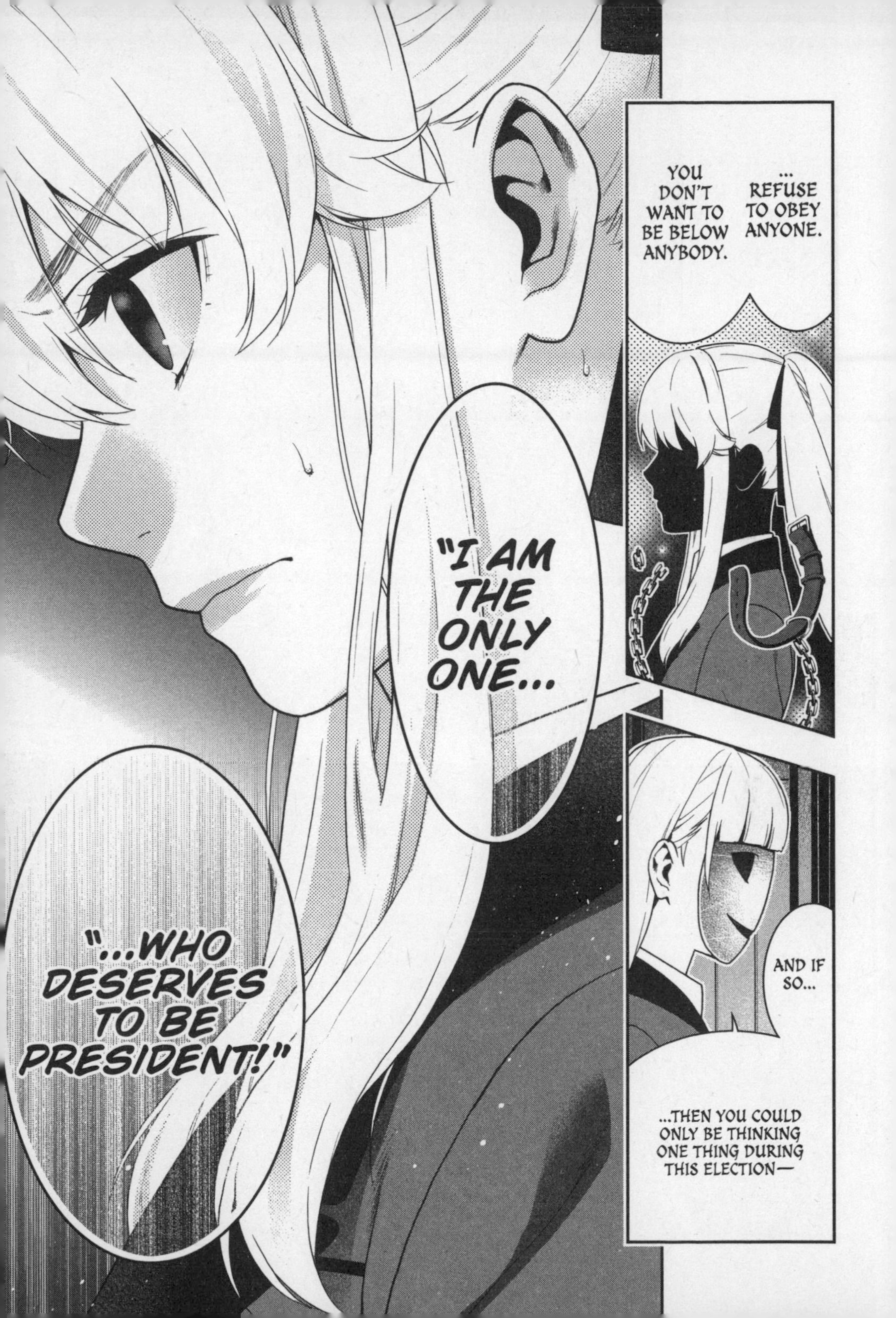
YOU DON'T WANT TO BE BELOW ANYBODY.
... REFUSE TO OBEY ANYONE.
AND IF SO...
...THEN YOU COULD ONLY BE THINKING ONE THING DURING THIS ELECTION—
"I AM THE ONLY ONE...
"...WHO DESERVES TO BE PRESIDENT!"

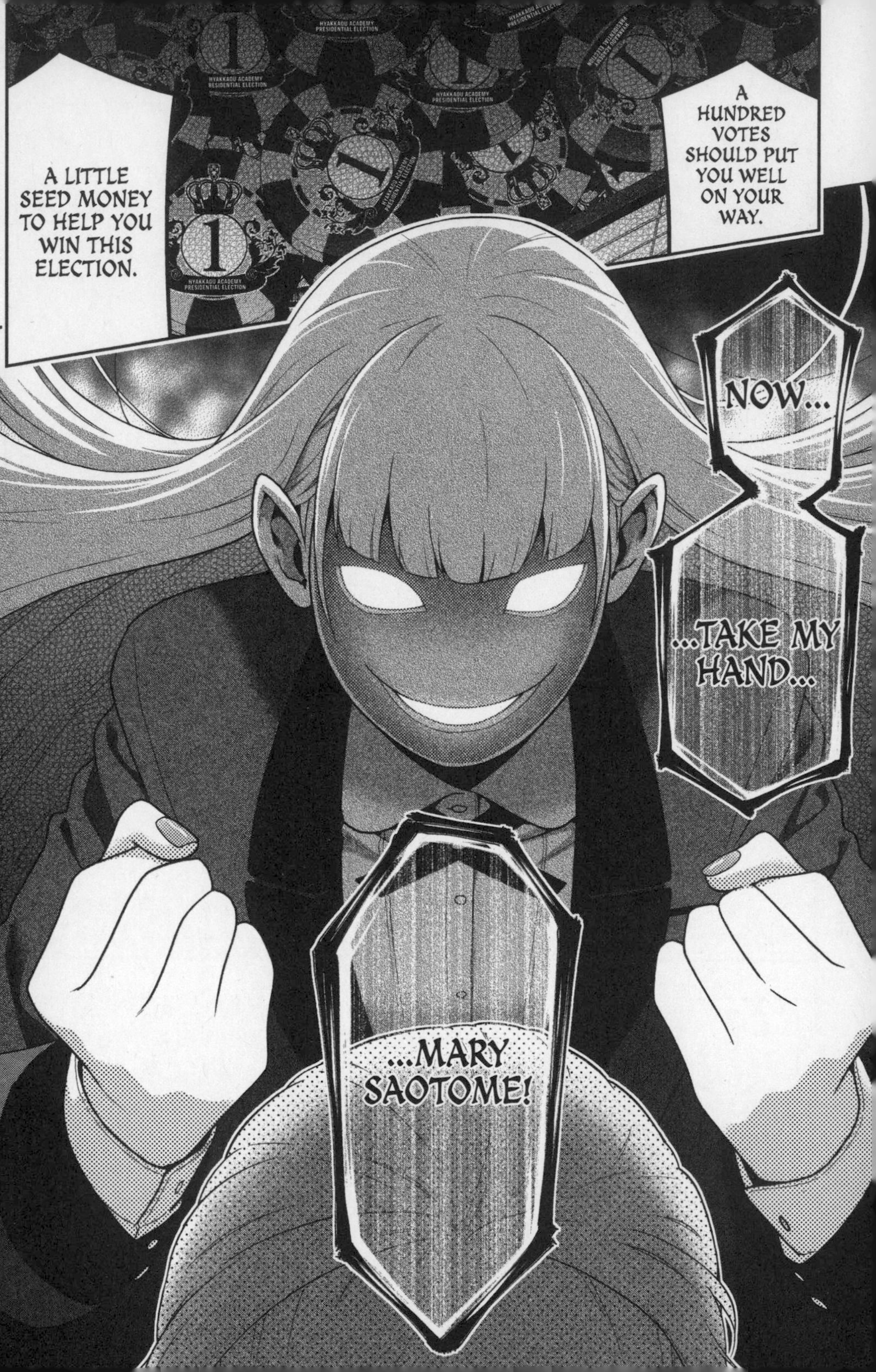
HYAKKAOU ACADEMY PRESIDENTIAL ELECTION
A HUNDRED VOTES SHOULD PUT YOU WELL ON YOUR WAY.
A LITTLE SEED MONEY TO HELP YOU WIN THIS ELECTION.
NOW...
...TAKE MY HAND...
...MARY SAOTOME!

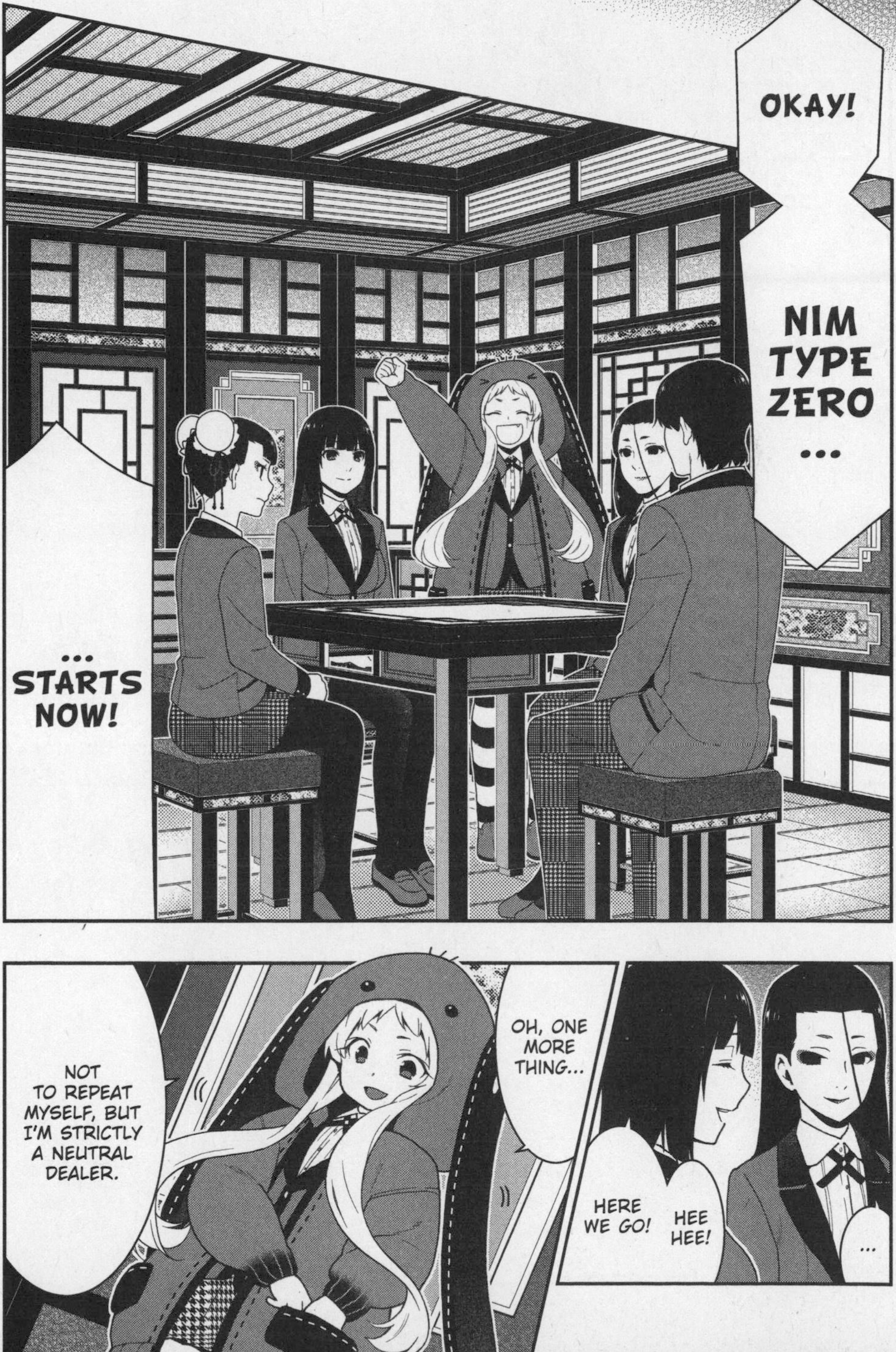
OKAY!
NIM TYPE ZERO ...
... STARTS NOW!
OH, ONE MORE THING...
NOT TO REPEAT MYSELF, BUT I'M STRICTLY A NEUTRAL DEALER.
HEE HEE!
HERE WE GO!
...

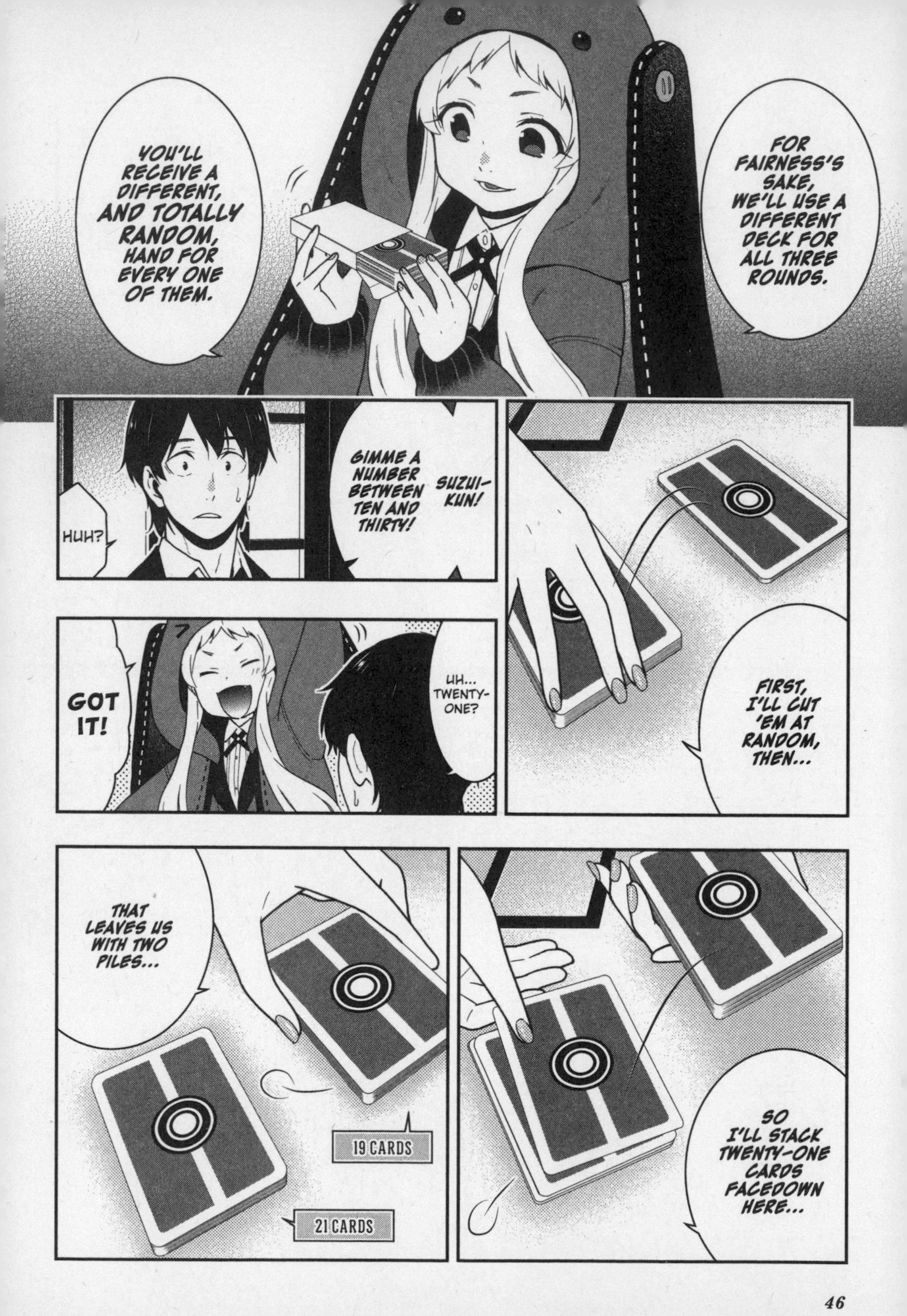
FOR FAIRNESS'S SAKE, WE'LL USE A DIFFERENT DECK FOR ALL THREE ROUNDS.
YOU'LL RECEIVE A DIFFERENT, AND TOTALLY RANDOM, HAND FOR EVERY ONE OF THEM.
FIRST, I'LL CUT 'EM AT RANDOM, THEN...
SUZUI-KUN!
GIMME A NUMBER BETWEEN TEN AND THIRTY!
HUH?
UH... TWENTY-ONE?
GOT IT!
SO I'LL STACK TWENTY-ONE CARDS FACEDOWN HERE...
THAT LEAVES US WITH TWO PILES...
19 CARDS
21 CARDS

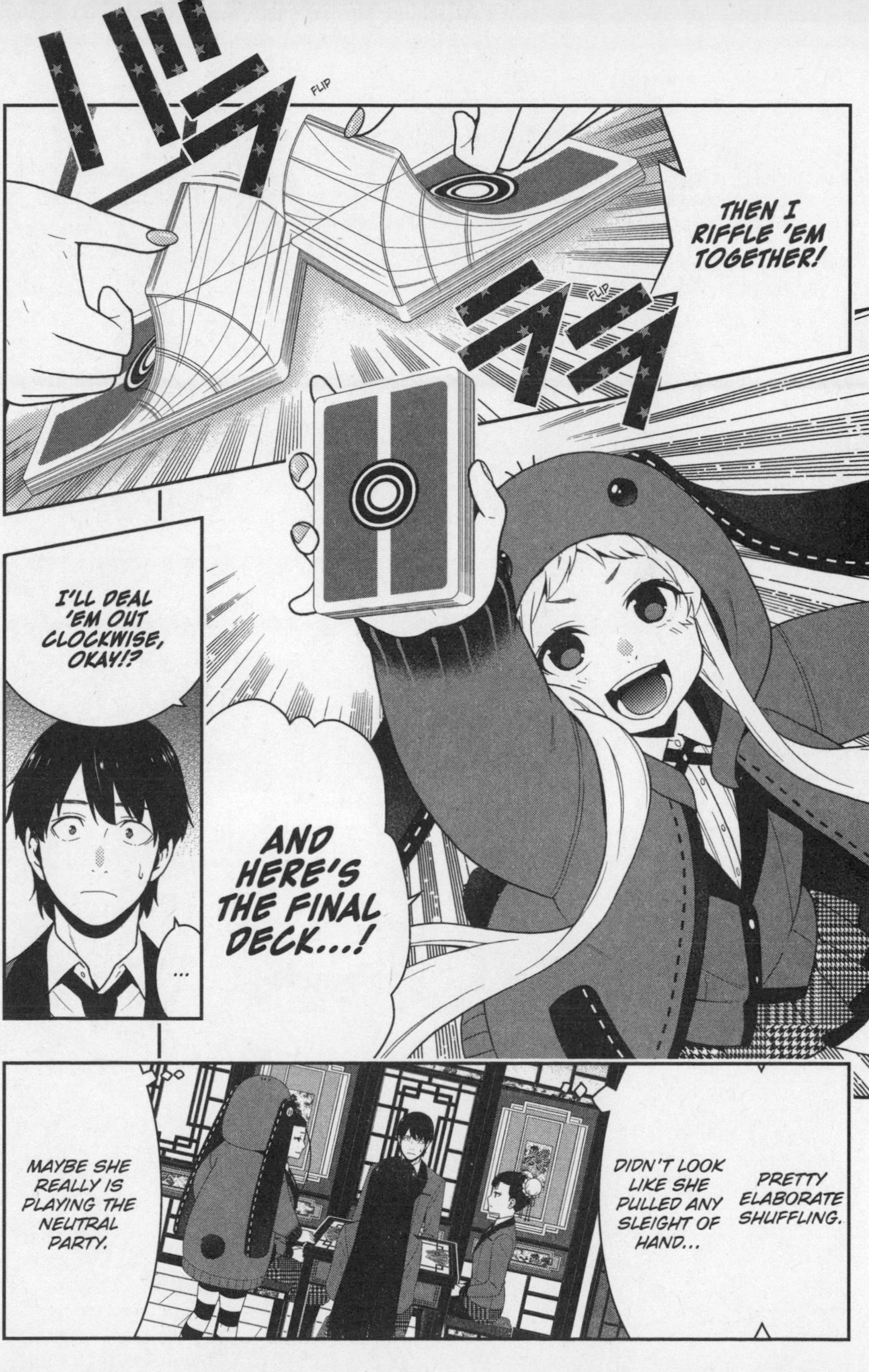
FLIP
THEN I RIFFLE 'EM TOGETHER!
FLIP
AND HERE'S THE FINAL DECK...!
I'LL DEAL 'EM OUT CLOCKWISE, OKAY!?
...
PRETTY ELABORATE SHUFFLING.
DIDN'T LOOK LIKE SHE PULLED ANY SLEIGHT OF HAND...
MAYBE SHE REALLY IS PLAYING THE NEUTRAL PARTY.

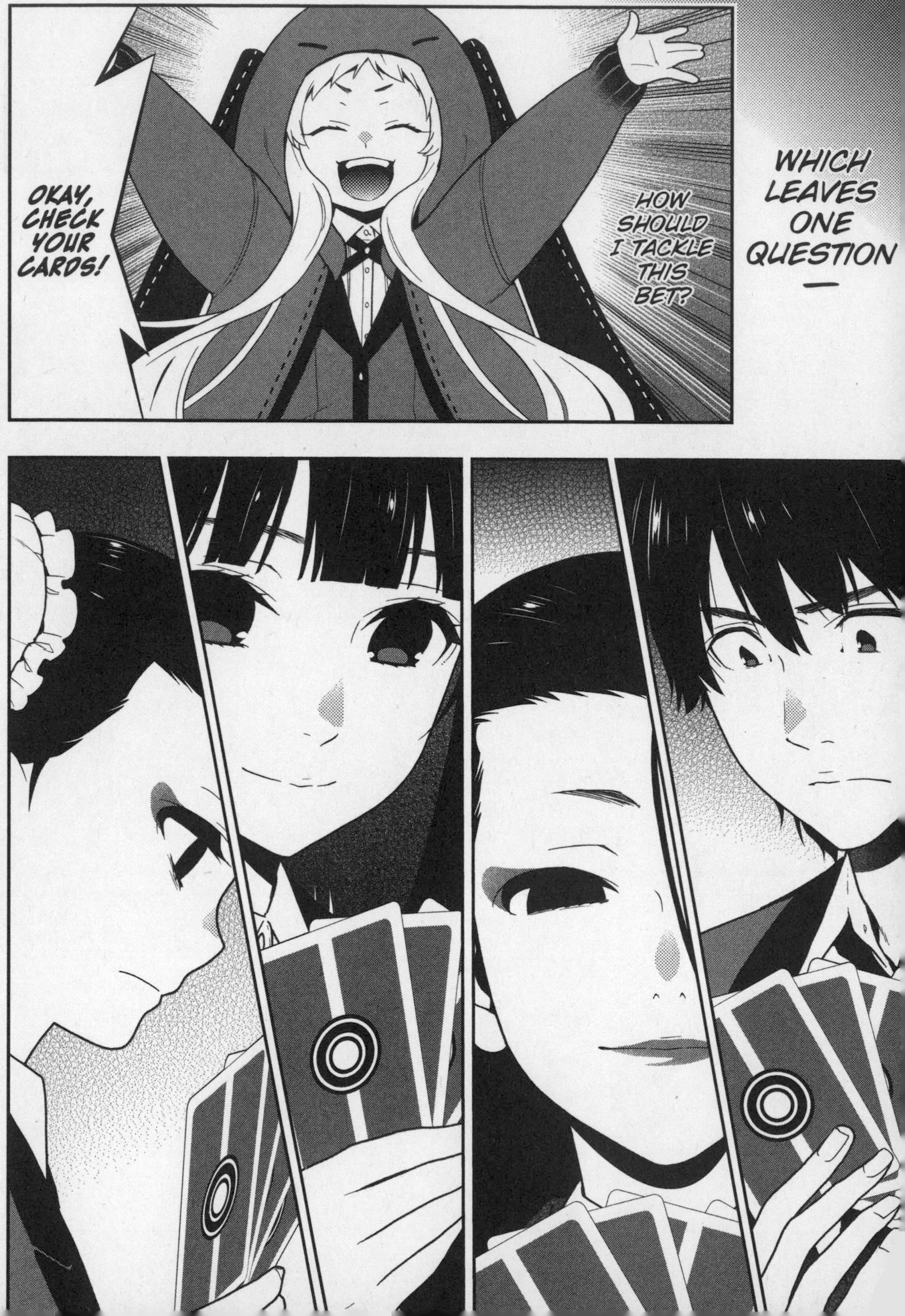
WHICH LEAVES ONE QUESTION —
HOW SHOULD I TACKLE THIS BET?
OKAY, CHECK YOUR CARDS!

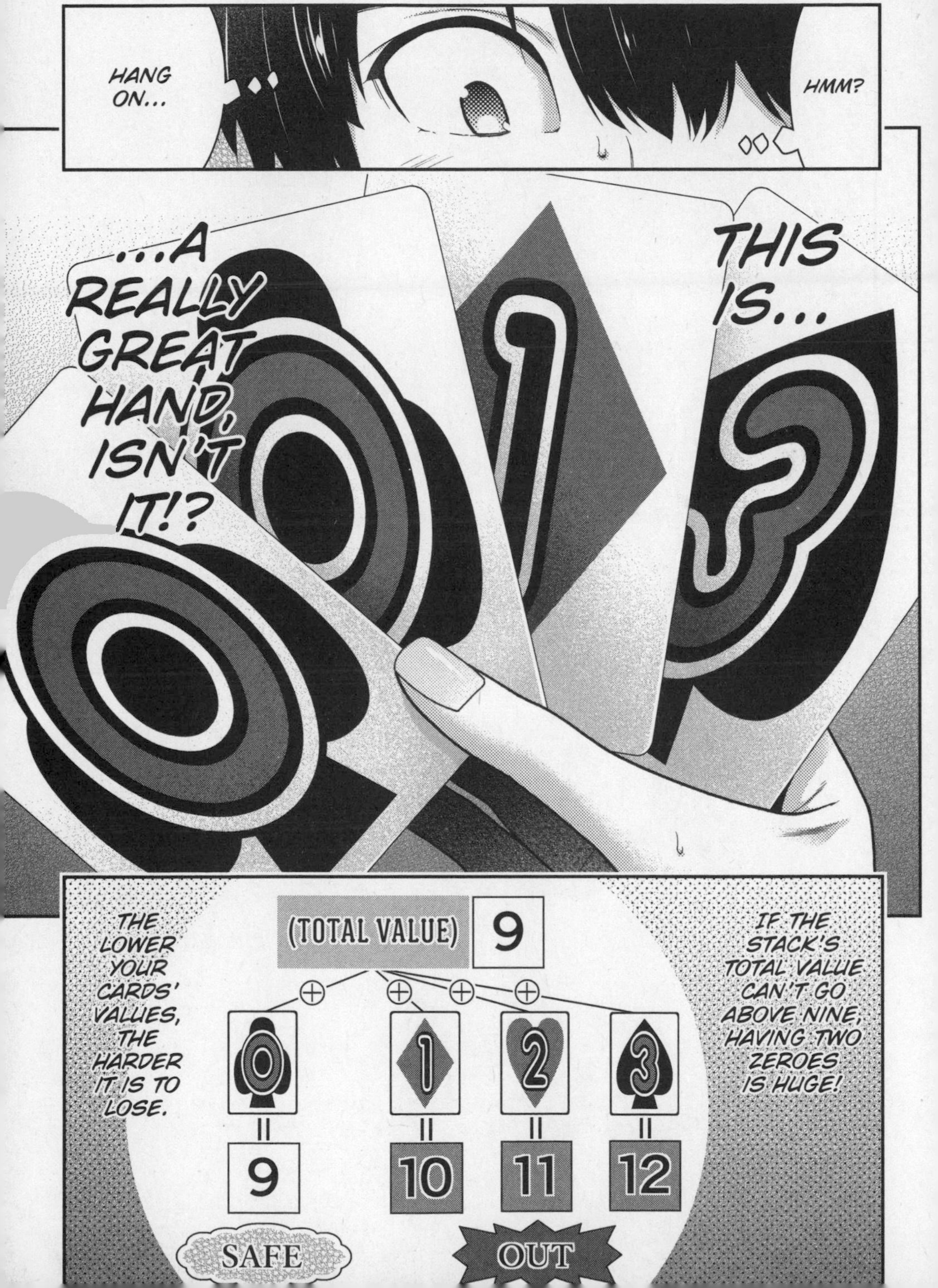
HMM?
HANG ON...
THIS IS...
...A REALLY GREAT HAND, ISN'T IT!?
IF THE STACK'S TOTAL VALUE CAN'T GO ABOVE NINE, HAVING TWO ZEROES IS HUGE!
THE LOWER YOUR CARDS' VALUES, THE HARDER IT IS TO LOSE.
(TOTAL VALUE) 9
0
1
2
3
9
10
11
12
SAFE
OUT

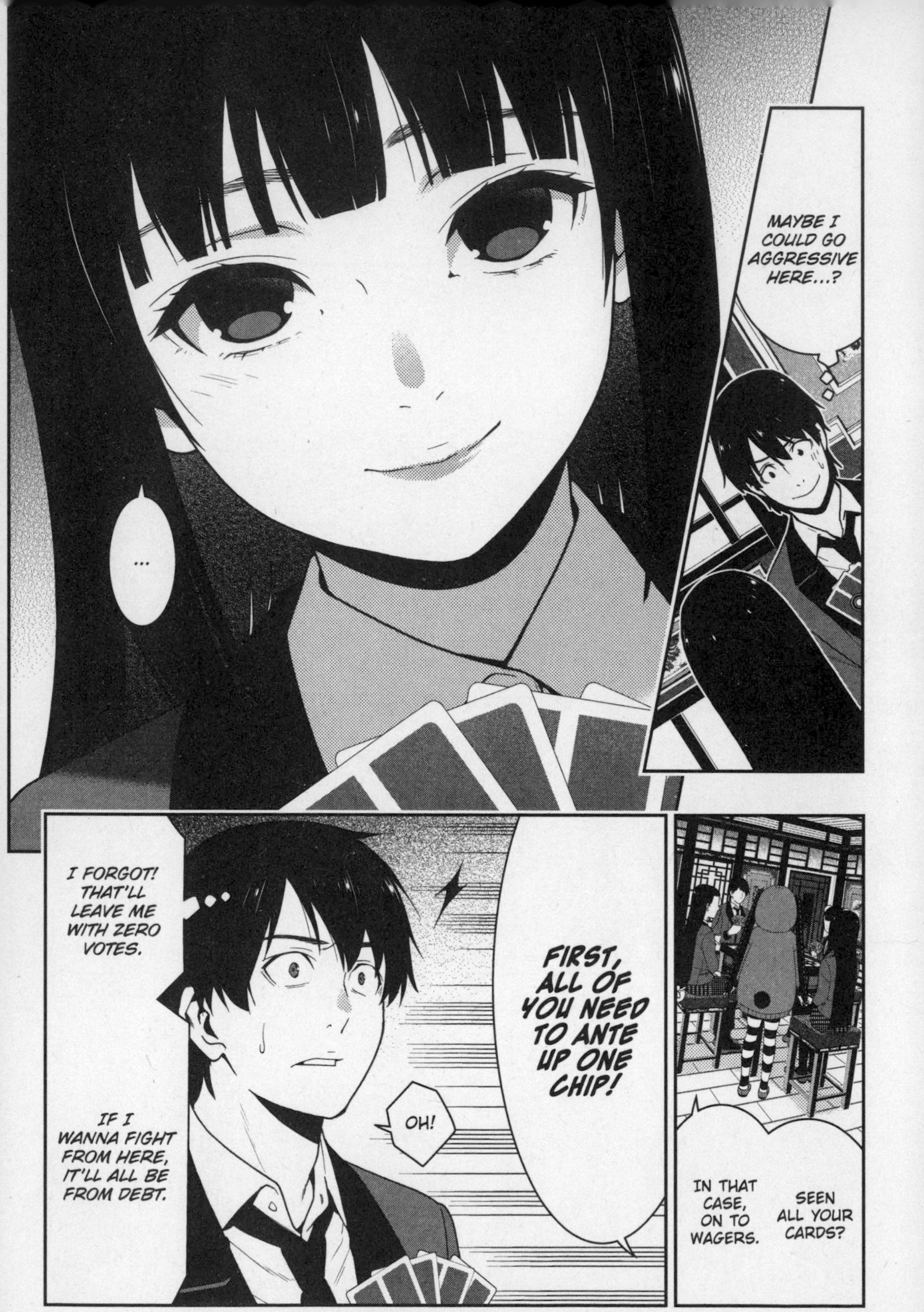
MAYBE I COULD GO AGGRESSIVE HERE...?
...
SEEN ALL YOUR CARDS?
IN THAT CASE, ON TO WAGERS.
FIRST, ALL OF YOU NEED TO ANTE UP ONE CHIP!
OH!
I FORGOT! THAT'LL LEAVE ME WITH ZERO VOTES.
IF I WANNA FIGHT FROM HERE, IT'LL ALL BE FROM DEBT.

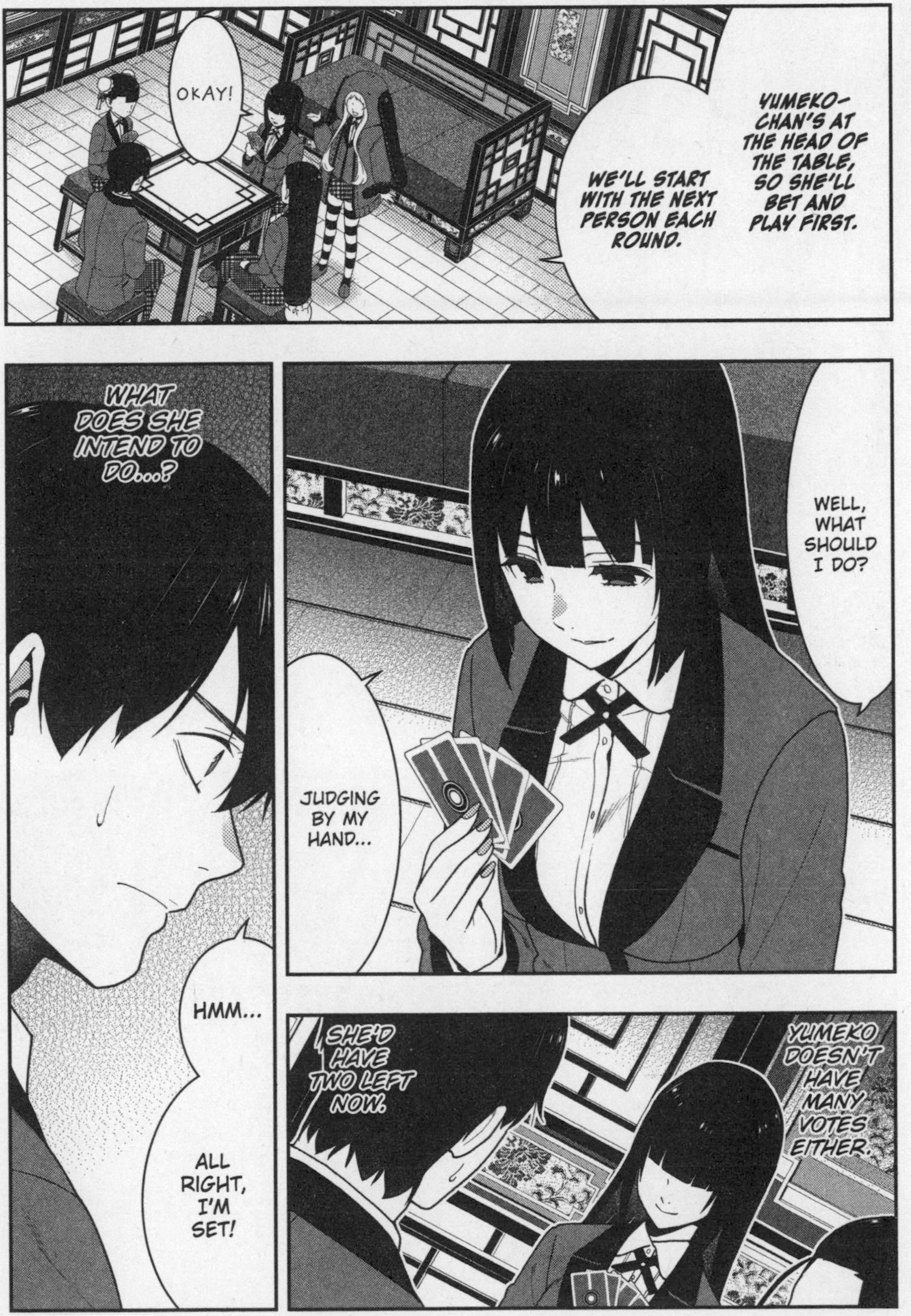
YUMEKO-CHAN'S AT THE HEAD OF THE TABLE, SO SHE'LL BET AND PLAY FIRST.
WE'LL START WITH THE NEXT PERSON EACH ROUND.
OKAY!
WELL, WHAT SHOULD I DO?
JUDGING BY MY HAND...
YUMEKO DOESN'T HAVE MANY VOTES EITHER.
SHE'D HAVE TWO LEFT NOW.
WHAT DOES SHE INTEND TO DO...?
HMM...
ALL RIGHT, I'M SET!

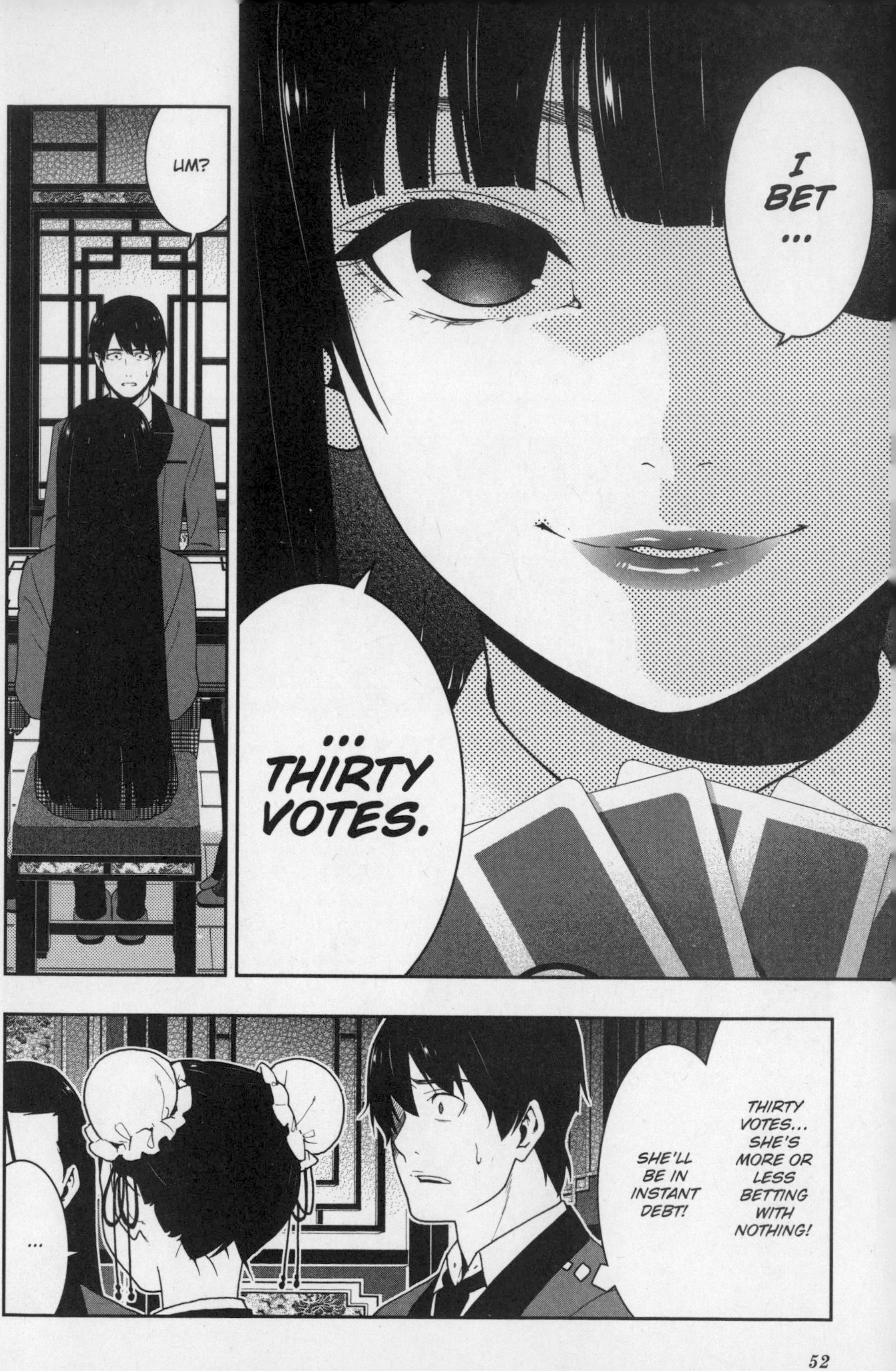
I BET ...
... THIRTY VOTES.
UM?
THIRTY VOTES... SHE'S MORE OR LESS BETTING WITH NOTHING!
SHE'LL BE IN INSTANT DEBT!
...

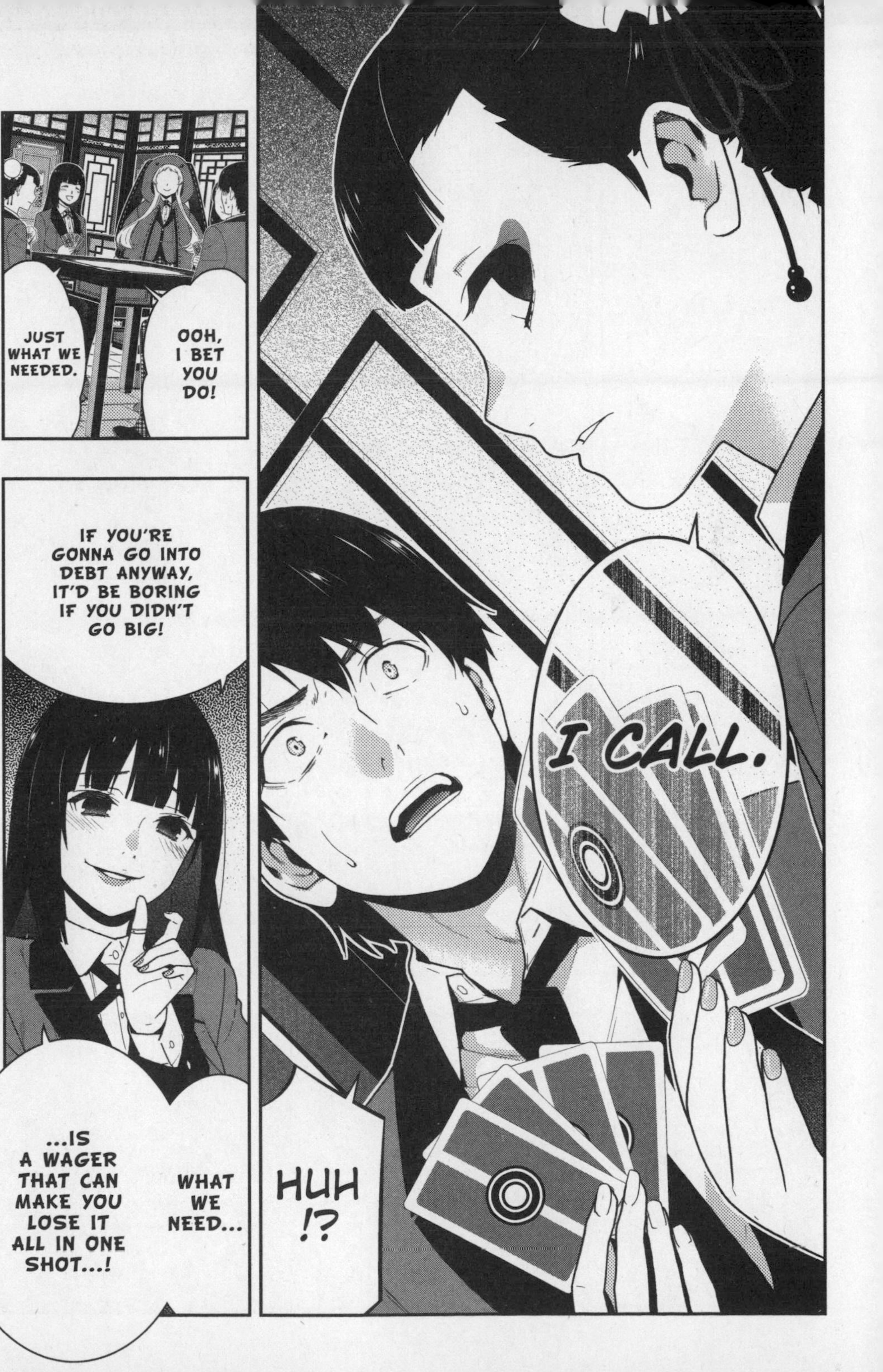
I CALL.
HUH !?
OOH, I BET YOU DO!
JUST WHAT WE NEEDED.
IF YOU'RE GONNA GO INTO DEBT ANYWAY, IT'D BE BORING IF YOU DIDN'T GO BIG!
WHAT WE NEED...
...IS A WAGER THAT CAN MAKE YOU LOSE IT ALL IN ONE SHOT...!

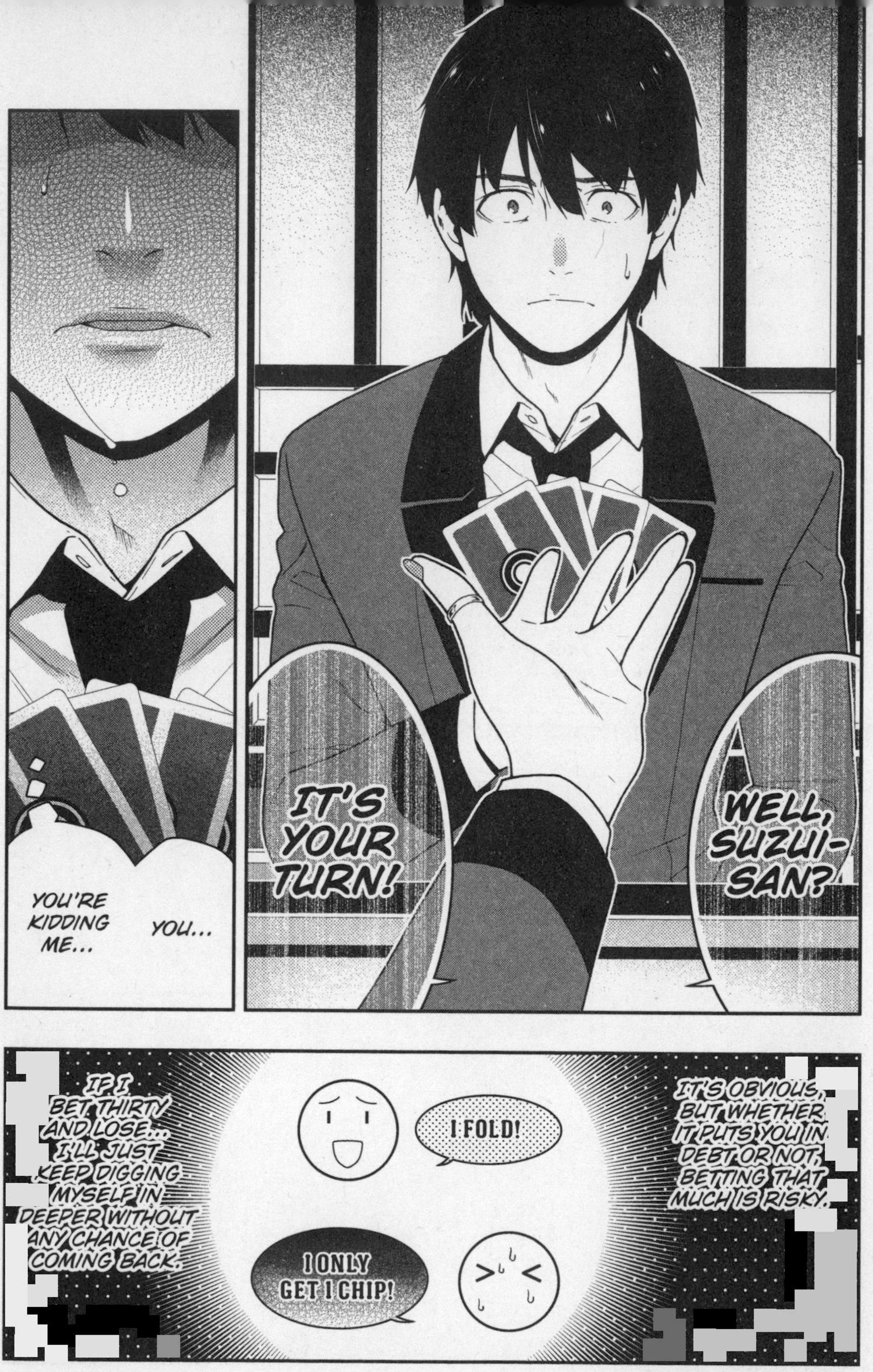
WELL, SUZUI-SAN?
IT'S YOUR TURN!
YOU...
YOU'RE KIDDING ME...
IT'S OBVIOUS, BUT WHETHER IT PUTS YOU IN DEBT OR NOT, BETTING THAT MUCH IS RISKY.
I FOLD!
I ONLY GET 1 CHIP!
IF I BET THIRTY AND LOSE... I'LL JUST KEEP DIGGING MYSELF IN DEEPER WITHOUT ANY CHANCE OF COMING BACK.

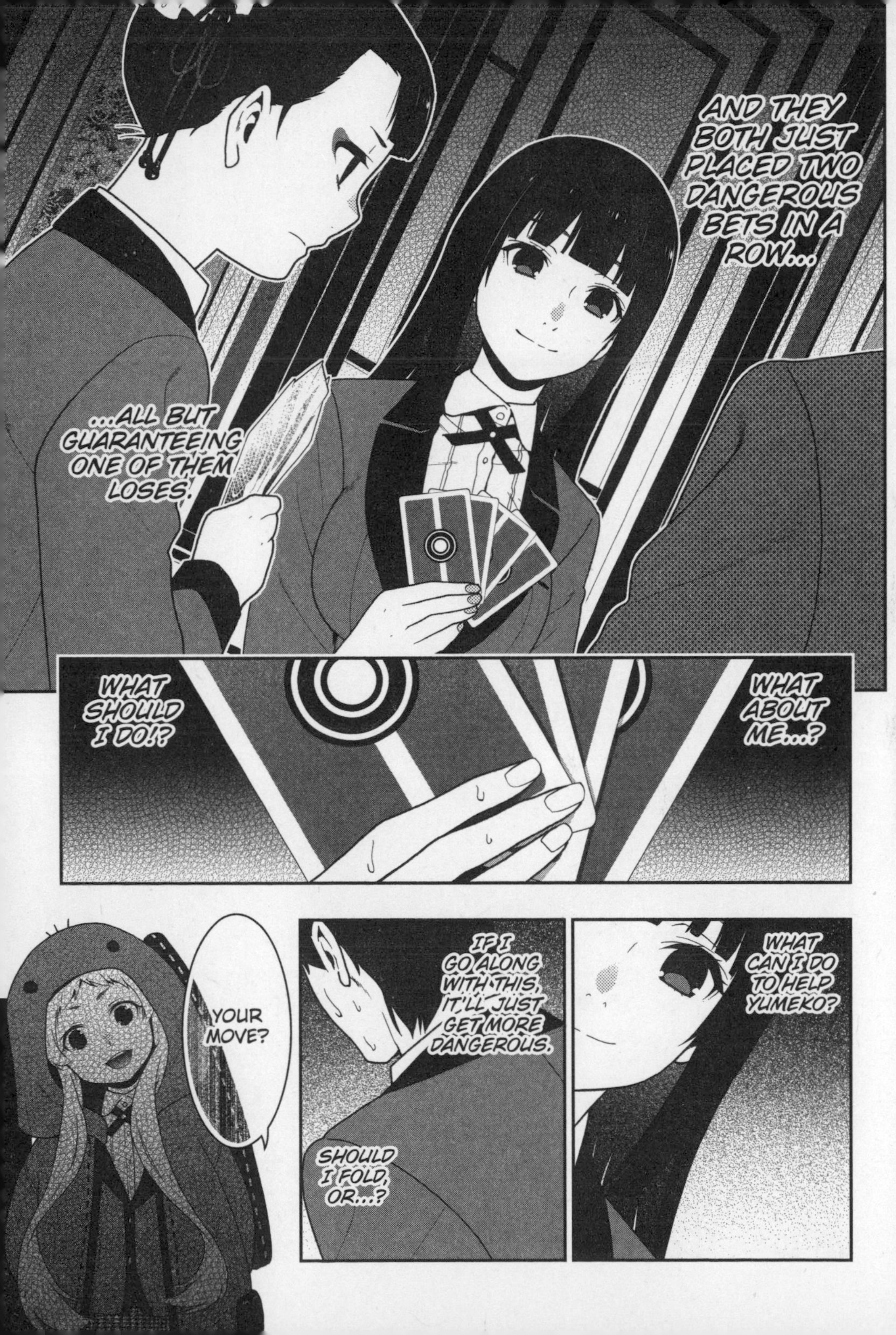
AND THEY BOTH JUST PLACED TWO DANGEROUS BETS IN A ROW...
...ALL BUT GUARANTEEING ONE OF THEM LOSES.
WHAT ABOUT ME...?
WHAT SHOULD I DO!?
WHAT CAN I DO TO HELP YUMEKO?
IF I GO ALONG WITH THIS, IT'LL JUST GET MORE DANGEROUS.
SHOULD I FOLD, OR...?
YOUR MOVE?

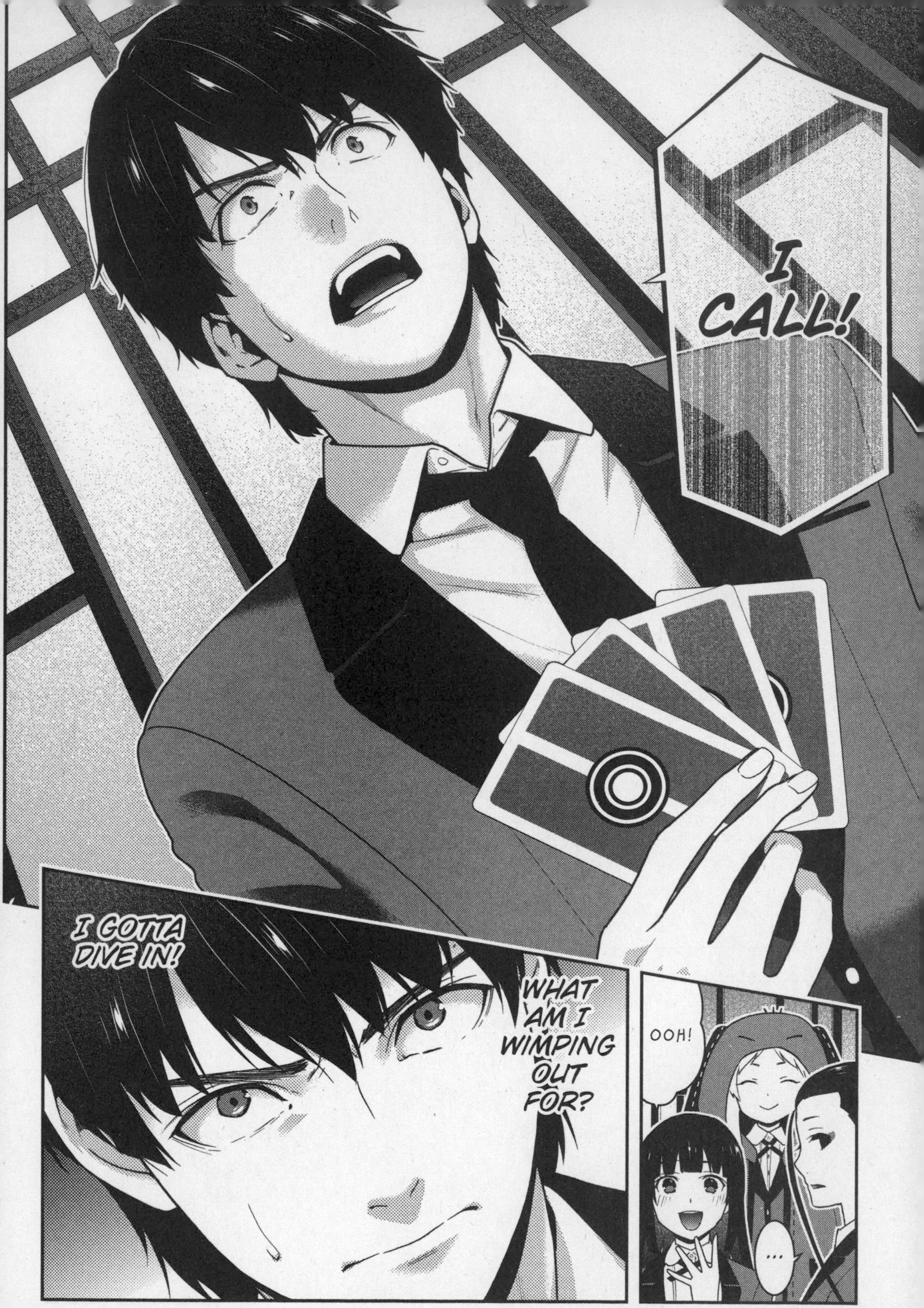
I CALL!
OOH!
...
WHAT AM I WIMPING OUT FOR?
I GOTTA DIVE IN!

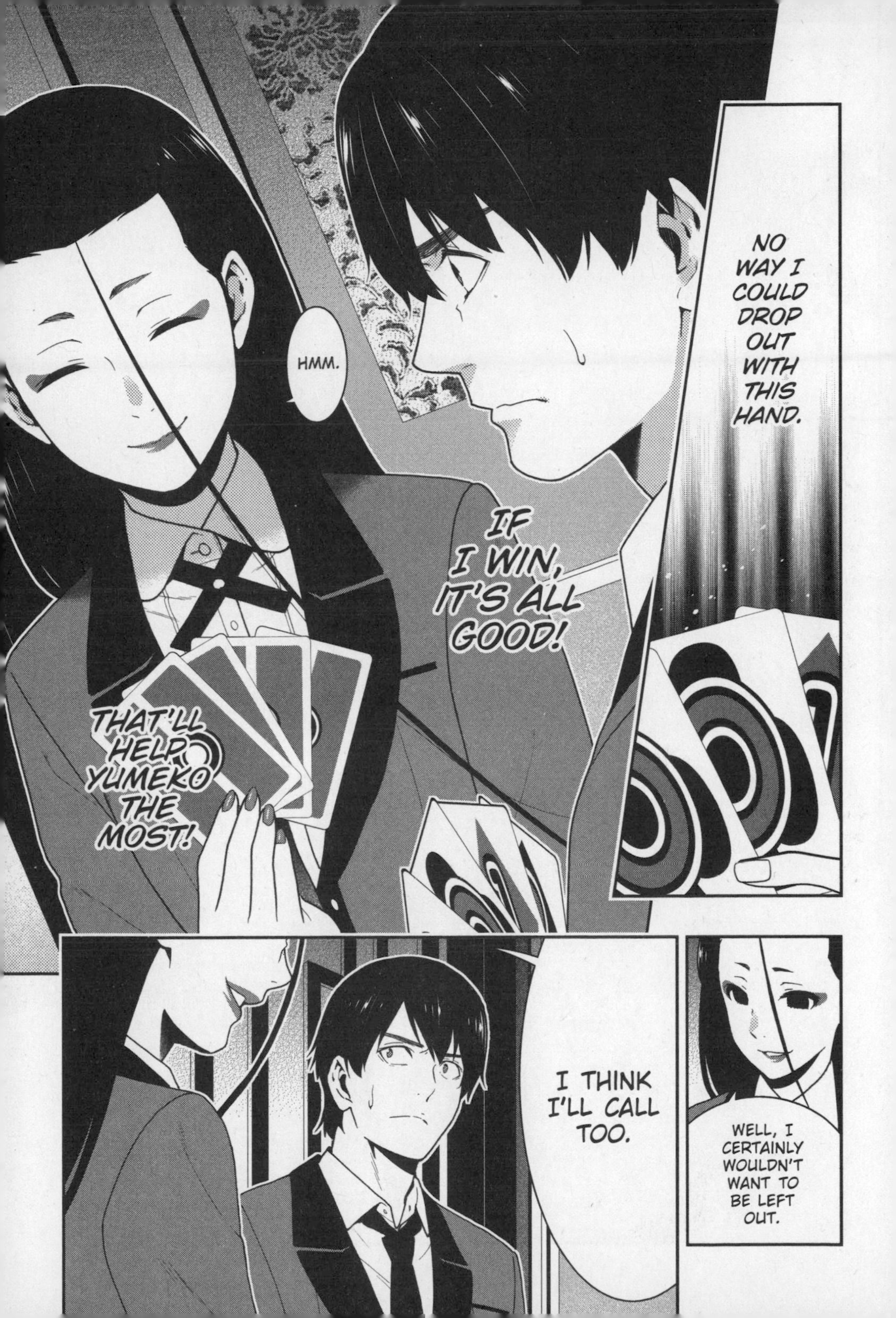
NO WAY I COULD DROP OUT WITH THIS HAND.
HMM.
IF I WIN, IT'S ALL GOOD!
THAT'LL HELP YUMEKO THE MOST!
WELL, I CERTAINLY WOULDN'T WANT TO BE LEFT OUT.
I THINK I'LL CALL TOO.

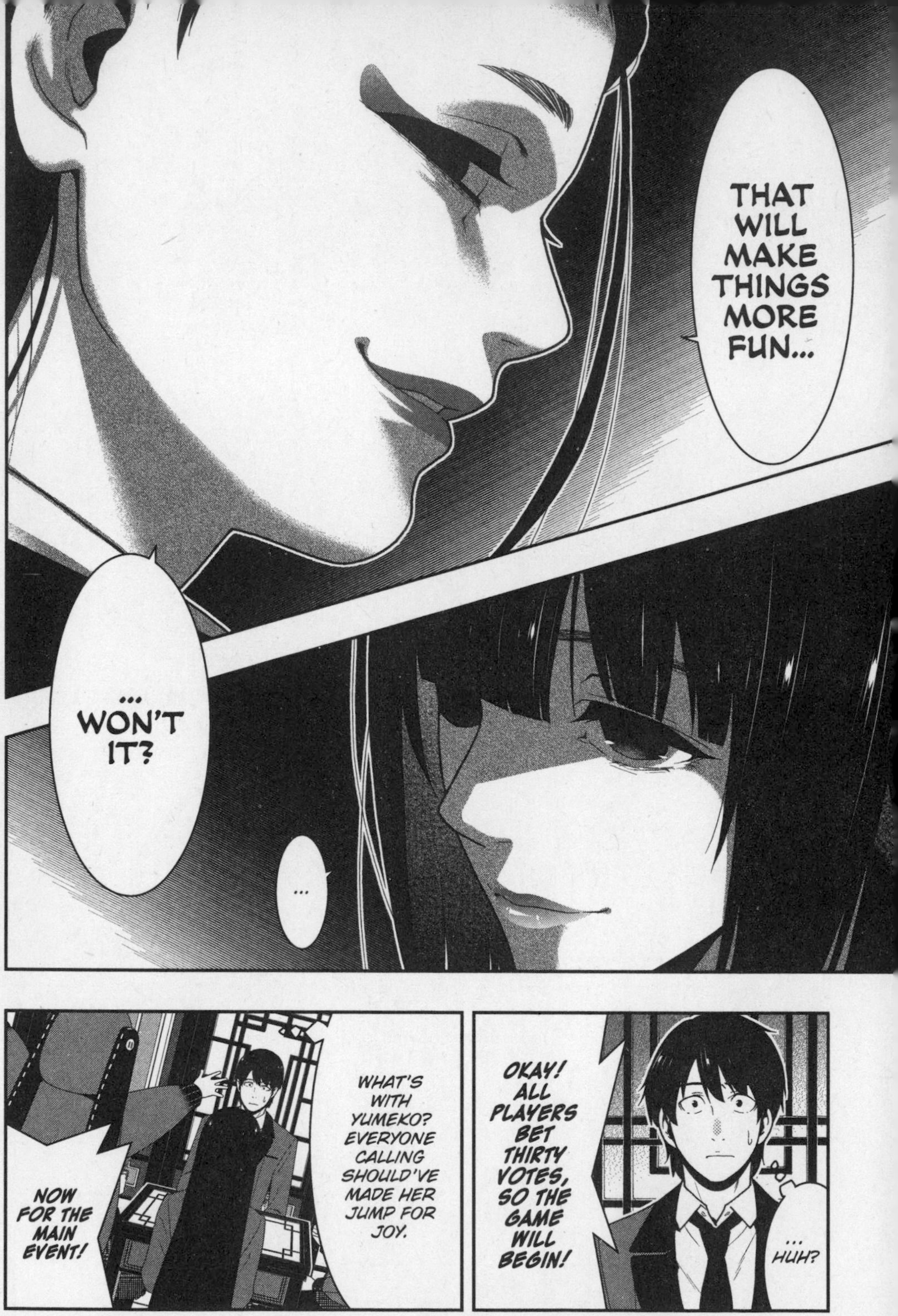
THAT WILL MAKE THINGS MORE FUN...
...WON'T IT?
...
OKAY! ALL PLAYERS BET THIRTY VOTES, SO THE GAME WILL BEGIN!
...HUH?
WHAT'S WITH YUMEKO? EVERYONE CALLING SHOULD'VE MADE HER JUMP FOR JOY.
NOW FOR THE MAIN EVENT!

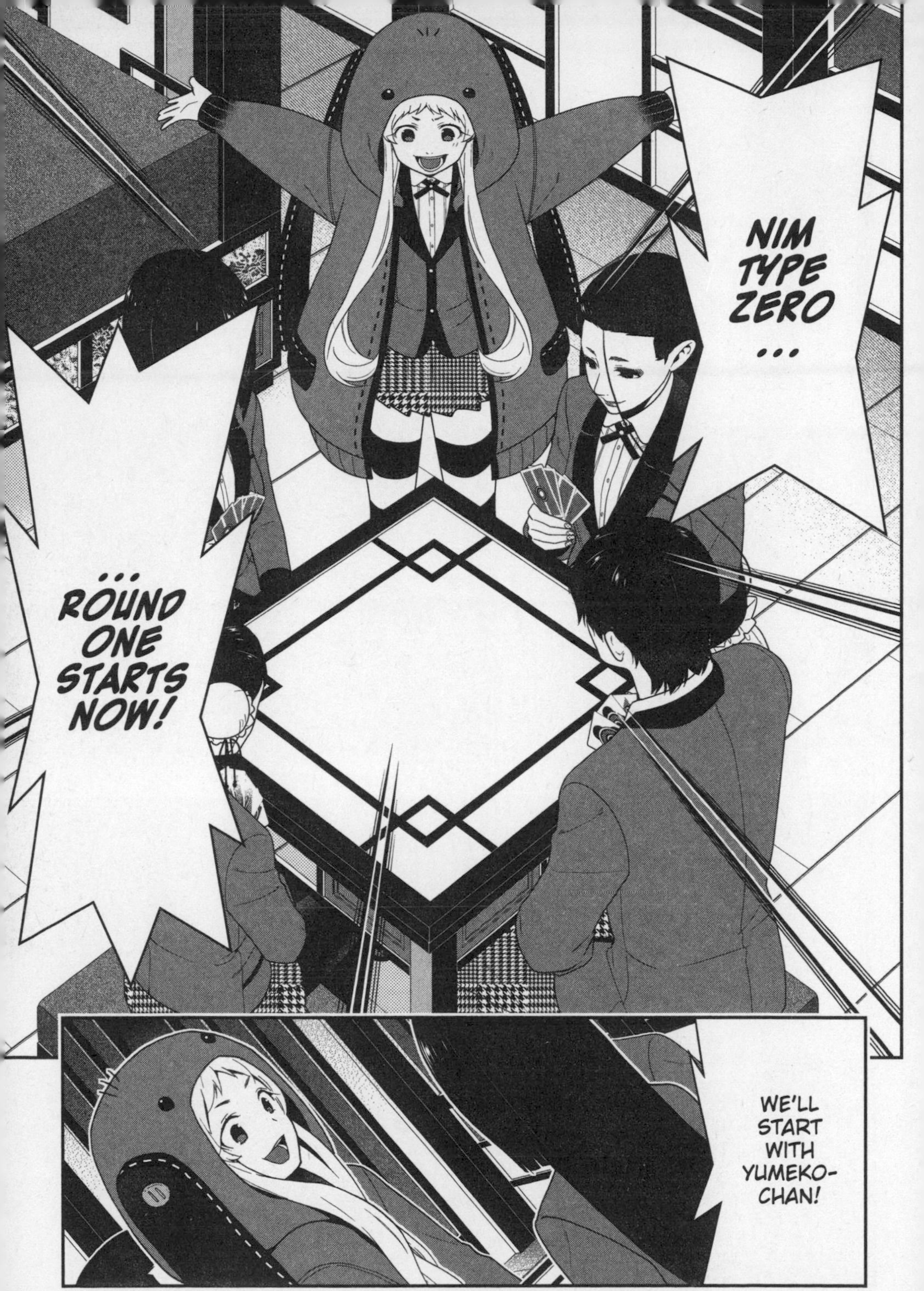
NIM TYPE ZERO ...
... RÖUND ONE STARTS NOW!
WE'LL START WITH YUMEKO-CHAN!

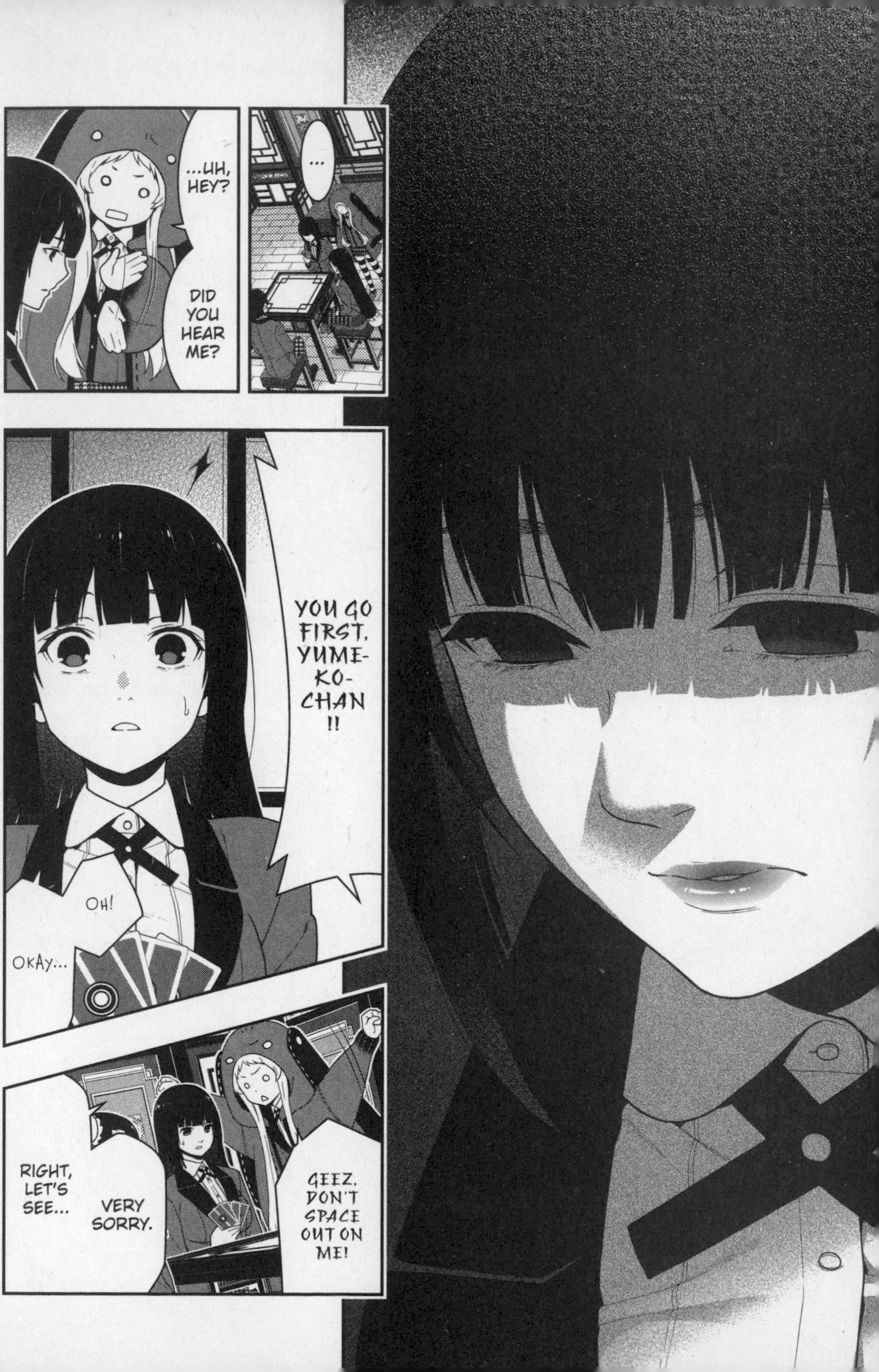
...
...UH, HEY?
DID YOU HEAR ME?
YOU GO FIRST, YUME-KO-CHAN !!
OH!
OKAY...
GEEZ. DON'T SPACE OUT ON ME!
VERY SORRY.
RIGHT, LET'S SEE...

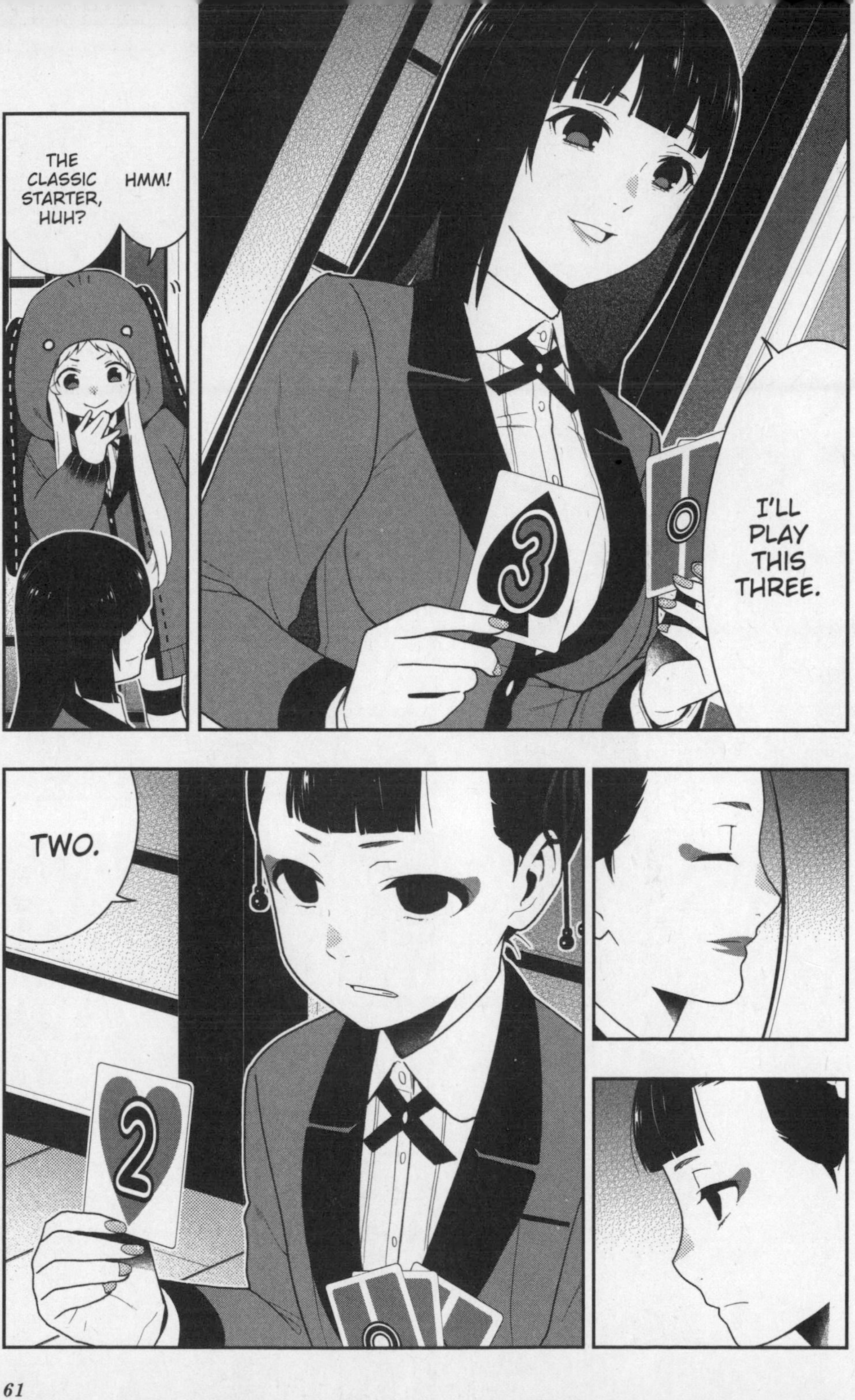
I'LL PLAY THIS THREE.
HMM!
THE CLASSIC STARTER, HUH?
TWO.

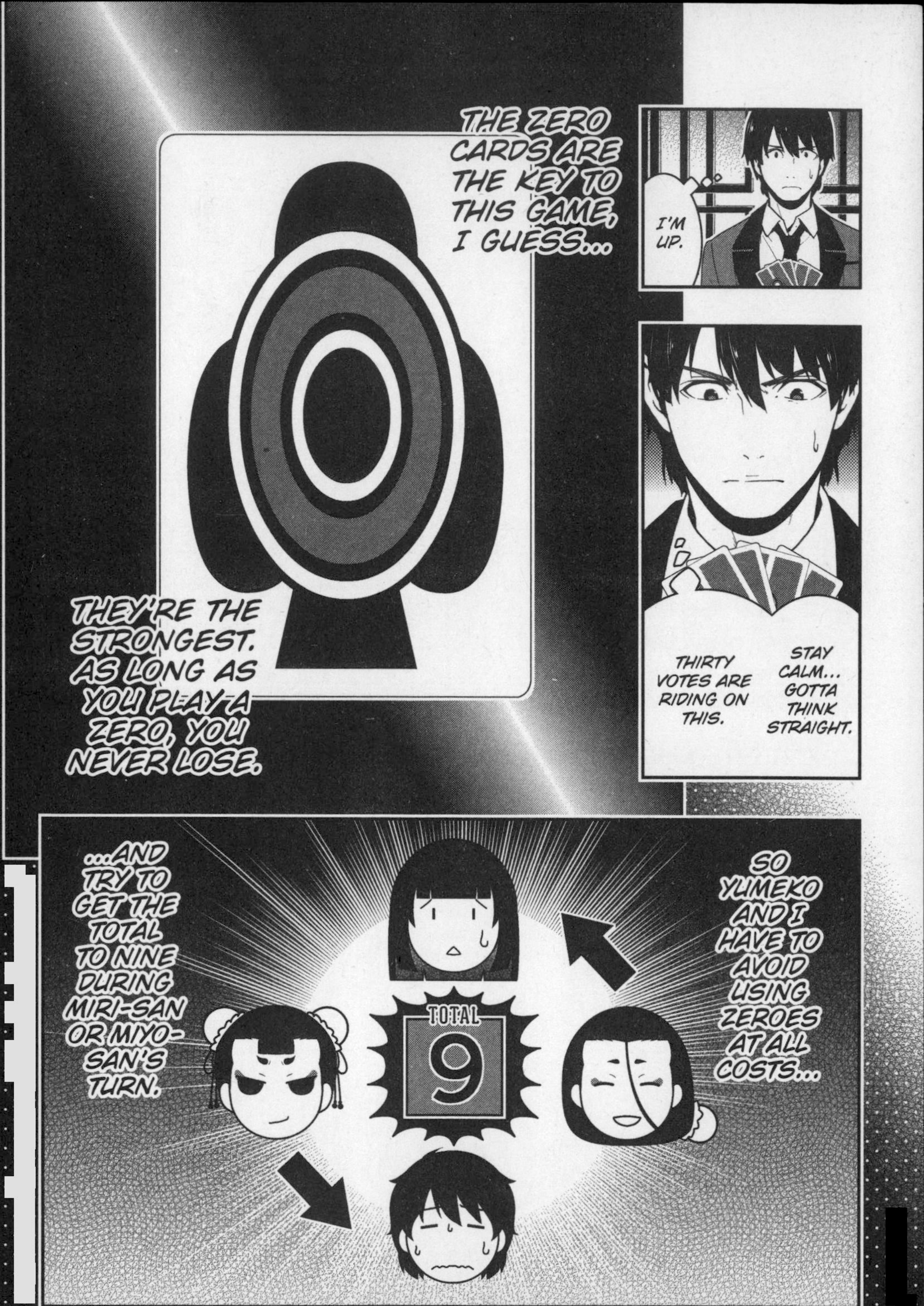
I'M UP.
STAY CALM... GOTTA THINK STRAIGHT.
THIRTY VOTES ARE RIDING ON THIS.
THE ZERO CARDS ARE THE KEY TO THIS GAME, I GUESS...
THEY'RE THE STRONGEST. AS LONG AS YOU PLAY A ZERO, YOU NEVER LOSE.
SO YUMEKO AND I HAVE TO AVOID USING ZEROES AT ALL COSTS...
...AND TRY TO GET THE TOTAL TO NINE DURING MIRI-SAN OR MIYO-SAN'S TURN.
TOTAL
9

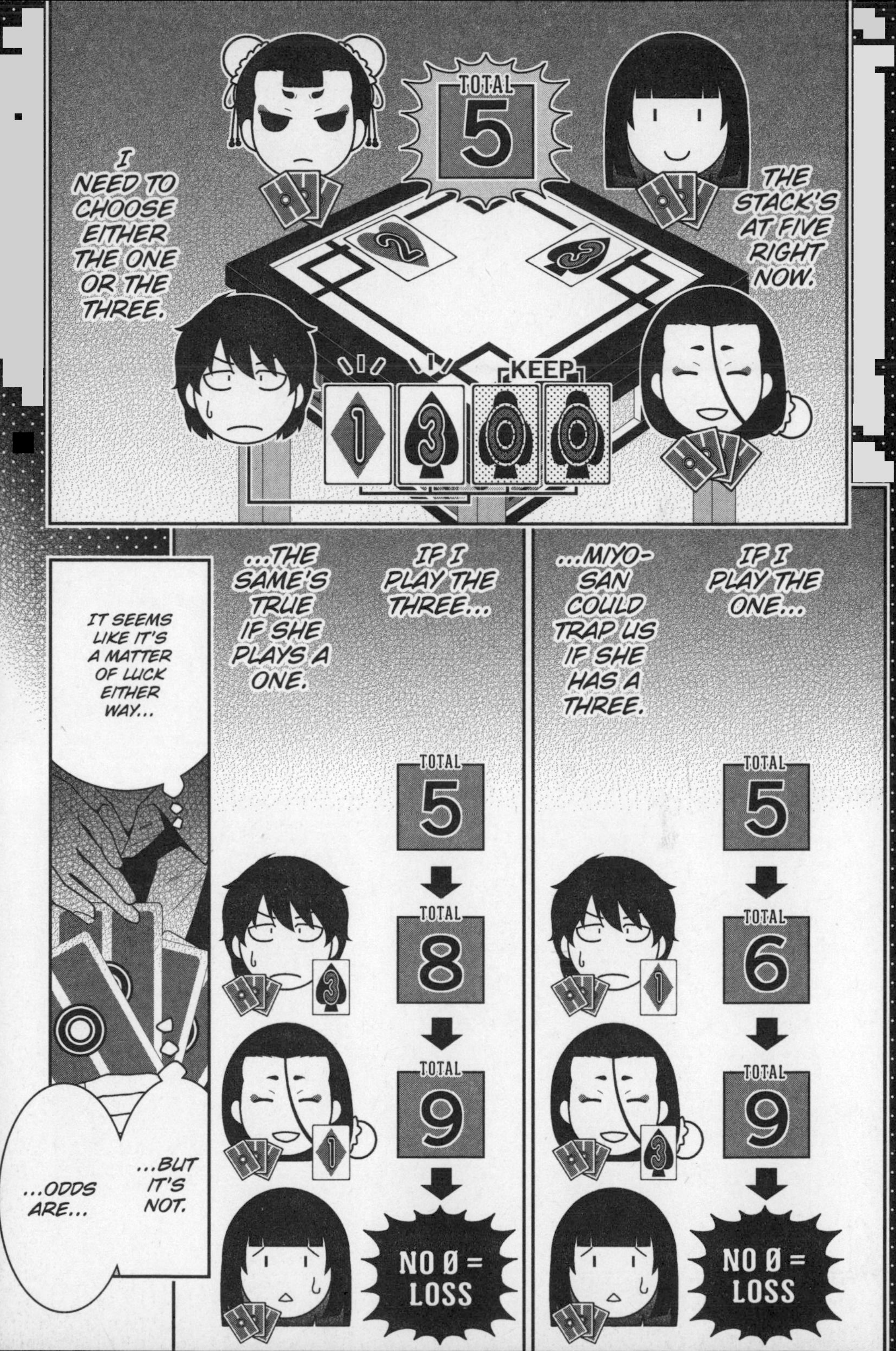
TOTAL 5
THE STACK'S AT FIVE RIGHT NOW.
I NEED TO CHOOSE EITHER THE ONE OR THE THREE.
KEEP
IF I PLAY THE ONE...
...MIYO-SAN COULD TRAP US IF SHE HAS A THREE.
TOTAL 5
TOTAL 6
TOTAL 9
NO 0 = LOSS
IF I PLAY THE THREE...
...THE SAME'S TRUE IF SHE PLAYS A ONE.
TOTAL 5
TOTAL 8
TOTAL 9
NO 0 = LOSS
IT SEEMS LIKE IT'S A MATTER OF LUCK EITHER WAY...
...BUT IT'S NOT.
...ODDS ARE...

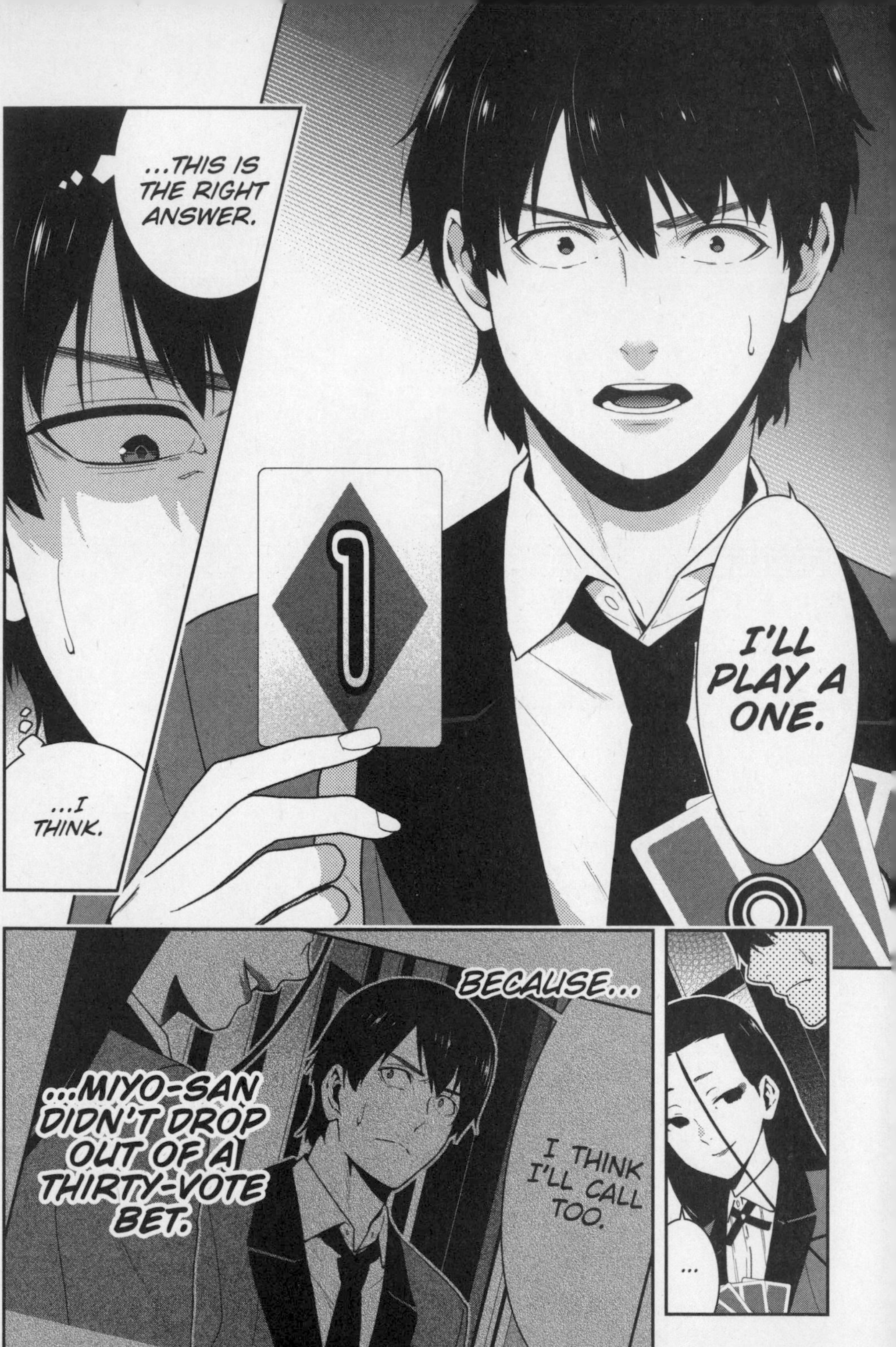
I'LL PLAY A ONE.
...THIS IS THE RIGHT ANSWER.
...I THINK.
...
BECAUSE...
...MIYO-SAN DIDN'T DROP OUT OF A THIRTY-VOTE BET.
I THINK I'LL CALL TOO.

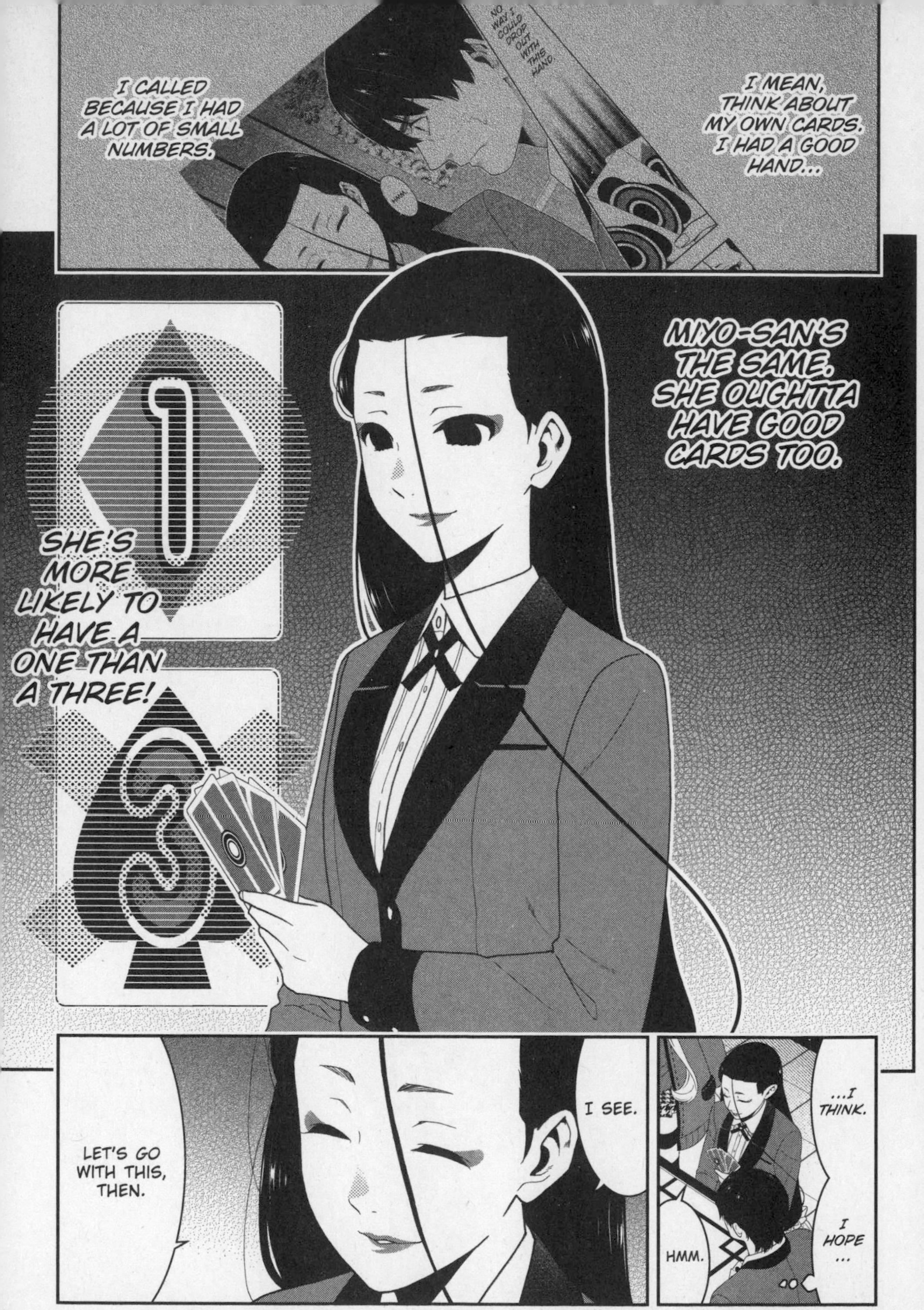
I MEAN, THINK ABOUT MY OWN CARDS. I HAD A GOOD HAND...
NO WAY I COULD DROP OUT WITH THIS HAND.
I CALLED BECAUSE I HAD A LOT OF SMALL NUMBERS.
MIYO-SAN'S THE SAME. SHE OUGHTTA HAVE GOOD CARDS TOO.
SHE'S MORE LIKELY TO HAVE A ONE THAN A THREE!
...I THINK.
I HOPE...
HMM.
I SEE.
LET'S GO WITH THIS, THEN.

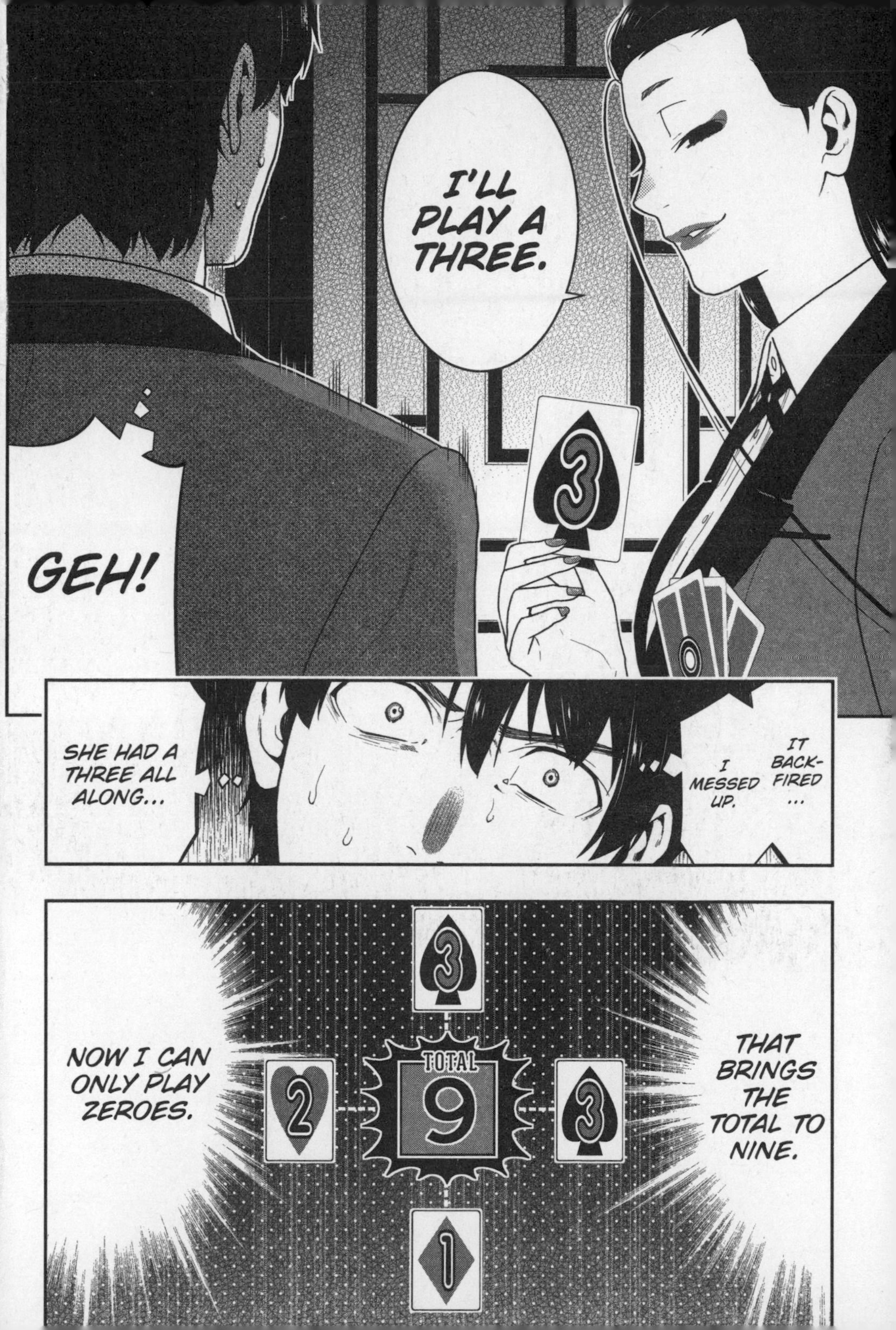
I'LL PLAY A THREE.
GEH!
IT BACK-FIRED...
I MESSED UP.
SHE HAD A THREE ALL ALONG...
TOTAL
THAT BRINGS THE TOTAL TO NINE.
NOW I CAN ONLY PLAY ZEROES.

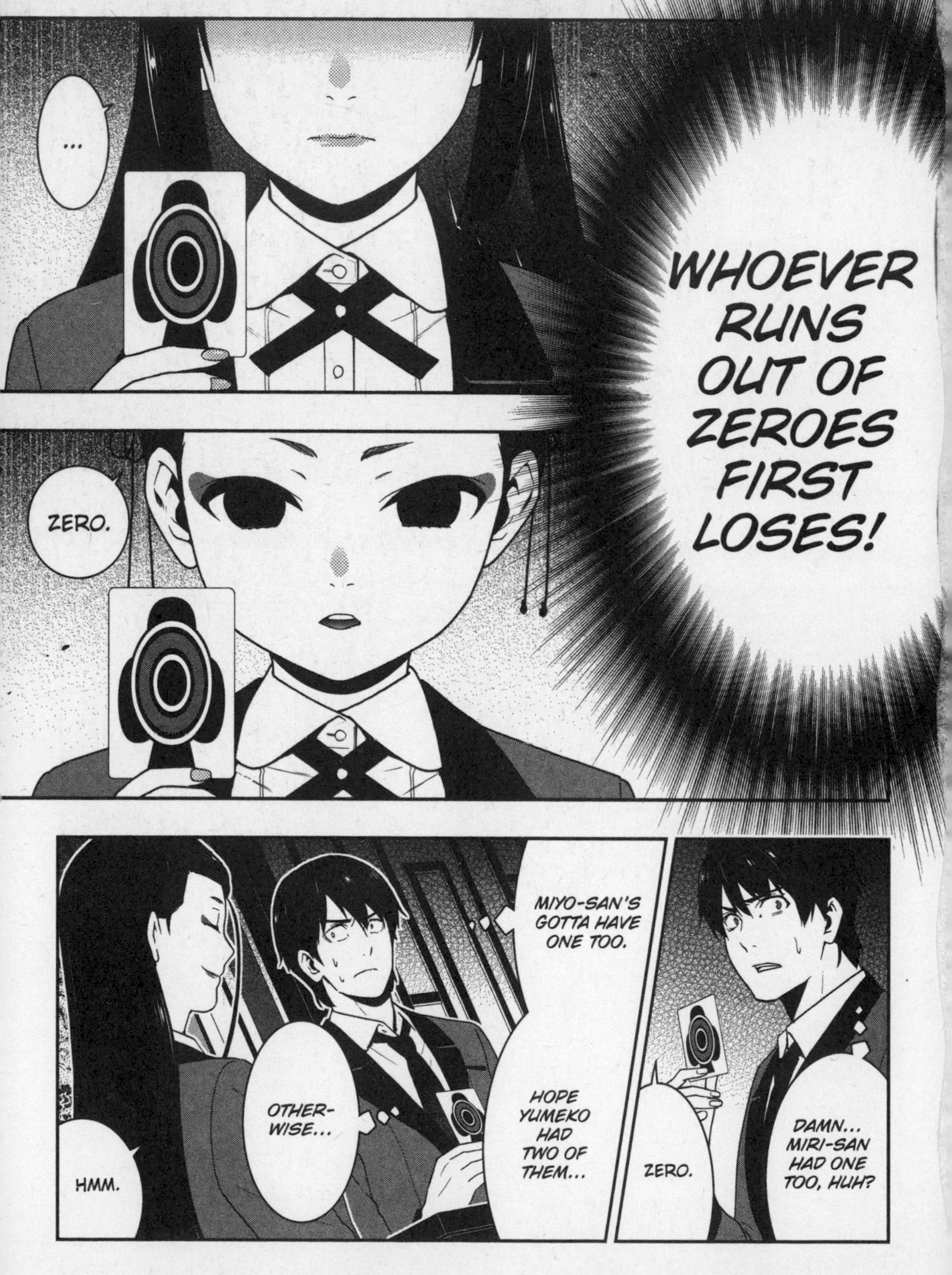

WHOEVER RUNS OUT OF ZEROES FIRST LOSES!
...
ZERO.
DAMN... MIRI-SAN HAD ONE TOO, HUH?
ZERO.
MIYO-SAN'S GOTTA HAVE ONE TOO.
HOPE YUMEKO HAD TWO OF THEM...
OTHER-WISE...
HMM.

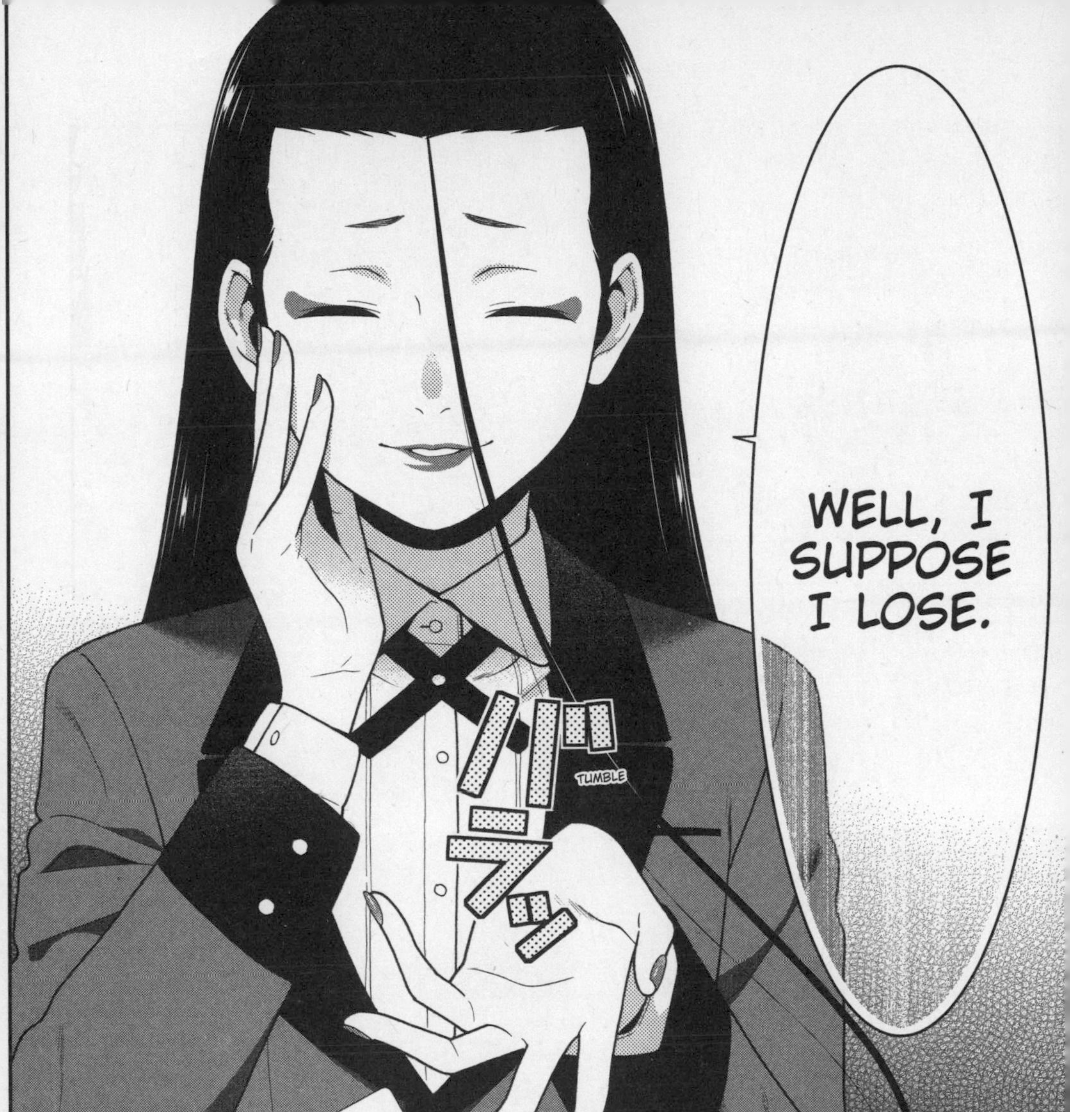
WELL, I SUPPOSE I LOSE.
TUMBLE

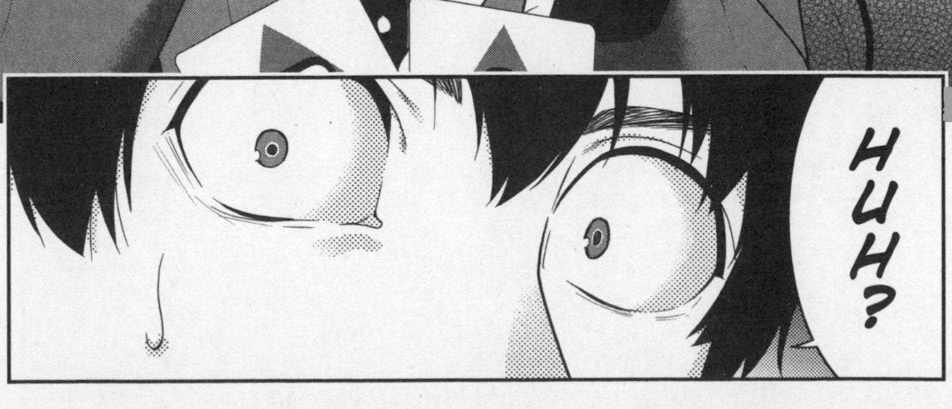
HUH?

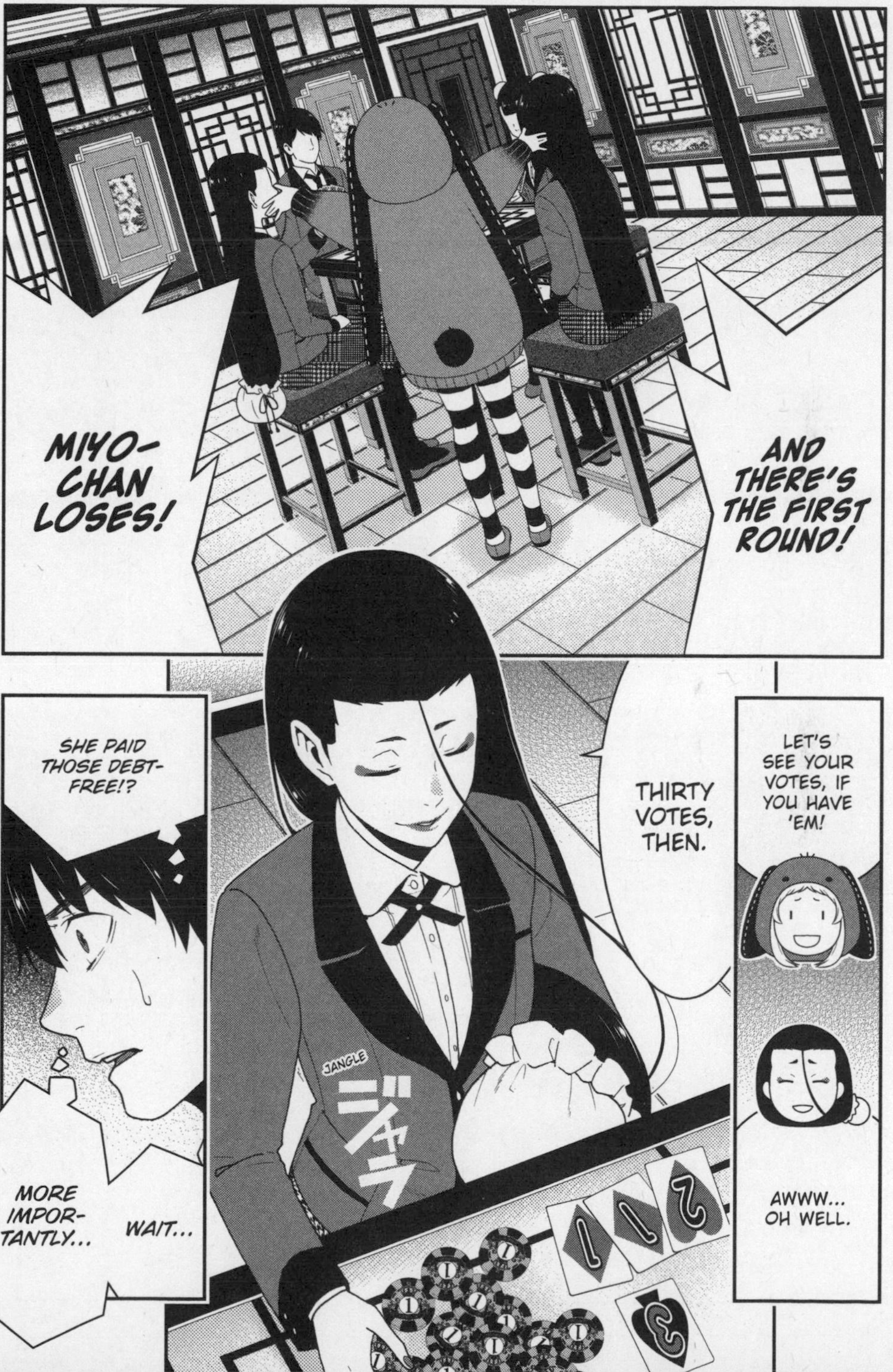
AND THERE'S THE FIRST ROUND!
MIYO-CHAN LOSES!
LET'S SEE YOUR VOTES, IF YOU HAVE 'EM!
AWWW... OH WELL.
THIRTY VOTES, THEN.
JANGLE
SHE PAID THOSE DEBT-FREE!?
WAIT...
MORE IMPORTANTLY...

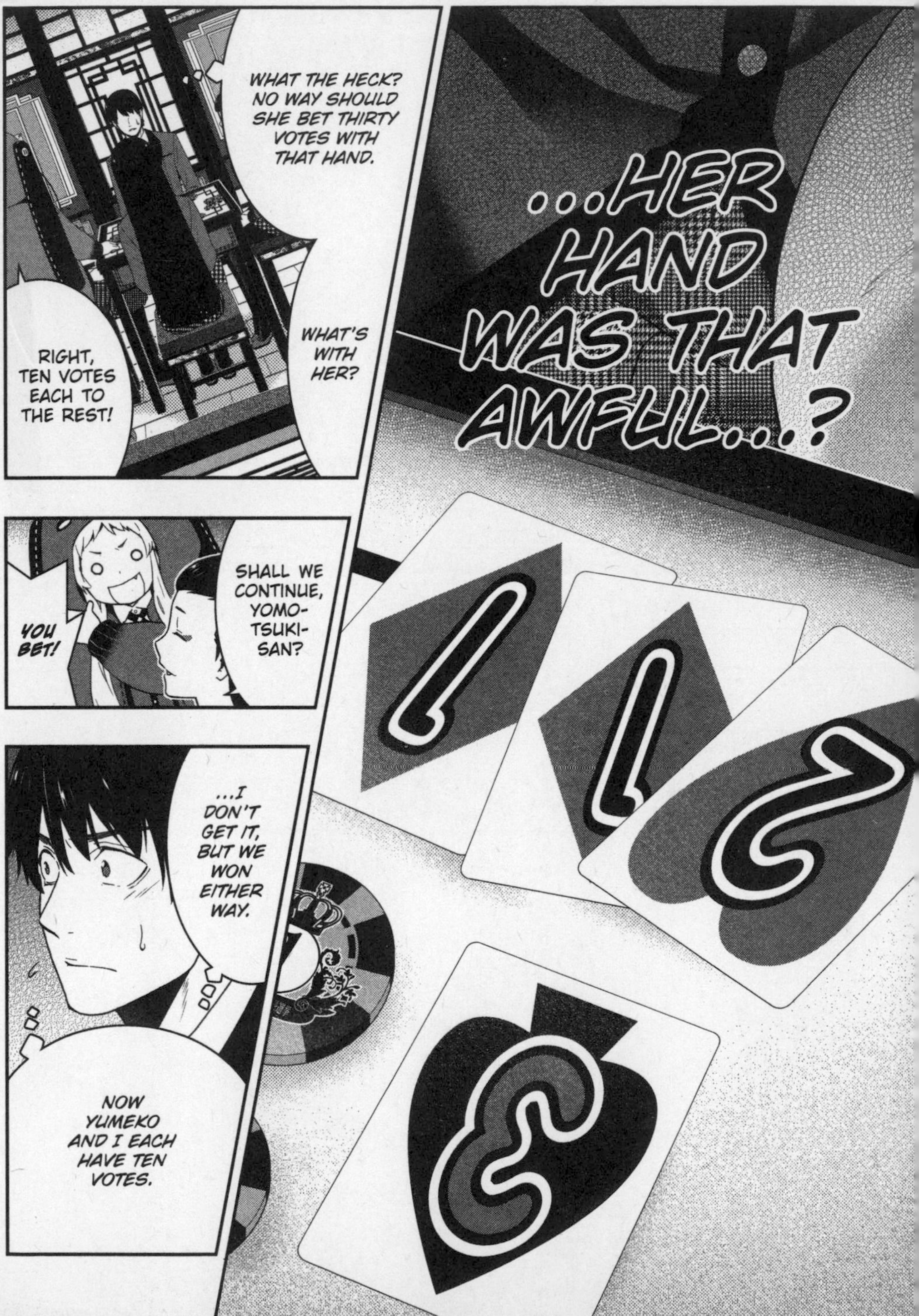
...HER HAND WAS THAT AWFUL...?
WHAT THE HECK? NO WAY SHOULD SHE BET THIRTY VOTES WITH THAT HAND.
WHAT'S WITH HER?
RIGHT, TEN VOTES EACH TO THE REST!
SHALL WE CONTINUE, YOMOTSUKI-SAN?
YOU BET!
...I DON'T GET IT, BUT WE WON EITHER WAY.
NOW YUMEKO AND I EACH HAVE TEN VOTES.

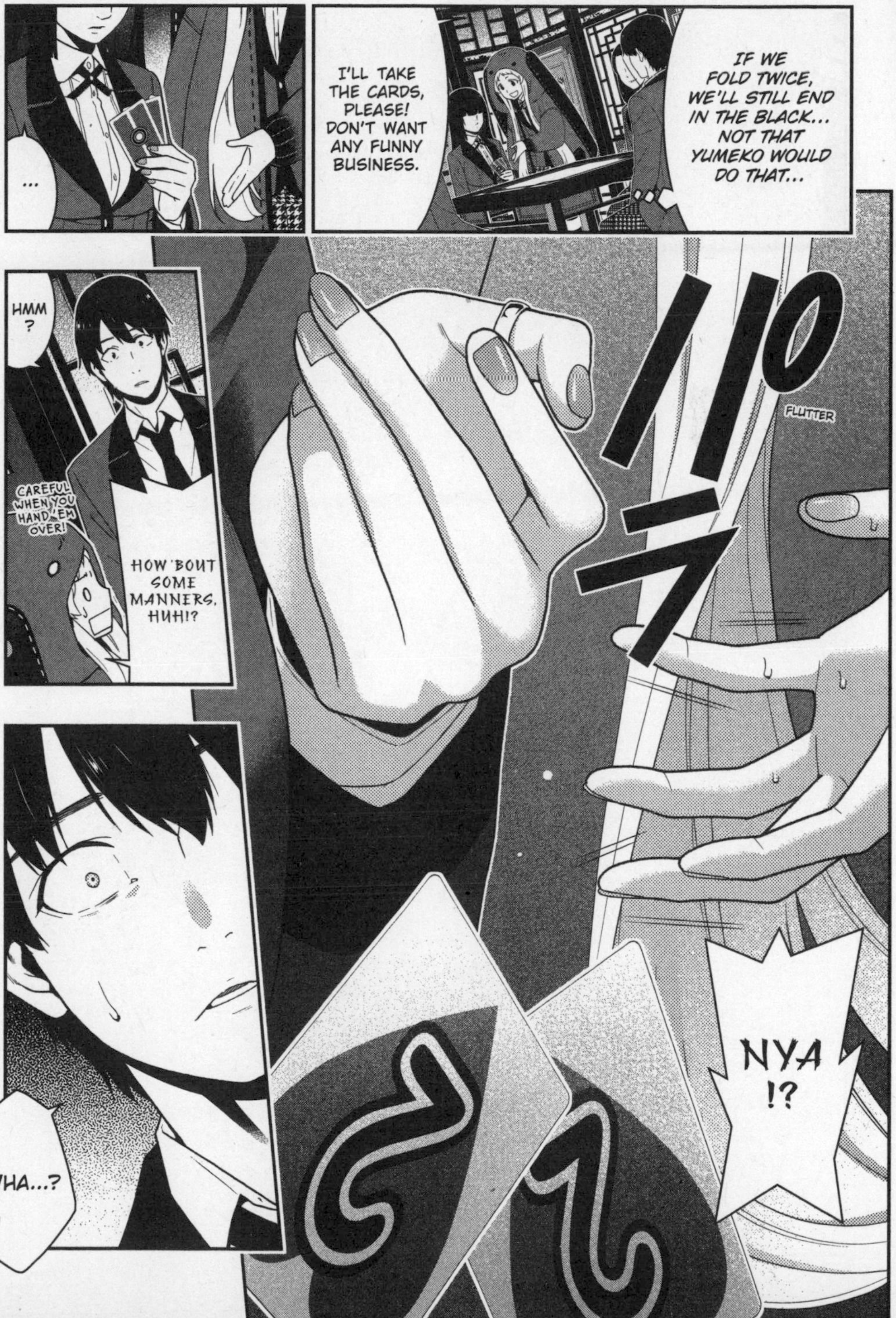
IF WE FOLD TWICE, WE'LL STILL END IN THE BLACK... NOT THAT YUMEKO WOULD DO THAT...
I'LL TAKE THE CARDS, PLEASE! DON'T WANT ANY FUNNY BUSINESS.
...
FLUTTER
NYA !?
HMM ?
HOW 'BOUT SOME MANNERS, HUH!?
CAREFUL WHEN YOU HAND 'EM OVER!
WHA...?

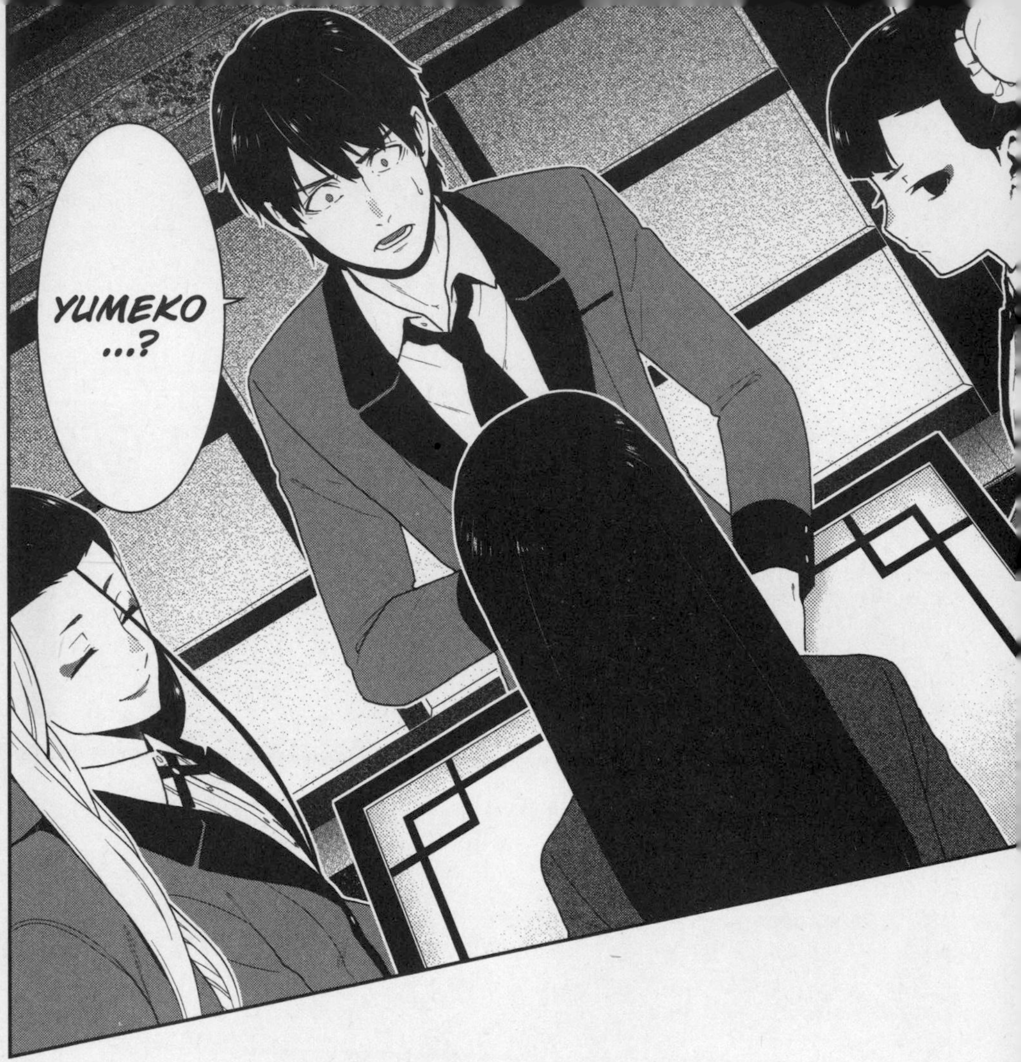
YUMEKO ...?
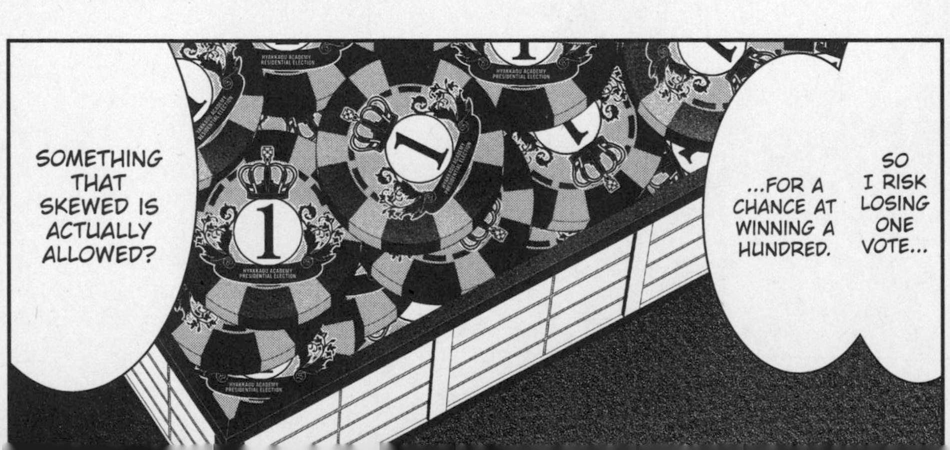
SO I RISK LOSING ONE VOTE...
...FOR A CHANCE AT WINNING A HUNDRED.
SOMETHING THAT SKEWED IS ACTUALLY ALLOWED?

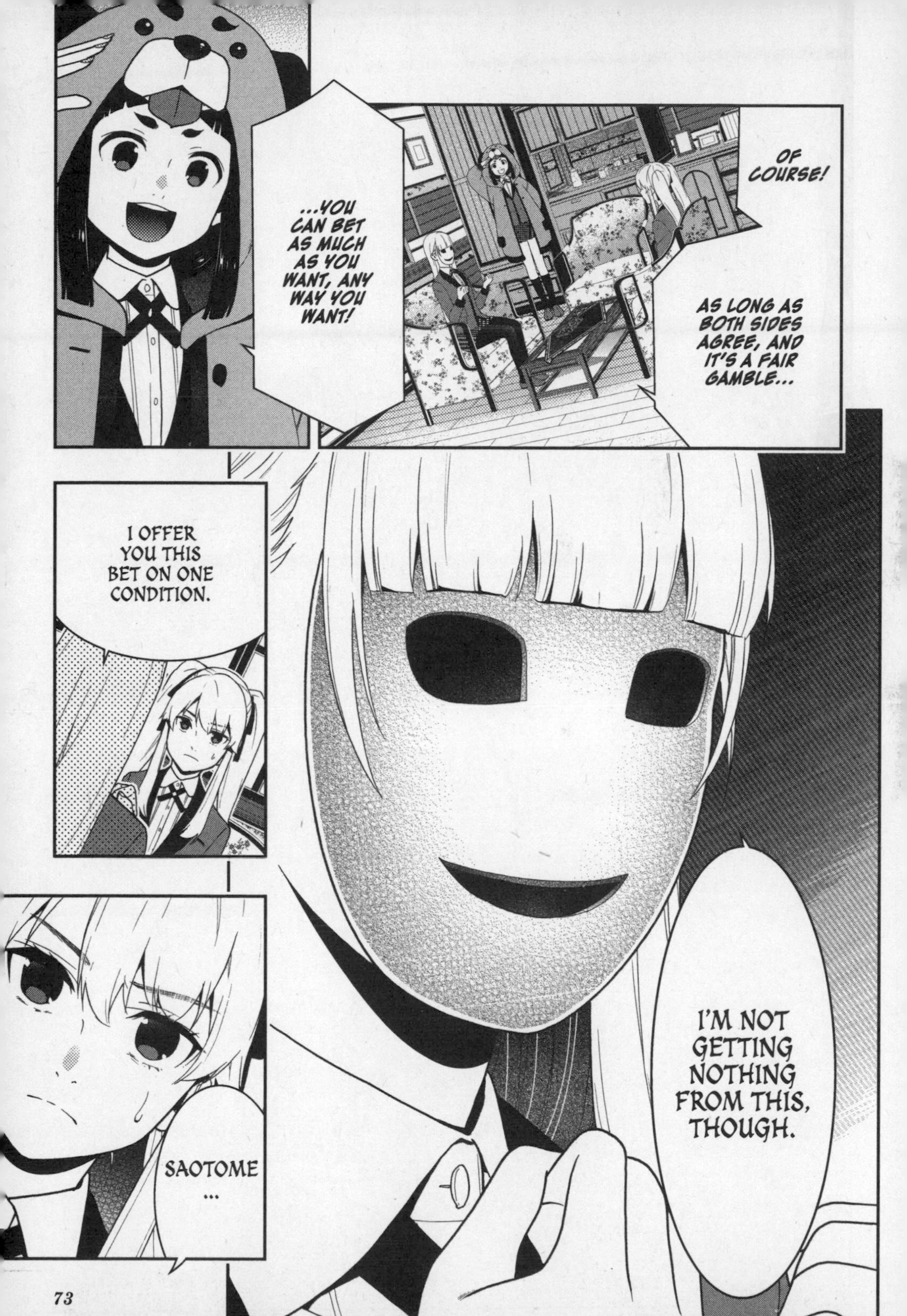
OF COURSE!
AS LONG AS BOTH SIDES AGREE, AND IT'S A FAIR GAMBLE...
...YOU CAN BET AS MUCH AS YOU WANT, ANY WAY YOU WANT!
I'M NOT GETTING NOTHING FROM THIS, THOUGH.
I OFFER YOU THIS BET ON ONE CONDITION.
SAOTOME ...

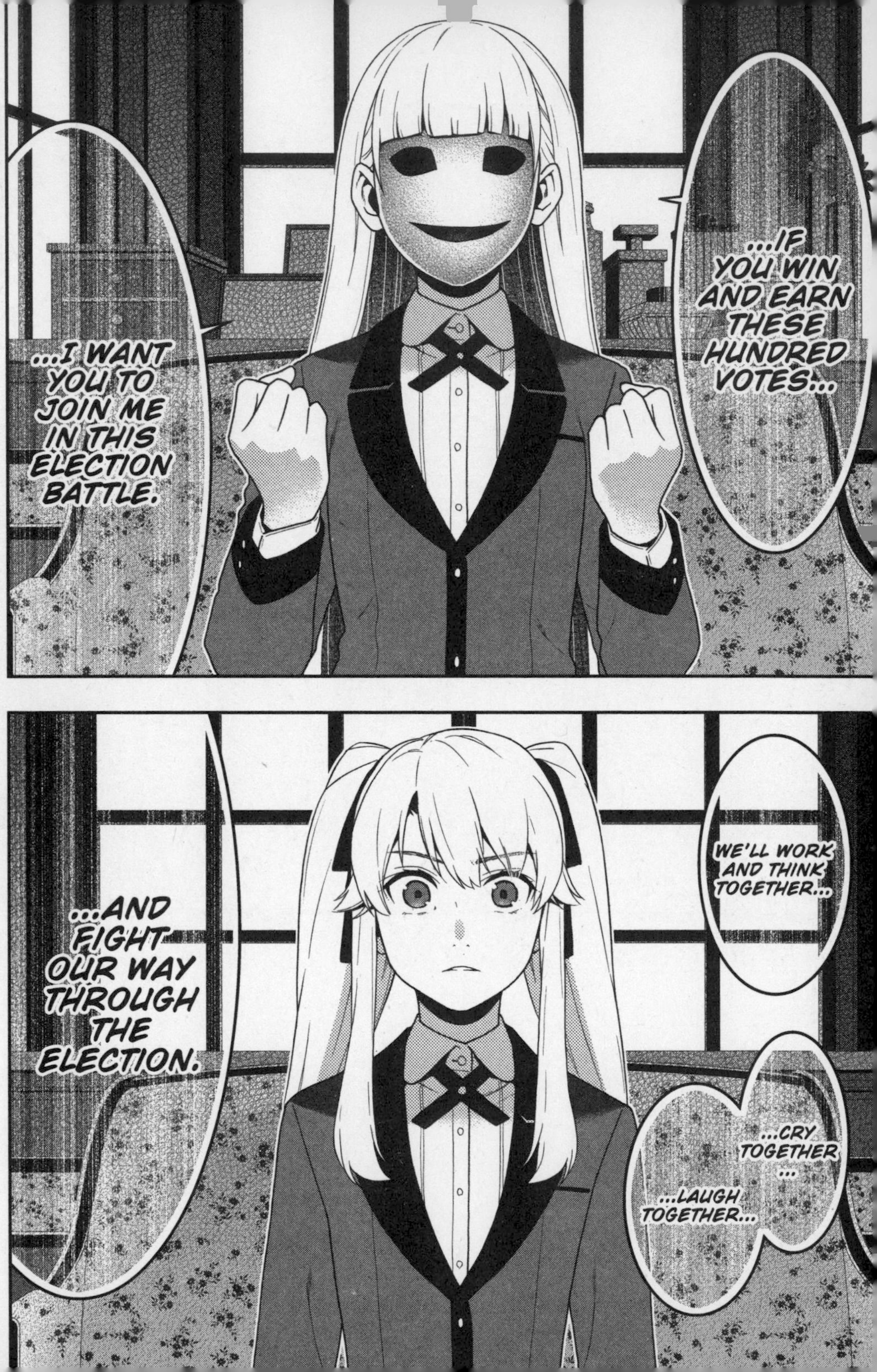
...IF YOU WIN AND EARN THESE HUNDRED VOTES...
...I WANT YOU TO JOIN ME IN THIS ELECTION BATTLE.
WE'LL WORK AND THINK TOGETHER...
...CRY TOGETHER...
...LAUGH TOGETHER...
...AND FIGHT OUR WAY THROUGH THE ELECTION.

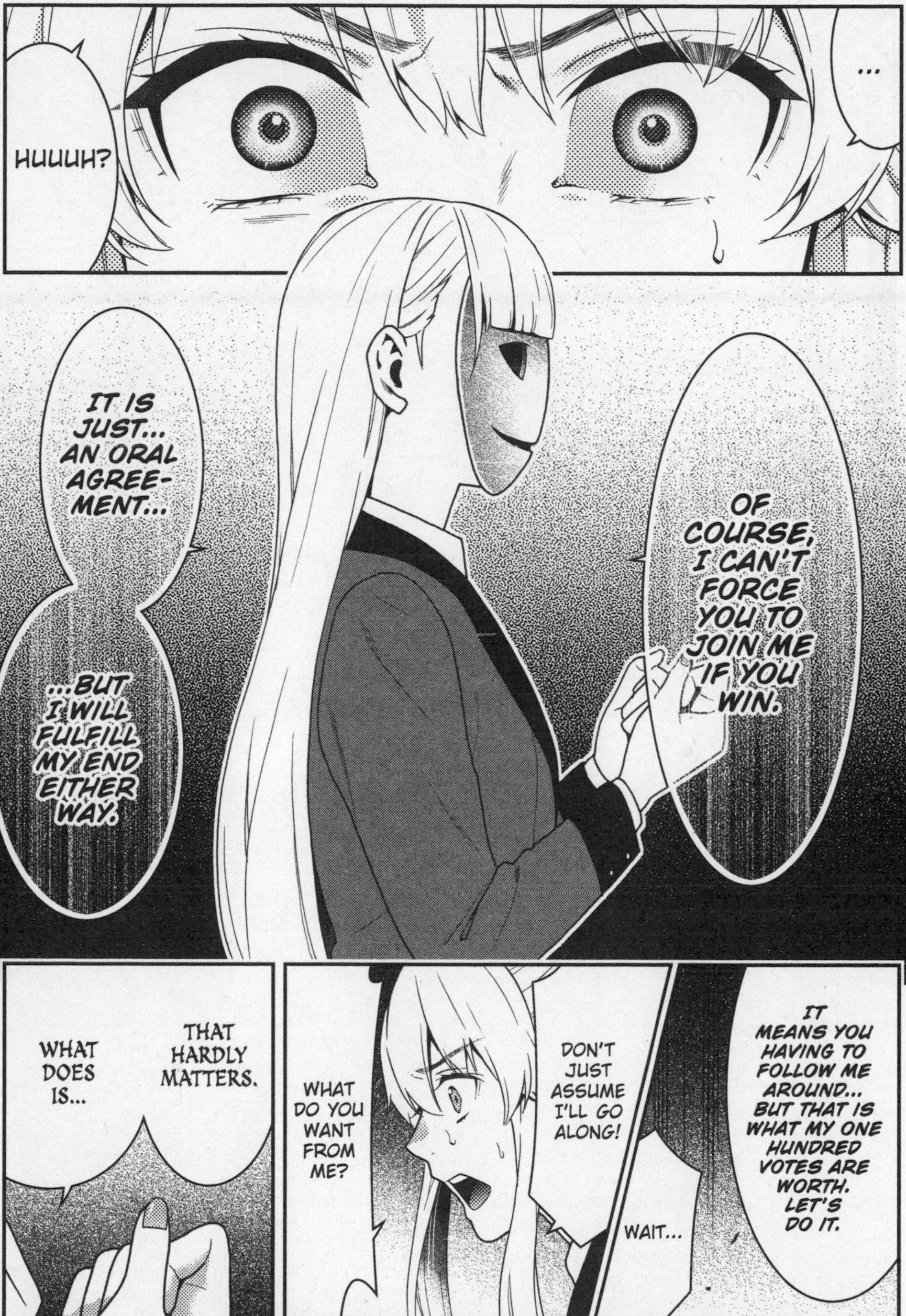
...
HUUUH?
OF COURSE, I CAN'T FORCE YOU TO JOIN ME IF YOU WIN.
IT IS JUST... AN ORAL AGREEMENT...
...BUT I WILL FULFILL MY END EITHER WAY.
IT MEANS YOU HAVING TO FOLLOW ME AROUND... BUT THAT IS WHAT MY ONE HUNDRED VOTES ARE WORTH. LET'S DO IT.
WAIT...
DON'T JUST ASSUME I'LL GO ALONG!
WHAT DO YOU WANT FROM ME?
THAT HARDLY MATTERS.
WHAT DOES IS...

...IF YOU JOIN HANDS WITH ME...

...YOU WILL BE WITHIN ARM'S REACH OF THE PRESIDENT'S CHAIR.

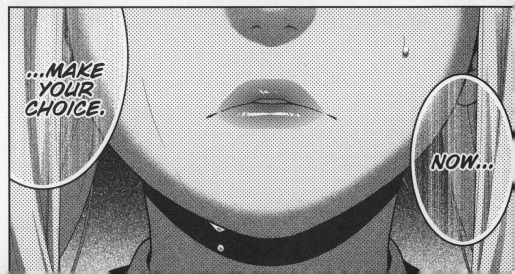

...MAKE YOUR CHOICE.

NOW...

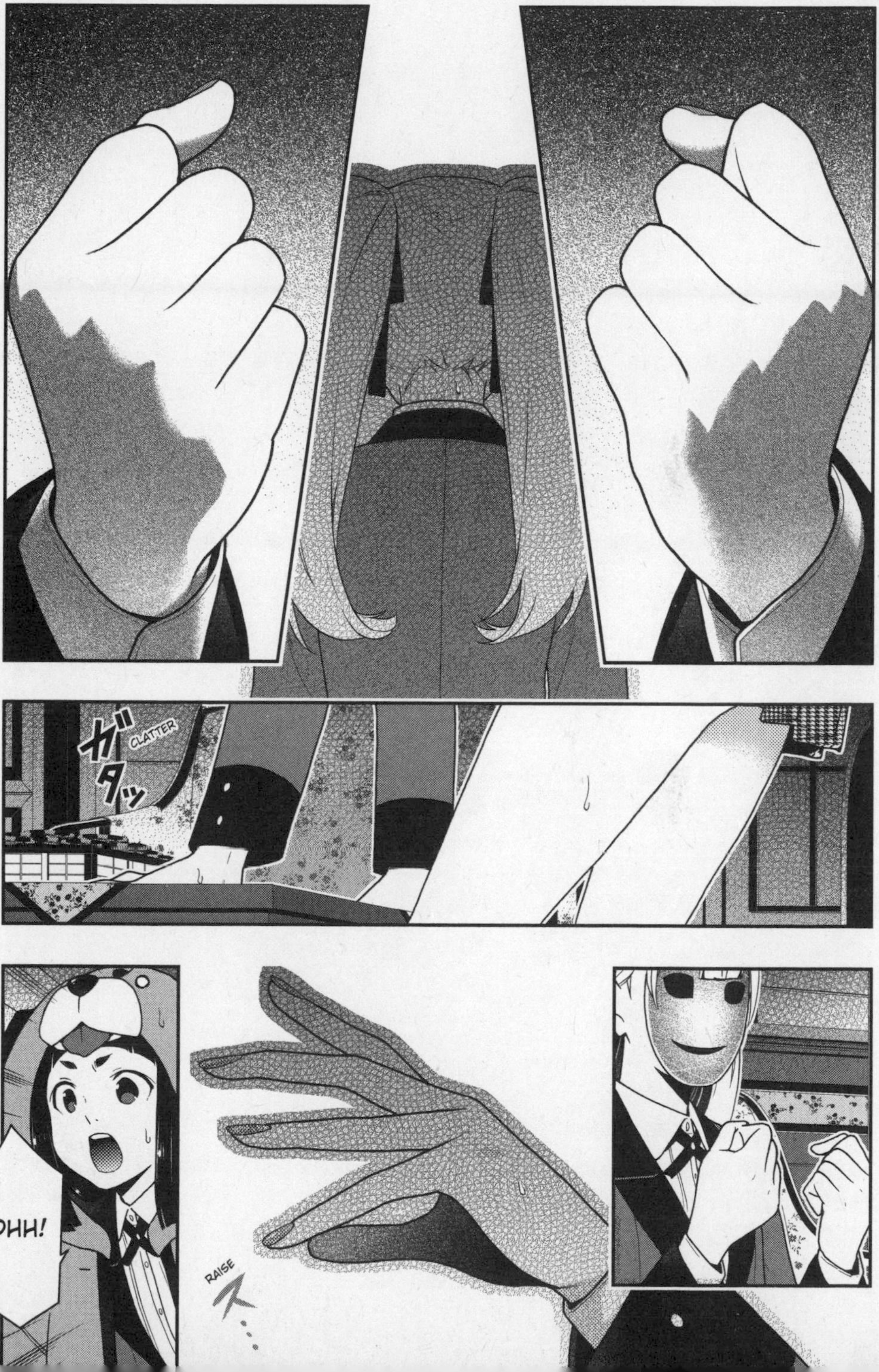
ガタッ
CLATTER
RAISE
ス
OHH!

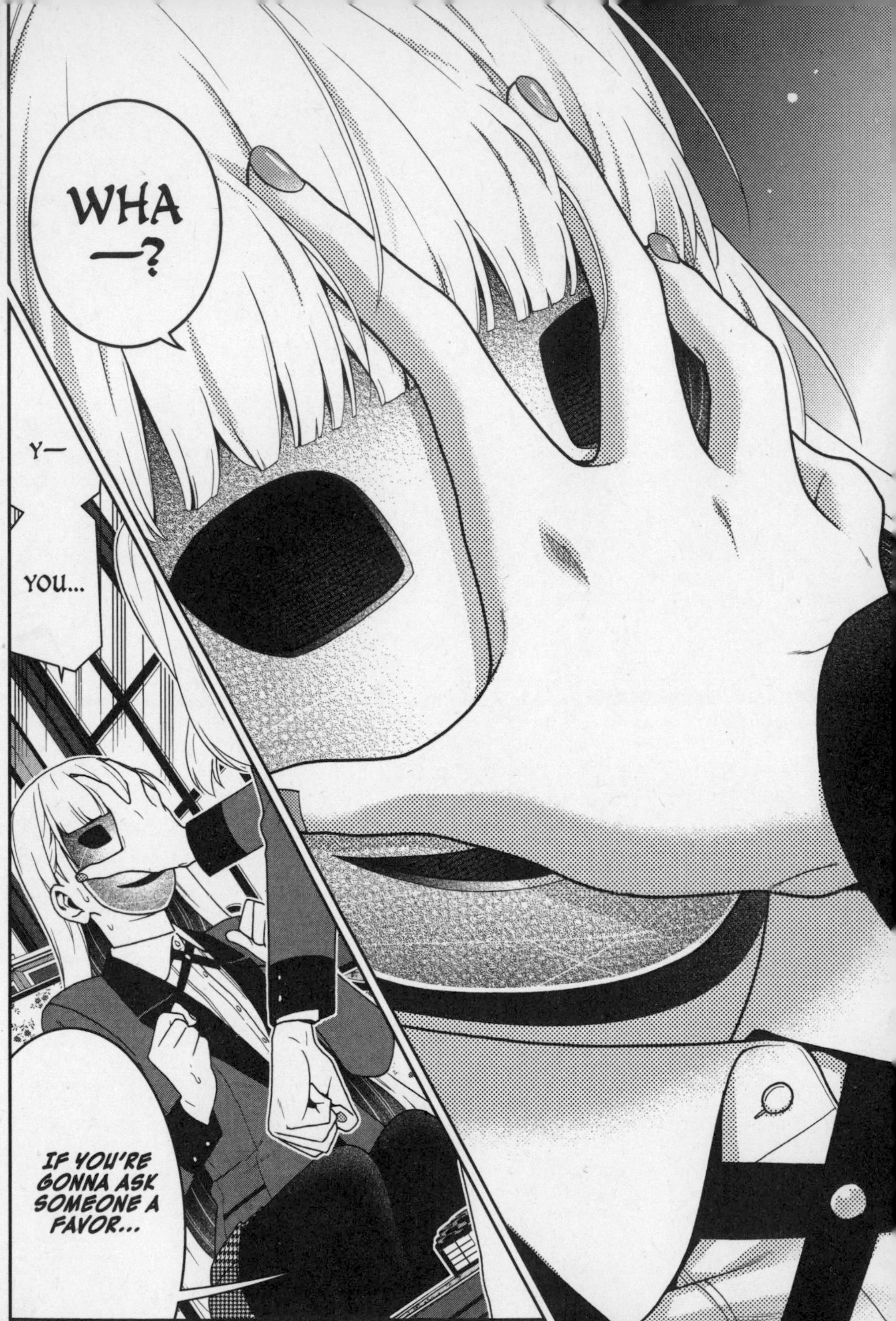
WHA—?
Y—
YOU...
IF YOU'RE GONNA ASK SOMEONE A FAVOR...

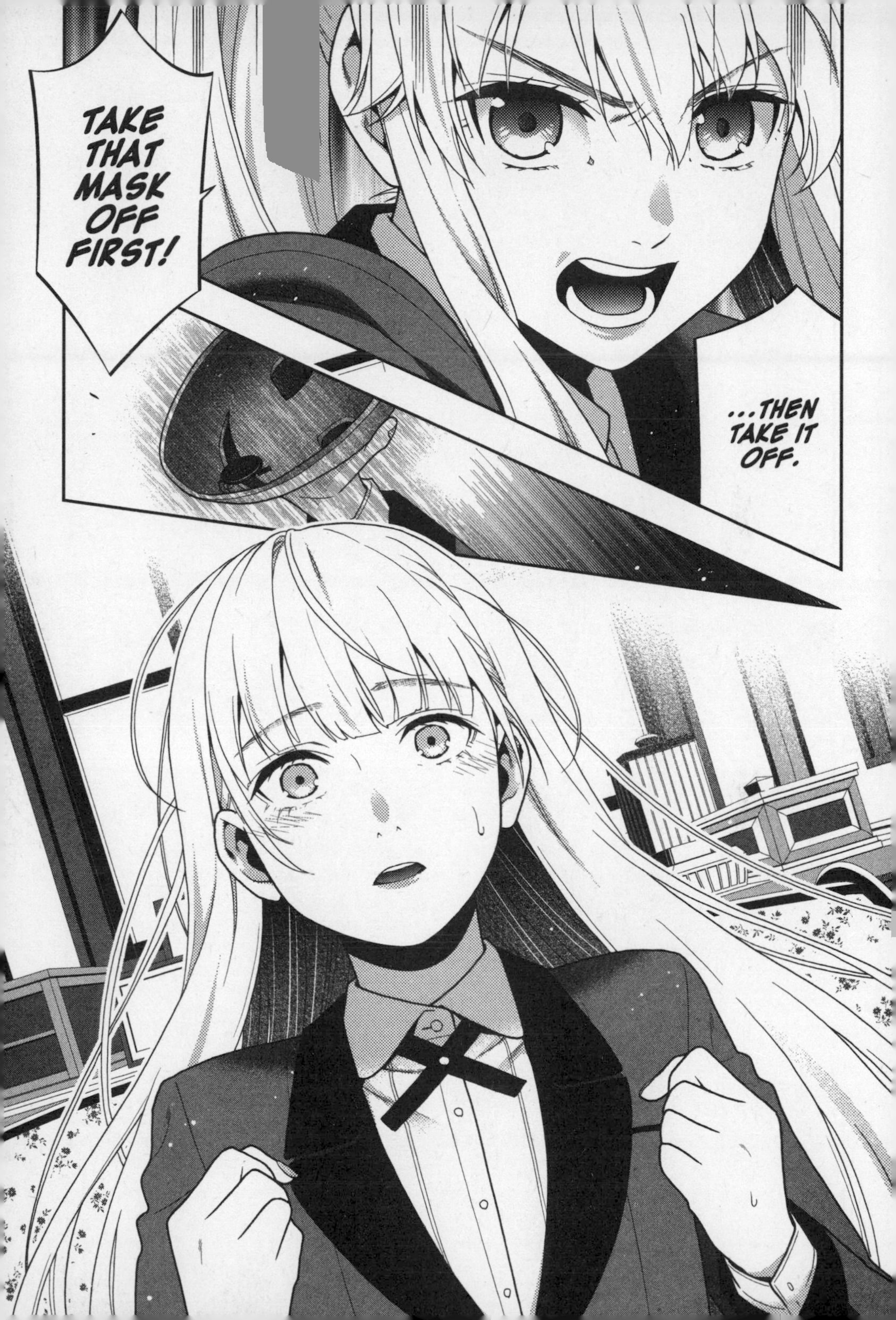
...THEN TAKE IT OFF.
TAKE THAT MASK OFF FIRST!

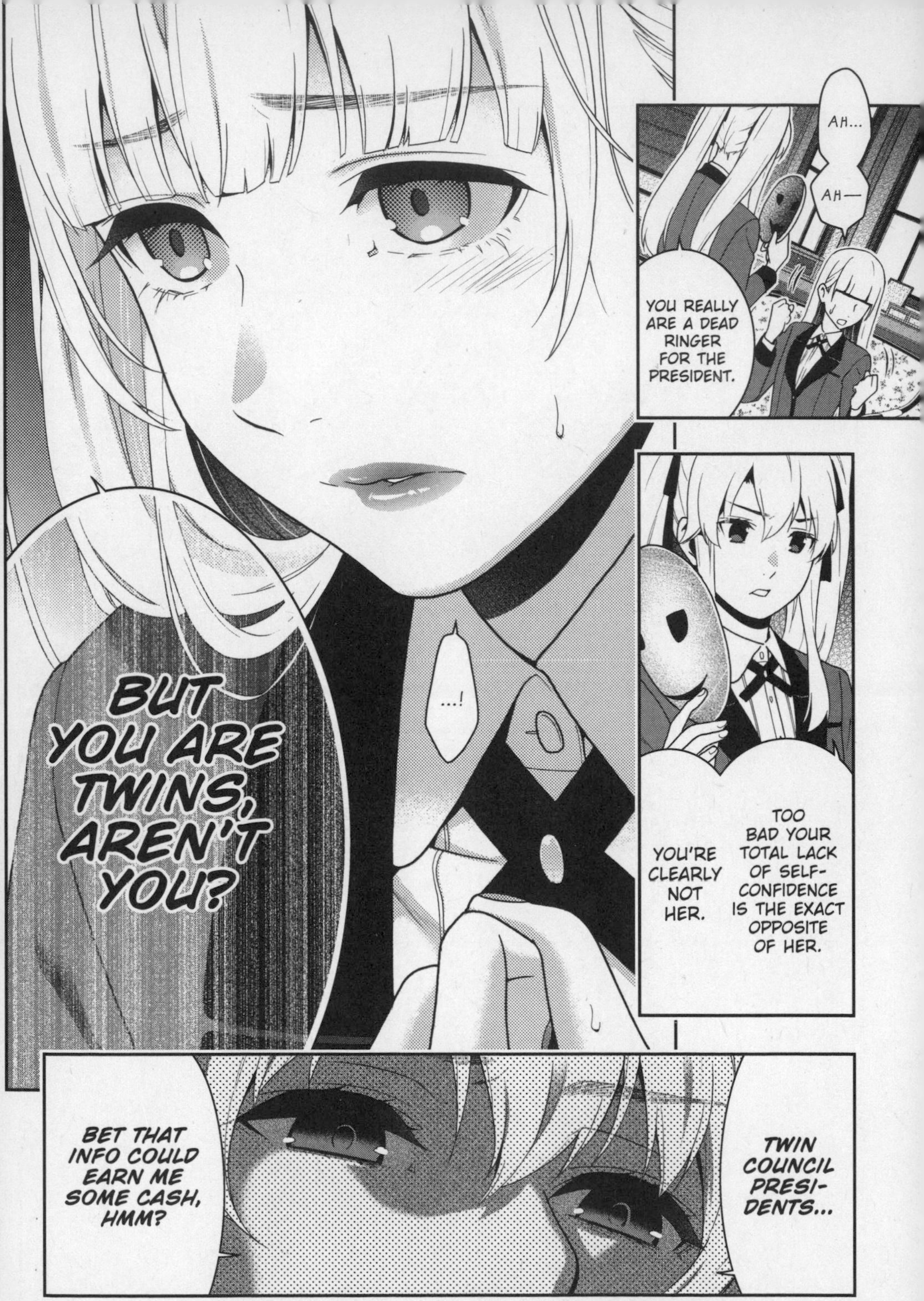
AH...
AH—
YOU REALLY ARE A DEAD RINGER FOR THE PRESIDENT.
YOU'RE CLEARLY NOT HER.
TOO BAD YOUR TOTAL LACK OF SELF-CONFIDENCE IS THE EXACT OPPOSITE OF HER.
...!
BUT YOU ARE TWINS, AREN'T YOU?
TWIN COUNCIL PRESI-DENTS...
BET THAT INFO COULD EARN ME SOME CASH, HMM?

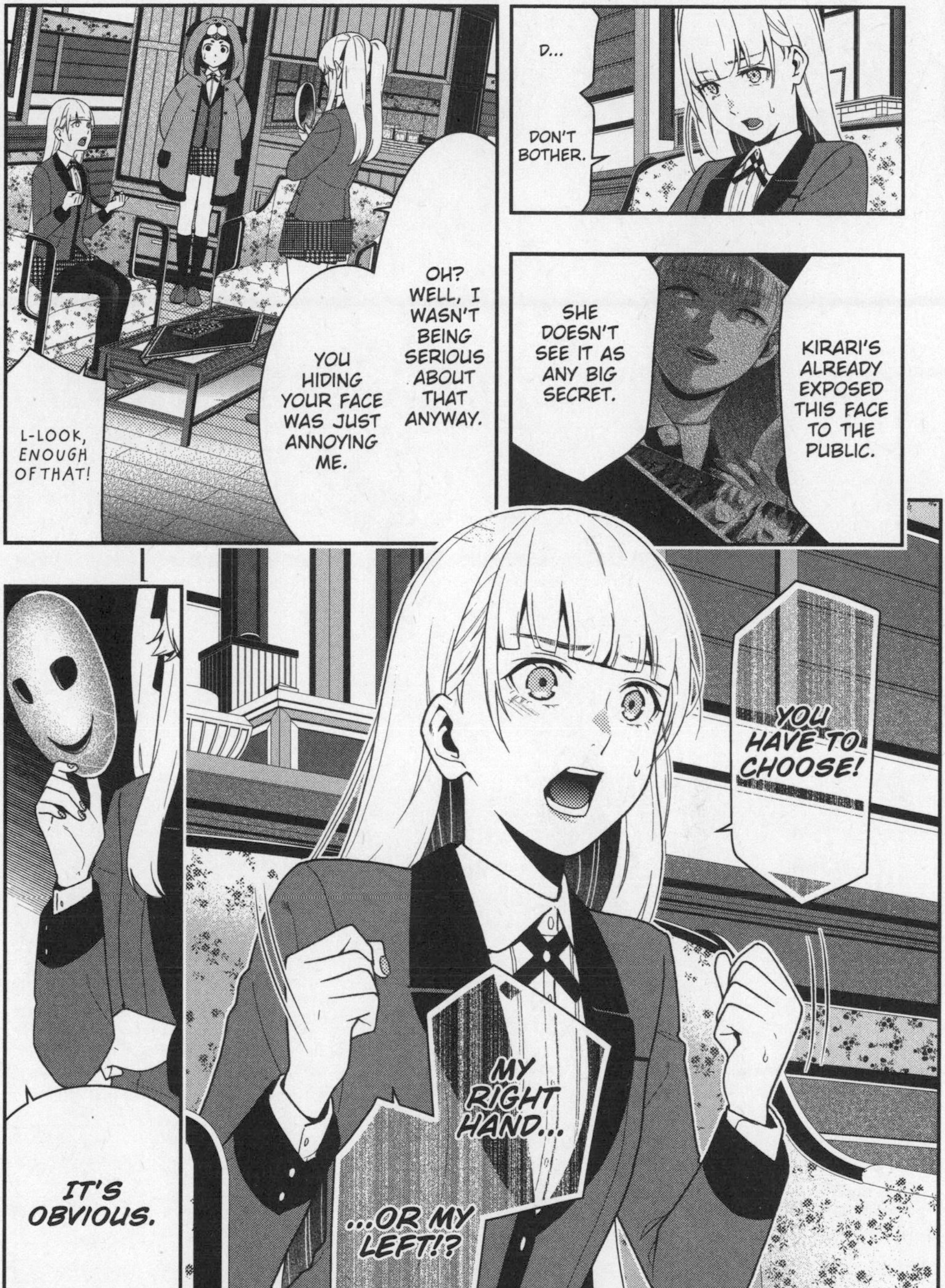
D...
DON'T BOTHER.
KIRARI'S ALREADY EXPOSED THIS FACE TO THE PUBLIC.
SHE DOESN'T SEE IT AS ANY BIG SECRET.
OH? WELL, I WASN'T BEING SERIOUS ABOUT THAT ANYWAY.
YOU HIDING YOUR FACE WAS JUST ANNOYING ME.
L-LOOK, ENOUGH OF THAT!
YOU HAVE TO CHOOSE!
MY RIGHT HAND...
...OR MY LEFT!?
IT'S OBVIOUS.

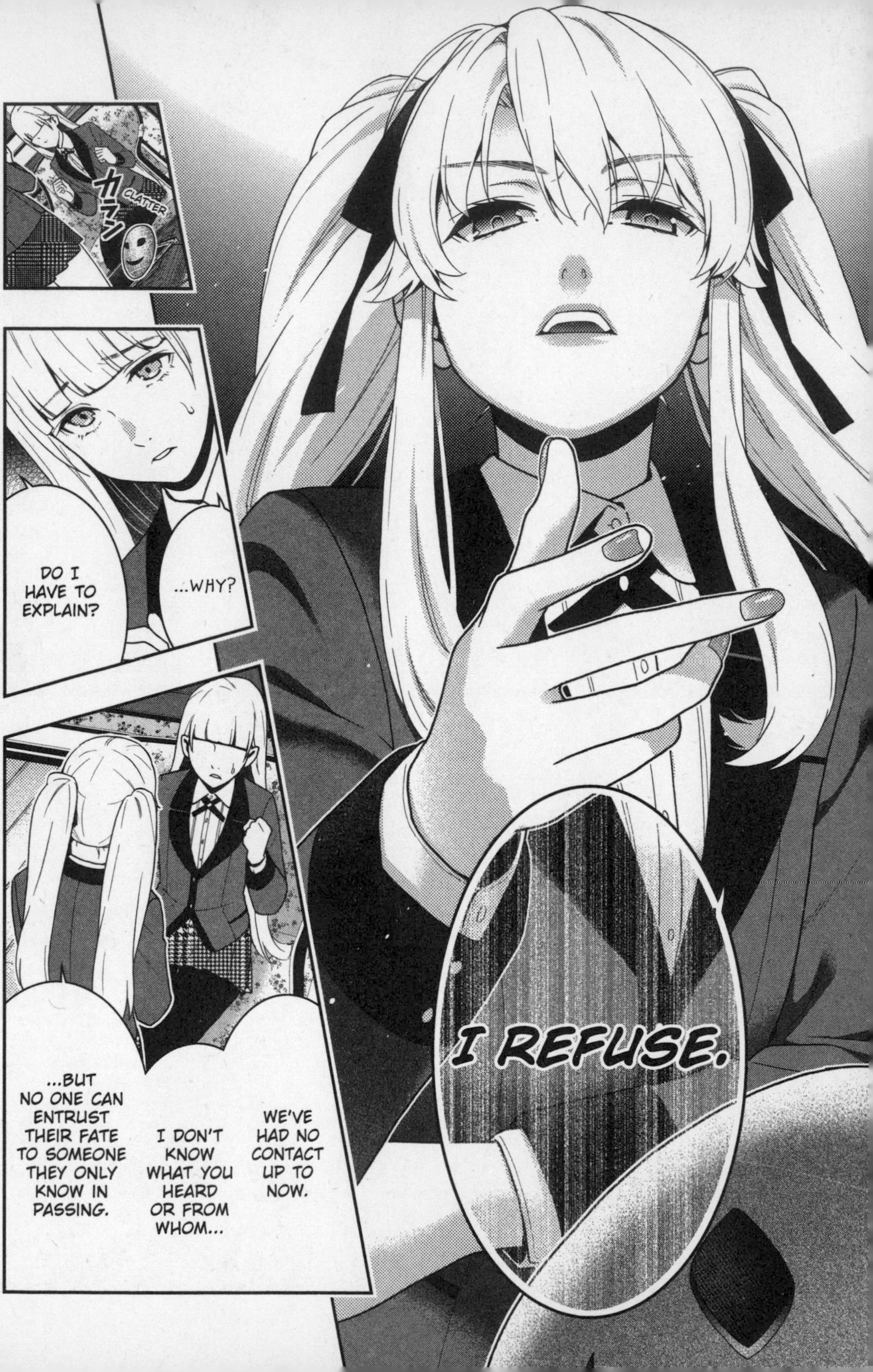
I REFUSE.
カラン
CLATTER
...WHY?
DO I HAVE TO EXPLAIN?
WE'VE HAD NO CONTACT UP TO NOW.
I DON'T KNOW WHAT YOU HEARD OR FROM WHOM...
...BUT NO ONE CAN ENTRUST THEIR FATE TO SOMEONE THEY ONLY KNOW IN PASSING.

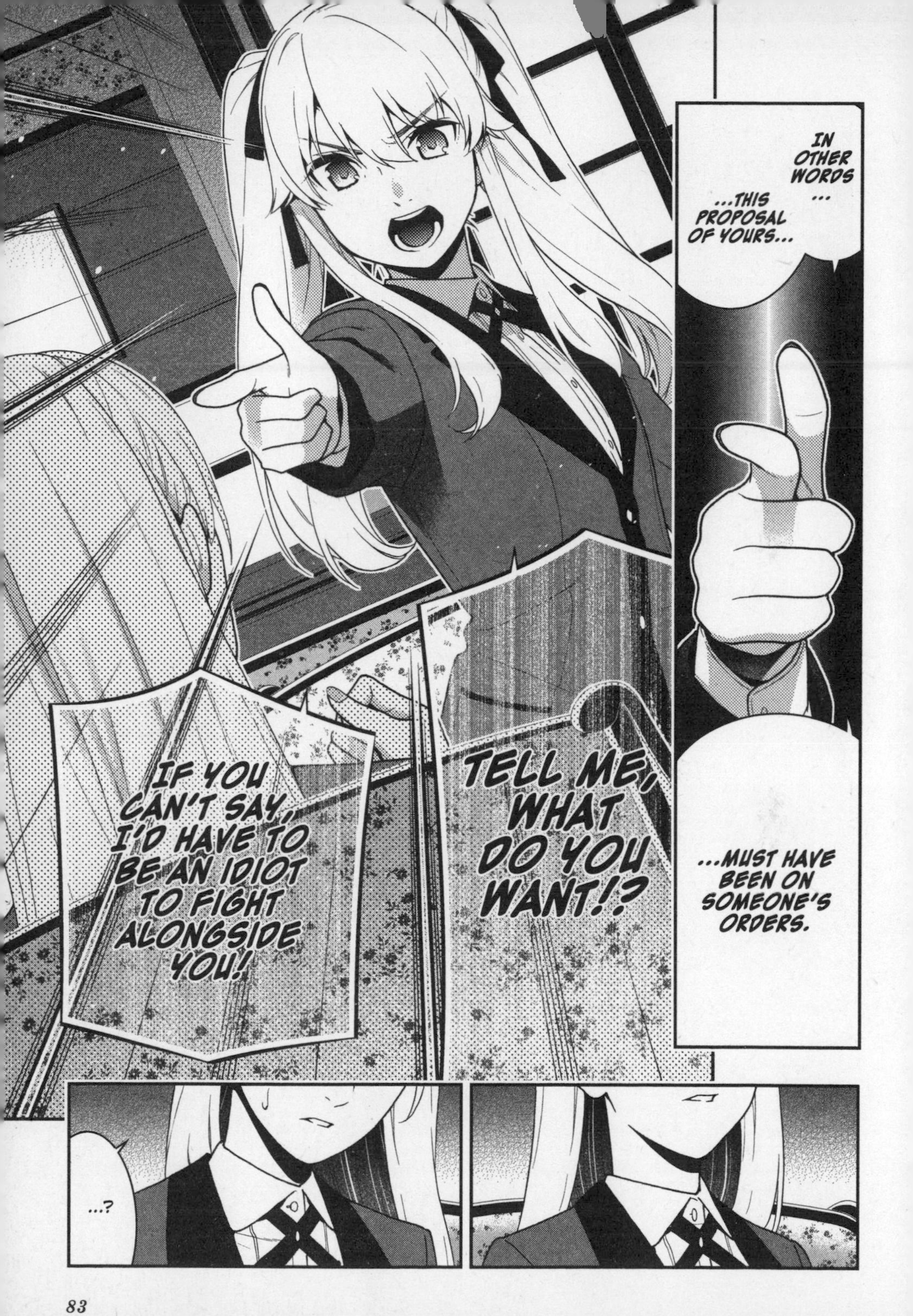
IN OTHER WORDS...
...THIS PROPOSAL OF YOURS...
...MUST HAVE BEEN ON SOMEONE'S ORDERS.
TELL ME, WHAT DO YOU WANT!?
IF YOU CAN'T SAY, I'D HAVE TO BE AN IDIOT TO FIGHT ALONGSIDE YOU!
...?

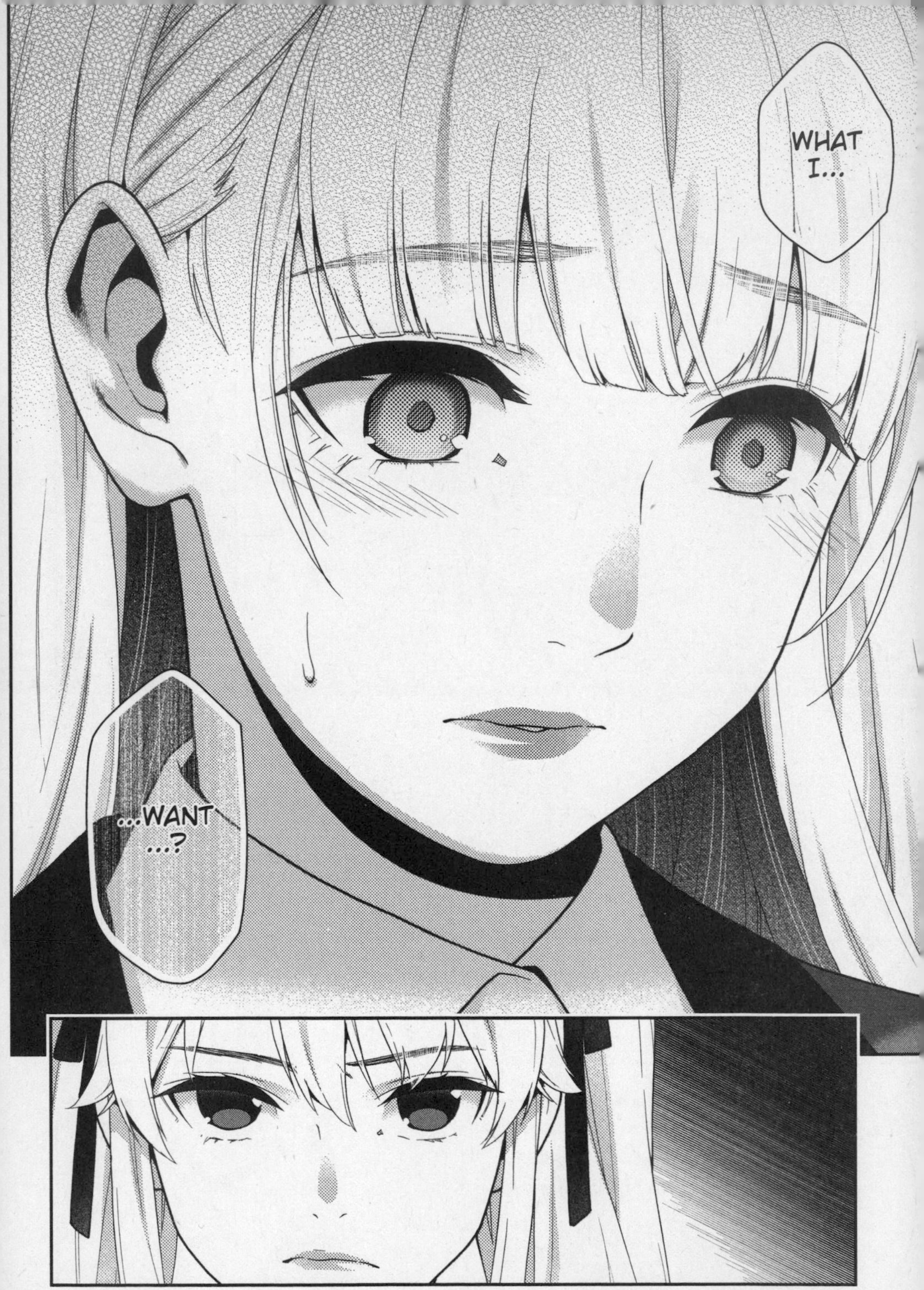
WHAT I...
...WANT ...?

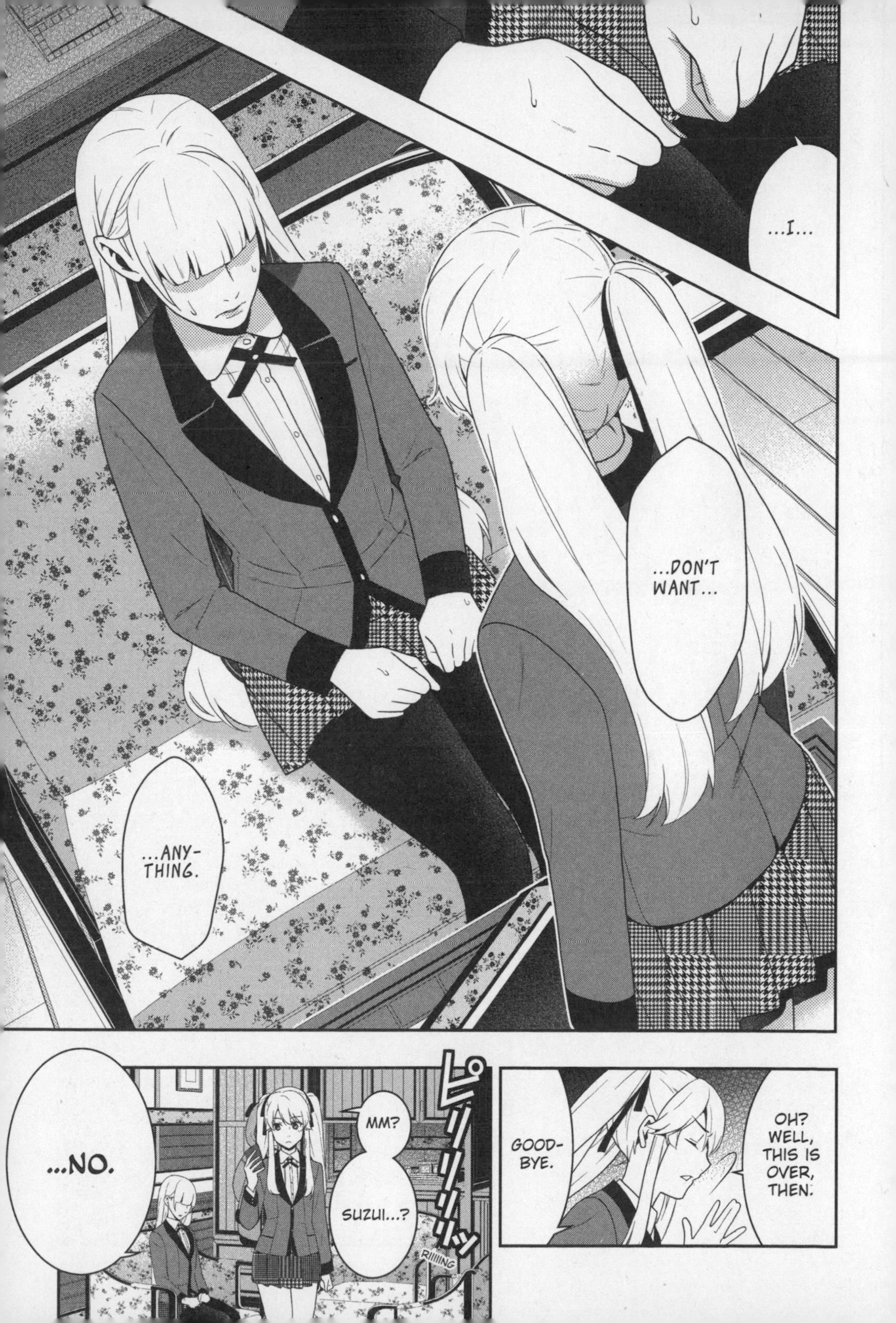
...I...
...DON'T WANT...
...ANY-THING.
OH? WELL, THIS IS OVER, THEN.
GOOD-BYE.
MM?
SUZUI...?
RIIIING
...NO.

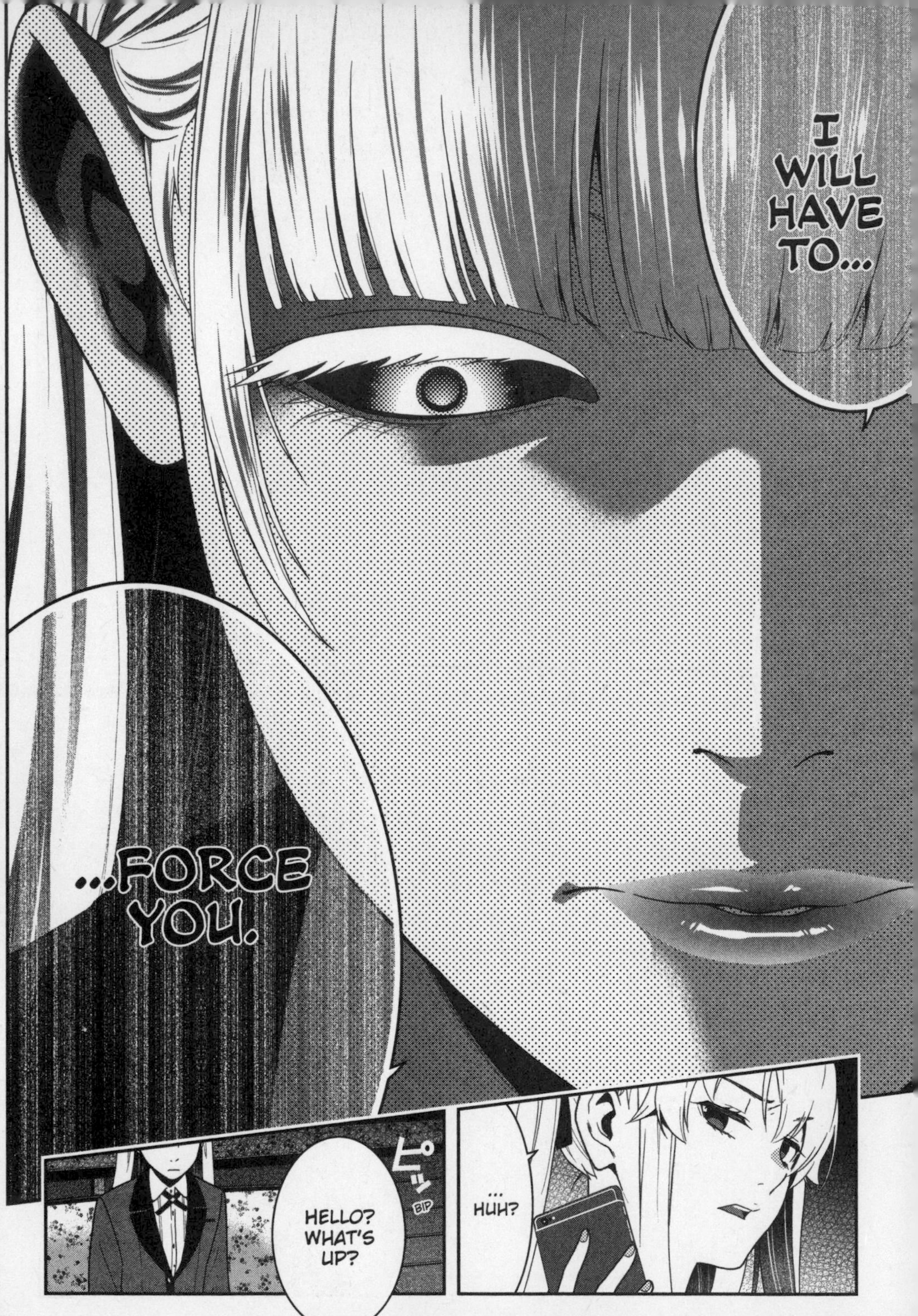
I WILL HAVE TO...
...FORCE YOU.
... HUH?
ピッ
BIP
HELLO? WHAT'S UP?

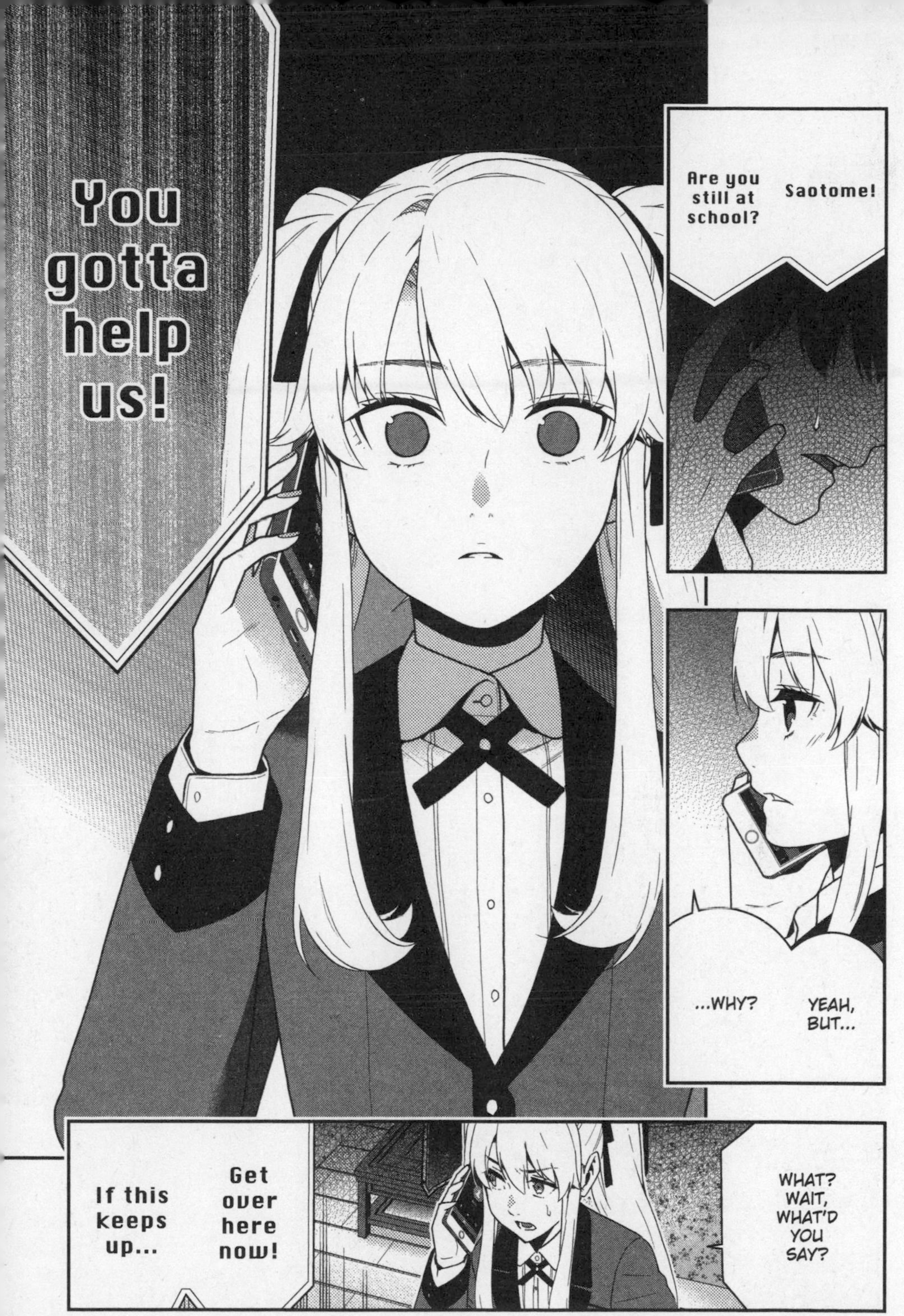
Saotome!
Are you still at school?
YEAH, BUT...
...WHY?
You gotta help us!
WHAT? WAIT, WHAT'D YOU SAY?
Get over here now!
If this keeps up...

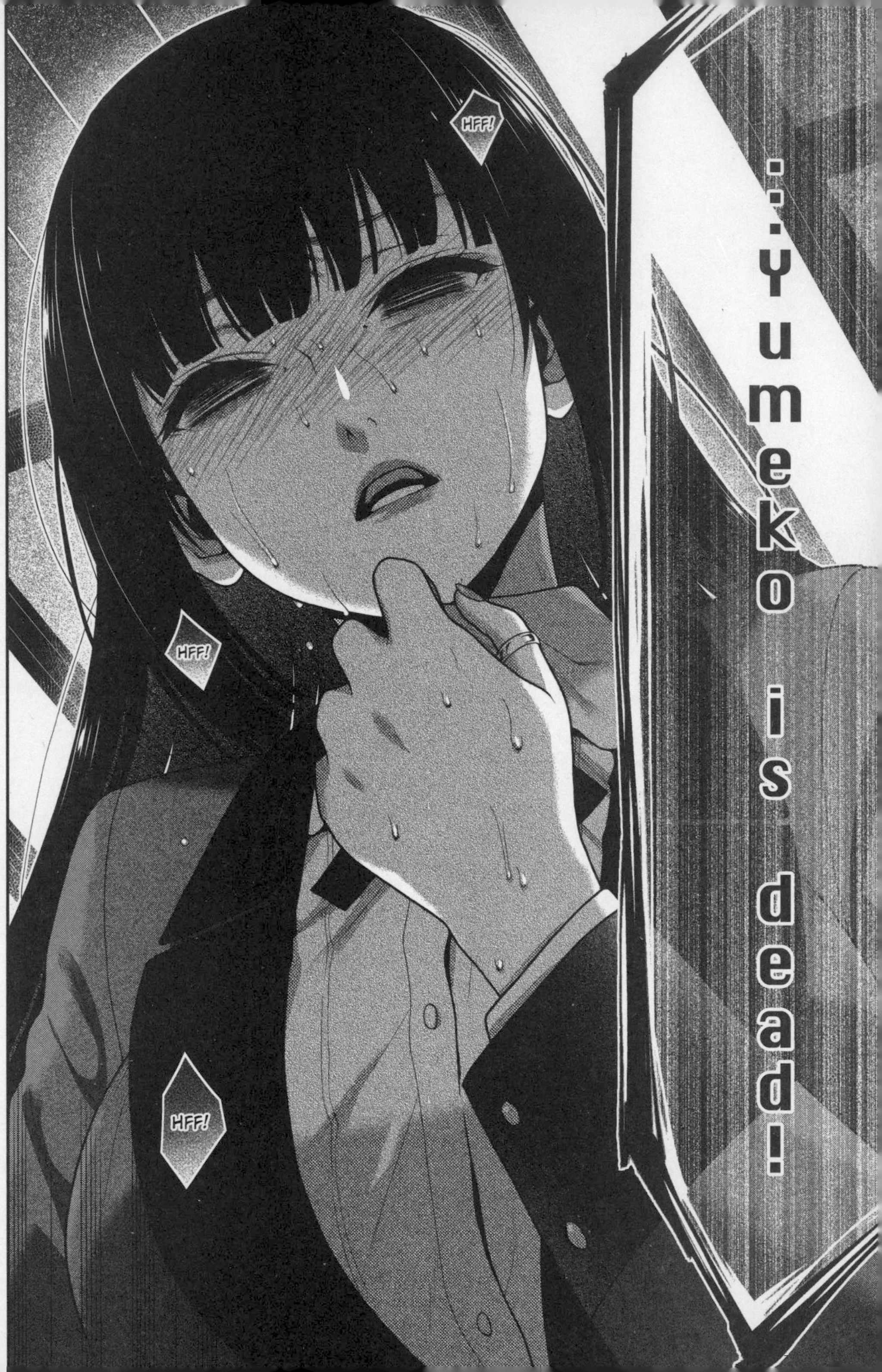
...Yumeko is dead!
HFF!
HFF!
HFF!

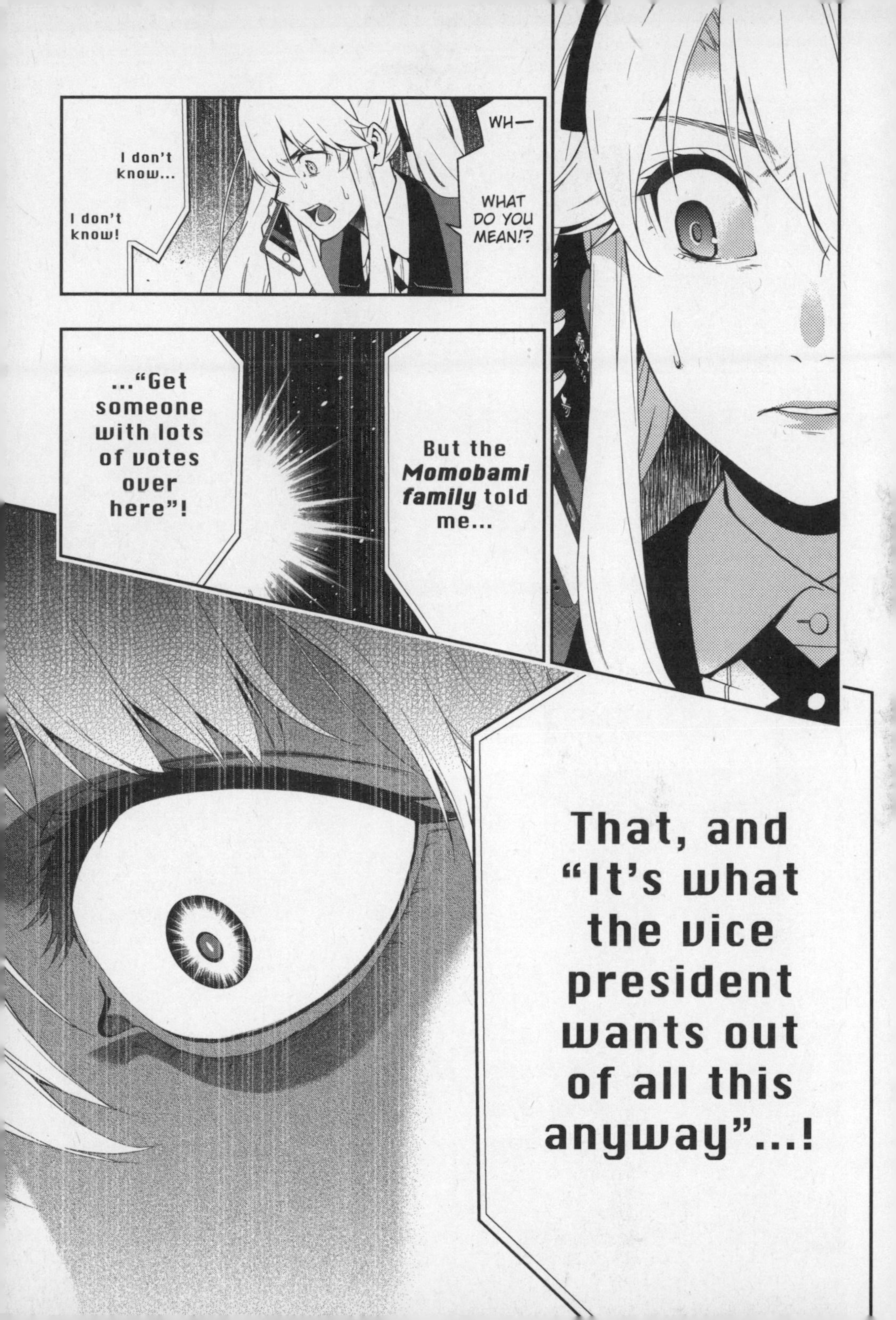
WH—
WHAT DO YOU MEAN!?
I don't know...
I don't know!
But the *Momobami family* told me...
..."Get someone with lots of votes over here"!
That, and "It's what the vice president wants out of all this anyway"...!

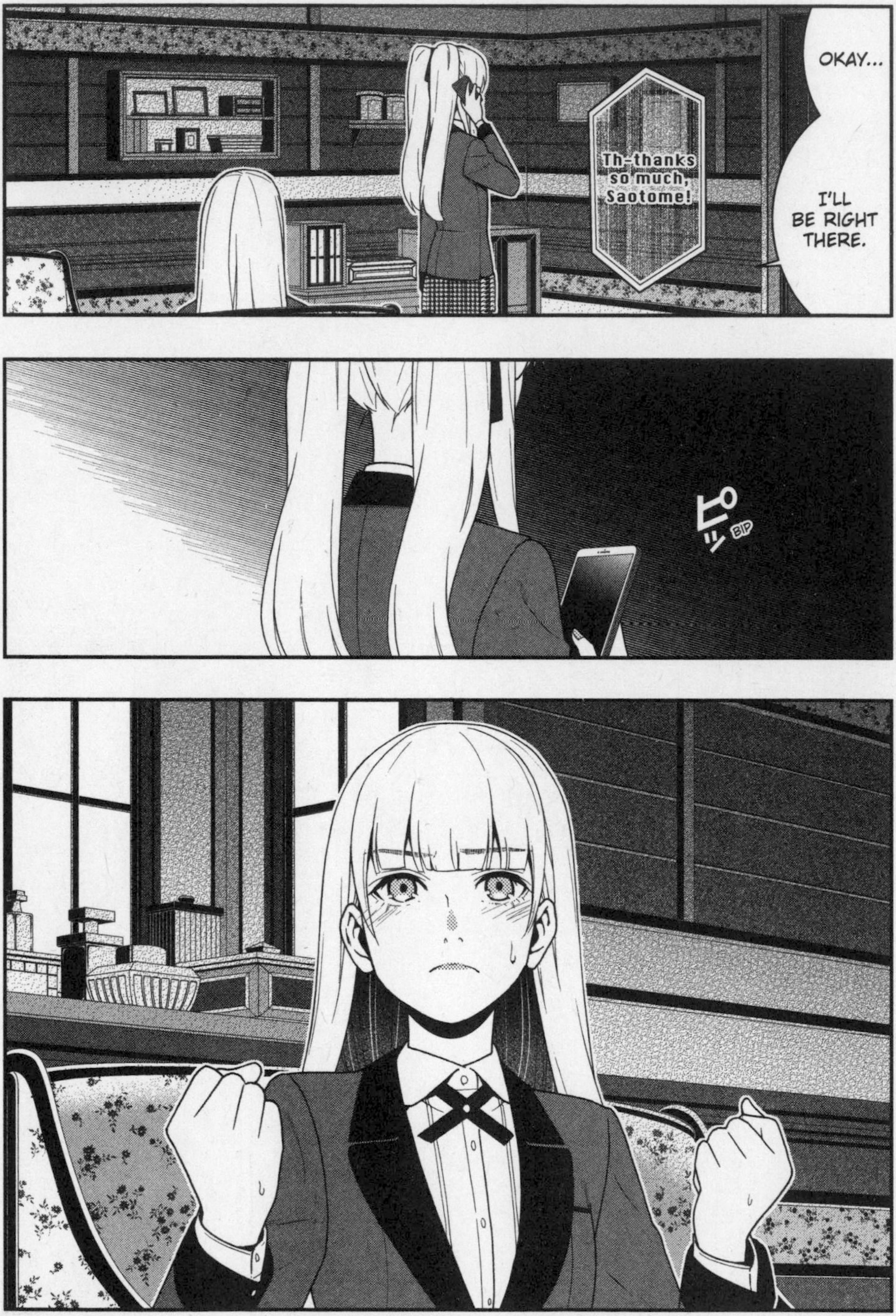
OKAY...
I'LL BE RIGHT THERE.
Th-thanks so much, Saotome!
ピッ
BIP

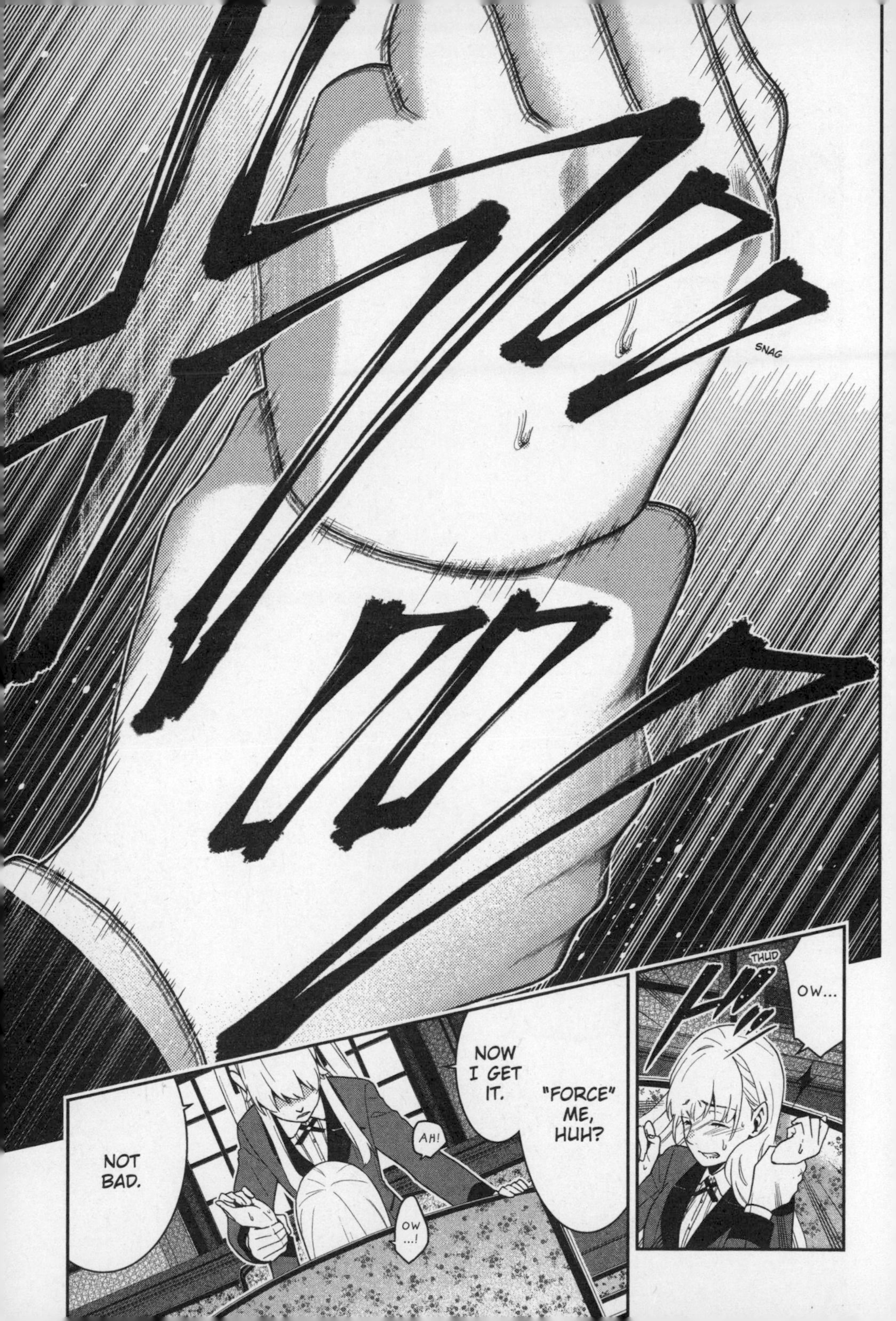
SNAG
THUD
OW...
"FORCE" ME, HUH?
NOW I GET IT.
AH!
NOT BAD.
OW ...!

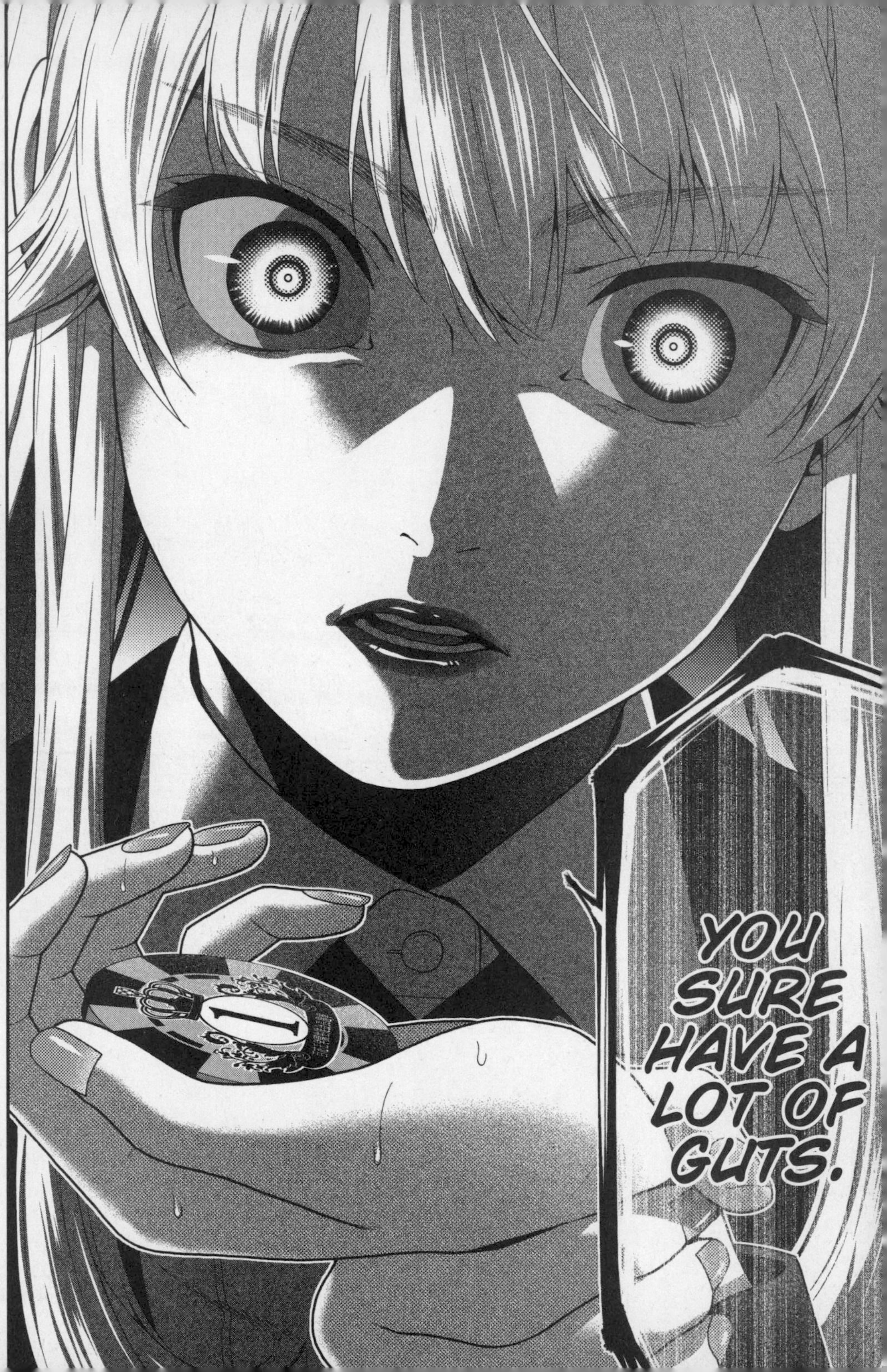
YOU SURE HAVE A LOT OF GUTS.

KAKEGURUI
— Compulsive Gambler —

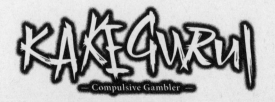

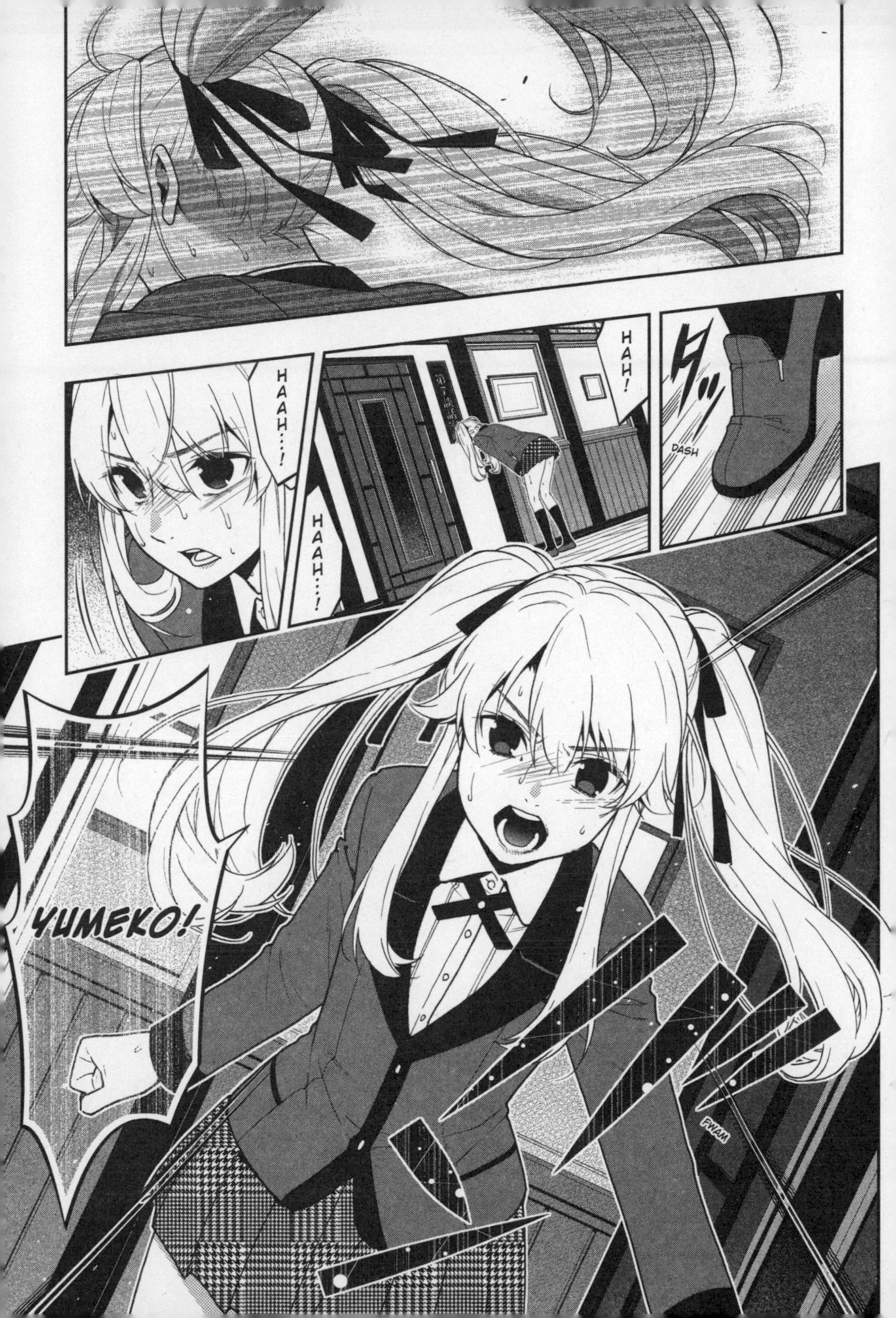
DASH
HAH!
HAAAH...!
HAAAH...!
YUMEKO!
PWAM

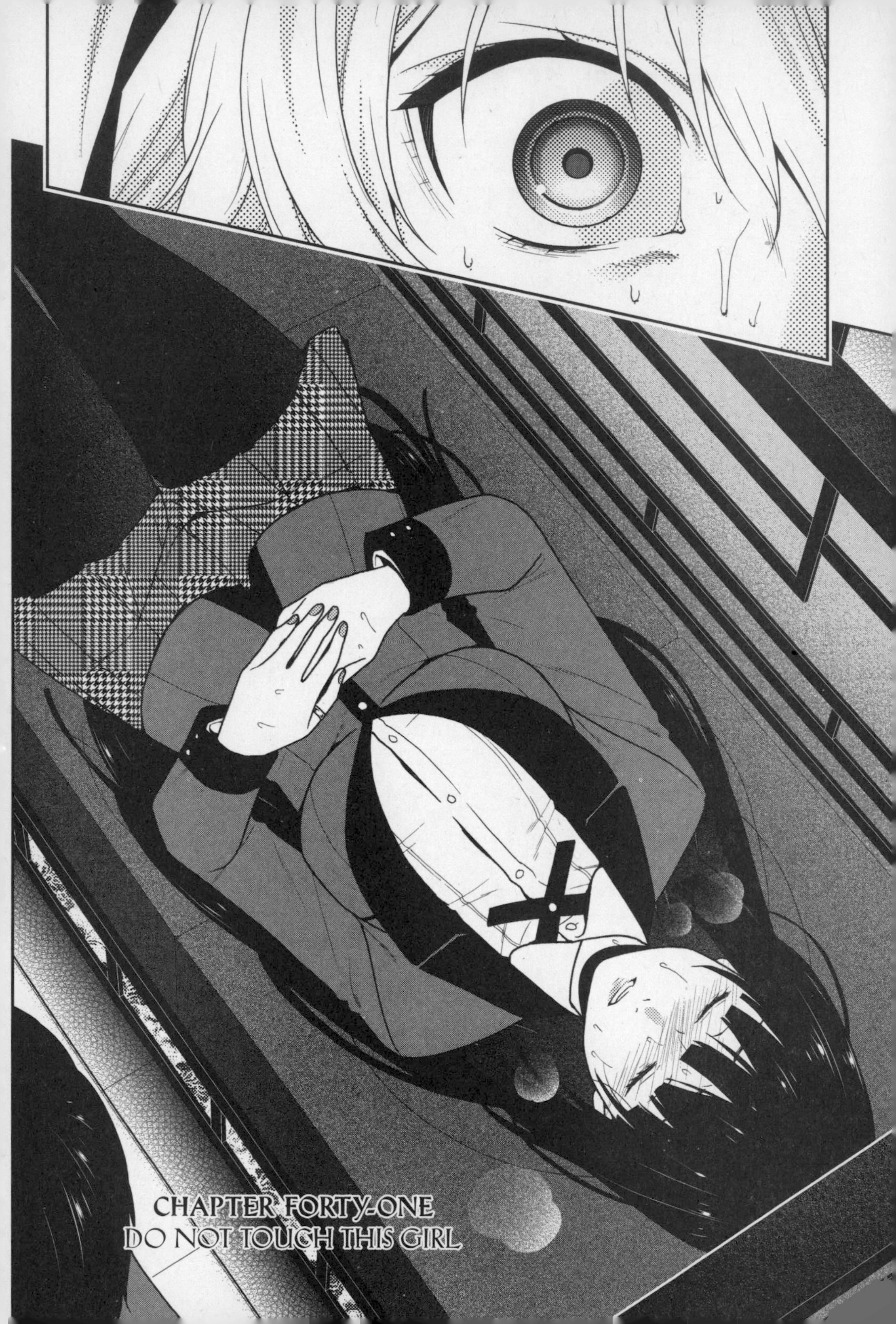
CHAPTER FORTY-ONE
DO NOT TOUCH THIS GIRL

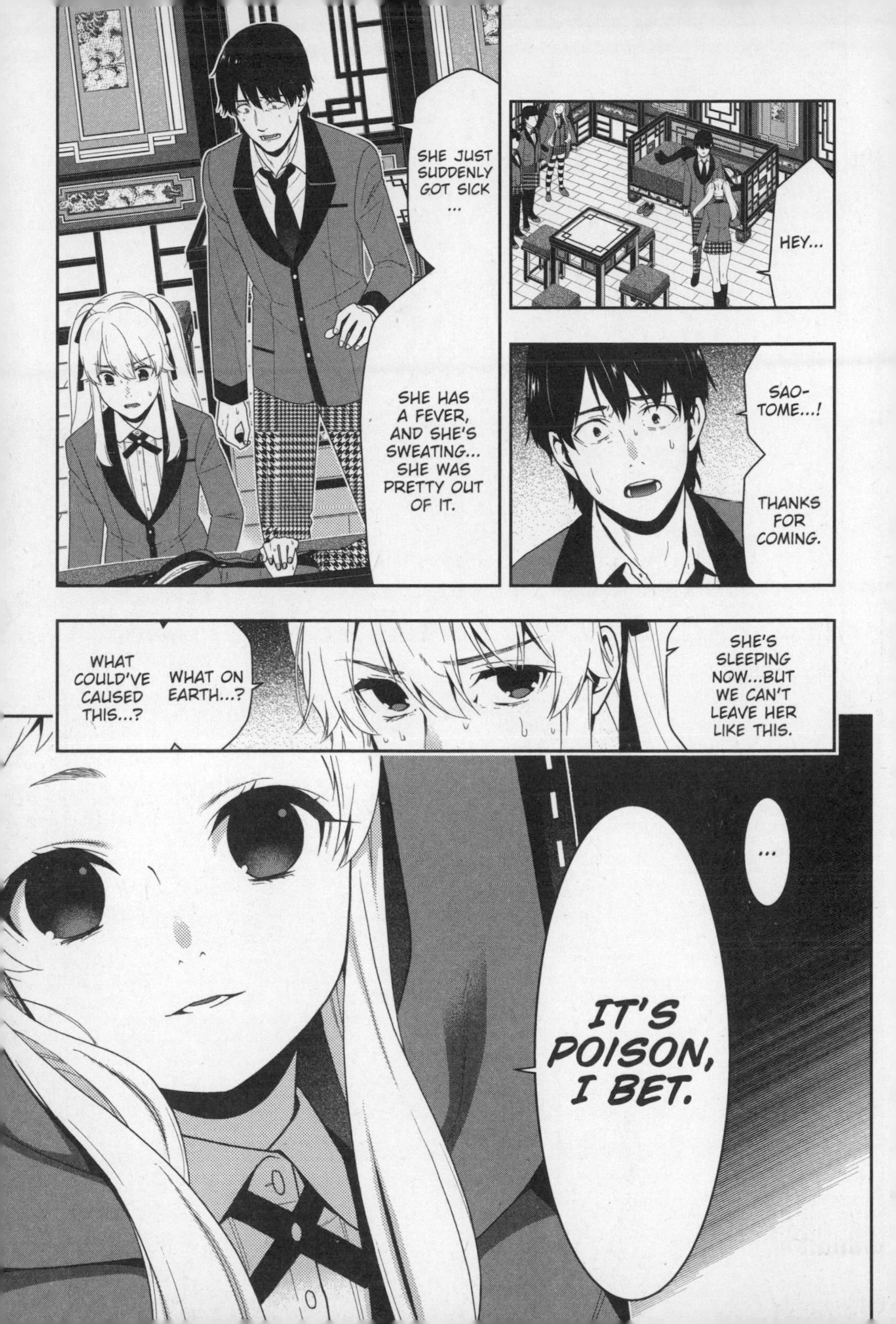
HEY...
SAO-TOME...!
THANKS FOR COMING.
SHE JUST SUDDENLY GOT SICK ...
SHE HAS A FEVER, AND SHE'S SWEATING... SHE WAS PRETTY OUT OF IT.
SHE'S SLEEPING NOW...BUT WE CAN'T LEAVE HER LIKE THIS.
WHAT ON EARTH...?
WHAT COULD'VE CAUSED THIS...?
...
IT'S POISON, I BET.

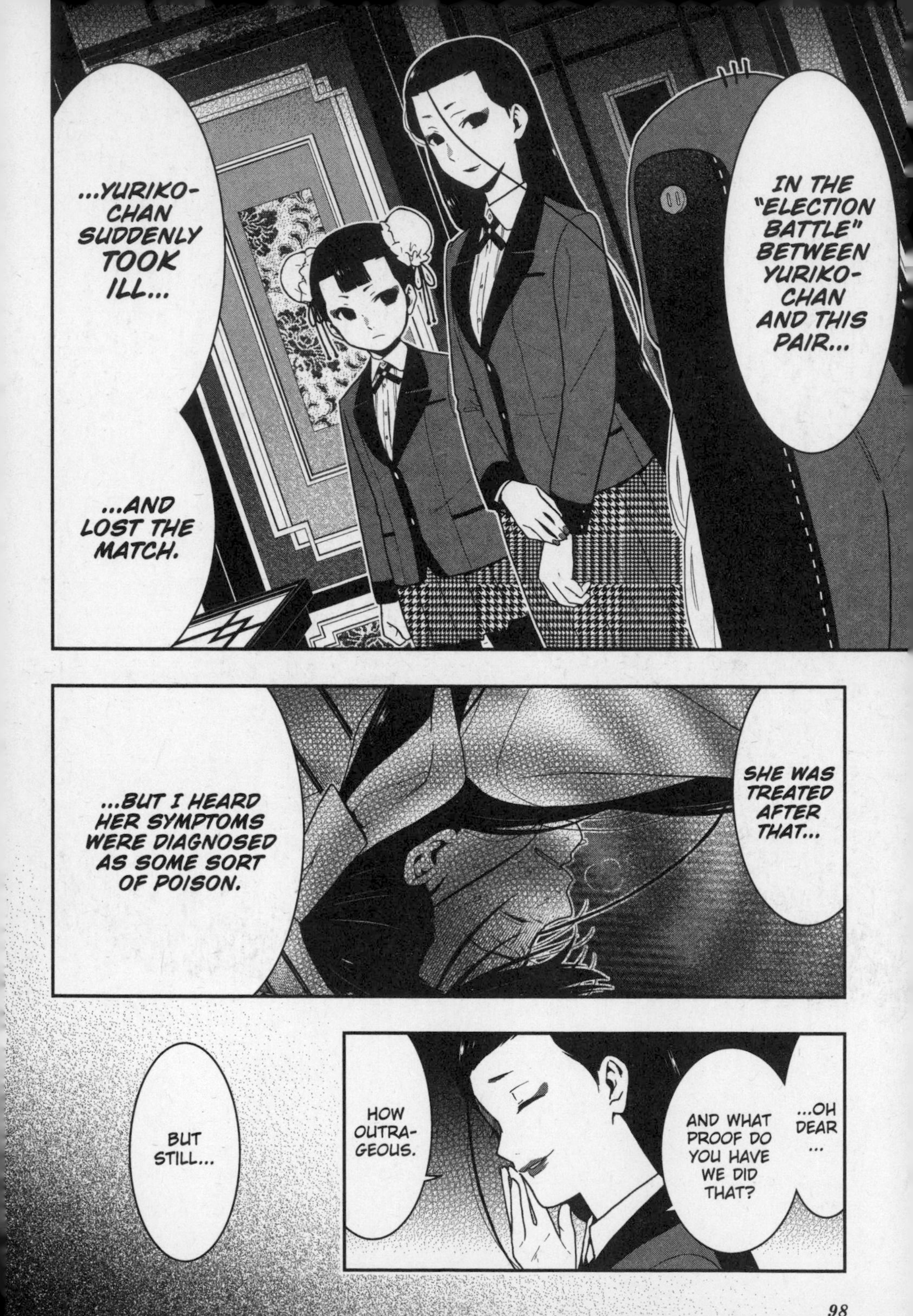
IN THE "ELECTION BATTLE" BETWEEN YURIKO-CHAN AND THIS PAIR...
...YURIKO-CHAN SUDDENLY TOOK ILL...
...AND LOST THE MATCH.
SHE WAS TREATED AFTER THAT...
...BUT I HEARD HER SYMPTOMS WERE DIAGNOSED AS SOME SORT OF POISON.
...OH DEAR ...
AND WHAT PROOF DO YOU HAVE WE DID THAT?
HOW OUTRAGEOUS.
BUT STILL...

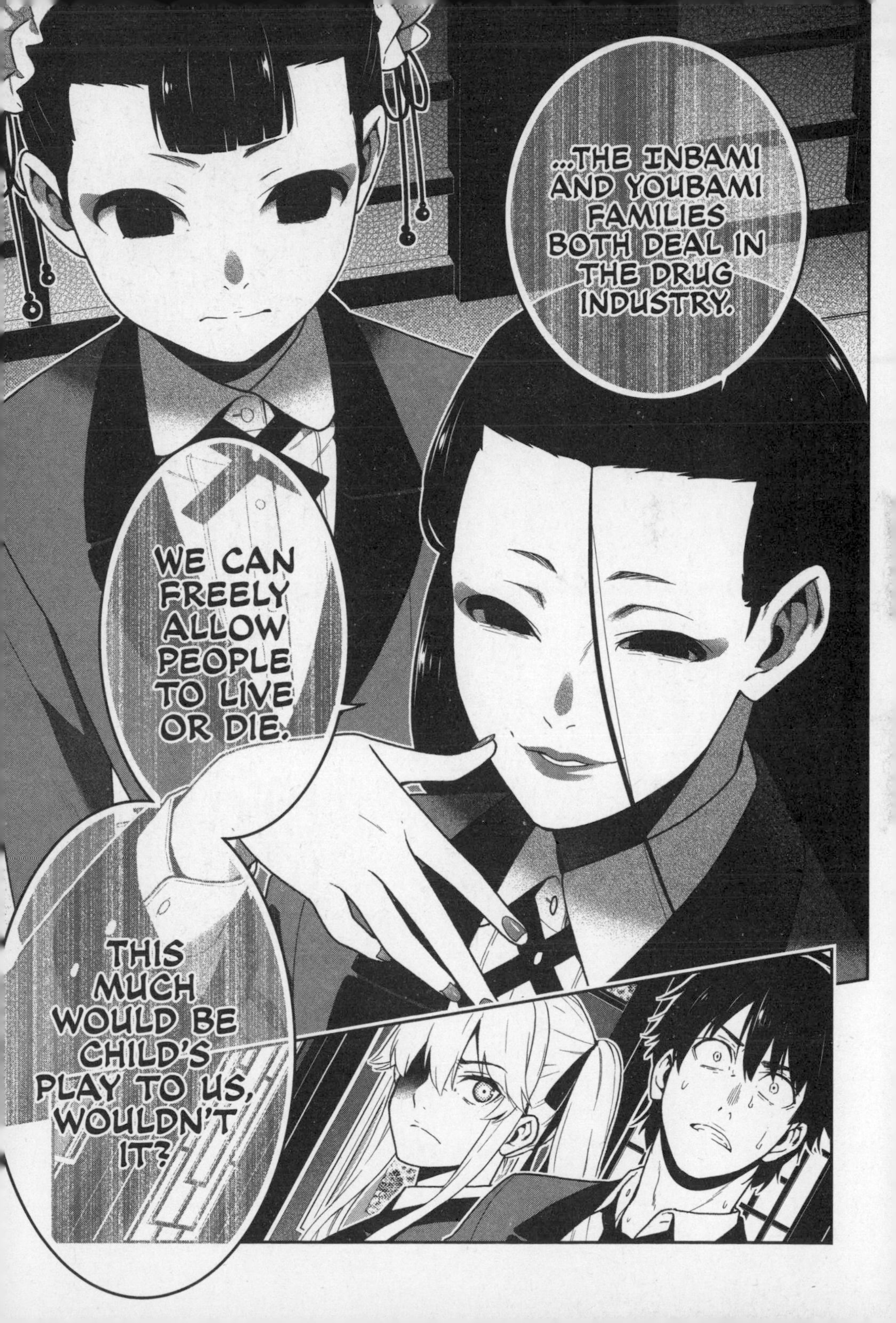
...THE INBAMI AND YOUBAMI FAMILIES BOTH DEAL IN THE DRUG INDUSTRY.
WE CAN FREELY ALLOW PEOPLE TO LIVE OR DIE.
THIS MUCH WOULD BE CHILD'S PLAY TO US, WOULDN'T IT?

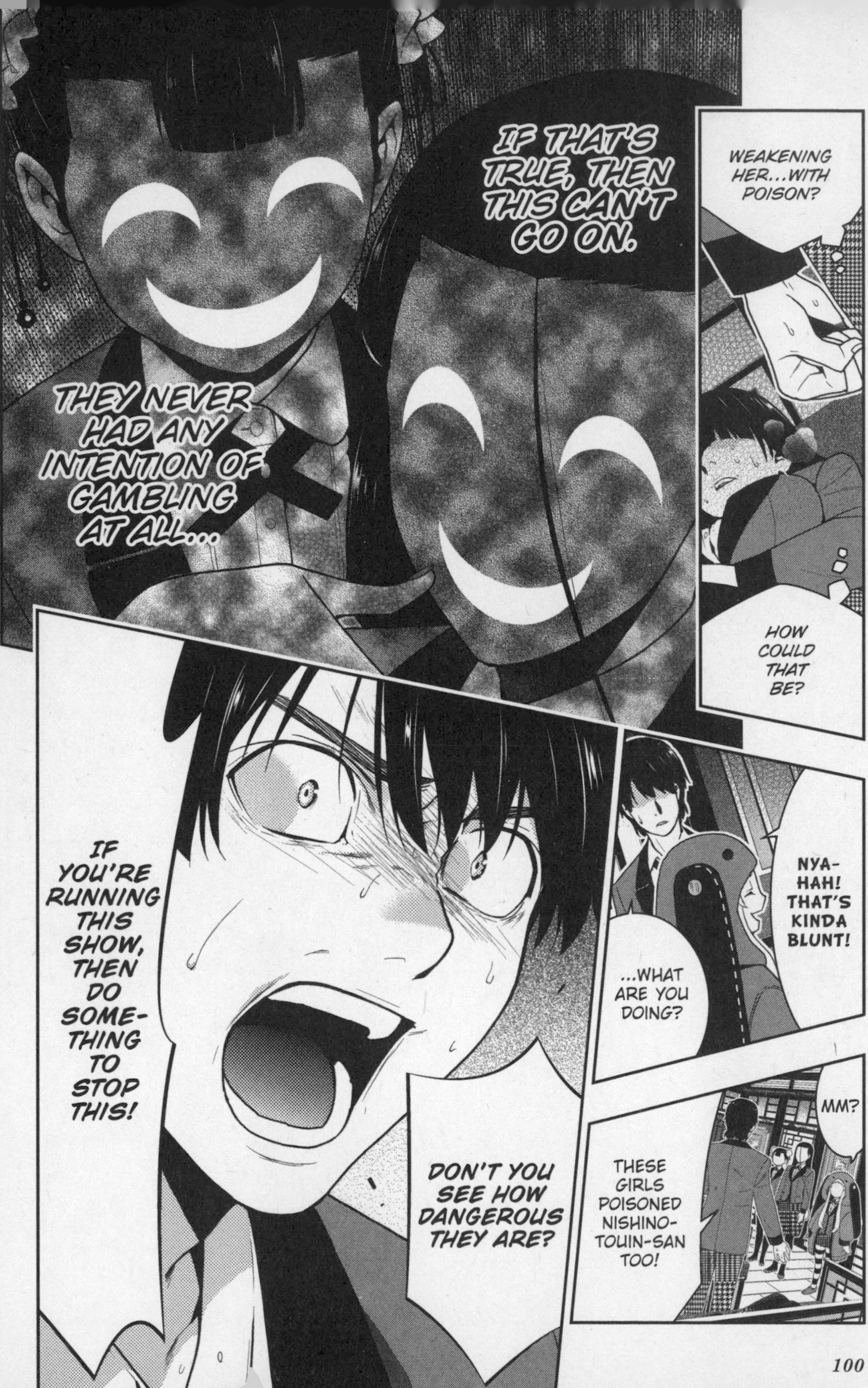
WEAKENING HER...WITH POISON?
HOW COULD THAT BE?
IF THAT'S TRUE, THEN THIS CAN'T GO ON.
THEY NEVER HAD ANY INTENTION OF GAMBLING AT ALL...
NYA-HAH! THAT'S KINDA BLUNT!
...WHAT ARE YOU DOING?
MM?
THESE GIRLS POISONED NISHINO-TOUIN-SAN TOO!
DON'T YOU SEE HOW DANGEROUS THEY ARE?
IF YOU'RE RUNNING THIS SHOW, THEN DO SOME-THING TO STOP THIS!

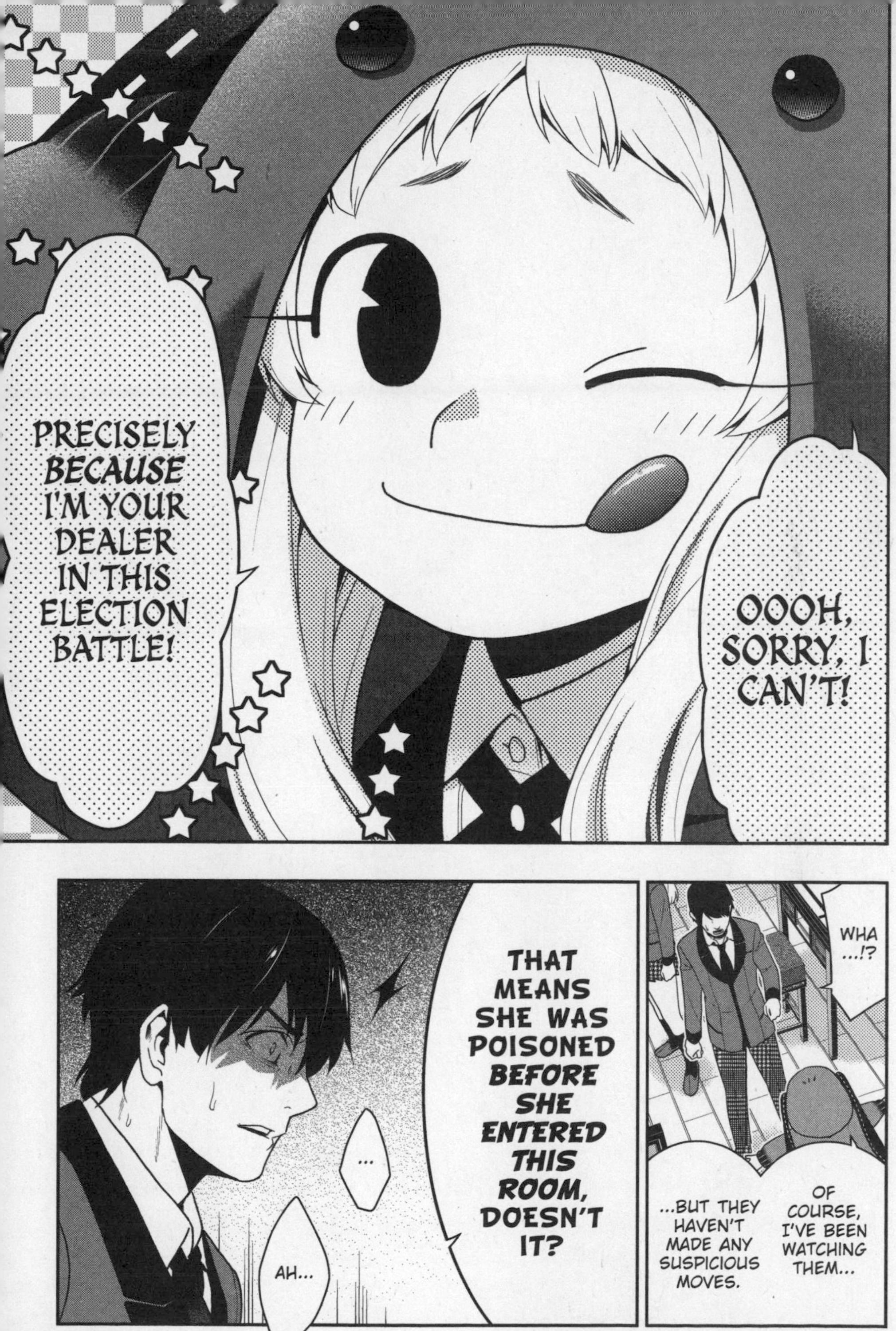
OOOH, SORRY, I CAN'T!
PRECISELY *BECAUSE* I'M YOUR DEALER IN THIS ELECTION BATTLE!
WHA ...!?
OF COURSE, I'VE BEEN WATCHING THEM...
...BUT THEY HAVEN'T MADE ANY SUSPICIOUS MOVES.
THAT MEANS SHE WAS POISONED *BEFORE* SHE ENTERED THIS ROOM, DOESN'T IT?
...
AH...

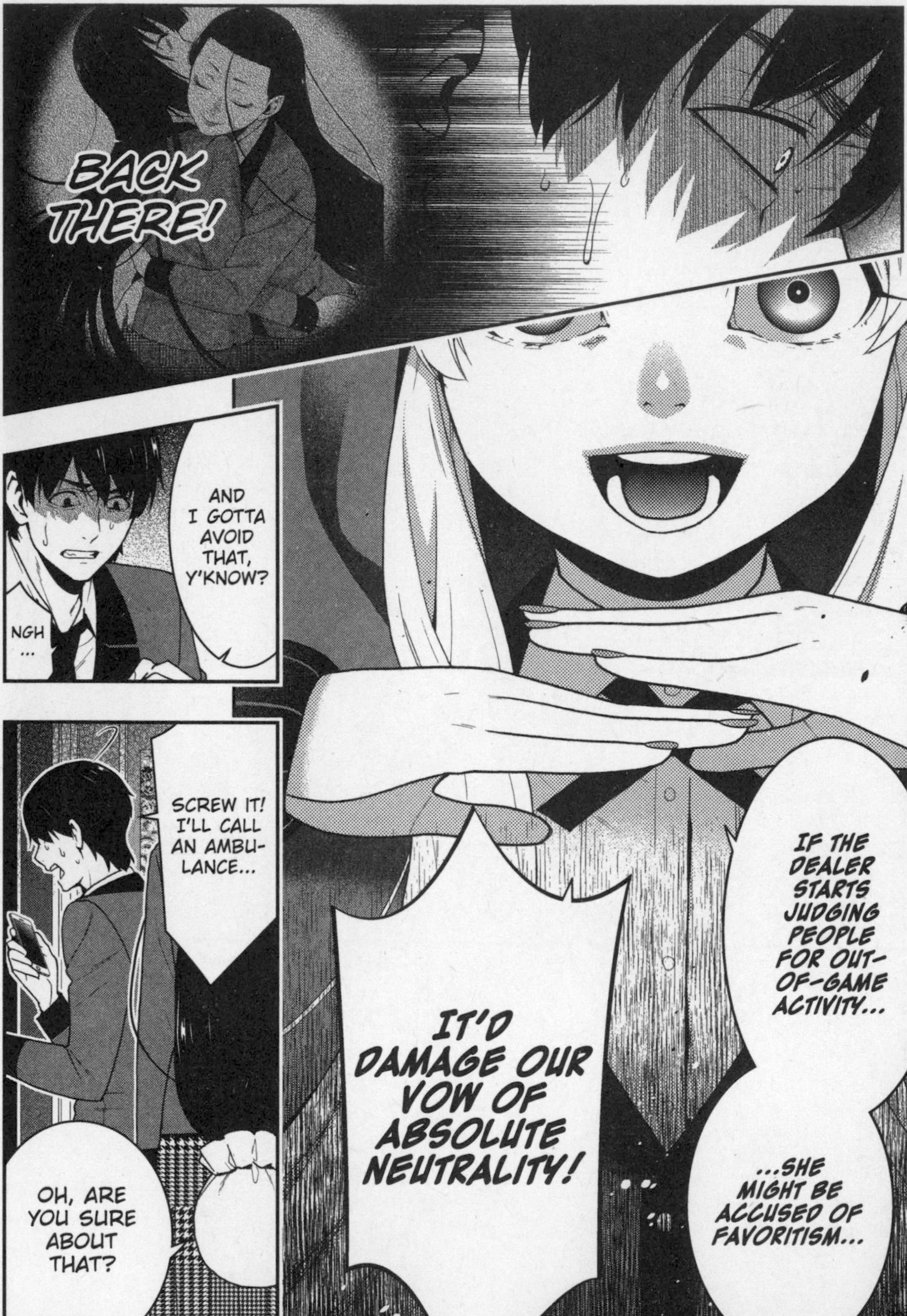
BACK THERE!
IF THE DEALER STARTS JUDGING PEOPLE FOR OUT-OF-GAME ACTIVITY...
...SHE MIGHT BE ACCUSED OF FAVORITISM...
IT'D DAMAGE OUR VOW OF ABSOLUTE NEUTRALITY!
AND I GOTTA AVOID THAT, Y'KNOW?
NGH...
SCREW IT! I'LL CALL AN AMBULANCE...
OH, ARE YOU SURE ABOUT THAT?

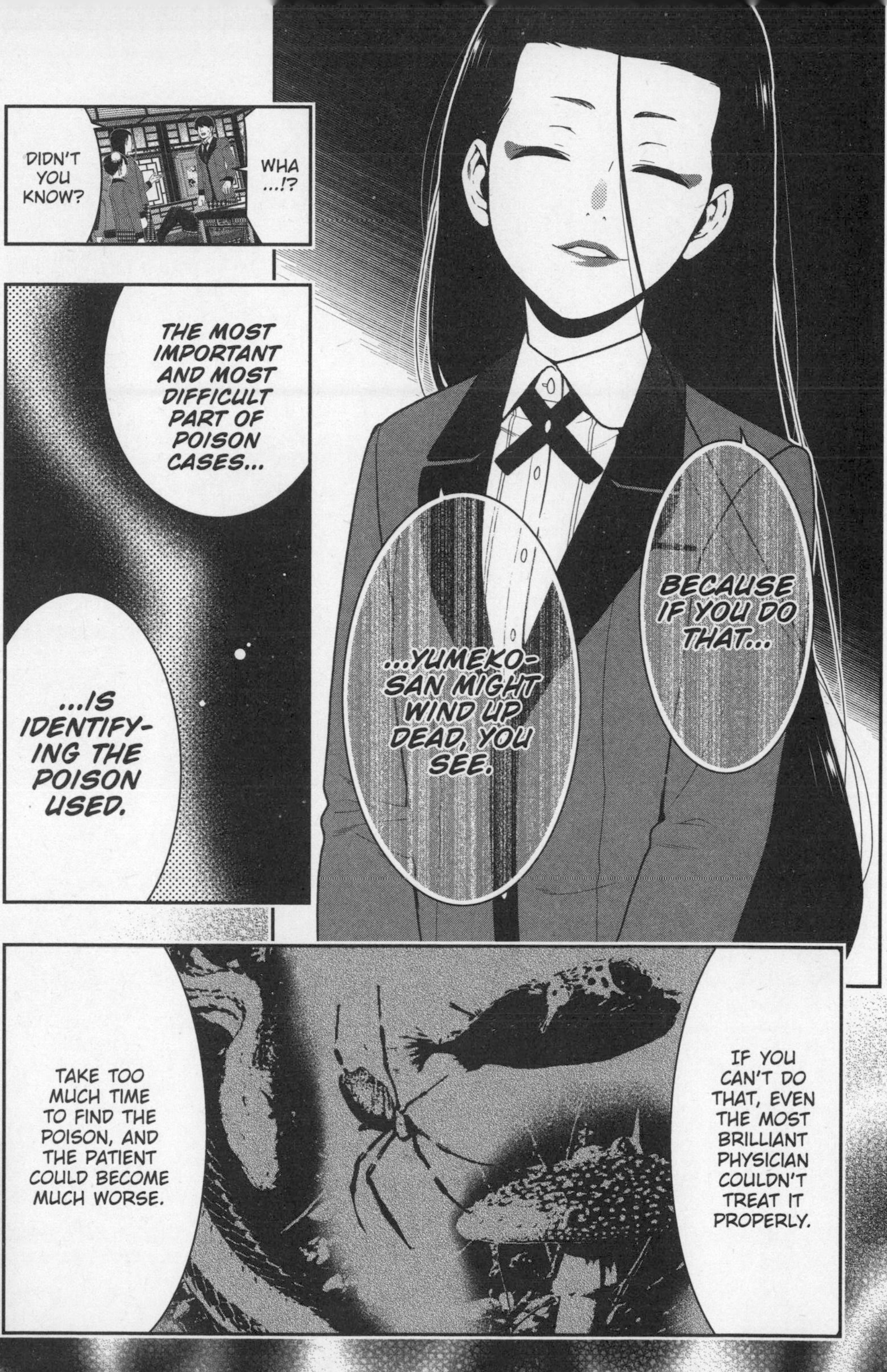
BECAUSE IF YOU DO THAT...
...YUMEKO-SAN MIGHT WIND UP DEAD, YOU SEE.
WHA ...!?
DIDN'T YOU KNOW?
THE MOST IMPORTANT AND MOST DIFFICULT PART OF POISON CASES...
...IS IDENTIFYING THE POISON USED.
IF YOU CAN'T DO THAT, EVEN THE MOST BRILLIANT PHYSICIAN COULDN'T TREAT IT PROPERLY.
TAKE TOO MUCH TIME TO FIND THE POISON, AND THE PATIENT COULD BECOME MUCH WORSE.

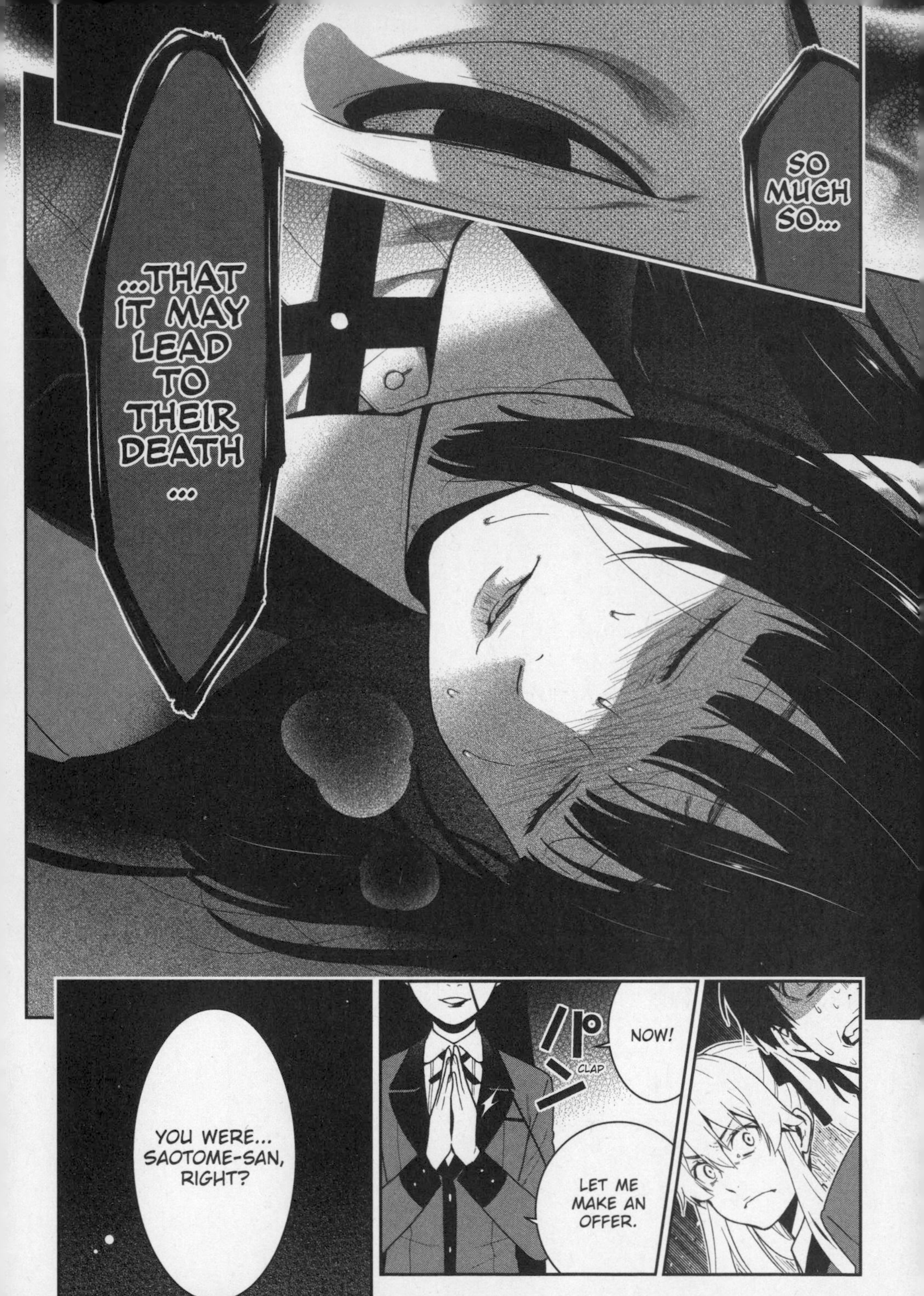

SO MUCH SO...
...THAT IT MAY LEAD TO THEIR DEATH...
NOW!
CLAP
LET ME MAKE AN OFFER.
YOU WERE... SAOTOME-SAN, RIGHT?

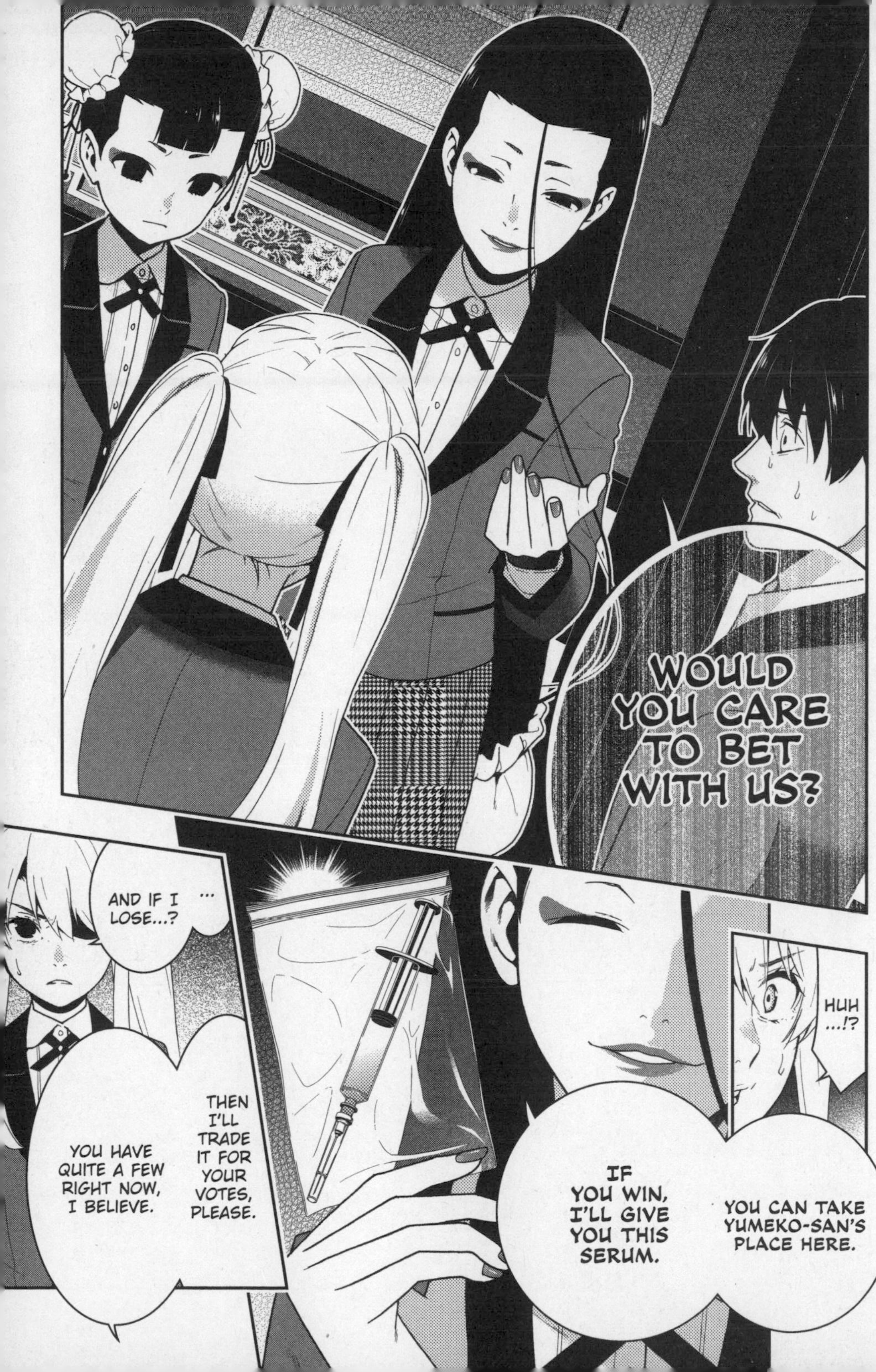
WOULD YOU CARE TO BET WITH US?
HUH ...!?
YOU CAN TAKE YUMEKO-SAN'S PLACE HERE.
IF YOU WIN, I'LL GIVE YOU THIS SERUM.
...
AND IF I LOSE...?
THEN I'LL TRADE IT FOR YOUR VOTES, PLEASE.
YOU HAVE QUITE A FEW RIGHT NOW, I BELIEVE.

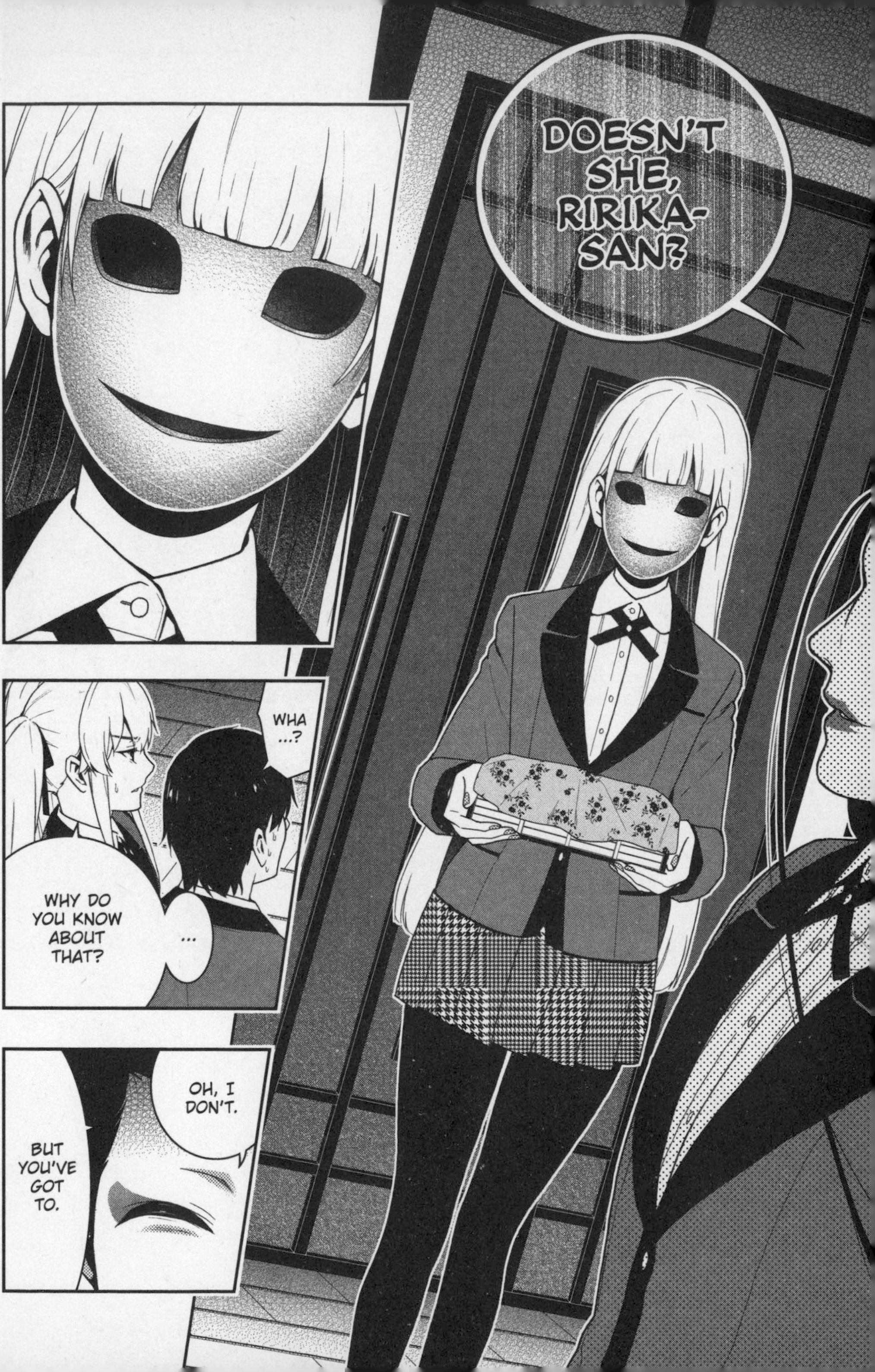
DOESN'T SHE, RIRIKA-SAN?
WHA ...?
...
WHY DO YOU KNOW ABOUT THAT?
OH, I DON'T.
BUT YOU'VE GOT TO.

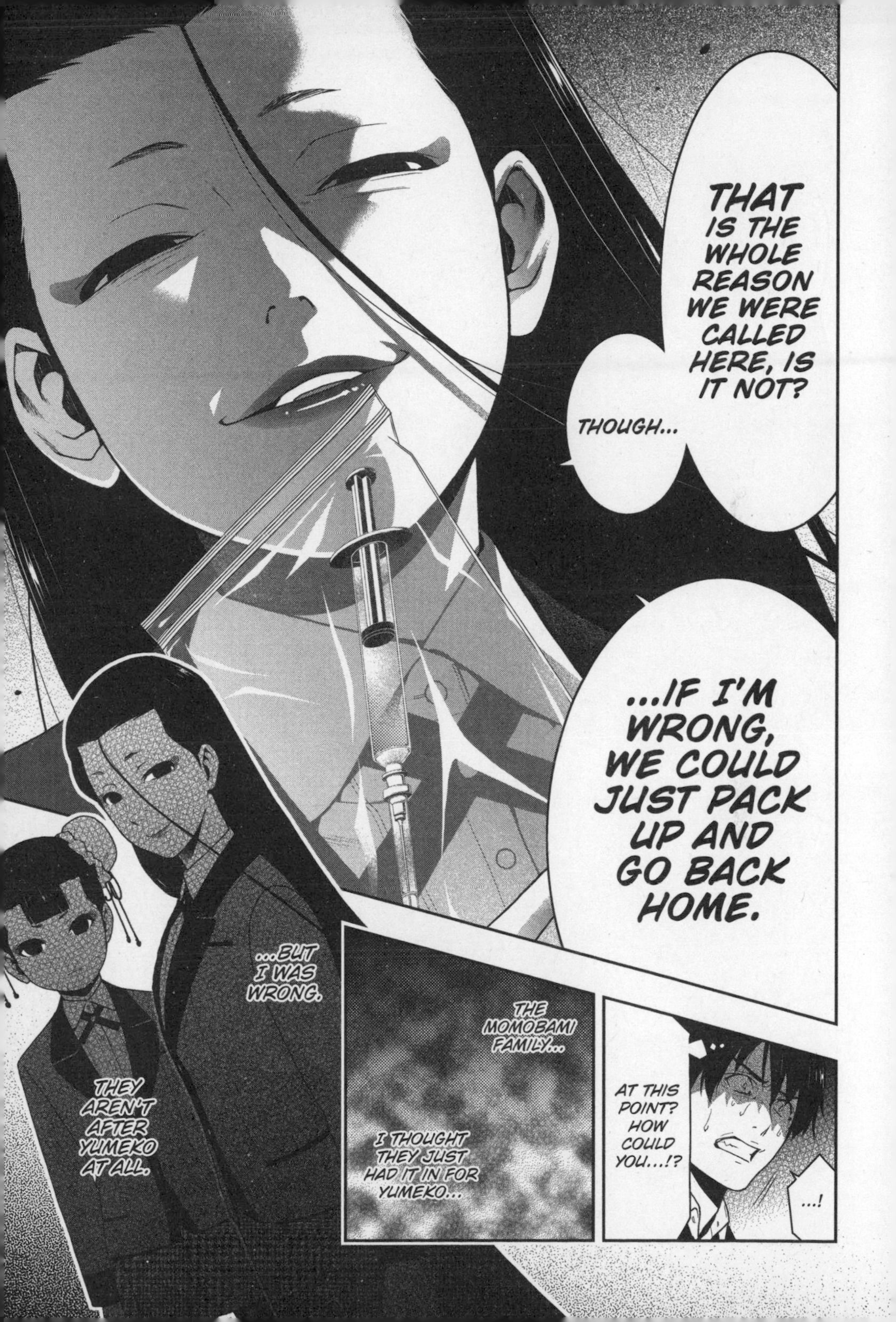
THAT IS THE WHOLE REASON WE WERE CALLED HERE, IS IT NOT?
THOUGH...
...IF I'M WRONG, WE COULD JUST PACK UP AND GO BACK HOME.
AT THIS POINT? HOW COULD YOU...!?
...!
THE MOMOBAMI FAMILY...
I THOUGHT THEY JUST HAD IT IN FOR YUMEKO...
...BUT I WAS WRONG.
THEY AREN'T AFTER YUMEKO AT ALL.

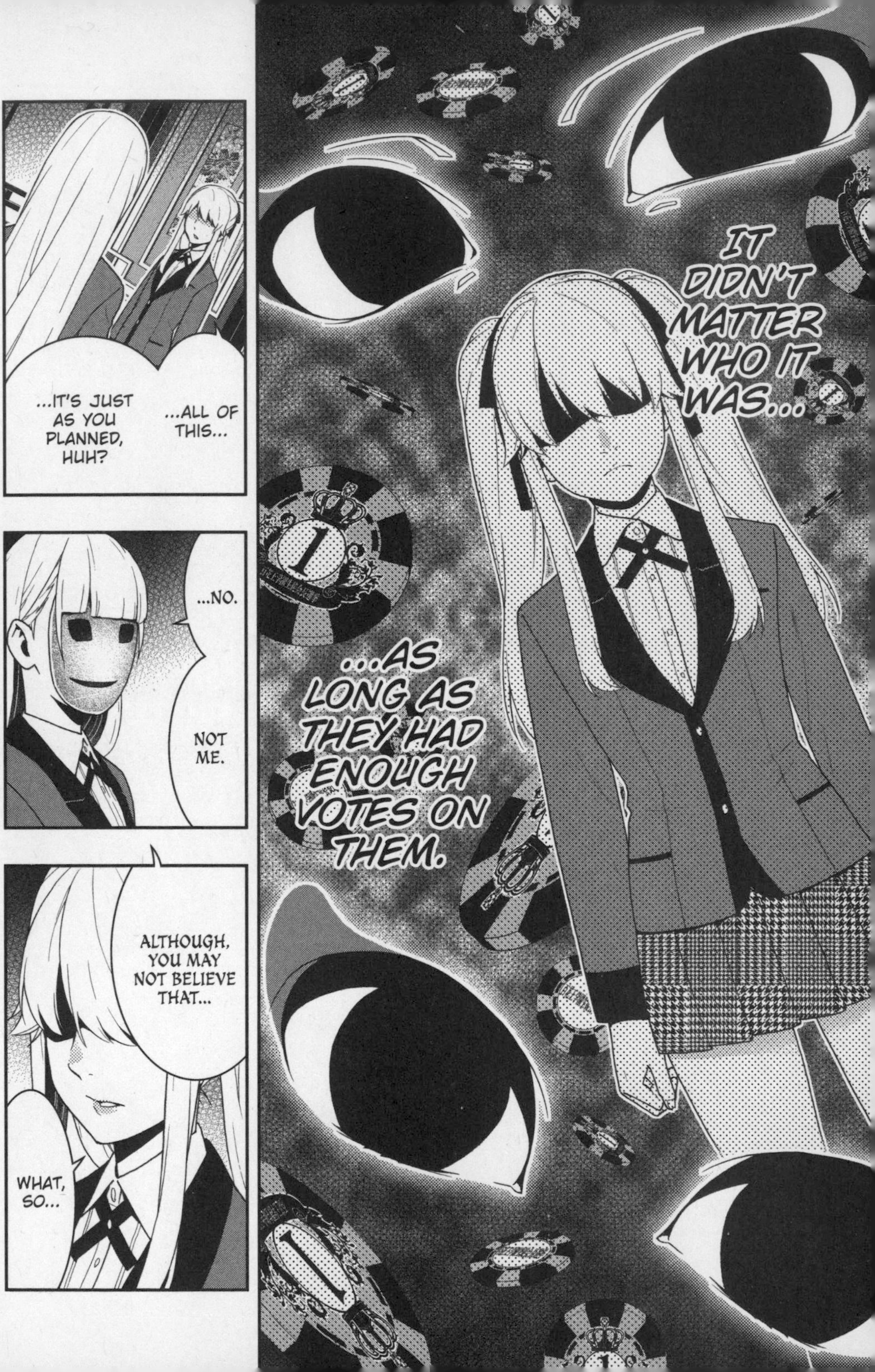
IT DIDN'T MATTER WHO IT WAS...
...AS LONG AS THEY HAD ENOUGH VOTES ON THEM.
...ALL OF THIS...
...IT'S JUST AS YOU PLANNED, HUH?
...NO.
NOT ME.
ALTHOUGH, YOU MAY NOT BELIEVE THAT...
WHAT, SO...

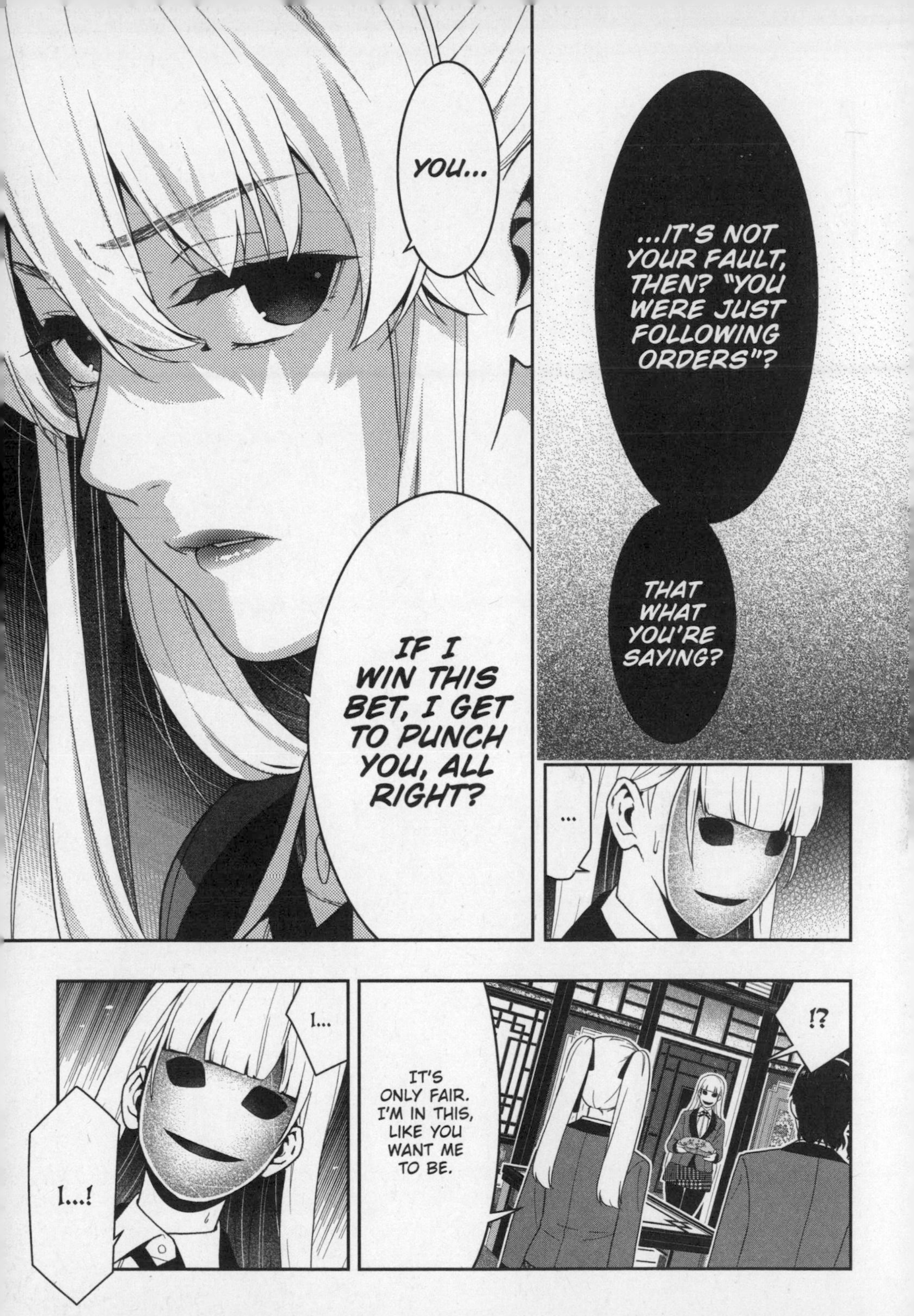
...IT'S NOT YOUR FAULT, THEN? "YOU WERE JUST FOLLOWING ORDERS"?
THAT WHAT YOU'RE SAYING?
...
YOU...
IF I WIN THIS BET, I GET TO PUNCH YOU, ALL RIGHT?
!?
IT'S ONLY FAIR. I'M IN THIS, LIKE YOU WANT ME TO BE.
I...
I...!

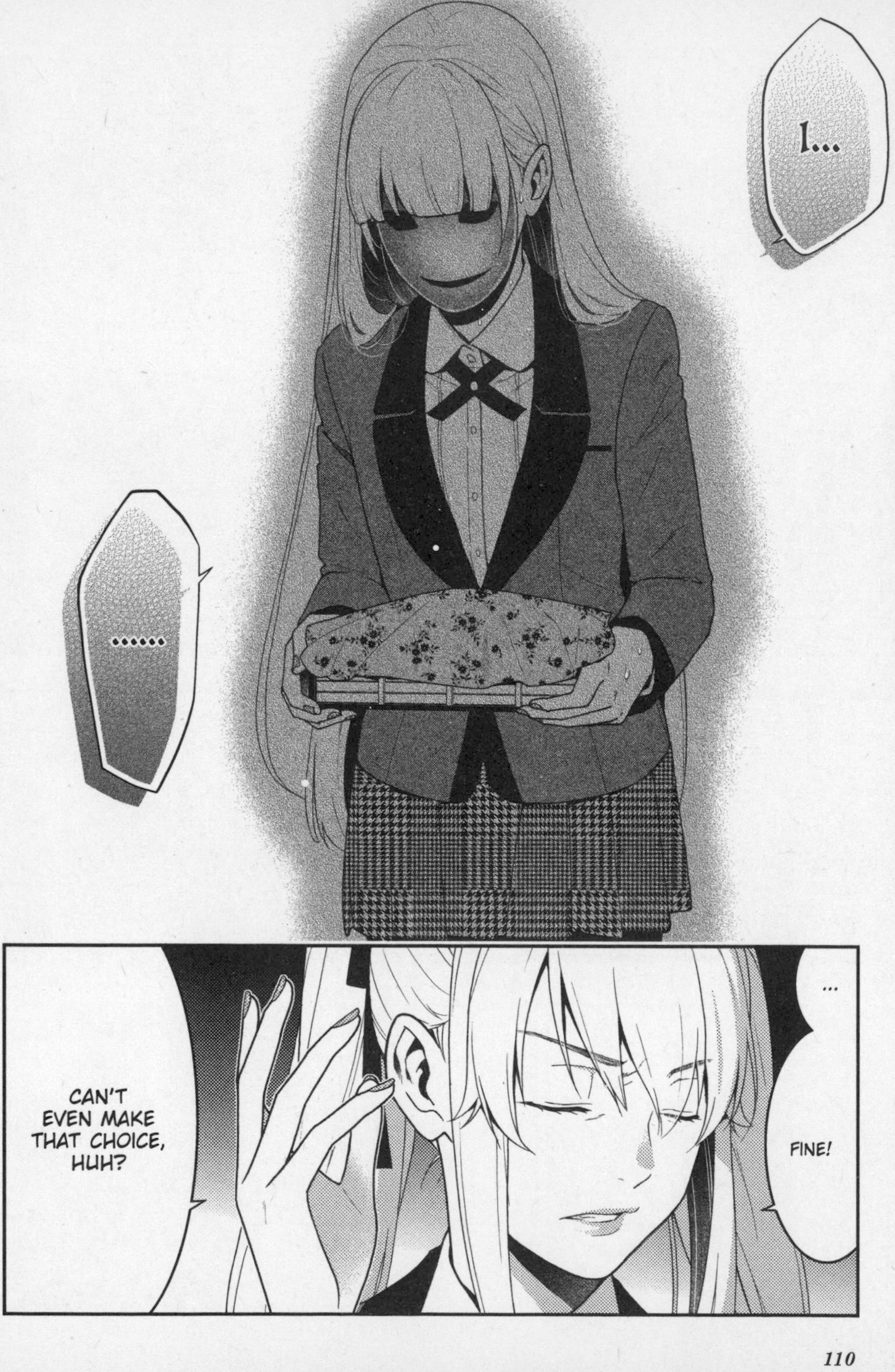
I...
......
... FINE!
CAN'T EVEN MAKE THAT CHOICE, HUH?

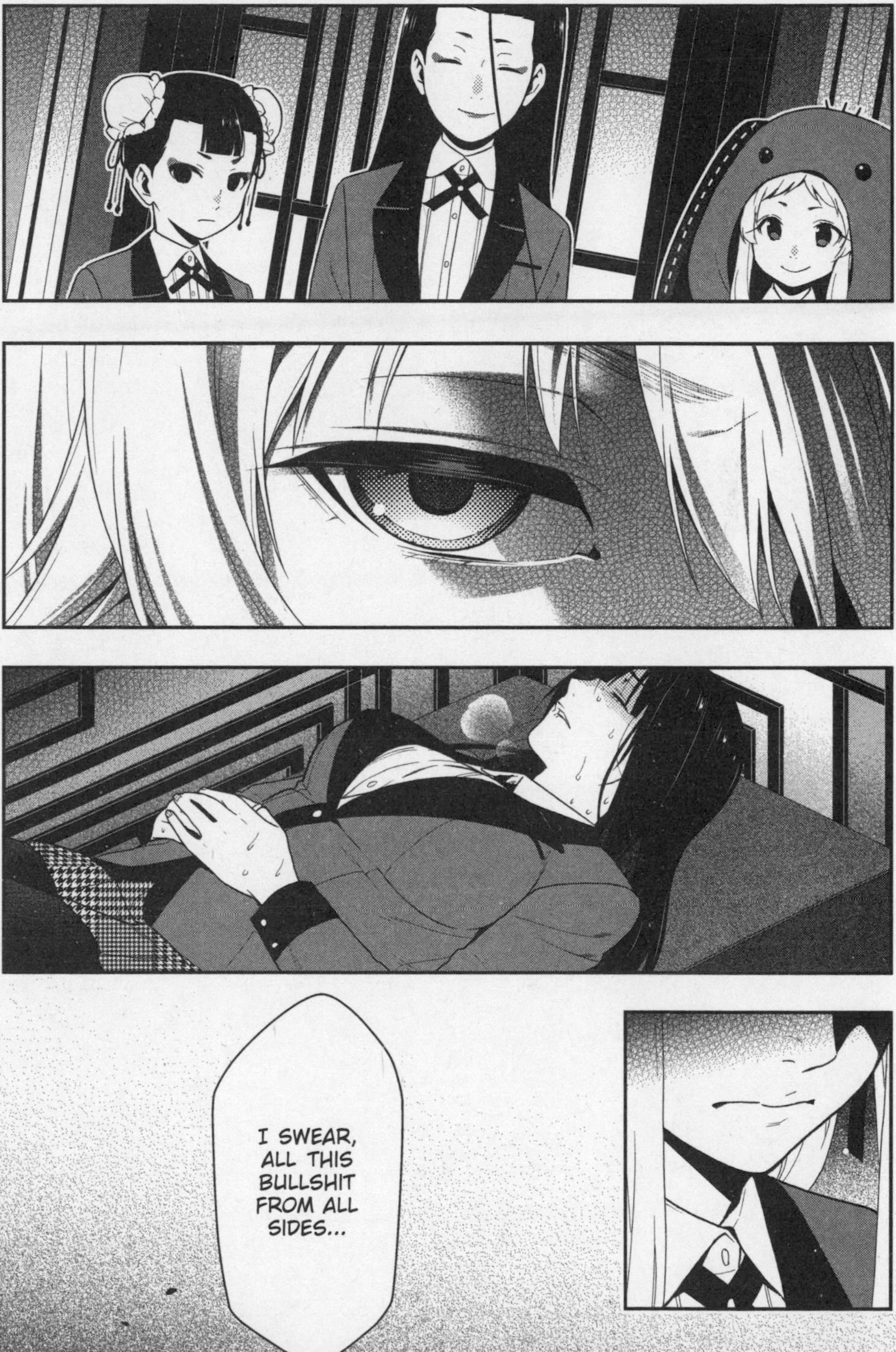
I SWEAR, ALL THIS BULLSHIT FROM ALL SIDES...

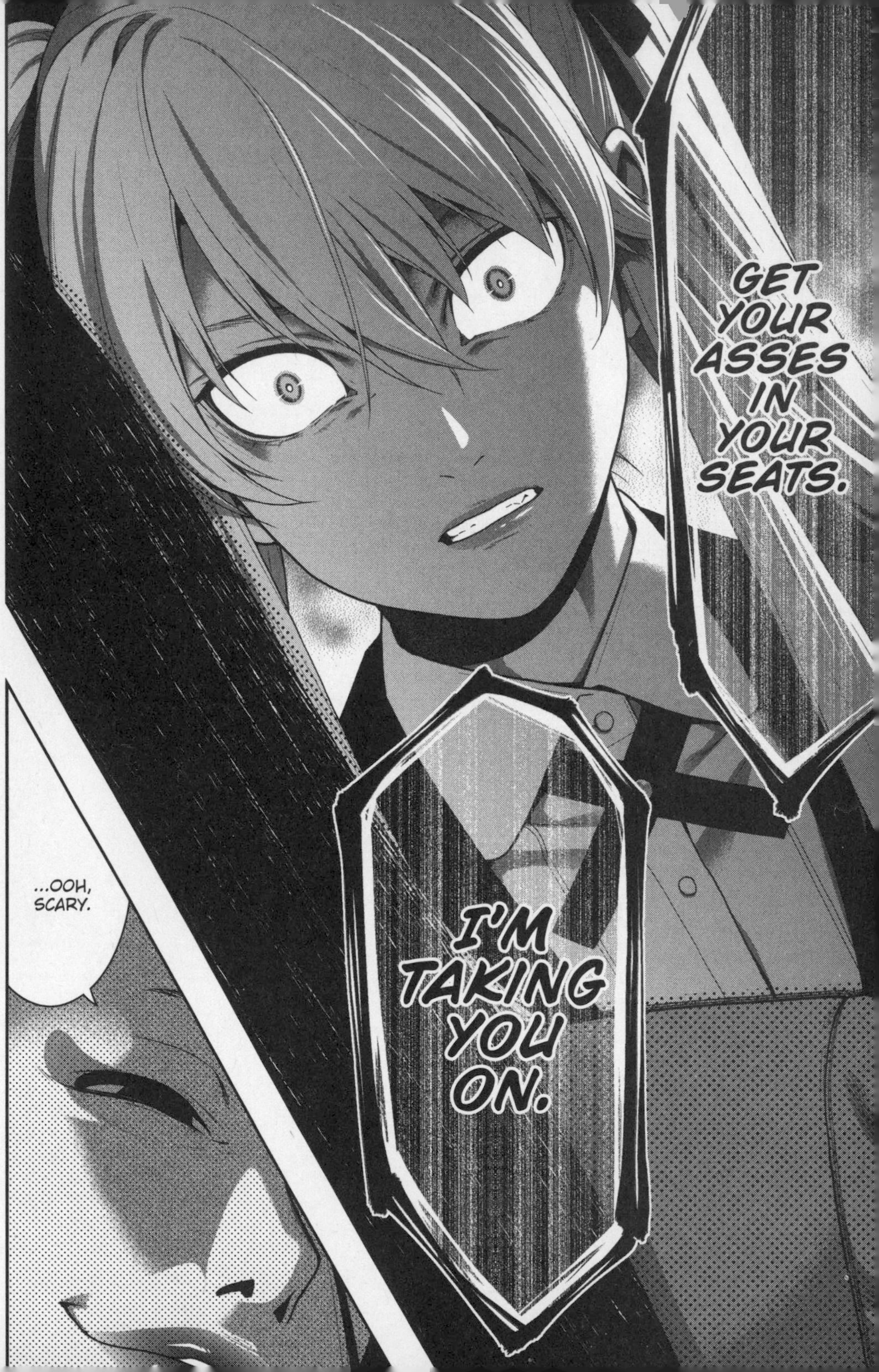
GET YOUR ASSES IN YOUR SEATS.
I'M TAKING YOU ON.
...OOH, SCARY.

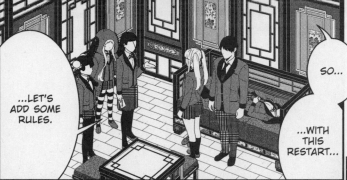

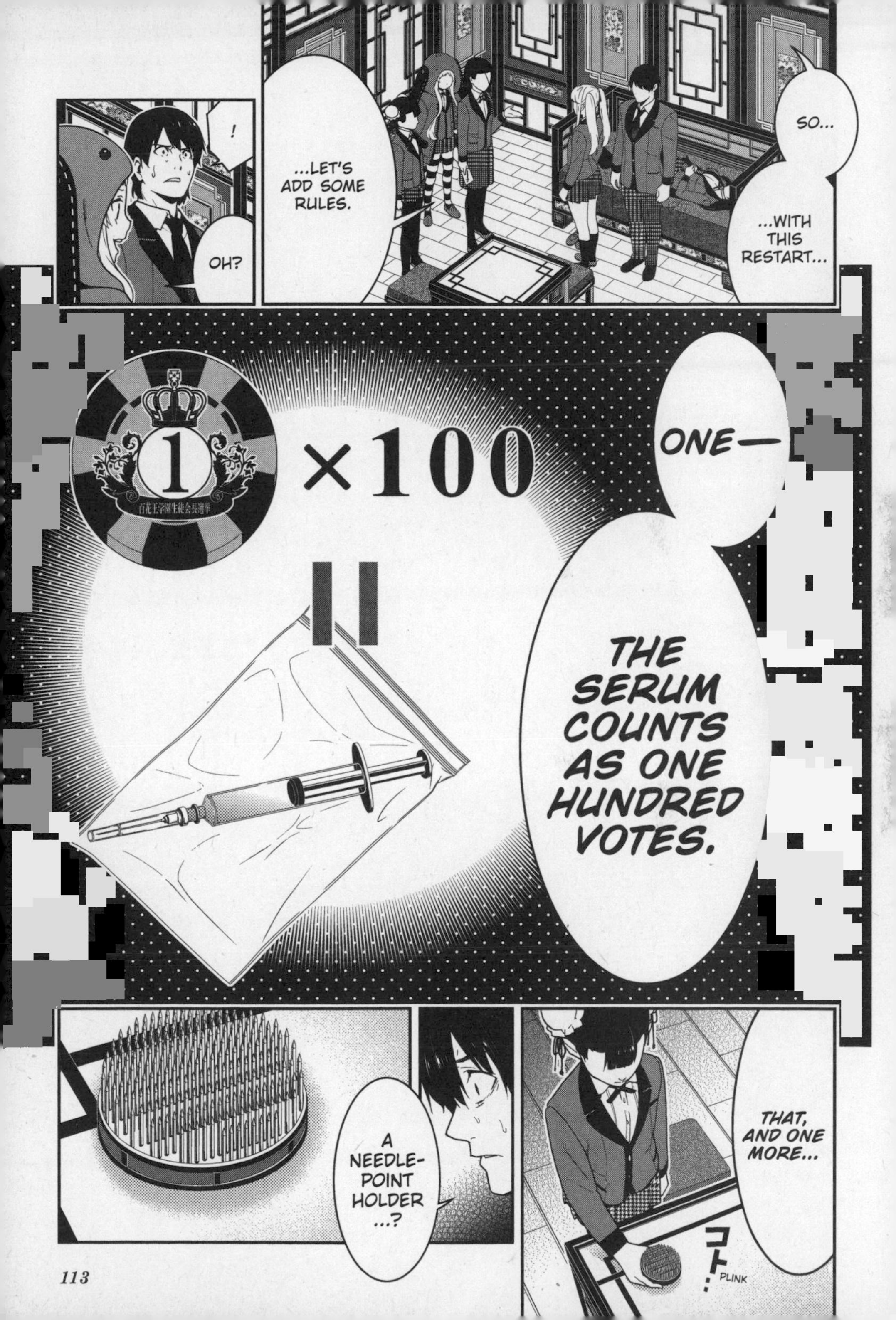

SO...
...WITH THIS RESTART...
...LET'S ADD SOME RULES.
!
OH?
ONE—
THE SERUM COUNTS AS ONE HUNDRED VOTES.
1
百花王学園生徒会長選挙
×100
THAT, AND ONE MORE...
コト
PLINK
A NEEDLE-POINT HOLDER ...?

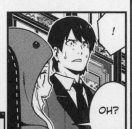

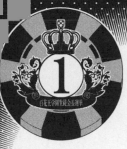

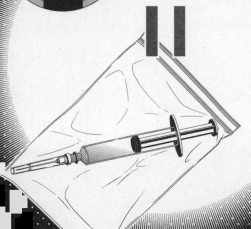

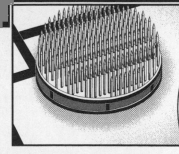

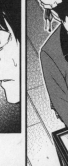

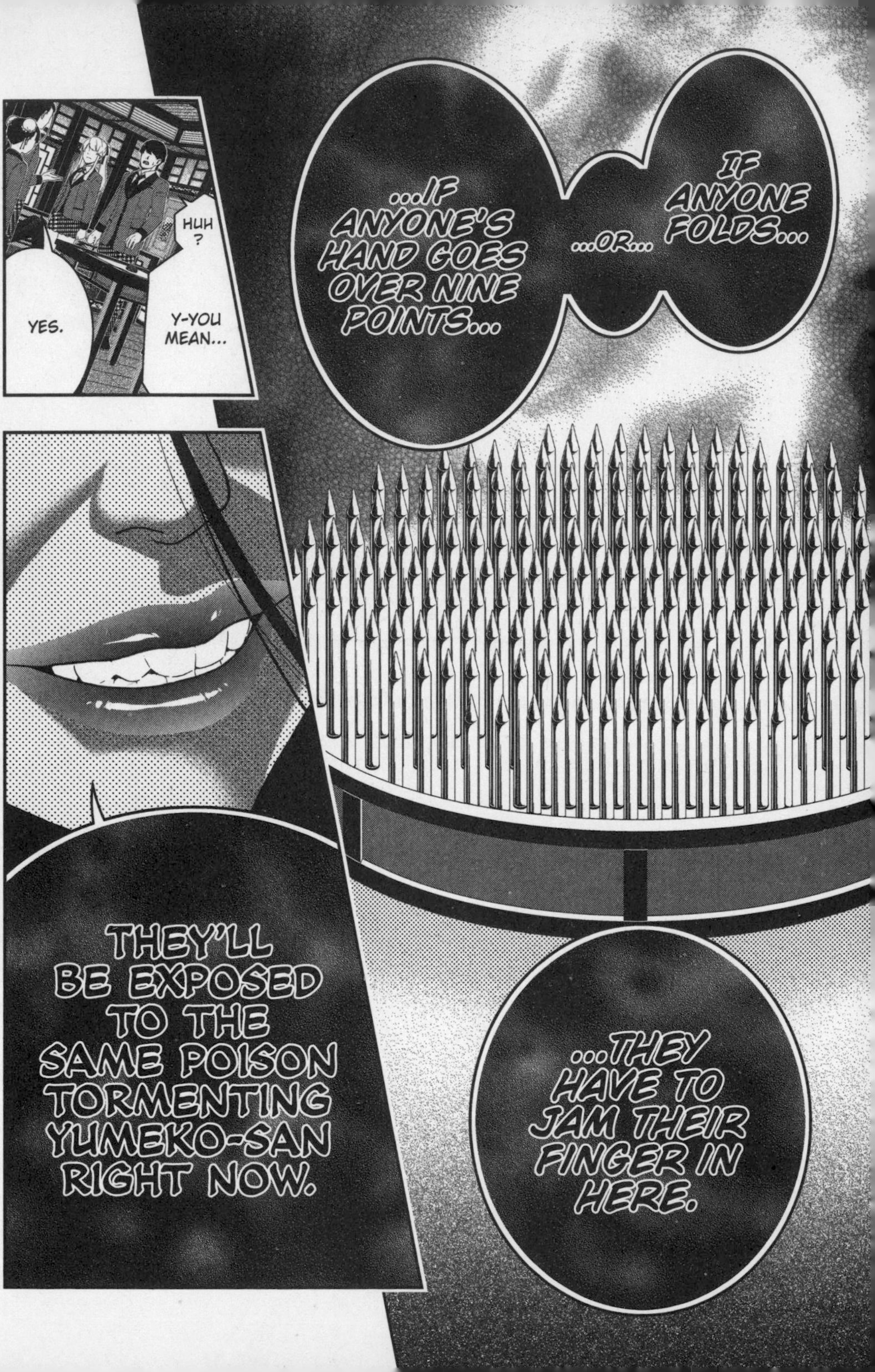
IF ANYONE FOLDS...
...OR...
...IF ANYONE'S HAND GOES OVER NINE POINTS...
...THEY HAVE TO JAM THEIR FINGER IN HERE.
HUH ?
Y-YOU MEAN...
YES.
THEY'LL BE EXPOSED TO THE SAME POISON TORMENTING YUMEKO-SAN RIGHT NOW.

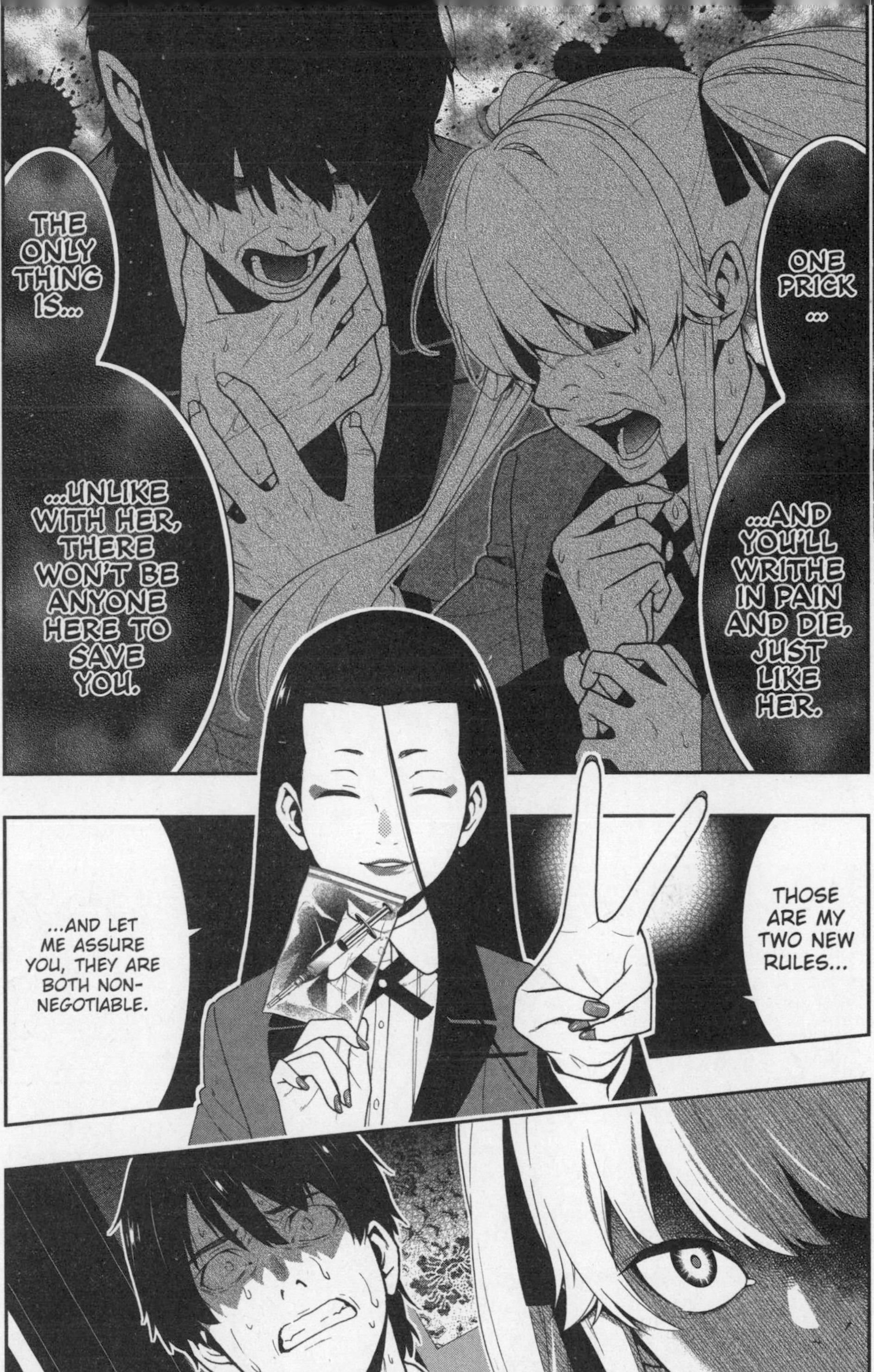
ONE PRICK ...
...AND YOU'LL WRITHE IN PAIN AND DIE, JUST LIKE HER.
THE ONLY THING IS...
...UNLIKE WITH HER, THERE WON'T BE ANYONE HERE TO SAVE YOU.
THOSE ARE MY TWO NEW RULES...
...AND LET ME ASSURE YOU, THEY ARE BOTH NON-NEGOTIABLE.

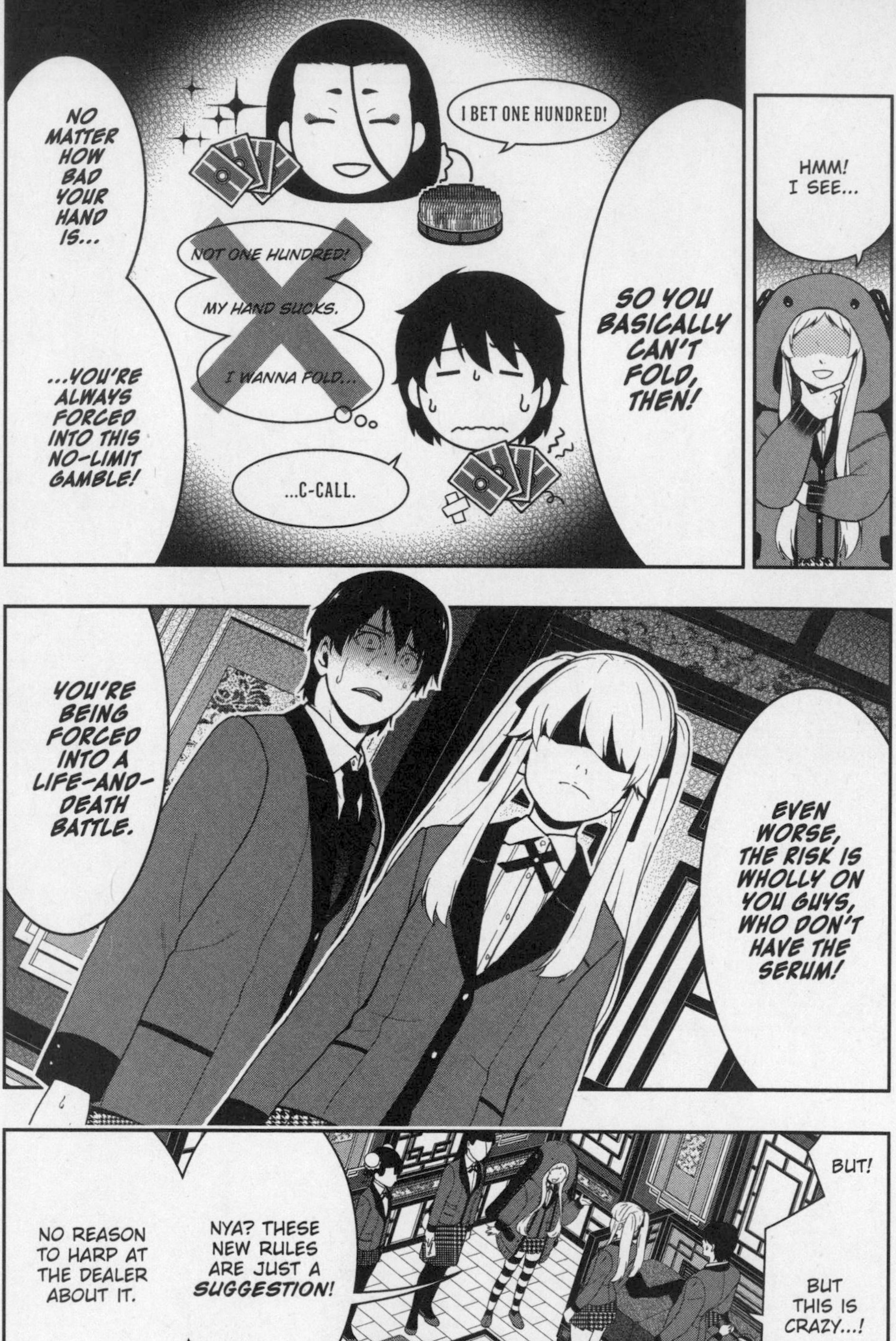
HMM! I SEE...
I BET ONE HUNDRED!
SO YOU BASICALLY CAN'T FOLD, THEN!
NO MATTER HOW BAD YOUR HAND IS...
NOT ONE HUNDRED!
MY HAND SUCKS.
I WANNA FOLD...
...YOU'RE ALWAYS FORCED INTO THIS NO-LIMIT GAMBLE!
...C-CALL.
EVEN WORSE, THE RISK IS WHOLLY ON YOU GUYS, WHO DON'T HAVE THE SERUM!
YOU'RE BEING FORCED INTO A LIFE-AND-DEATH BATTLE.
BUT!
BUT THIS IS CRAZY...!
NYA? THESE NEW RULES ARE JUST A SUGGESTION!
NO REASON TO HARP AT THE DEALER ABOUT IT.

SO, WHAT'S IT GONNA BE?

ARE YOU AGREEING TO THESE RULES...

...OR AREN'T YOU?

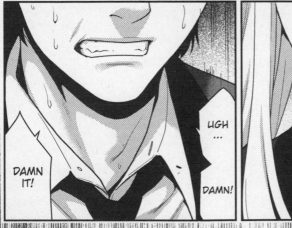

UGH...

DAMN IT!

DAMN!

STOP BEATING AROUND THE BUSH.

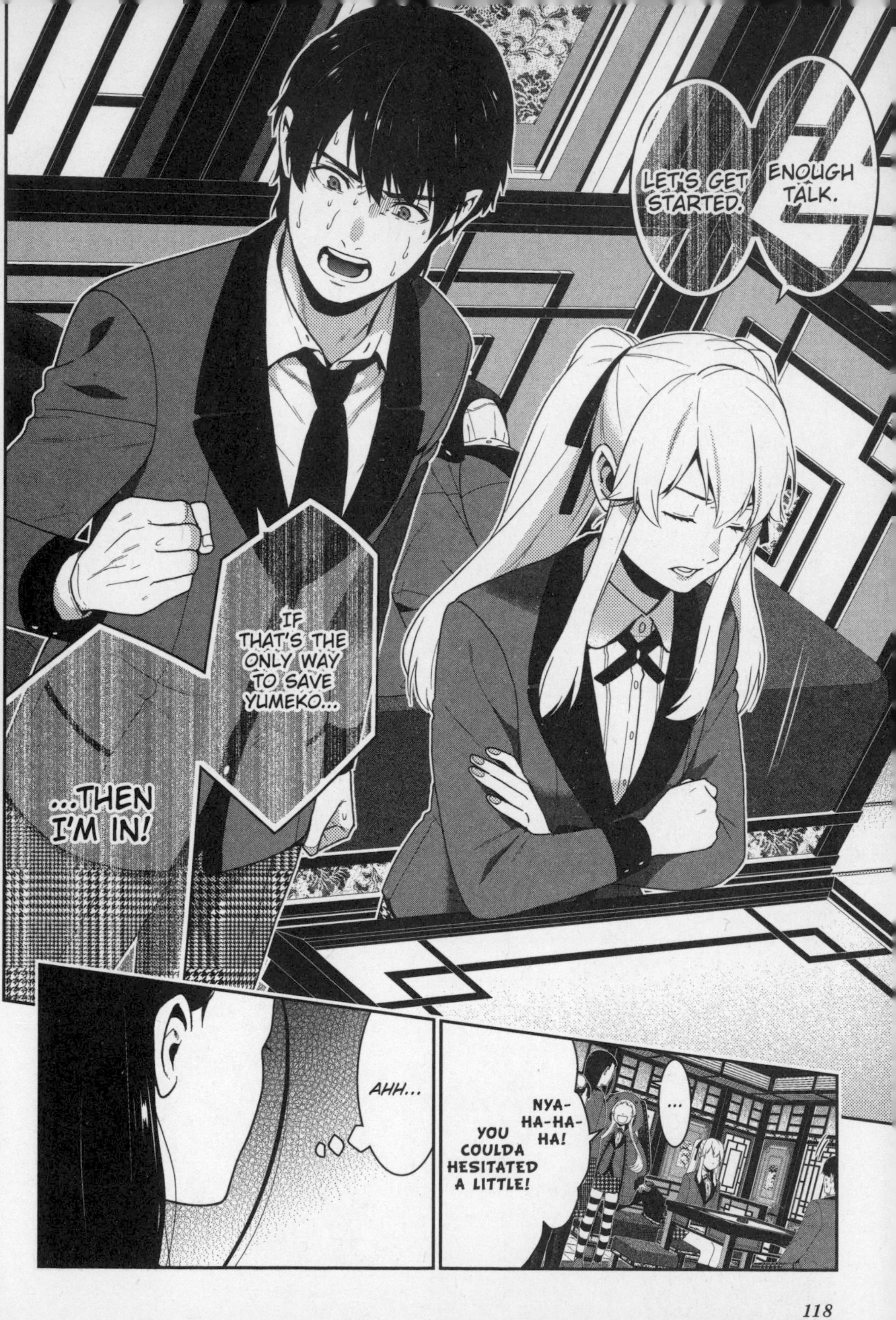
ENOUGH TALK.
LET'S GET STARTED.
IF THAT'S THE ONLY WAY TO SAVE YUMEKO...
...THEN I'M IN!
...
NYA-HA-HA-HA!
YOU COULDA HESITATED A LITTLE!
AHH...

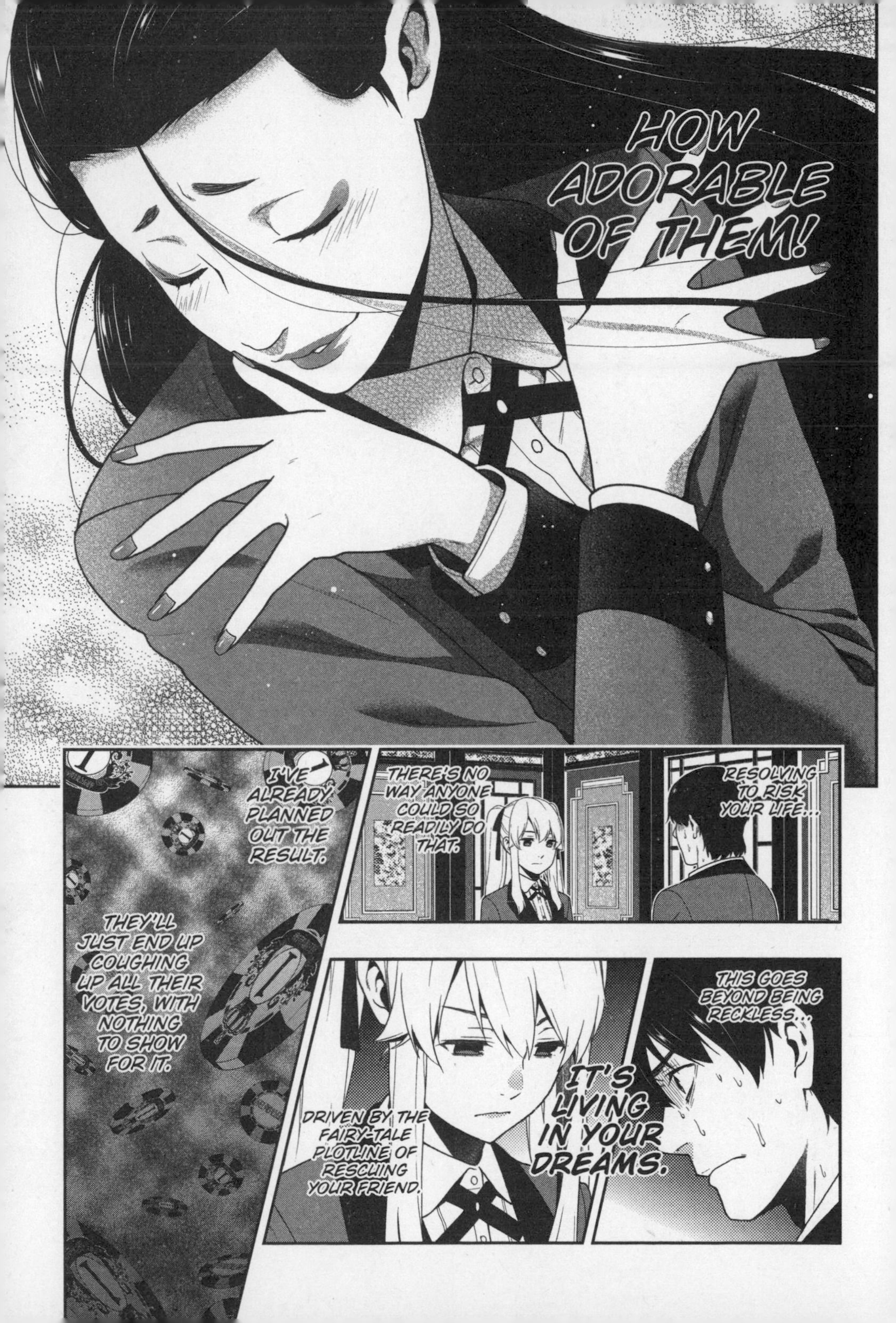
HOW ADORABLE OF THEM!
RESOLVING TO RISK YOUR LIFE...
THERE'S NO WAY ANYONE COULD SO READILY DO THAT.
THIS GOES BEYOND BEING RECKLESS...
IT'S LIVING IN YOUR DREAMS.
DRIVEN BY THE FAIRY-TALE PLOTLINE OF RESCUING YOUR FRIEND.
I'VE ALREADY PLANNED OUT THE RESULT.
THEY'LL JUST END UP COUGHING UP ALL THEIR VOTES, WITH NOTHING TO SHOW FOR IT.

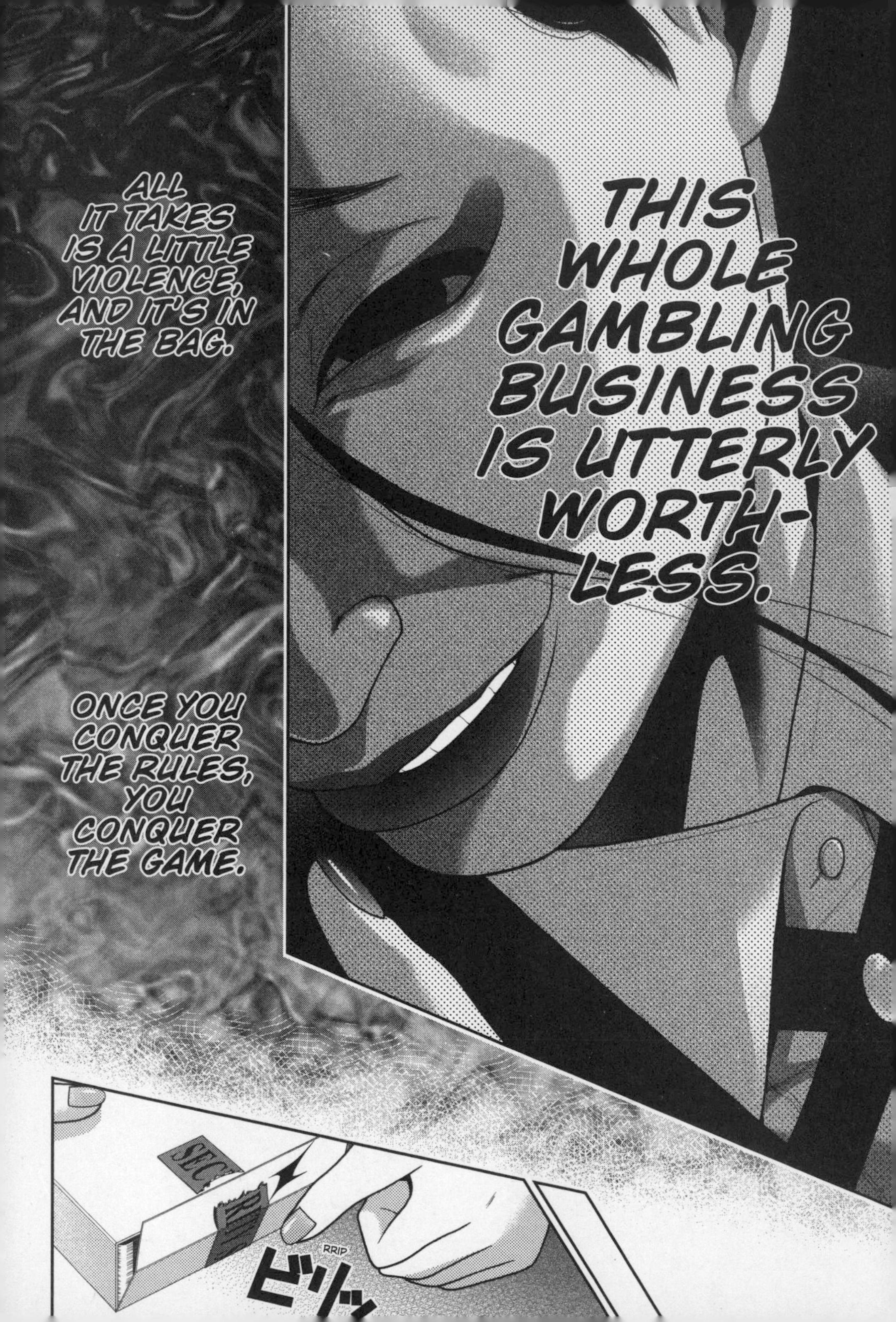
THIS WHOLE GAMBLING BUSINESS IS UTTERLY WORTH-LESS.
ALL IT TAKES IS A LITTLE VIOLENCE, AND IT'S IN THE BAG.
ONCE YOU CONQUER THE RULES, YOU CONQUER THE GAME.
RRIP
ビッ

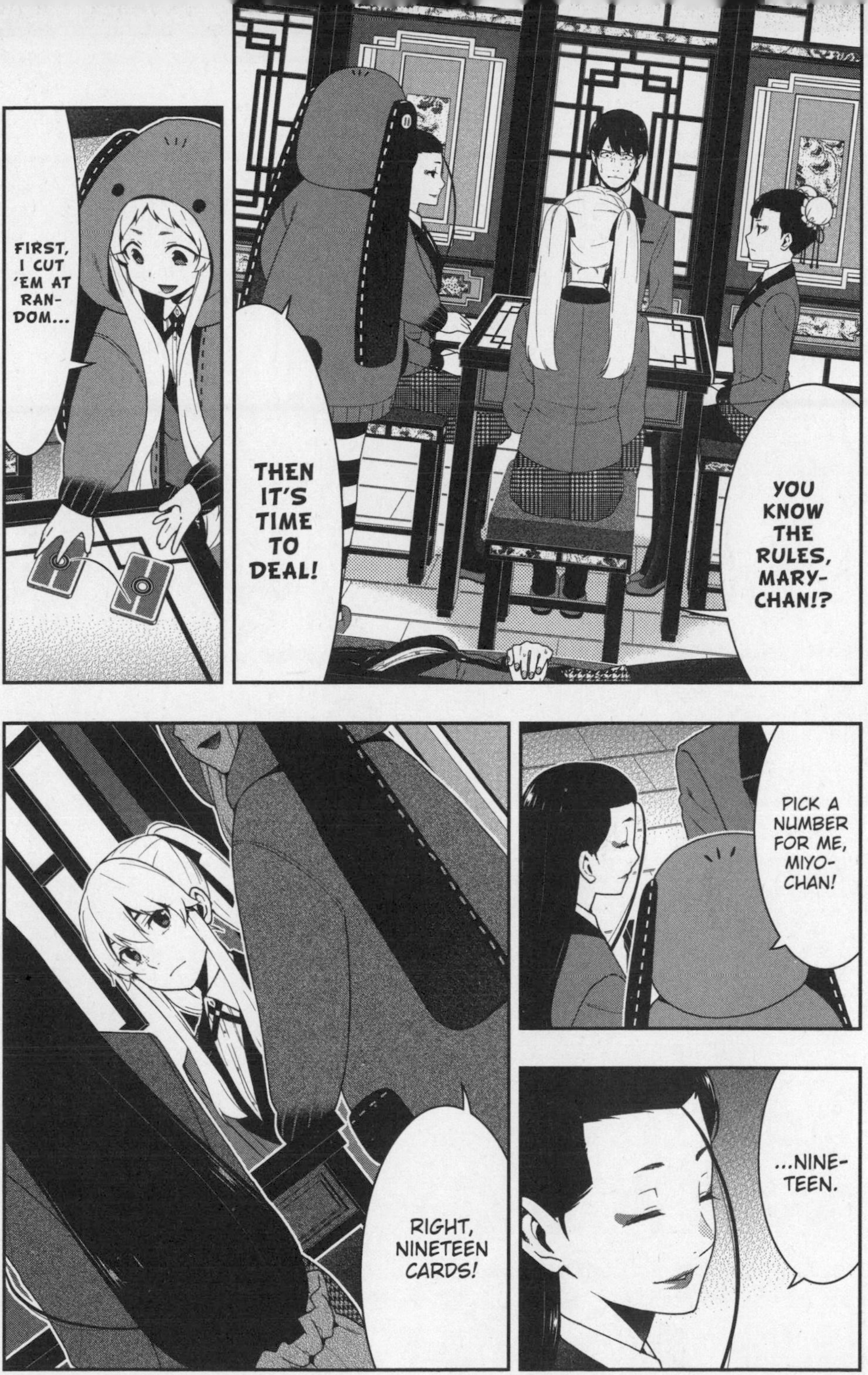
YOU KNOW THE RULES, MARY-CHAN!?
THEN IT'S TIME TO DEAL!
FIRST, I CUT 'EM AT RAN-DOM...
PICK A NUMBER FOR ME, MIYO-CHAN!
...NINE-TEEN.
RIGHT, NINETEEN CARDS!

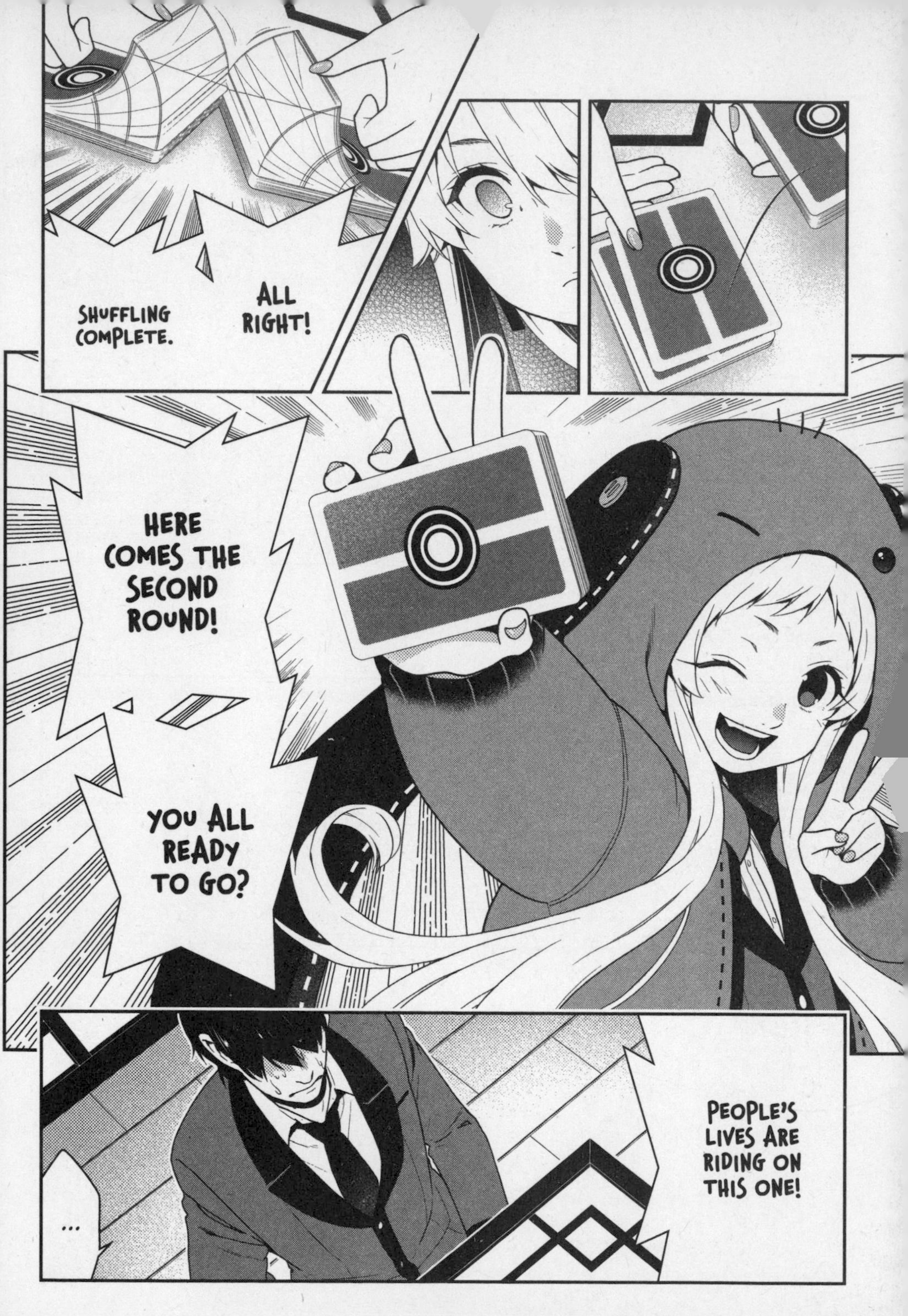
ALL RIGHT!
SHUFFLING COMPLETE.
HERE COMES THE SECOND ROUND!
YOU ALL READY TO GO?
PEOPLE'S LIVES ARE RIDING ON THIS ONE!
...

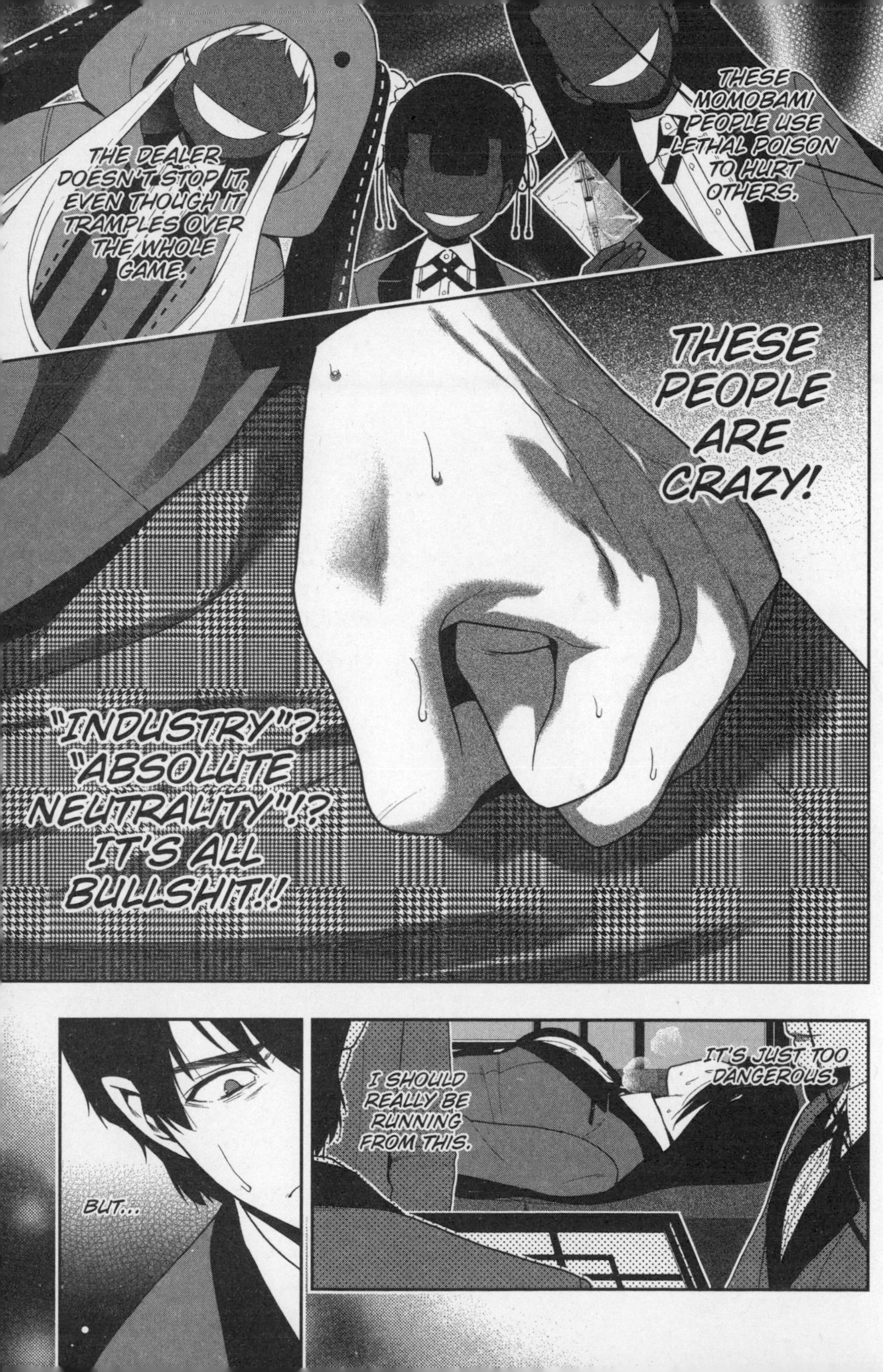
THESE MOMOBAMI PEOPLE USE LETHAL POISON TO HURT OTHERS.
THE DEALER DOESN'T STOP IT, EVEN THOUGH IT TRAMPLES OVER THE WHOLE GAME.
THESE PEOPLE ARE CRAZY!
"INDUSTRY"? "ABSOLUTE NEUTRALITY"!? IT'S ALL BULLSHIT!!
IT'S JUST TOO DANGEROUS.
I SHOULD REALLY BE RUNNING FROM THIS.
BUT...

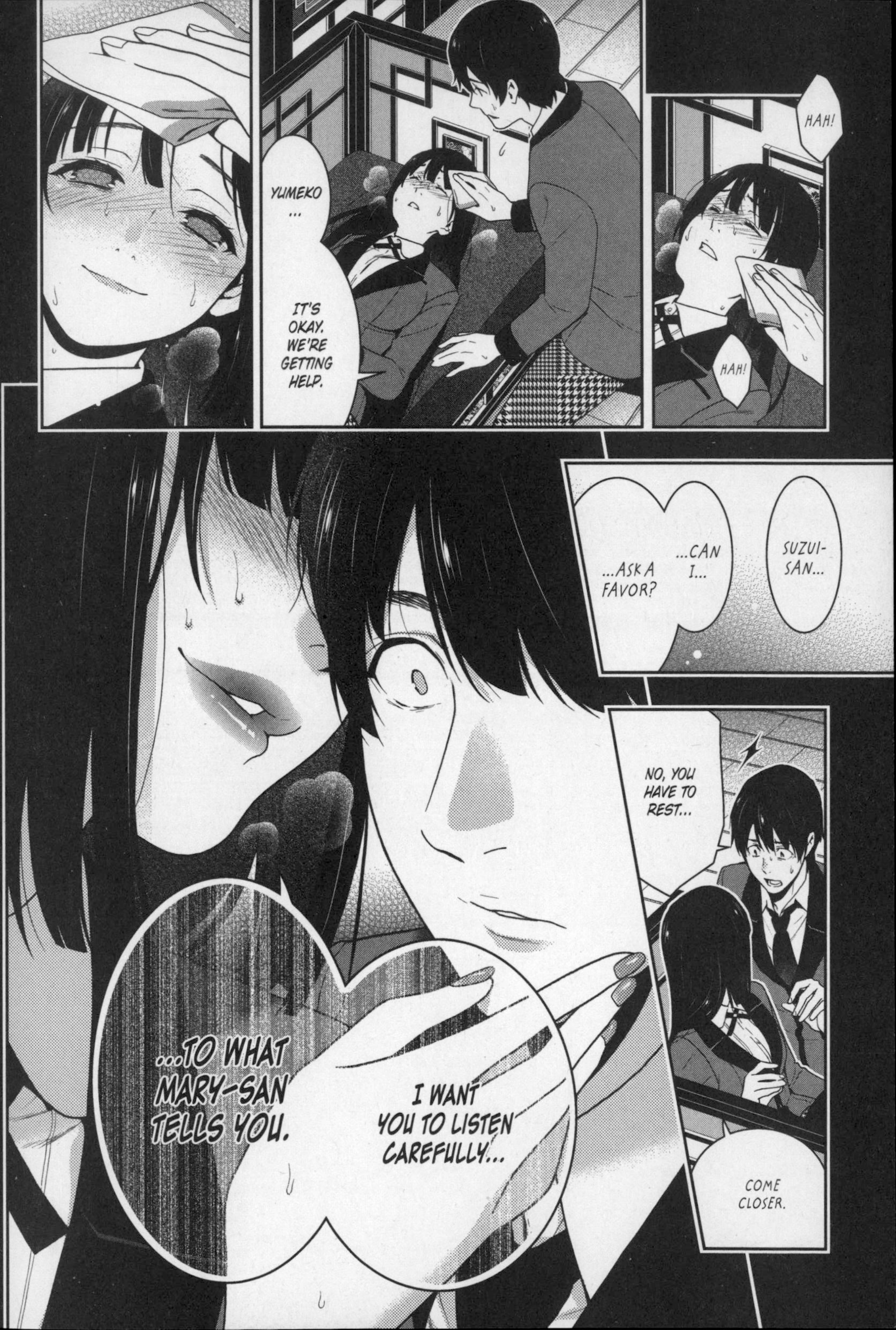
HAH!
HAH!
YUMEKO...
IT'S OKAY. WE'RE GETTING HELP.
SUZUI-SAN...
...CAN I...
...ASK A FAVOR?
NO, YOU HAVE TO REST...
COME CLOSER.
I WANT YOU TO LISTEN CAREFULLY...
...TO WHAT MARY-SAN TELLS YOU.

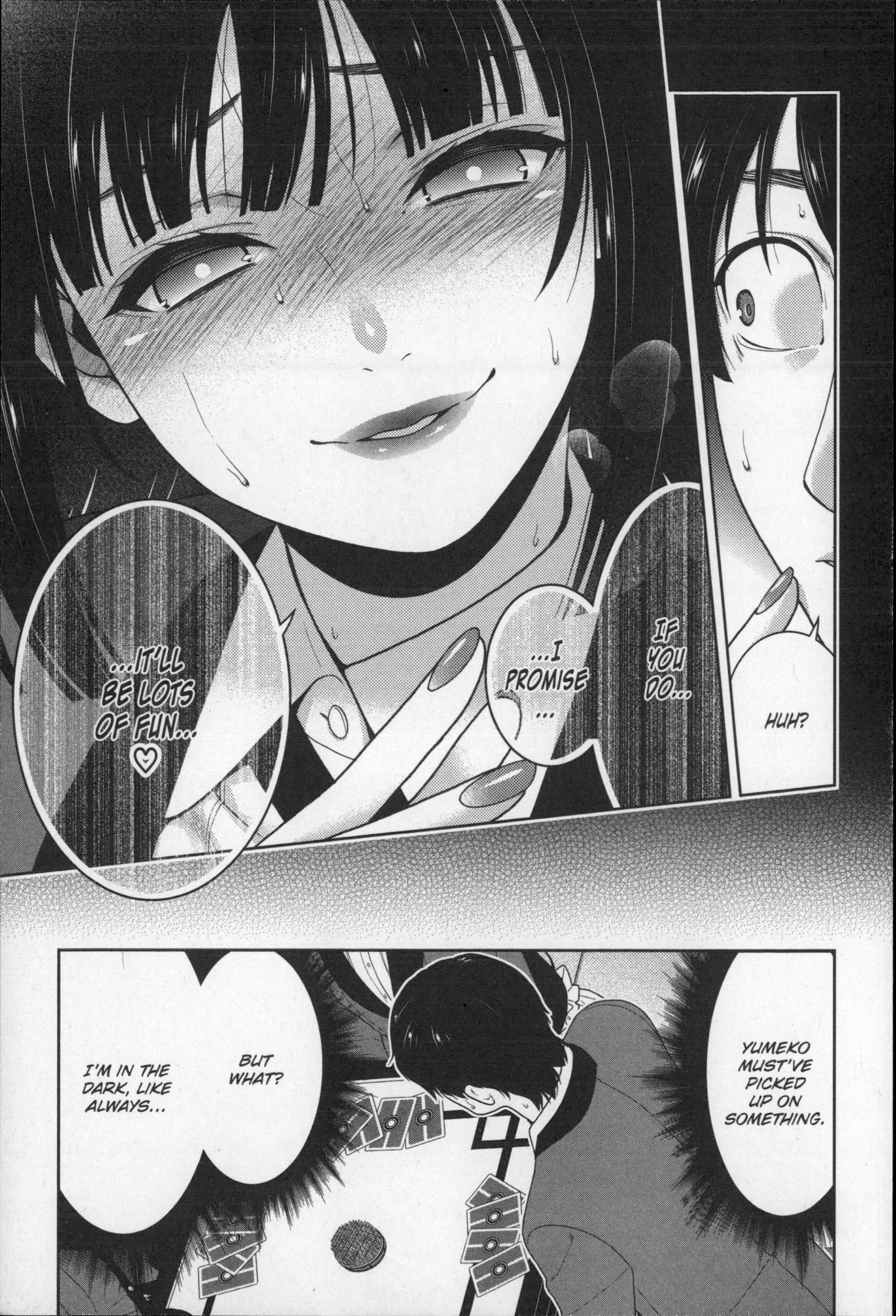
HUH?
IF YOU DO...
...I PROMISE ...
...IT'LL BE LOTS OF FUN... ♡
YUMEKO MUST'VE PICKED UP ON SOMETHING.
BUT WHAT?
I'M IN THE DARK, LIKE ALWAYS...

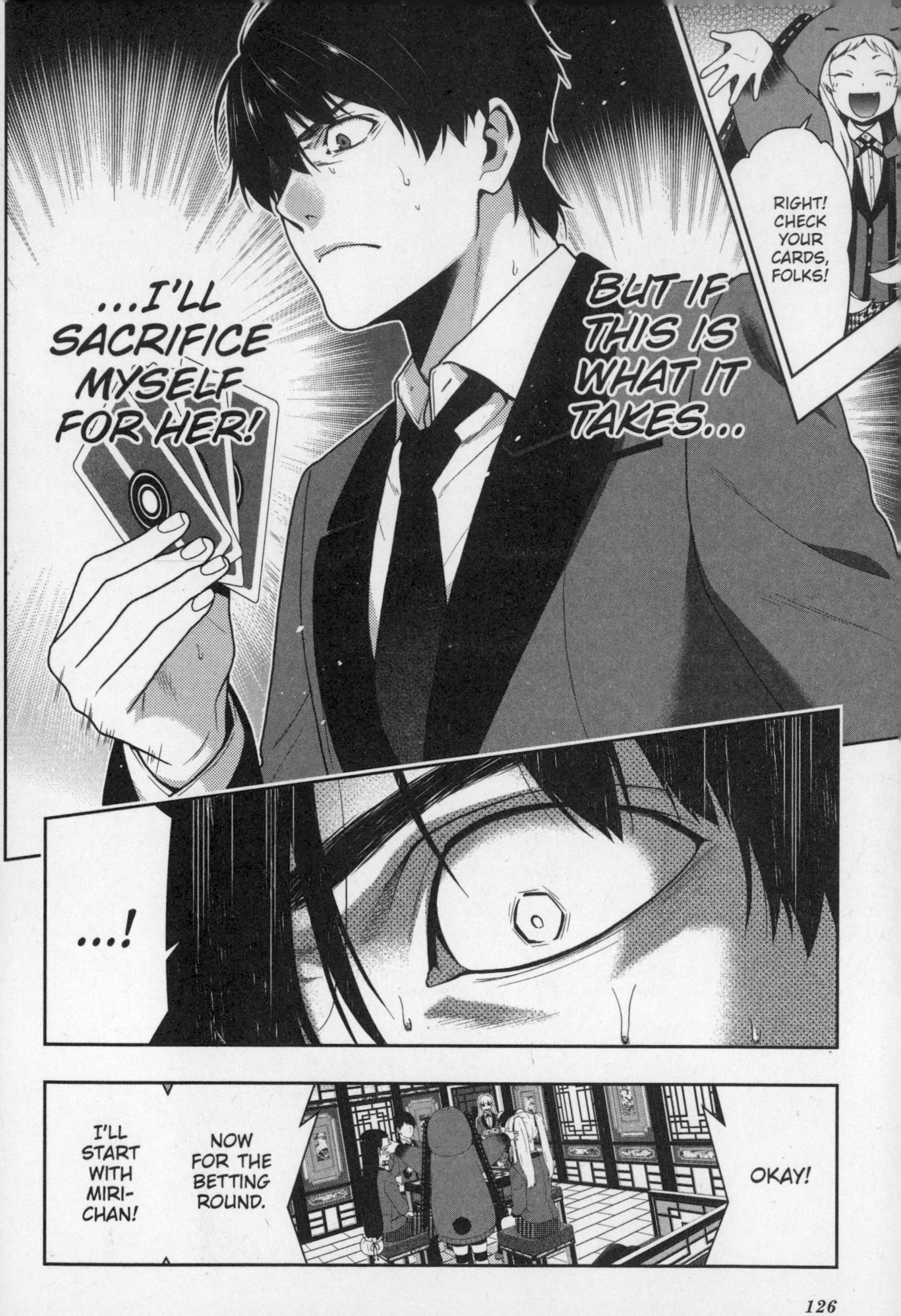
RIGHT! CHECK YOUR CARDS, FOLKS!
BUT IF THIS IS WHAT IT TAKES...
...I'LL SACRIFICE MYSELF FOR HER!
...!
OKAY!
NOW FOR THE BETTING ROUND.
I'LL START WITH MIRI-CHAN!

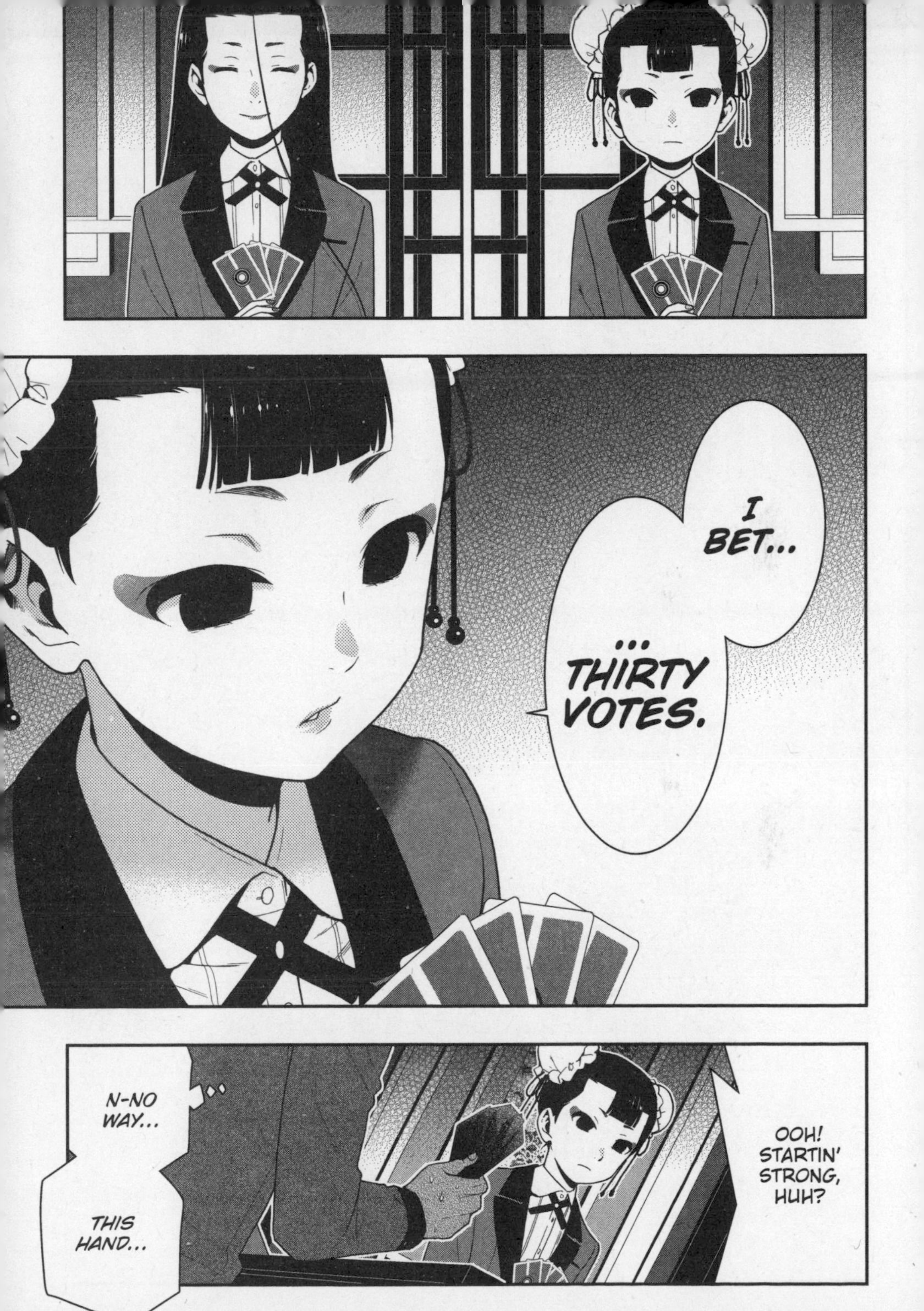
I BET...
... THIRTY VOTES.
OOH! STARTIN' STRONG, HUH?
...
N-NO WAY...
THIS HAND...

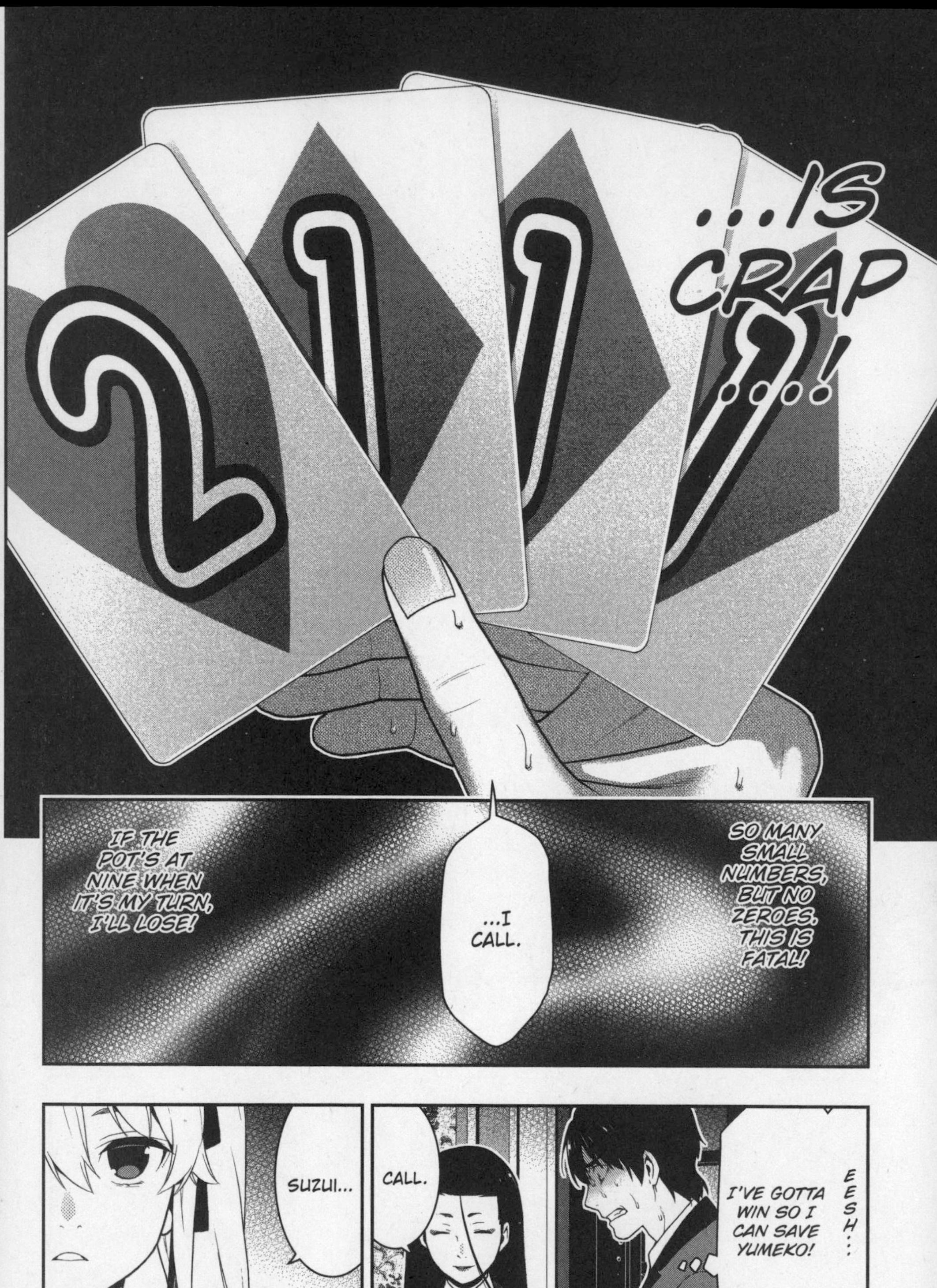
...IS CRAP...!
SO MANY SMALL NUMBERS, BUT NO ZEROES. THIS IS FATAL!
...I CALL.
IF THE POT'S AT NINE WHEN IT'S MY TURN, I'LL LOSE!
EESH...
I'VE GOTTA WIN SO I CAN SAVE YUMEKO!
CALL.
SUZUI...

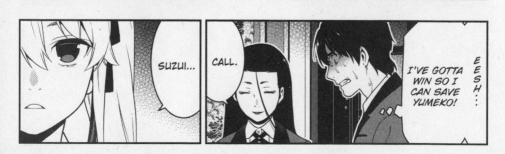

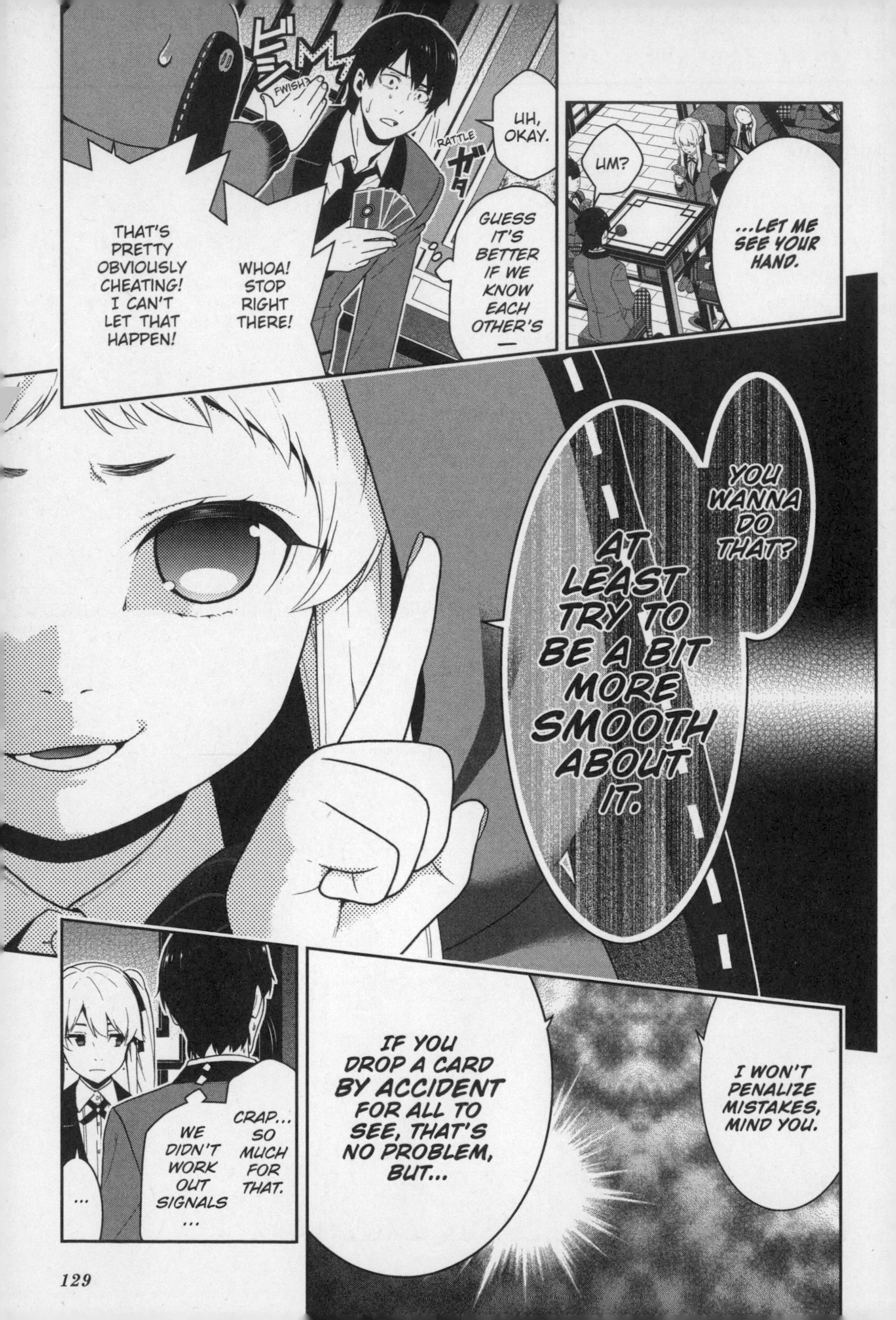
...LET ME SEE YOUR HAND.
UM?
UH, OKAY.
RATTLE
GUESS IT'S BETTER IF WE KNOW EACH OTHER'S —
FWISH
WHOA! STOP RIGHT THERE!
THAT'S PRETTY OBVIOUSLY CHEATING! I CAN'T LET THAT HAPPEN!
YOU WANNA DO THAT?
AT LEAST TRY TO BE A BIT MORE SMOOTH ABOUT IT.
I WON'T PENALIZE MISTAKES, MIND YOU.
IF YOU DROP A CARD BY ACCIDENT FOR ALL TO SEE, THAT'S NO PROBLEM, BUT...
CRAP... SO MUCH FOR THAT.
WE DIDN'T WORK OUT SIGNALS...
...

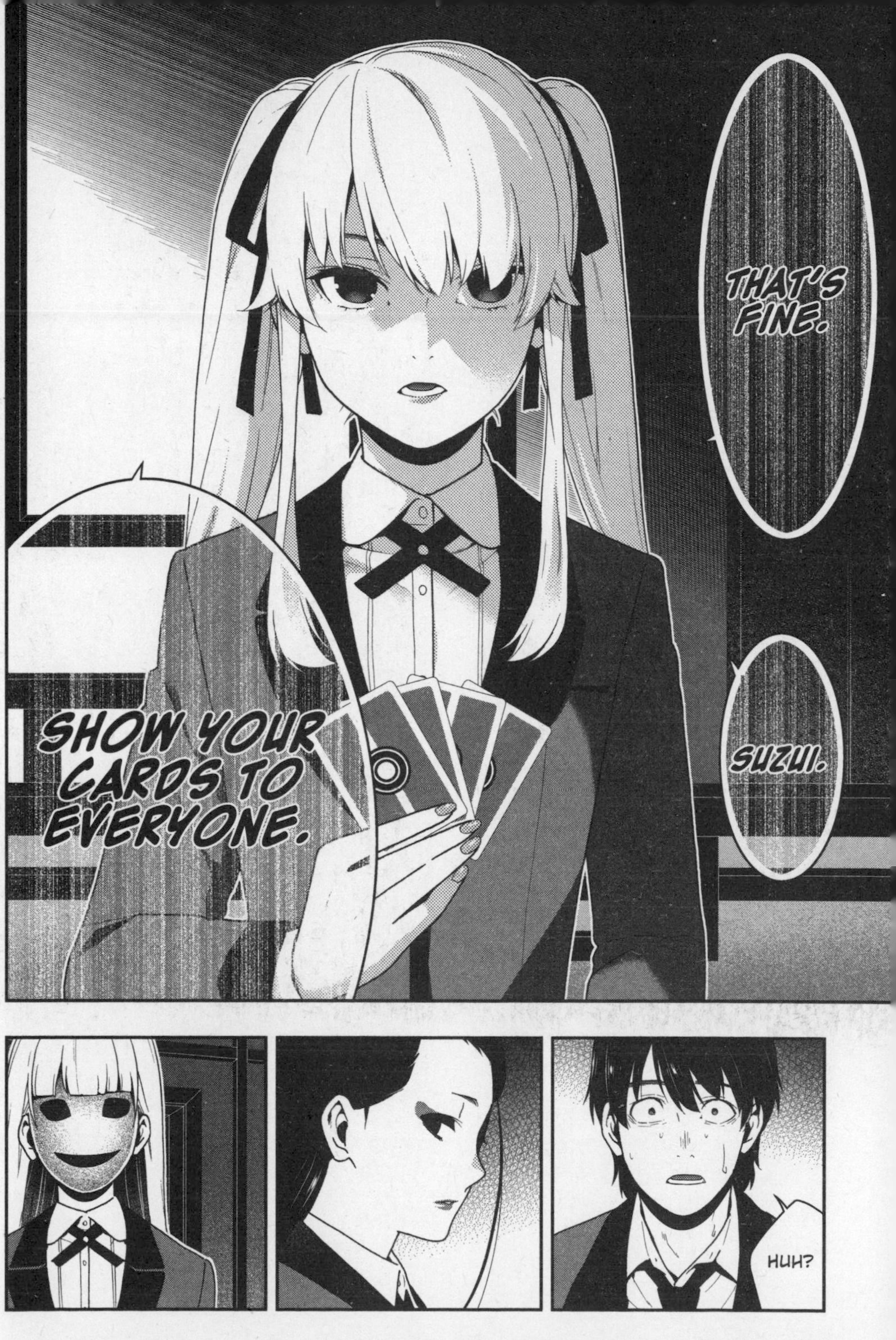
THAT'S FINE.
SUZUI.
SHOW YOUR CARDS TO EVERYONE.
HUH?

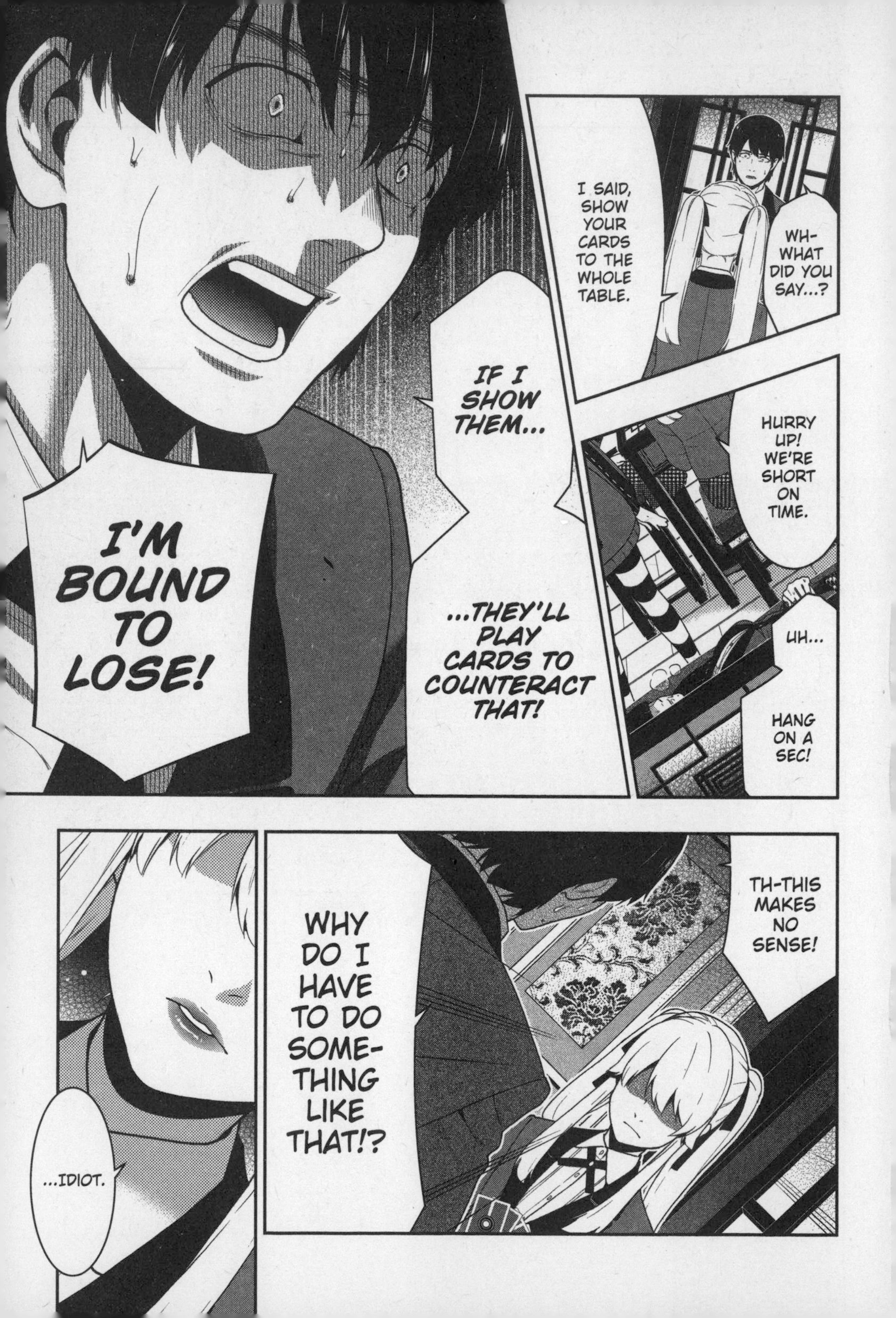
WH-WHAT DID YOU SAY...?
I SAID, SHOW YOUR CARDS TO THE WHOLE TABLE.
HURRY UP! WE'RE SHORT ON TIME.
UH...
HANG ON A SEC!
IF I SHOW THEM...
...THEY'LL PLAY CARDS TO COUNTERACT THAT!
I'M BOUND TO LOSE!
TH-THIS MAKES NO SENSE!
WHY DO I HAVE TO DO SOMETHING LIKE THAT!?
...IDIOT.

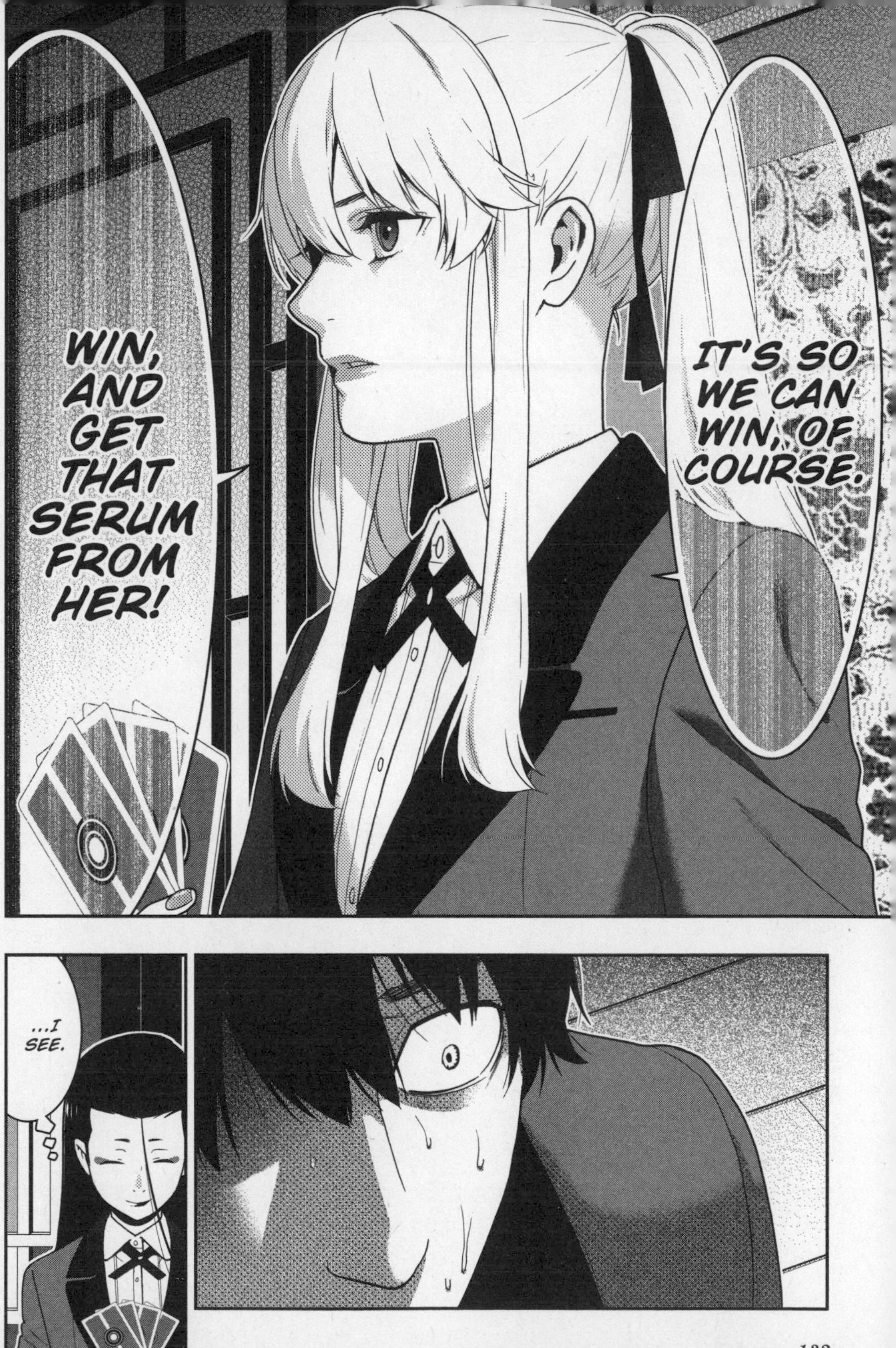
IT'S SO WE CAN WIN, OF COURSE.
WIN, AND GET THAT SERUM FROM HER!
...I SEE.

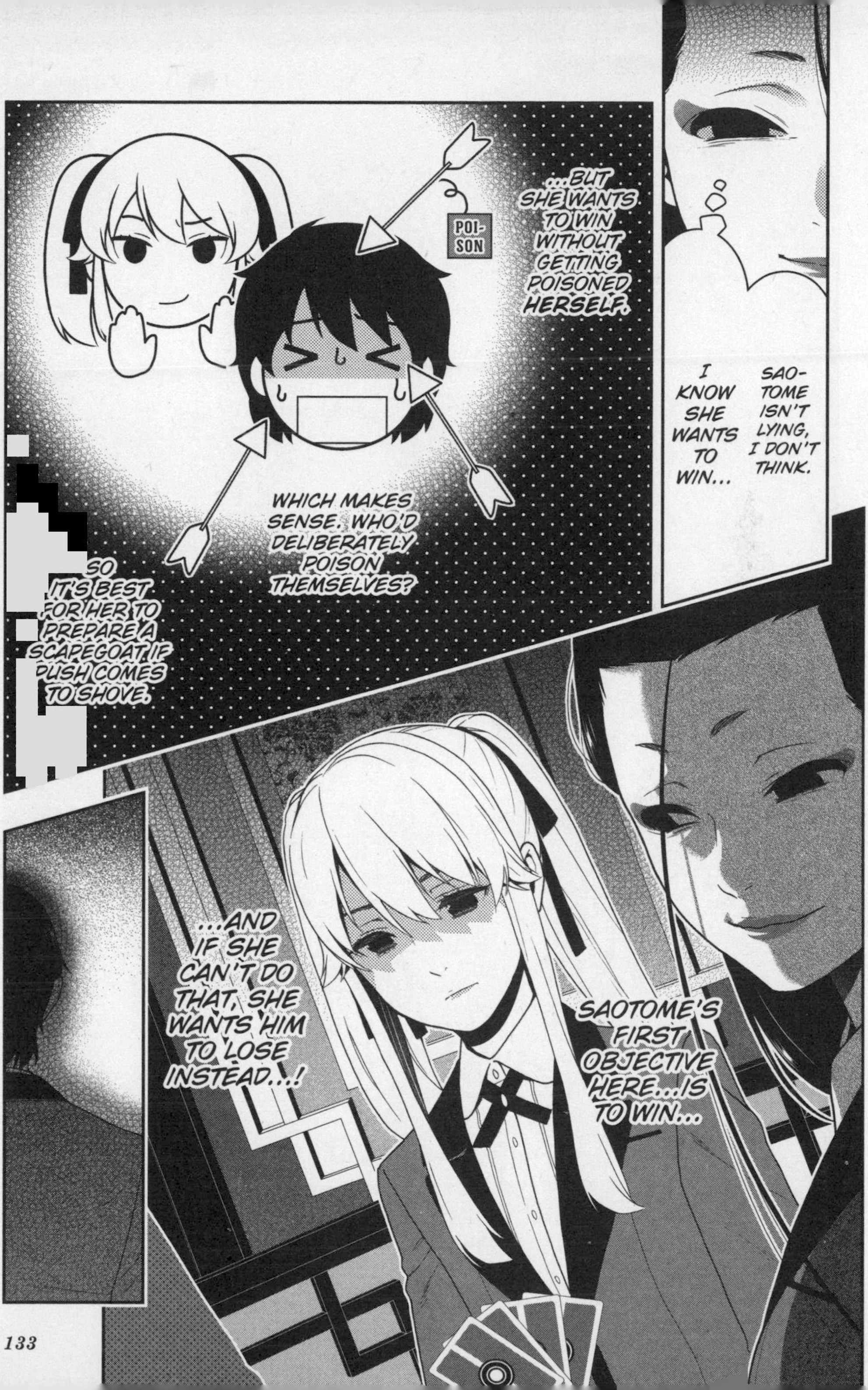
SAO-TOME ISN'T LYING, I DON'T THINK.
I KNOW SHE WANTS TO WIN...
...BUT SHE WANTS TO WIN WITHOUT GETTING POISONED HERSELF.
POI-SON
WHICH MAKES SENSE. WHO'D DELIBERATELY POISON THEMSELVES?
SO IT'S BEST FOR HER TO PREPARE A SCAPEGOAT IF PUSH COMES TO SHOVE.
SAOTOME'S FIRST OBJECTIVE HERE...IS TO WIN...
...AND IF SHE CAN'T DO THAT, SHE WANTS HIM TO LOSE INSTEAD...!

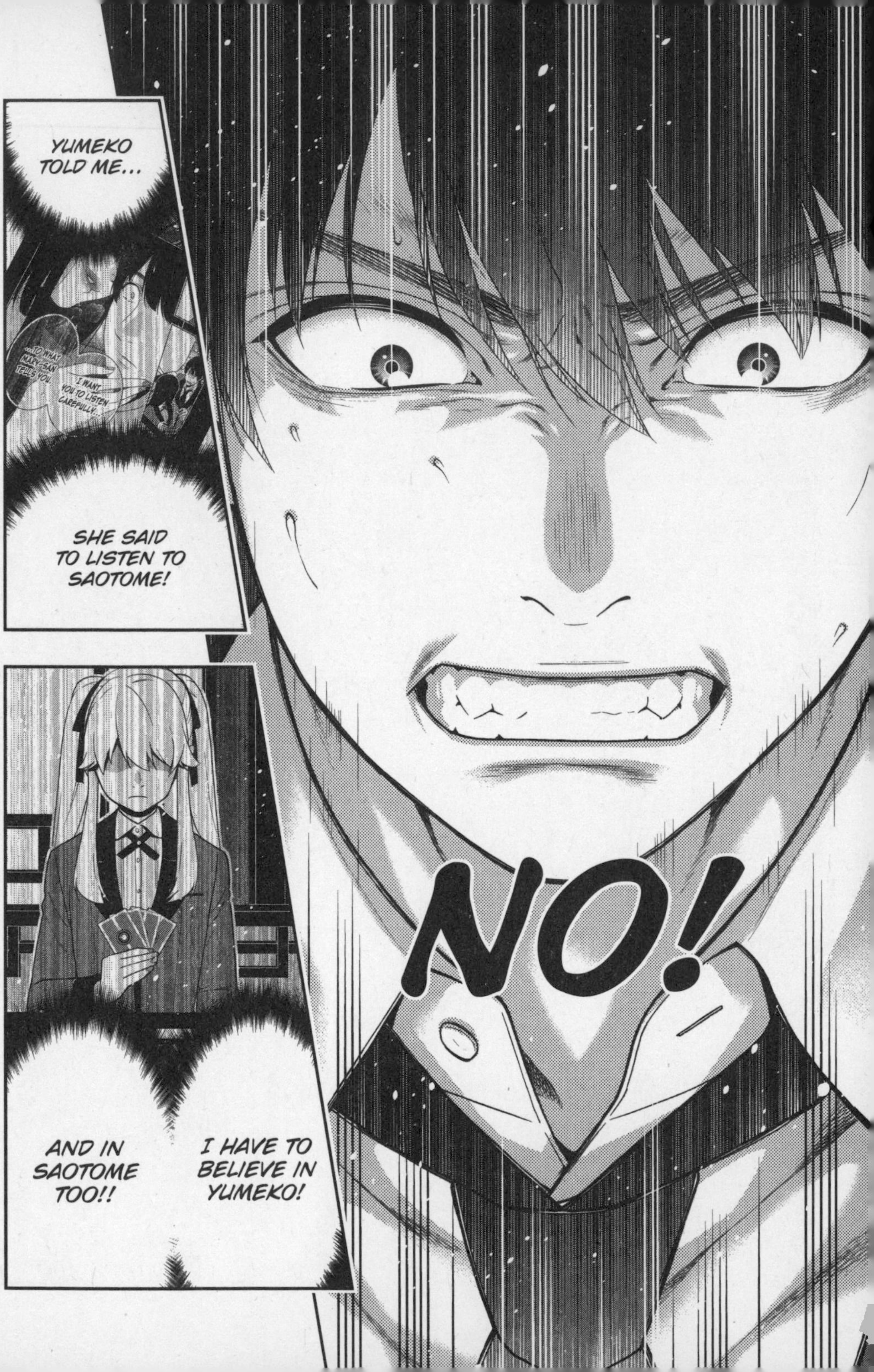
NO!
YUMEKO TOLD ME...
I WANT YOU TO LISTEN CAREFULLY...
...TO WHAT MARY-SAN TELLS YOU.
SHE SAID TO LISTEN TO SAOTOME!
I HAVE TO BELIEVE IN YUMEKO!
AND IN SAOTOME TOO!!

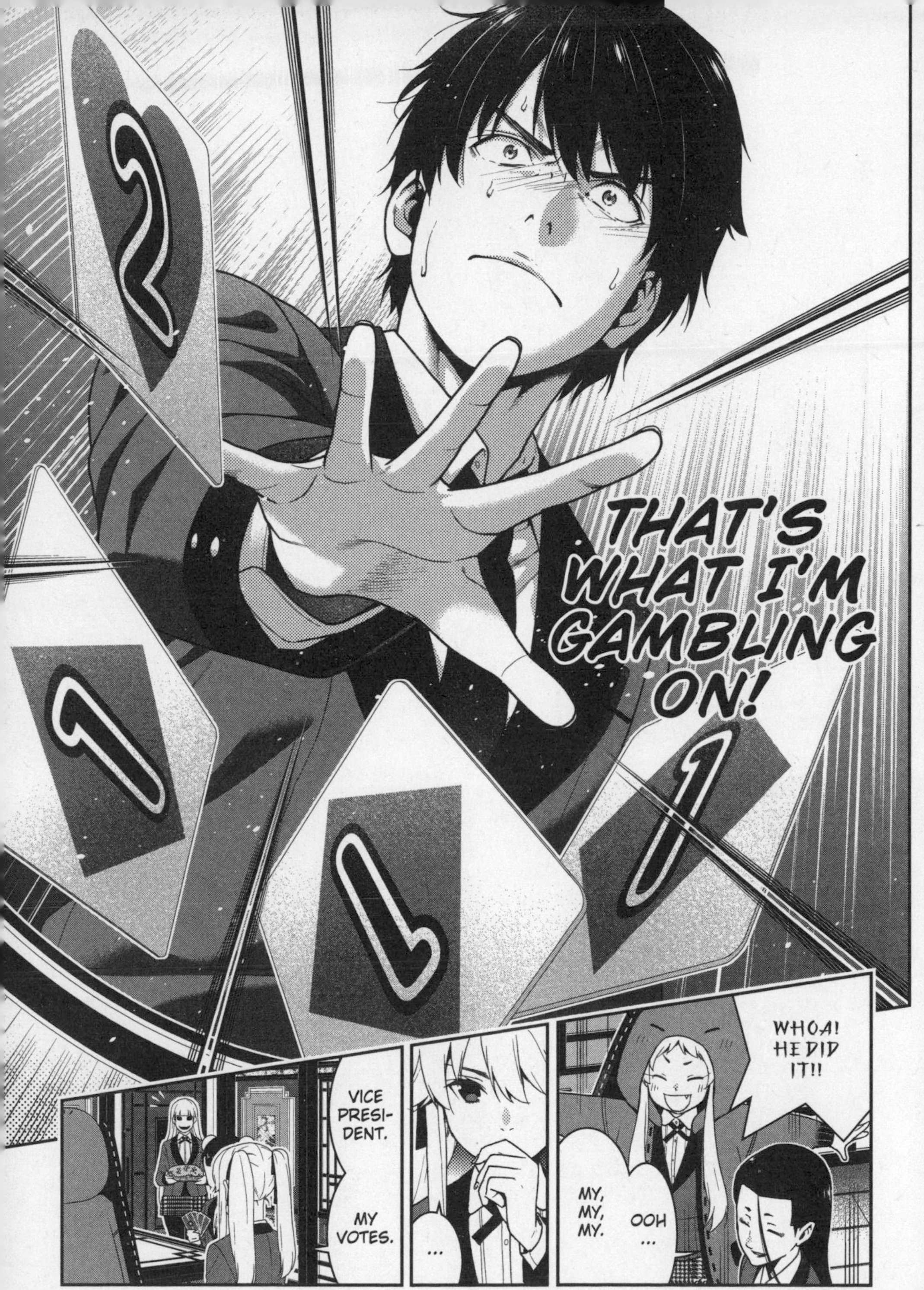
THAT'S WHAT I'M GAMBLING ON!
WHOA! HE DID IT!!
MY, MY, MY.
OOH ...
...
VICE PRESIDENT.
MY VOTES.

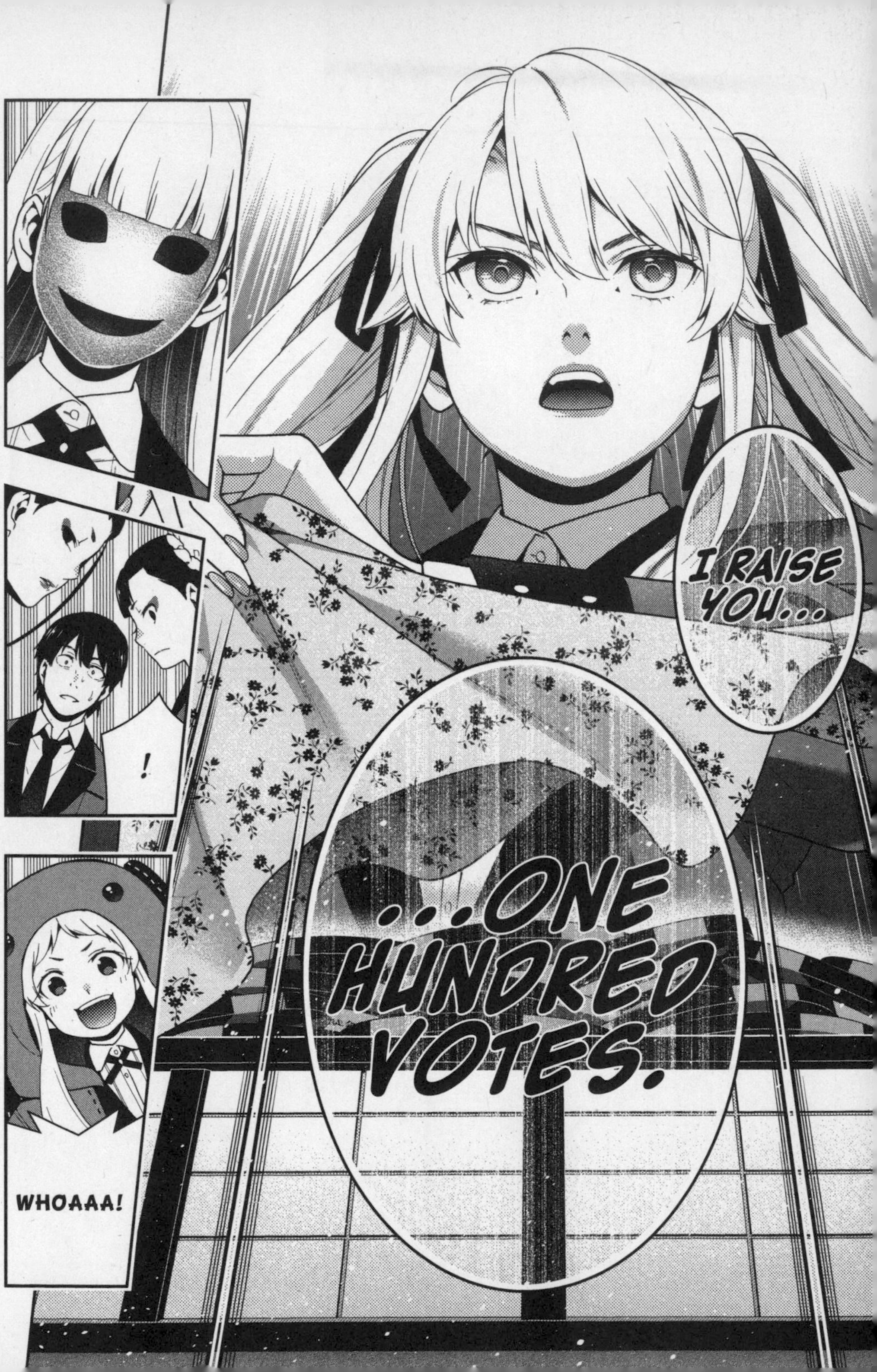
I RAISE YOU...
...ONE HUNDRED VOTES.
!
WHOAAA!

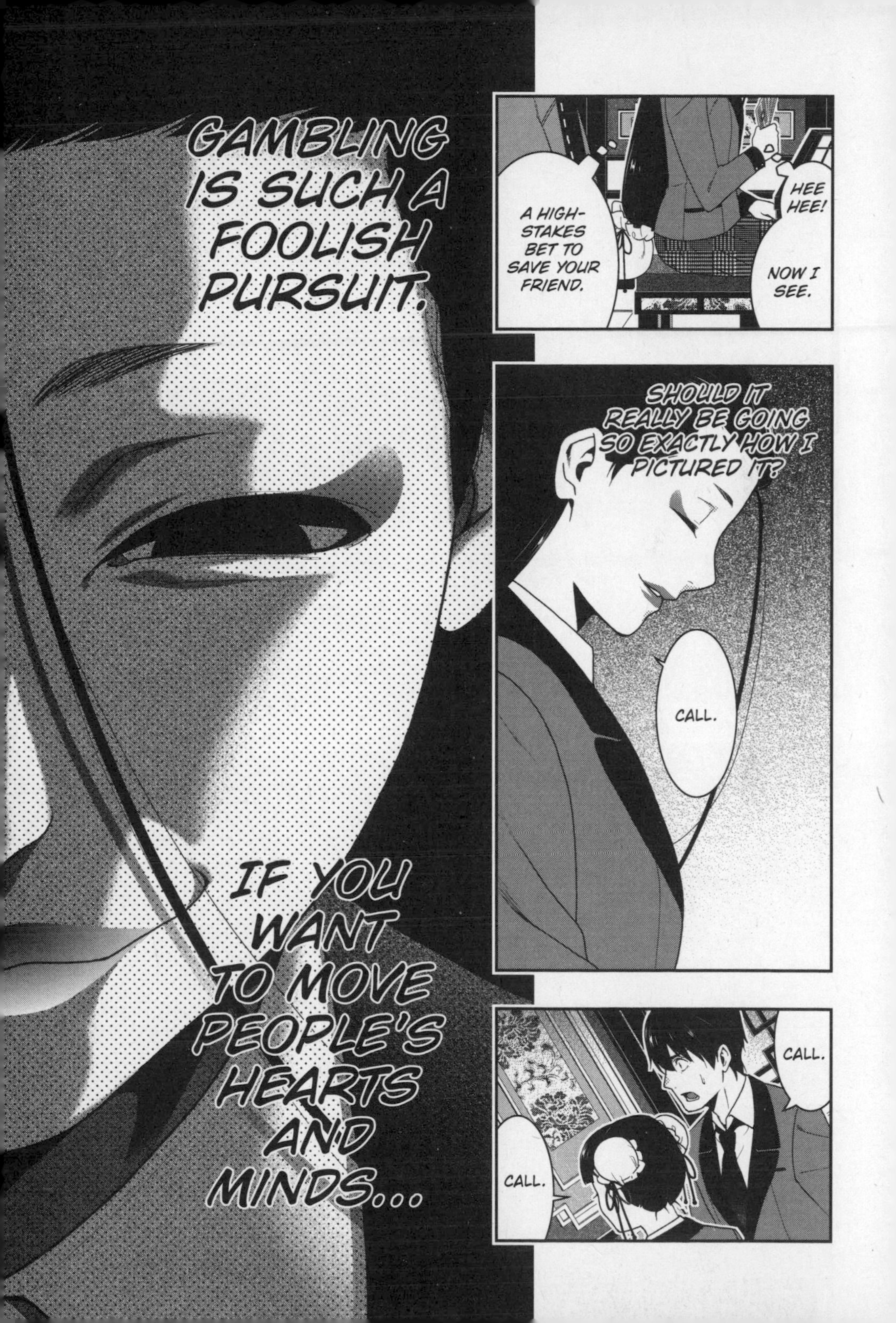
HEE HEE!
NOW I SEE.
A HIGH-STAKES BET TO SAVE YOUR FRIEND.
SHOULD IT REALLY BE GOING SO EXACTLY HOW I PICTURED IT?
CALL.
CALL.
CALL.
GAMBLING IS SUCH A FOOLISH PURSUIT.
IF YOU WANT TO MOVE PEOPLE'S HEARTS AND MINDS...

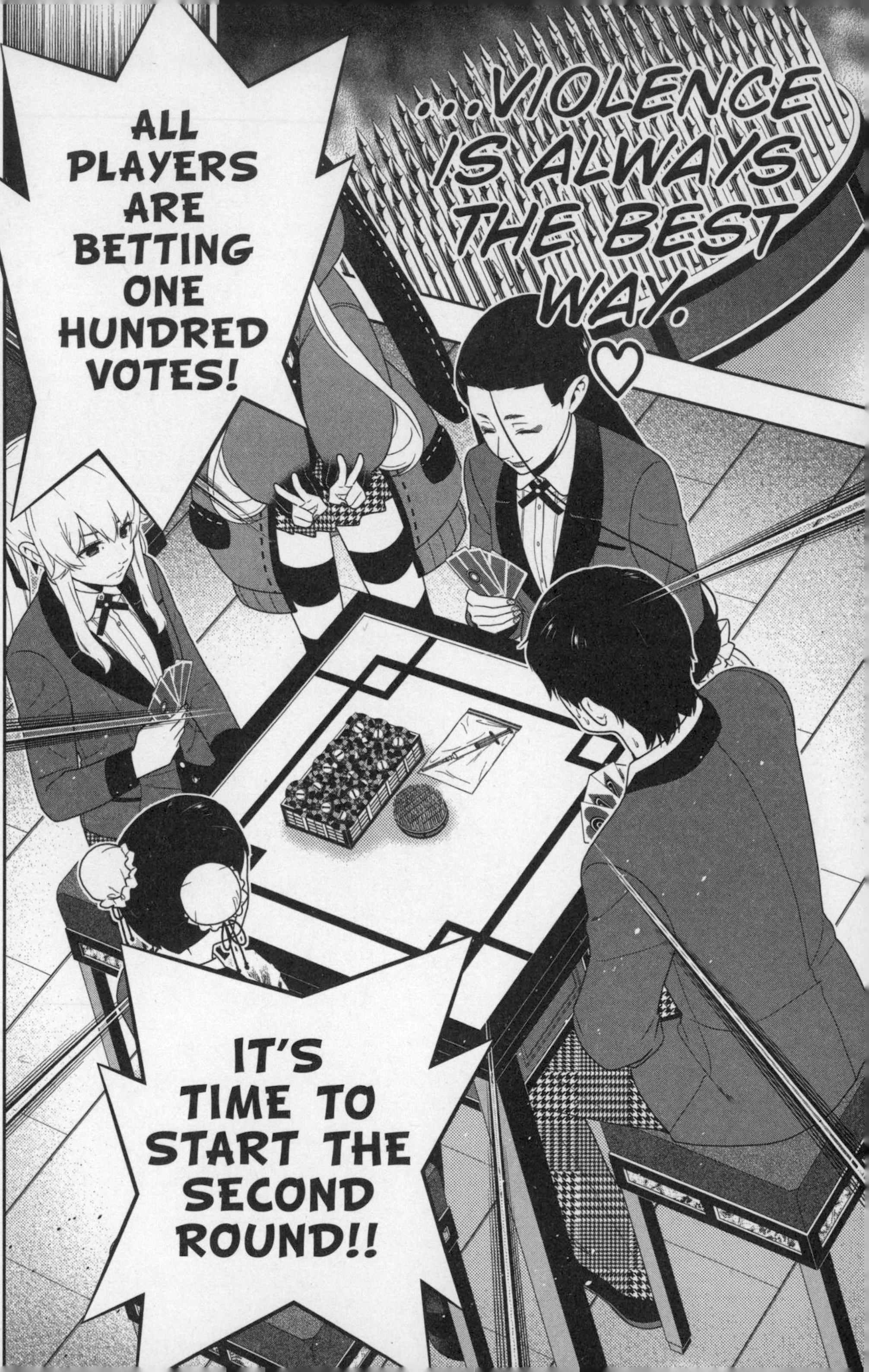
...VIOLENCE IS ALWAYS THE BEST WAY. ♥
ALL PLAYERS ARE BETTING ONE HUNDRED VOTES!
IT'S TIME TO START THE SECOND ROUND!!

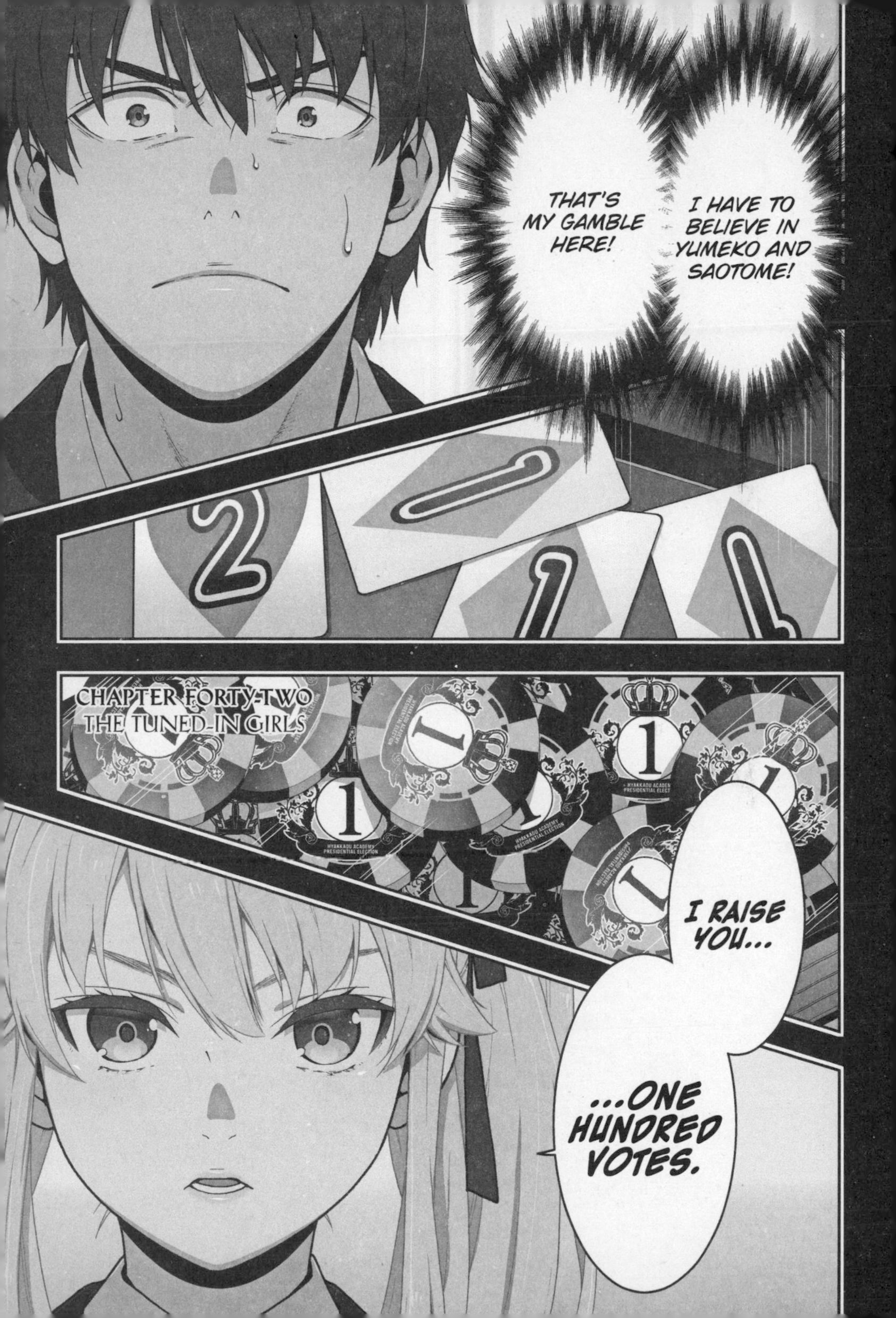
I HAVE TO BELIEVE IN YUMEKO AND SAOTOME!
THAT'S MY GAMBLE HERE!
CHAPTER FORTY-TWO
THE TUNED-IN GIRLS
HYAKKAOU ACADEMY PRESIDENTIAL ELECTION
I RAISE YOU...
...ONE HUNDRED VOTES.

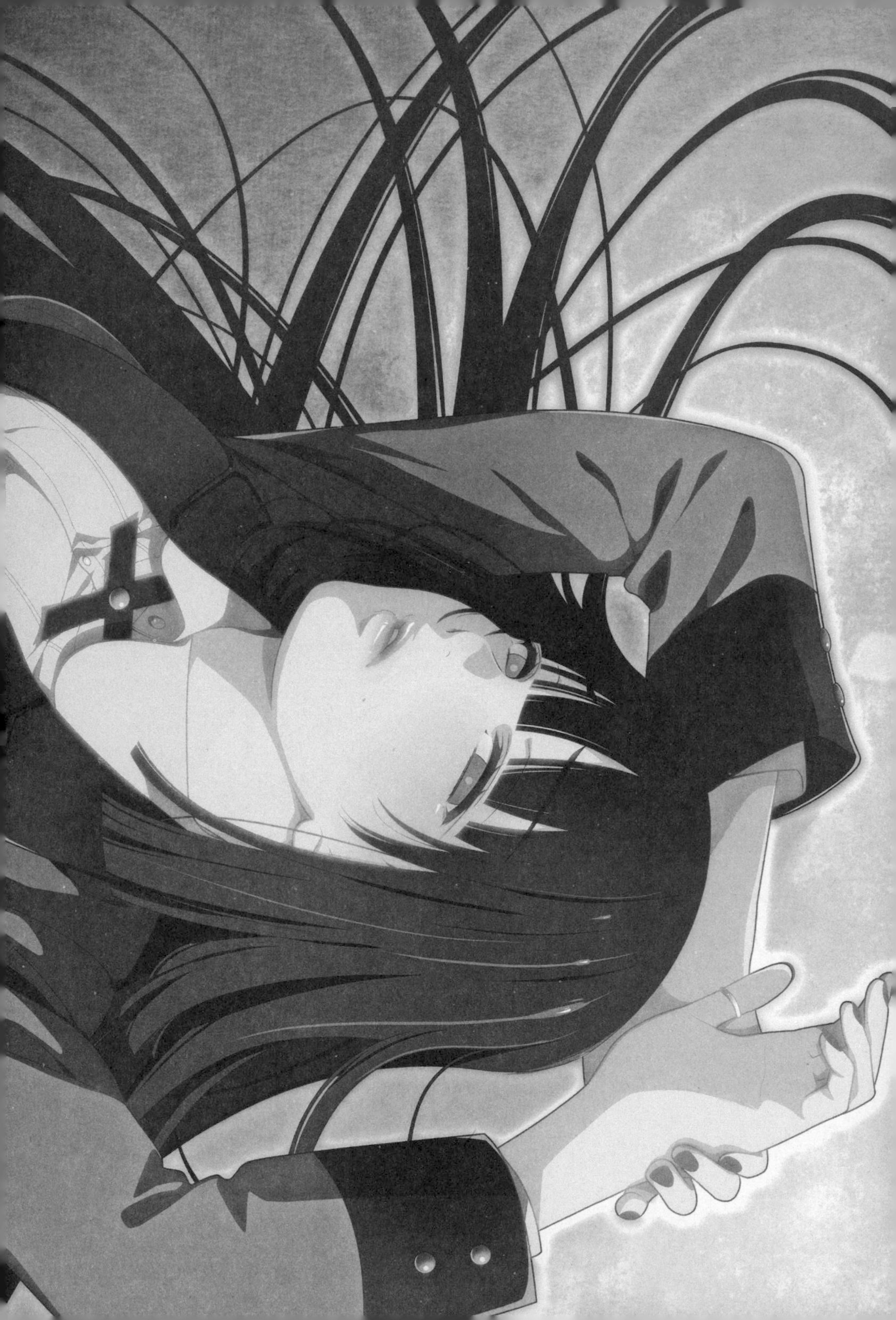

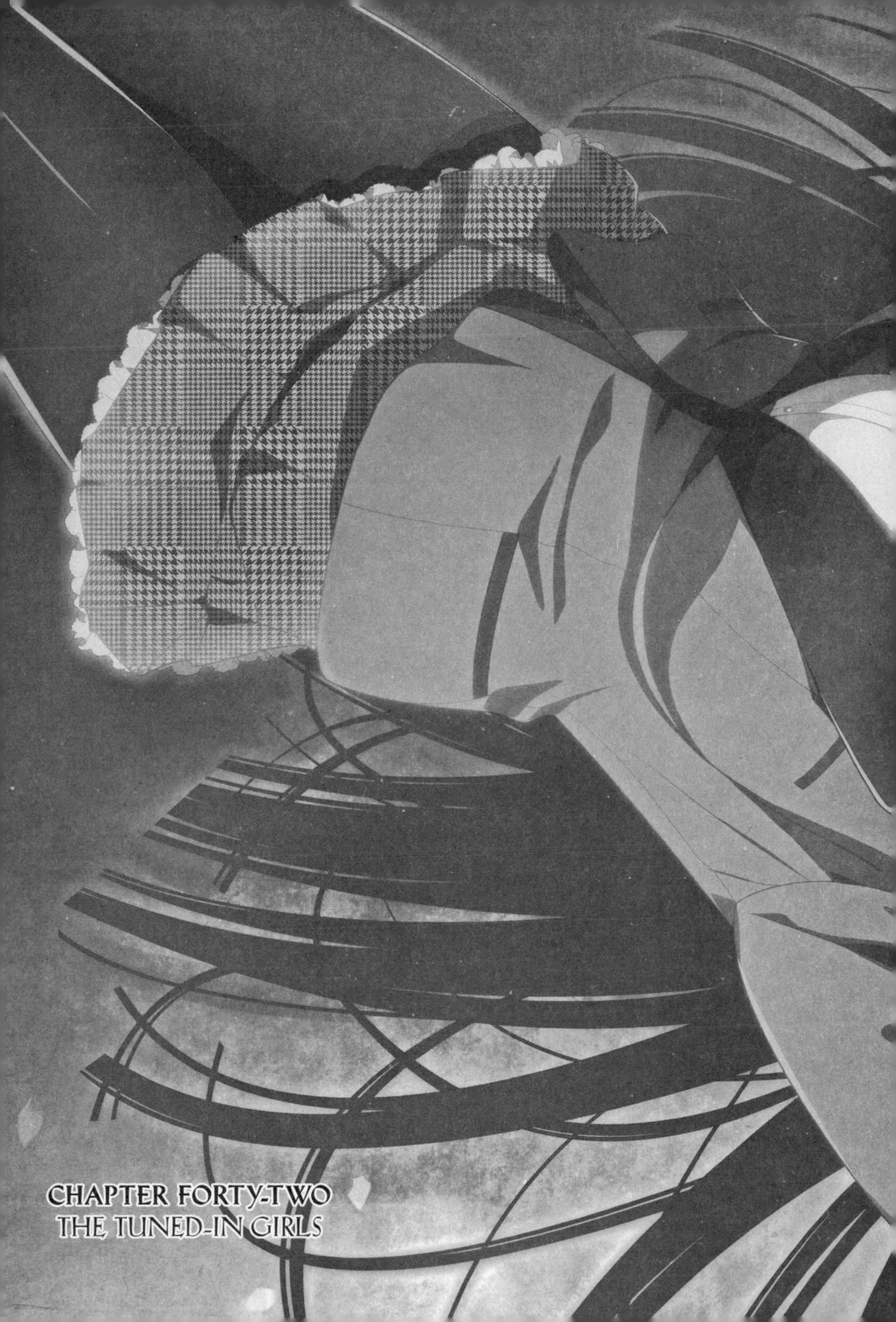

CHAPTER FORTY-TWO
THE TUNED-IN GIRLS

KAKEGURUI

— Compulsive Gambler —

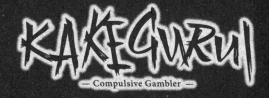

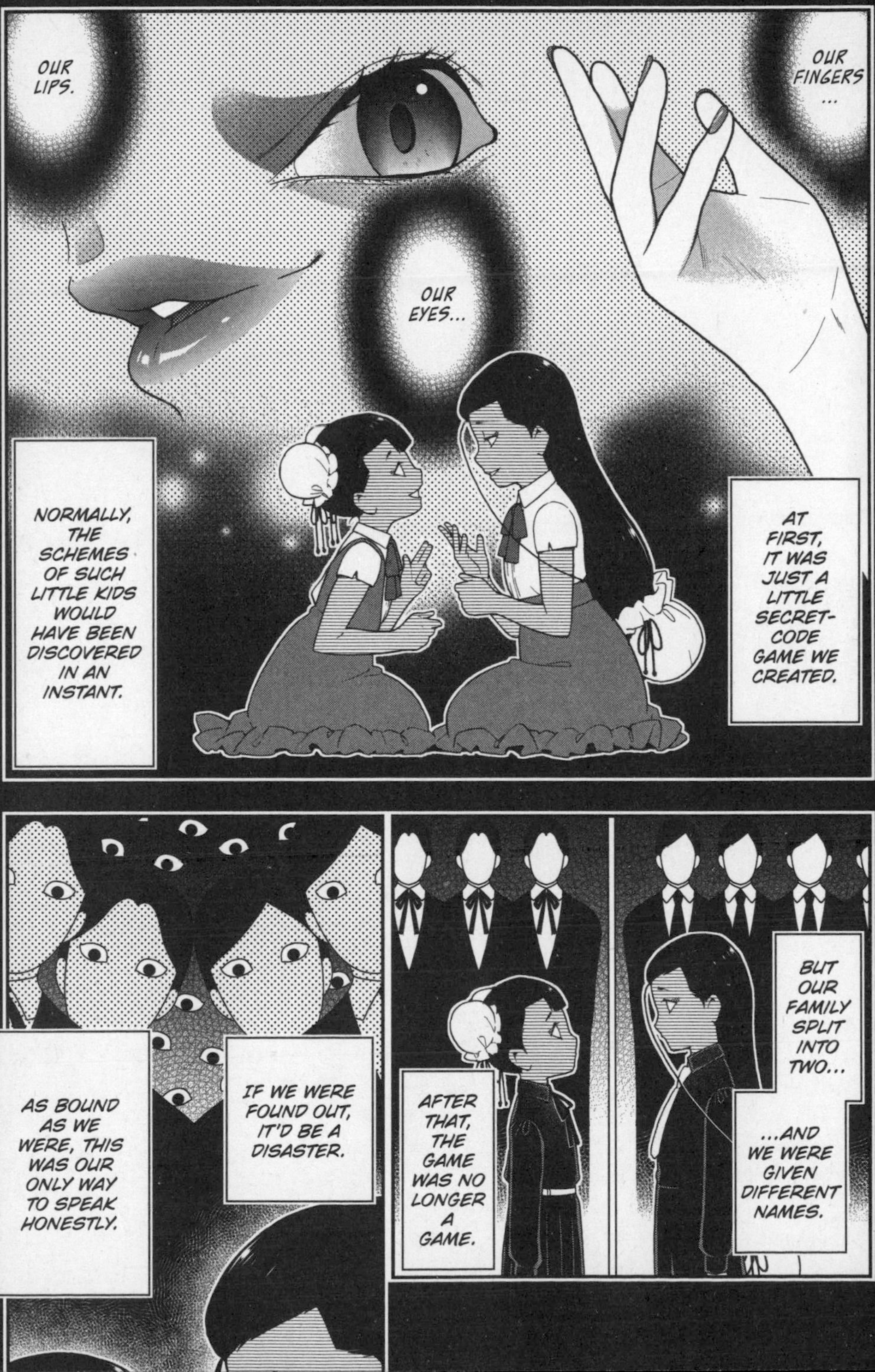
OUR FINGERS...
OUR LIPS.
OUR EYES...
AT FIRST, IT WAS JUST A LITTLE SECRET-CODE GAME WE CREATED.
NORMALLY, THE SCHEMES OF SUCH LITTLE KIDS WOULD HAVE BEEN DISCOVERED IN AN INSTANT.
BUT OUR FAMILY SPLIT INTO TWO...
...AND WE WERE GIVEN DIFFERENT NAMES.
AFTER THAT, THE GAME WAS NO LONGER A GAME.
IF WE WERE FOUND OUT, IT'D BE A DISASTER.
AS BOUND AS WE WERE, THIS WAS OUR ONLY WAY TO SPEAK HONESTLY.

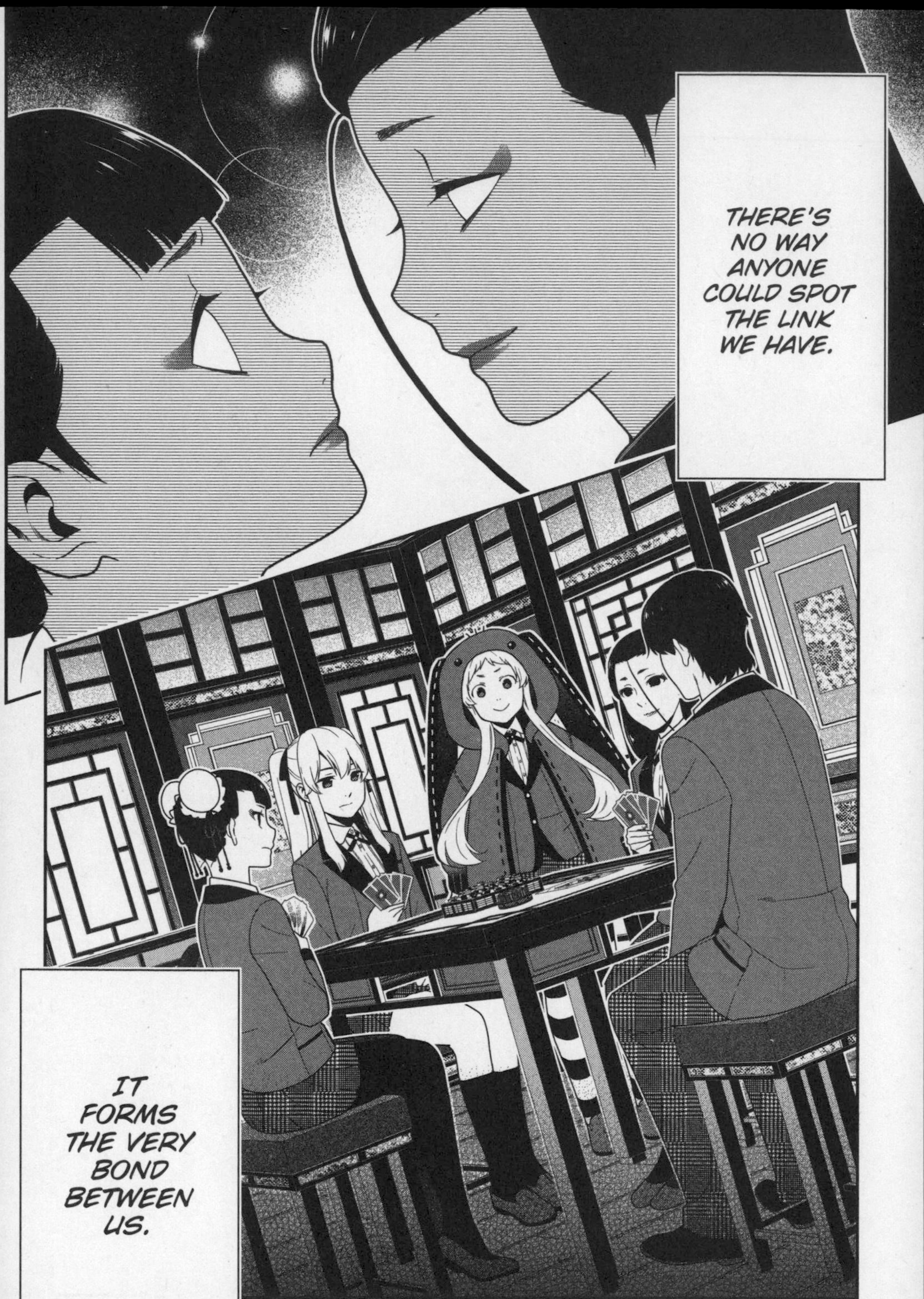
THERE'S NO WAY ANYONE COULD SPOT THE LINK WE HAVE.
IT FORMS THE VERY BOND BETWEEN US.

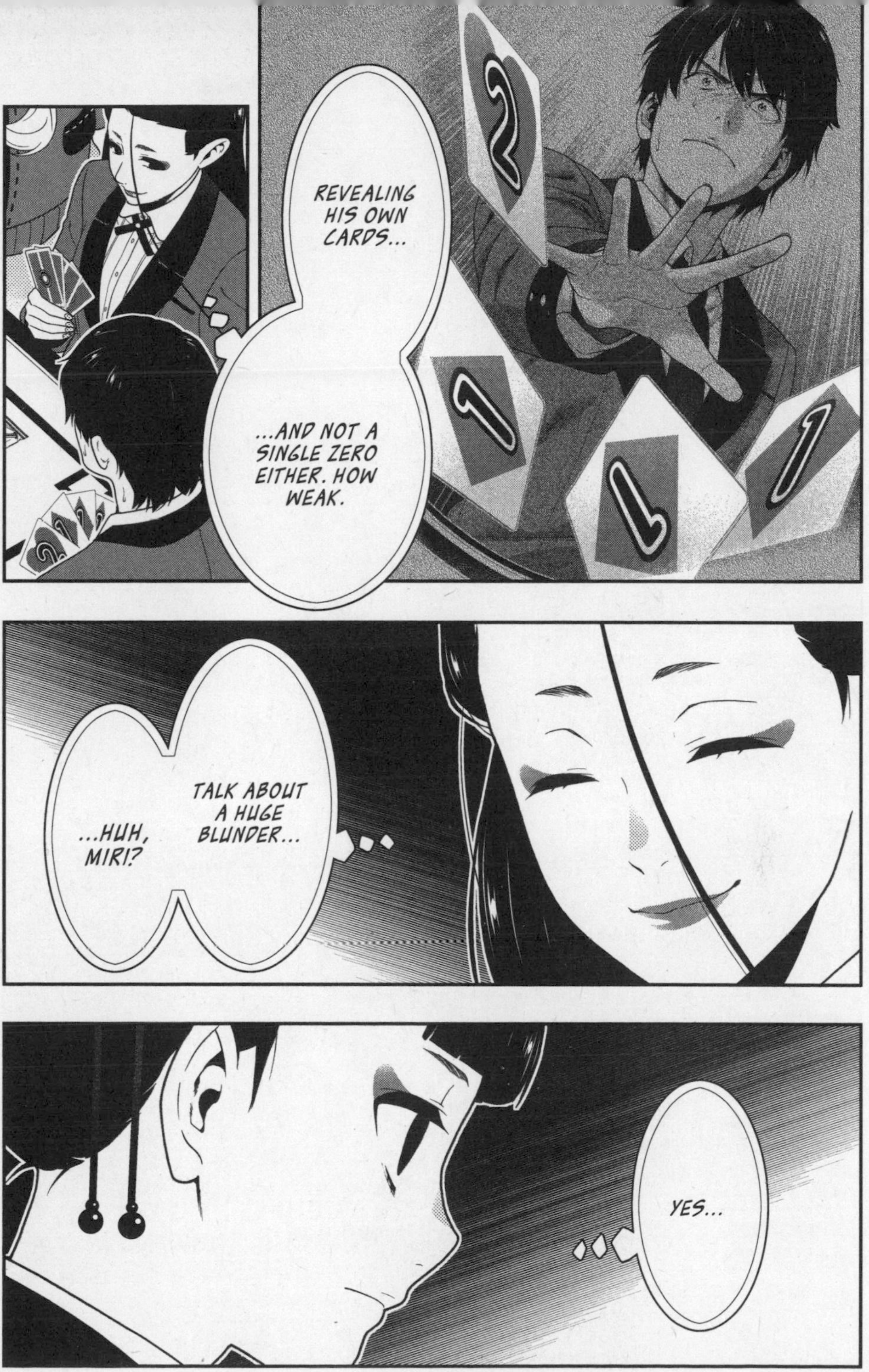
REVEALING HIS OWN CARDS...
...AND NOT A SINGLE ZERO EITHER. HOW WEAK.
TALK ABOUT A HUGE BLUNDER...
...HUH, MIRI?
YES...

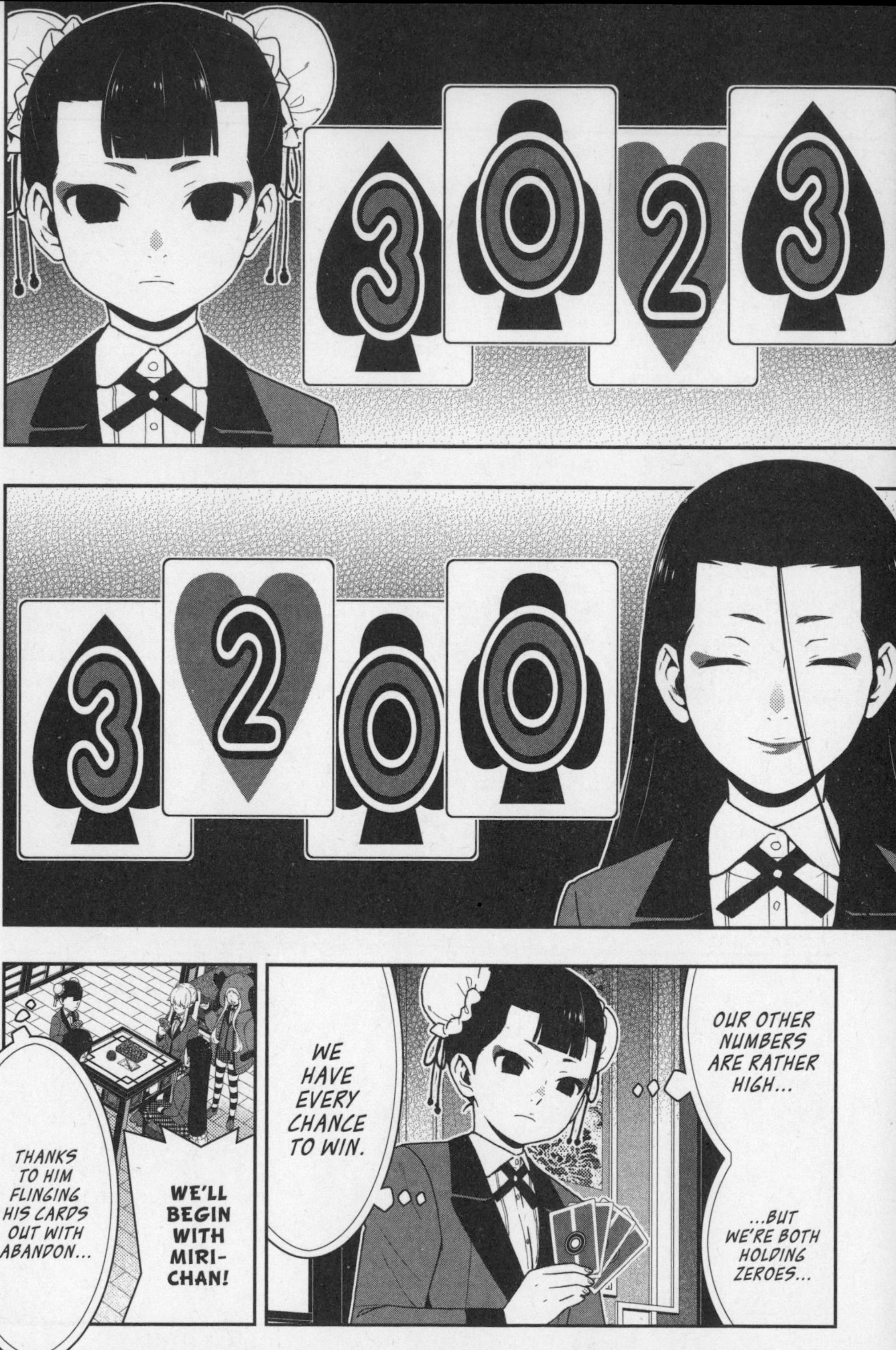
OUR OTHER NUMBERS ARE RATHER HIGH...
...BUT WE'RE BOTH HOLDING ZEROES...
WE HAVE EVERY CHANCE TO WIN.
WE'LL BEGIN WITH MIRI-CHAN!
THANKS TO HIM FLINGING HIS CARDS OUT WITH ABANDON...

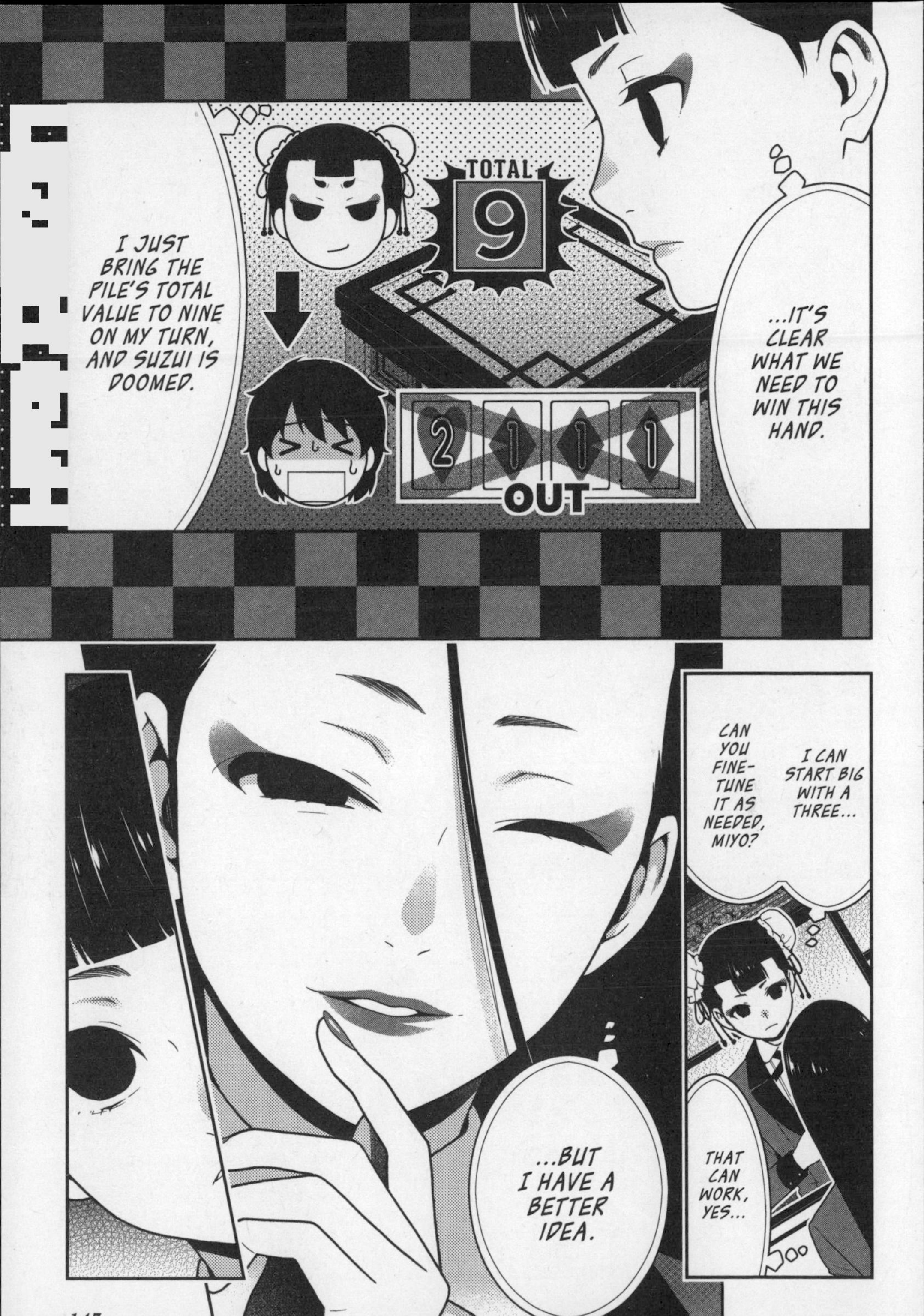
...IT'S CLEAR WHAT WE NEED TO WIN THIS HAND.
TOTAL
9
2 1 1 1
OUT
I JUST BRING THE PILE'S TOTAL VALUE TO NINE ON MY TURN, AND SUZUI IS DOOMED.
I CAN START BIG WITH A THREE...
CAN YOU FINE-TUNE IT AS NEEDED, MIYO?
THAT CAN WORK, YES...
...BUT I HAVE A BETTER IDEA.

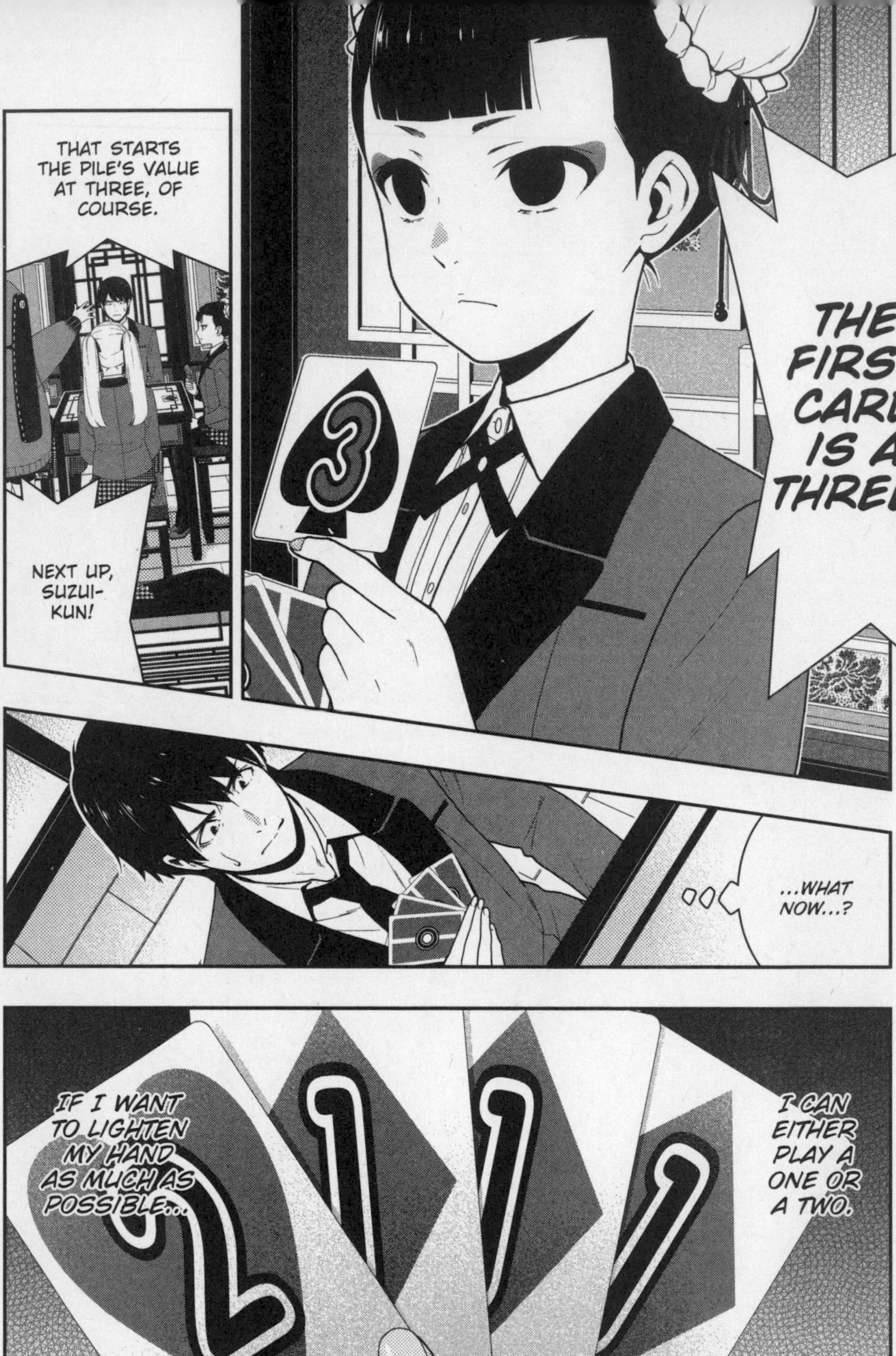
THE FIRST CARD IS A THREE!
THAT STARTS THE PILE'S VALUE AT THREE, OF COURSE.
NEXT UP, SUZUI-KUN!
...WHAT NOW...?
I CAN EITHER PLAY A ONE OR A TWO.
IF I WANT TO LIGHTEN MY HAND AS MUCH AS POSSIBLE...

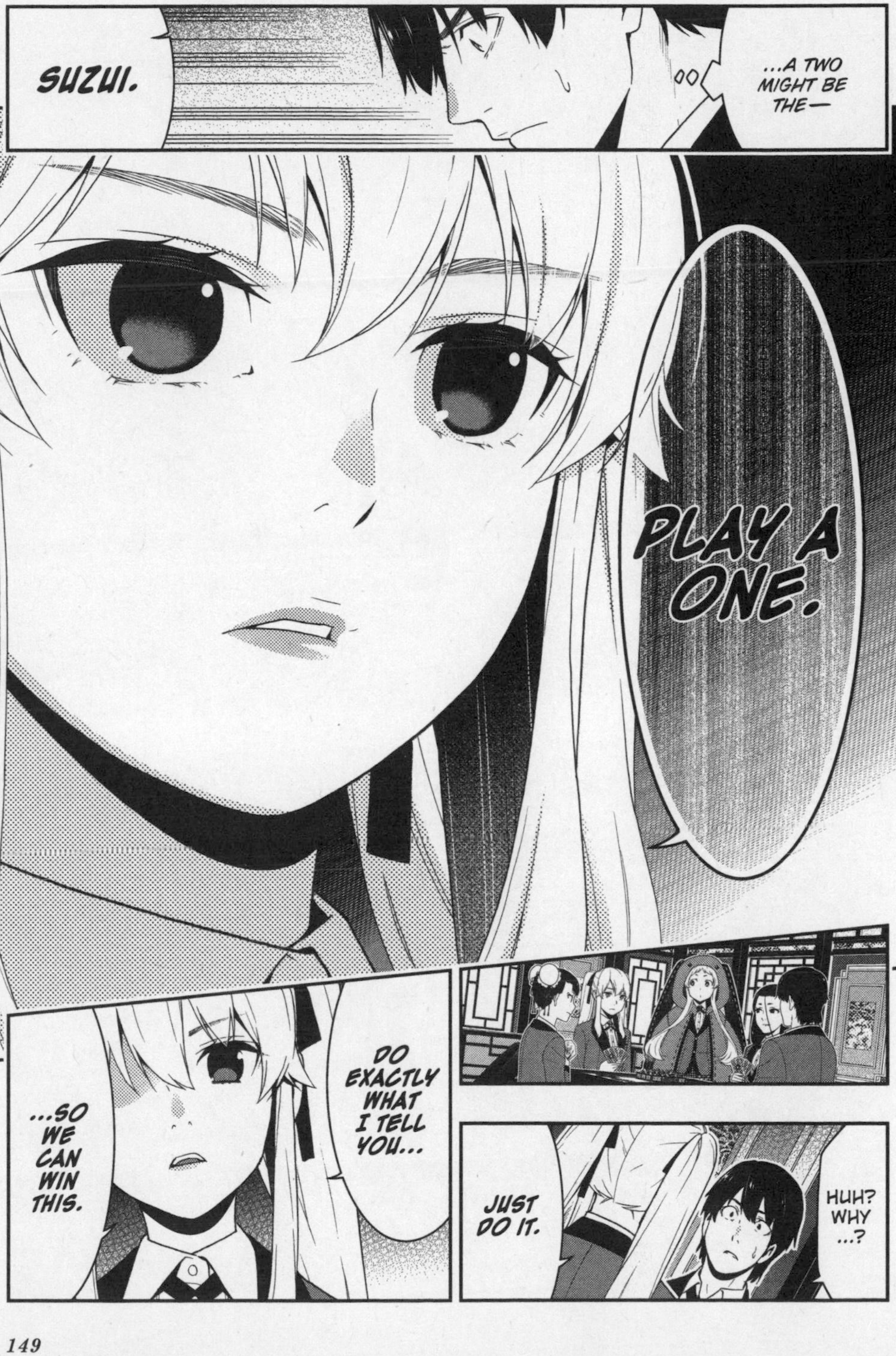
...A TWO MIGHT BE THE—
SUZUI.
PLAY A ONE.
HUH? WHY ...?
JUST DO IT.
DO EXACTLY WHAT I TELL YOU...
...SO WE CAN WIN THIS.

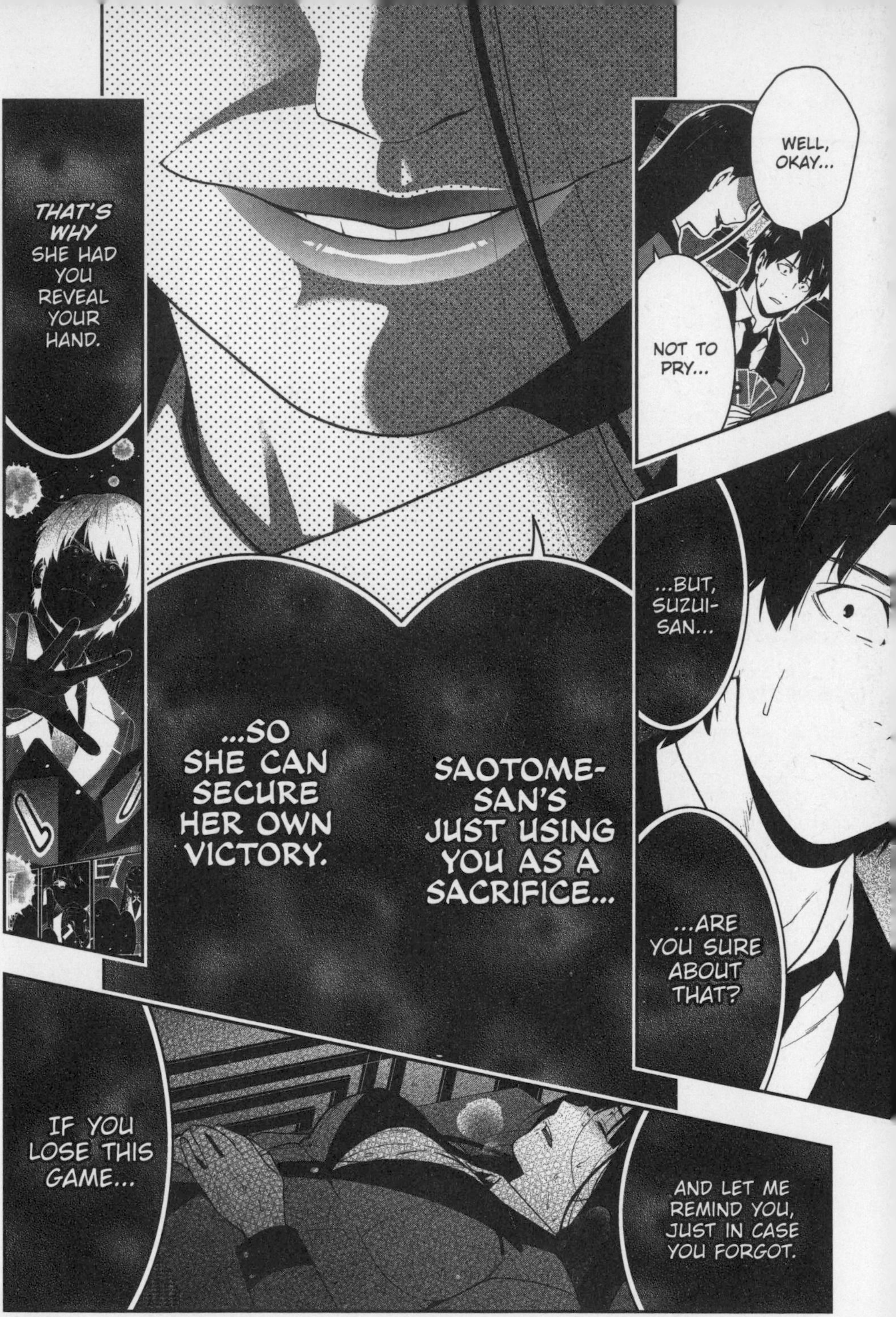
WELL, OKAY...
NOT TO PRY...
...BUT, SUZUI-SAN...
...ARE YOU SURE ABOUT THAT?
SAOTOME-SAN'S JUST USING YOU AS A SACRIFICE...
...SO SHE CAN SECURE HER OWN VICTORY.
THAT'S WHY SHE HAD YOU REVEAL YOUR HAND.
AND LET ME REMIND YOU, JUST IN CASE YOU FORGOT.
IF YOU LOSE THIS GAME...

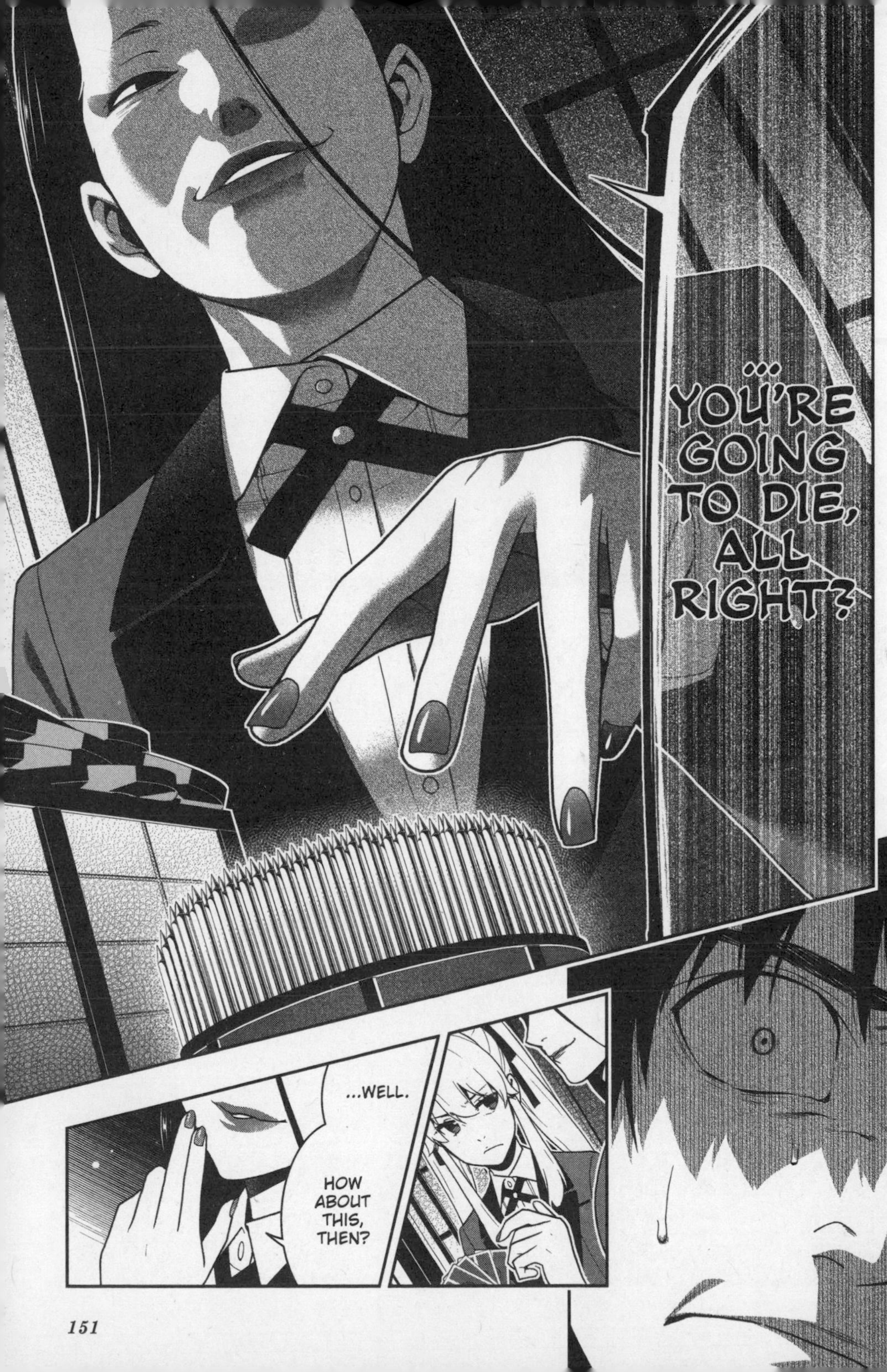
...YOU'RE GOING TO DIE, ALL RIGHT?
...WELL.
HOW ABOUT THIS, THEN?

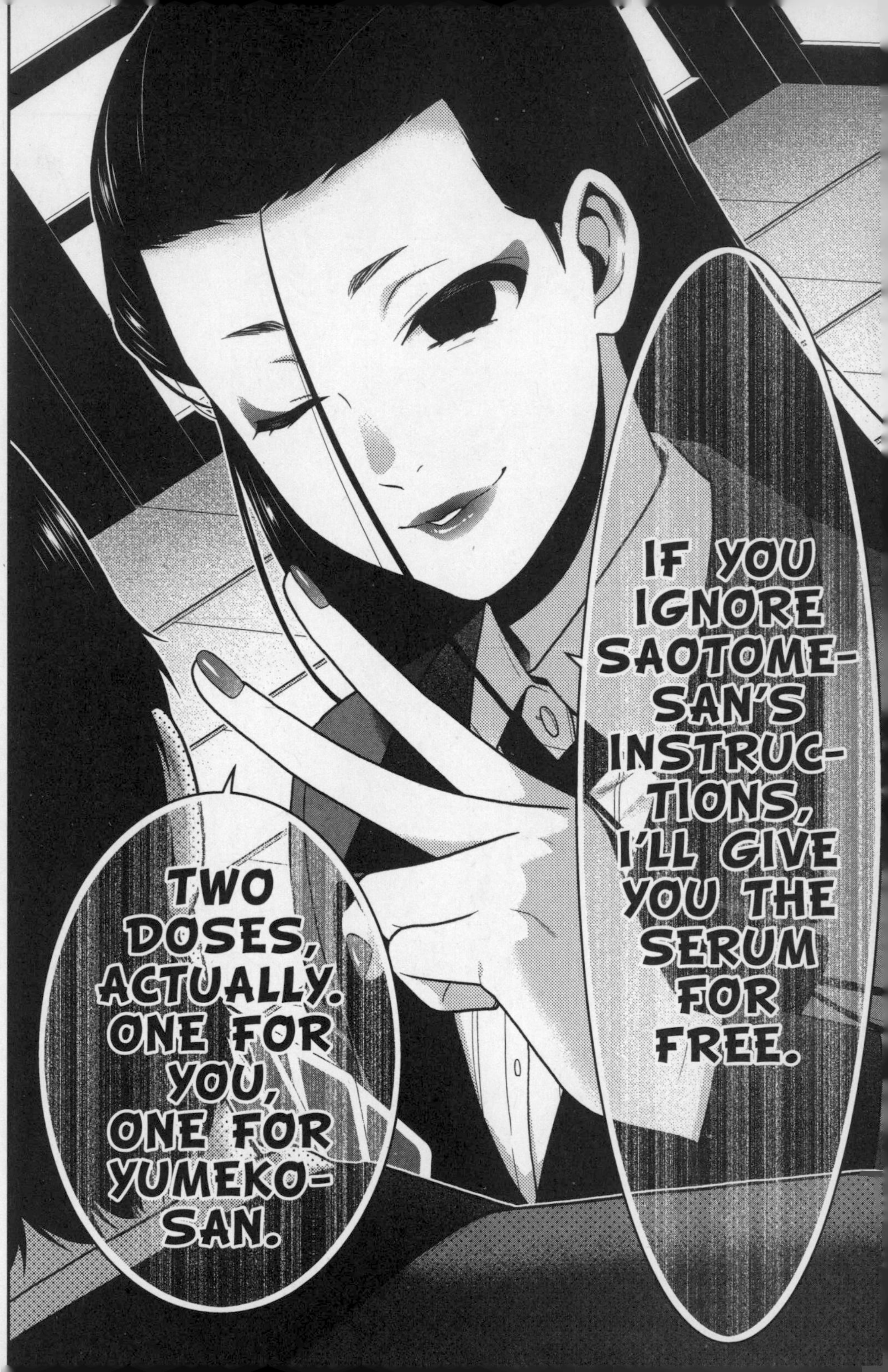
IF YOU IGNORE SAOTOME-SAN'S INSTRUCTIONS, I'LL GIVE YOU THE SERUM FOR FREE.
TWO DOSES, ACTUALLY. ONE FOR YOU, ONE FOR YUMEKO-SAN.

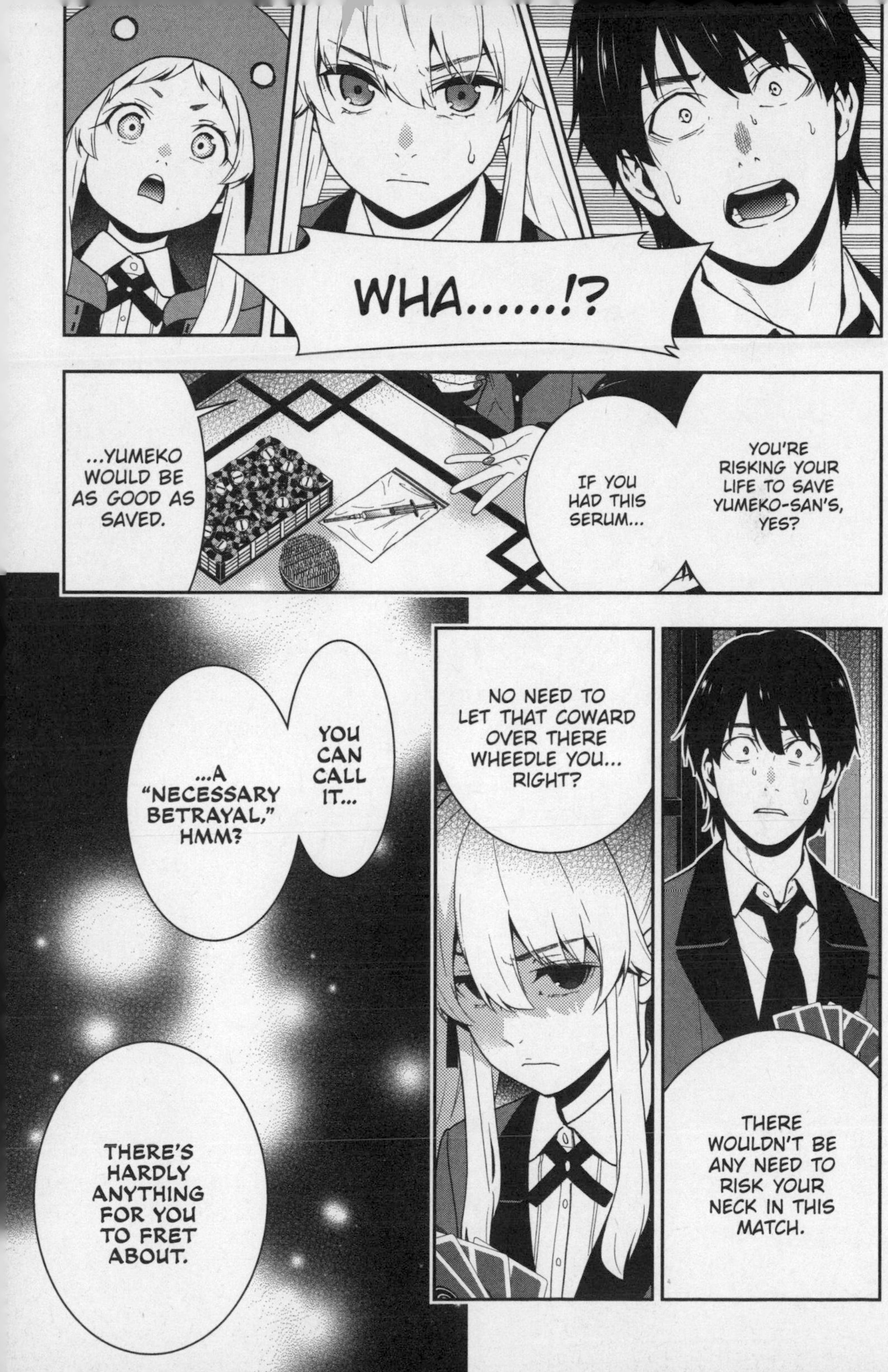
WHA......!?
YOU'RE RISKING YOUR LIFE TO SAVE YUMEKO-SAN'S, YES?
IF YOU HAD THIS SERUM...
...YUMEKO WOULD BE AS GOOD AS SAVED.
THERE WOULDN'T BE ANY NEED TO RISK YOUR NECK IN THIS MATCH.
NO NEED TO LET THAT COWARD OVER THERE WHEEDLE YOU... RIGHT?
YOU CAN CALL IT...
...A "NECESSARY BETRAYAL," HMM?
THERE'S HARDLY ANYTHING FOR YOU TO FRET ABOUT.

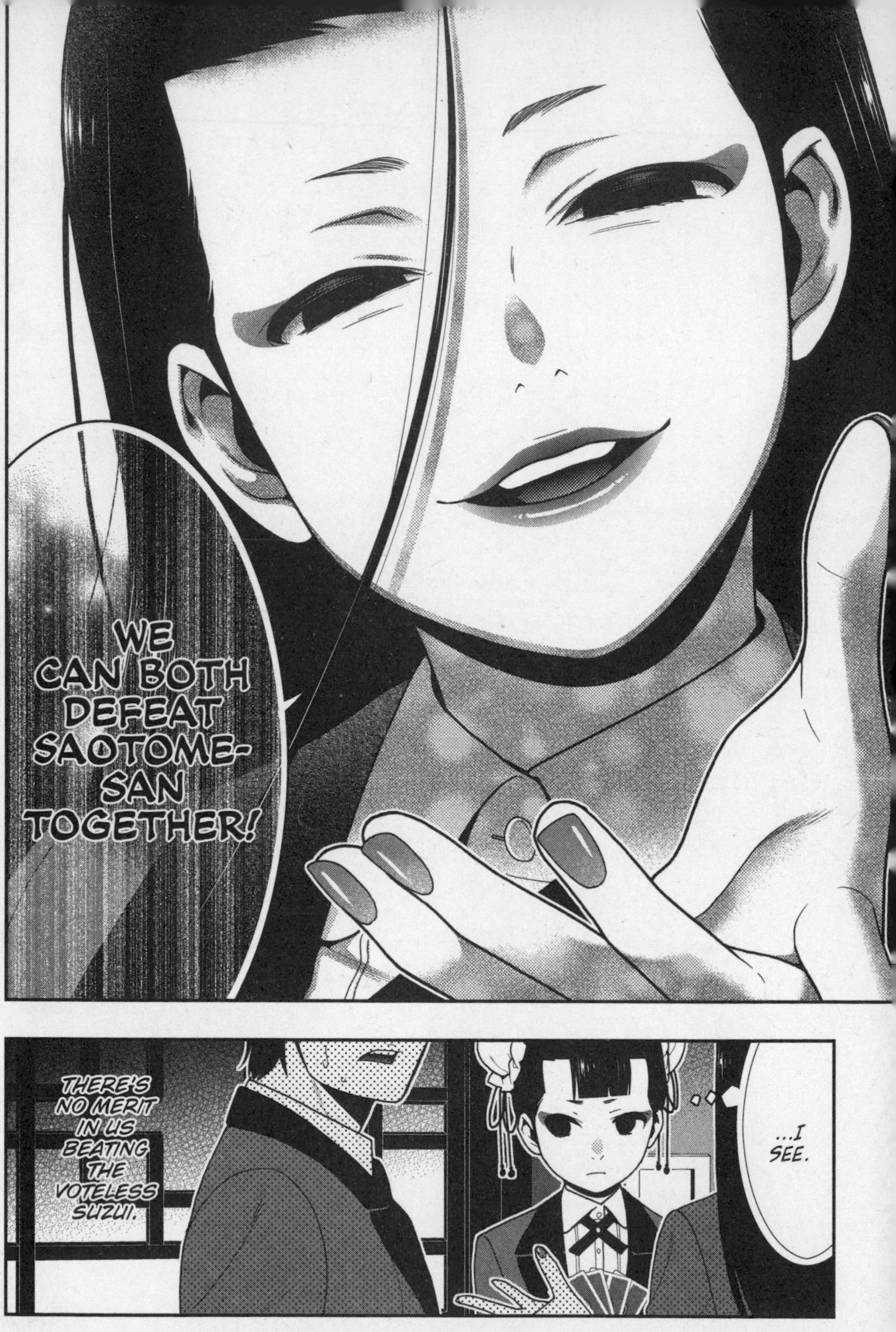
WE CAN BOTH DEFEAT SAOTOME-SAN TOGETHER!
...I SEE.
THERE'S NO MERIT IN US BEATING THE VOTELESS SUZUI.

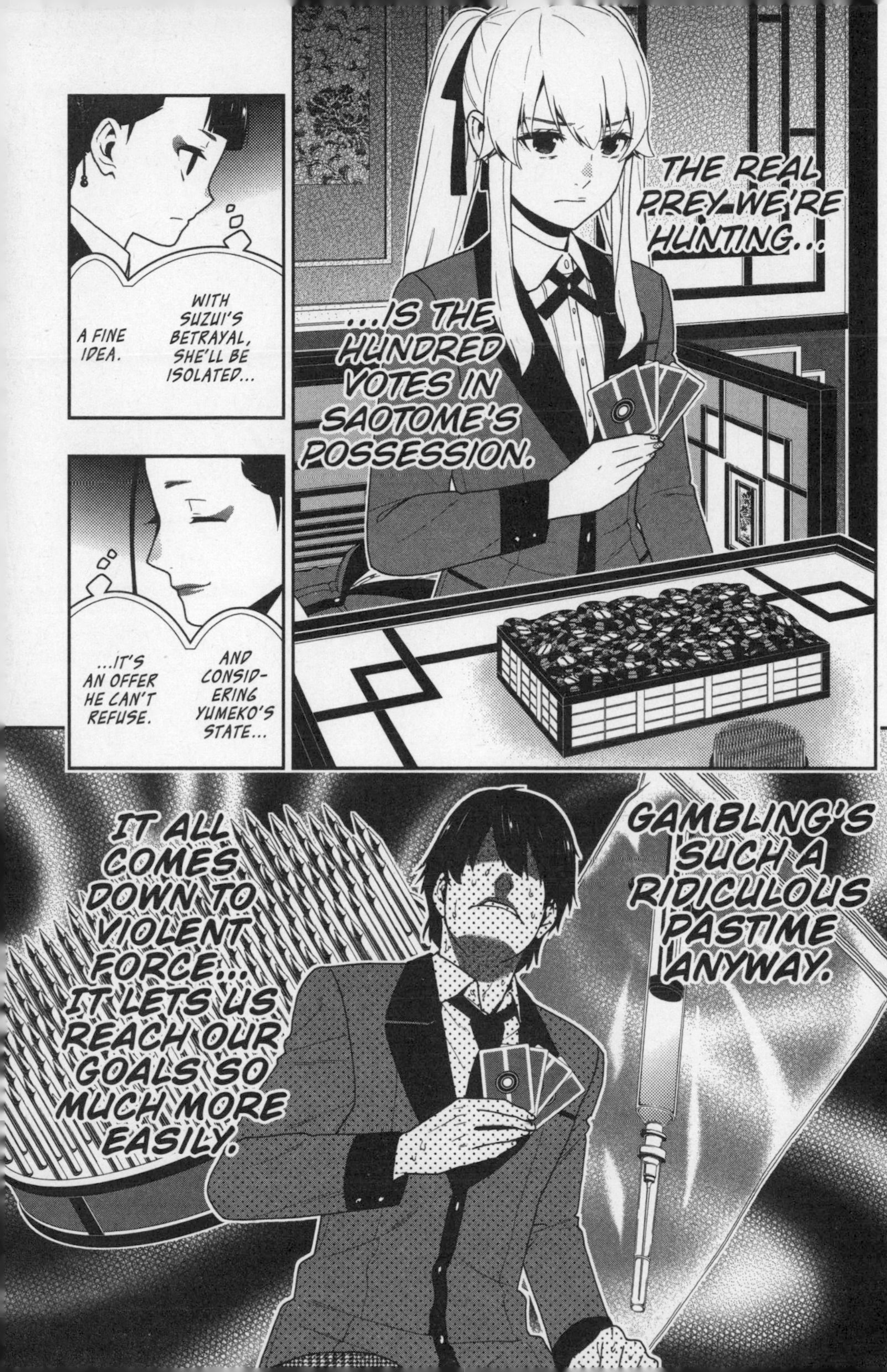
THE REAL PREY WE'RE HUNTING...
...IS THE HUNDRED VOTES IN SAOTOME'S POSSESSION.
WITH SUZUI'S BETRAYAL, SHE'LL BE ISOLATED...
A FINE IDEA.
AND CONSID-ERING YUMEKO'S STATE...
...IT'S AN OFFER HE CAN'T REFUSE.
GAMBLING'S SUCH A RIDICULOUS PASTIME ANYWAY.
IT ALL COMES DOWN TO VIOLENT FORCE... IT LETS US REACH OUR GOALS SO MUCH MORE EASILY.

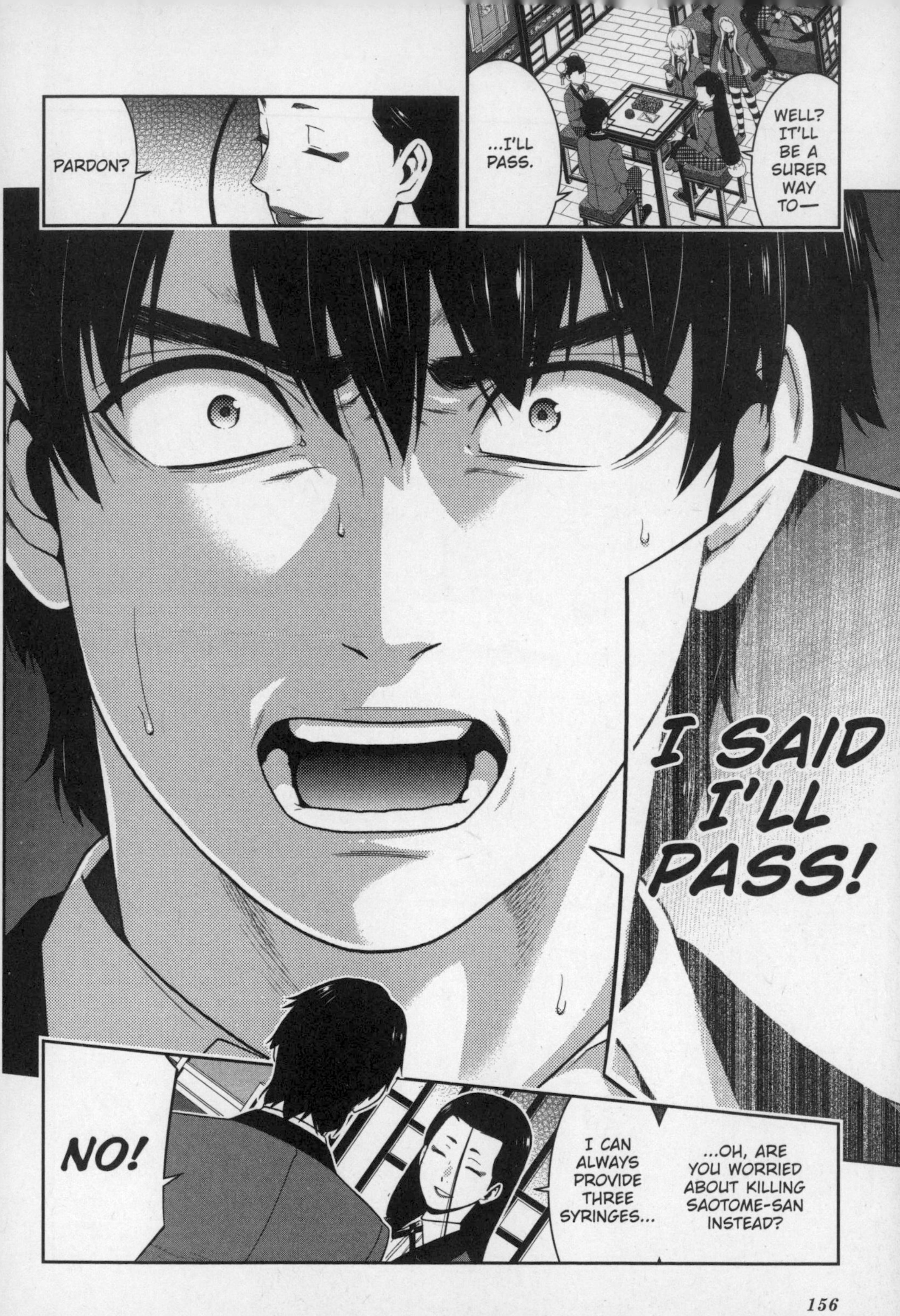
WELL? IT'LL BE A SURER WAY TO—
...I'LL PASS.
PARDON?
I SAID I'LL PASS!
...OH, ARE YOU WORRIED ABOUT KILLING SAOTOME-SAN INSTEAD?
I CAN ALWAYS PROVIDE THREE SYRINGES...
NO!

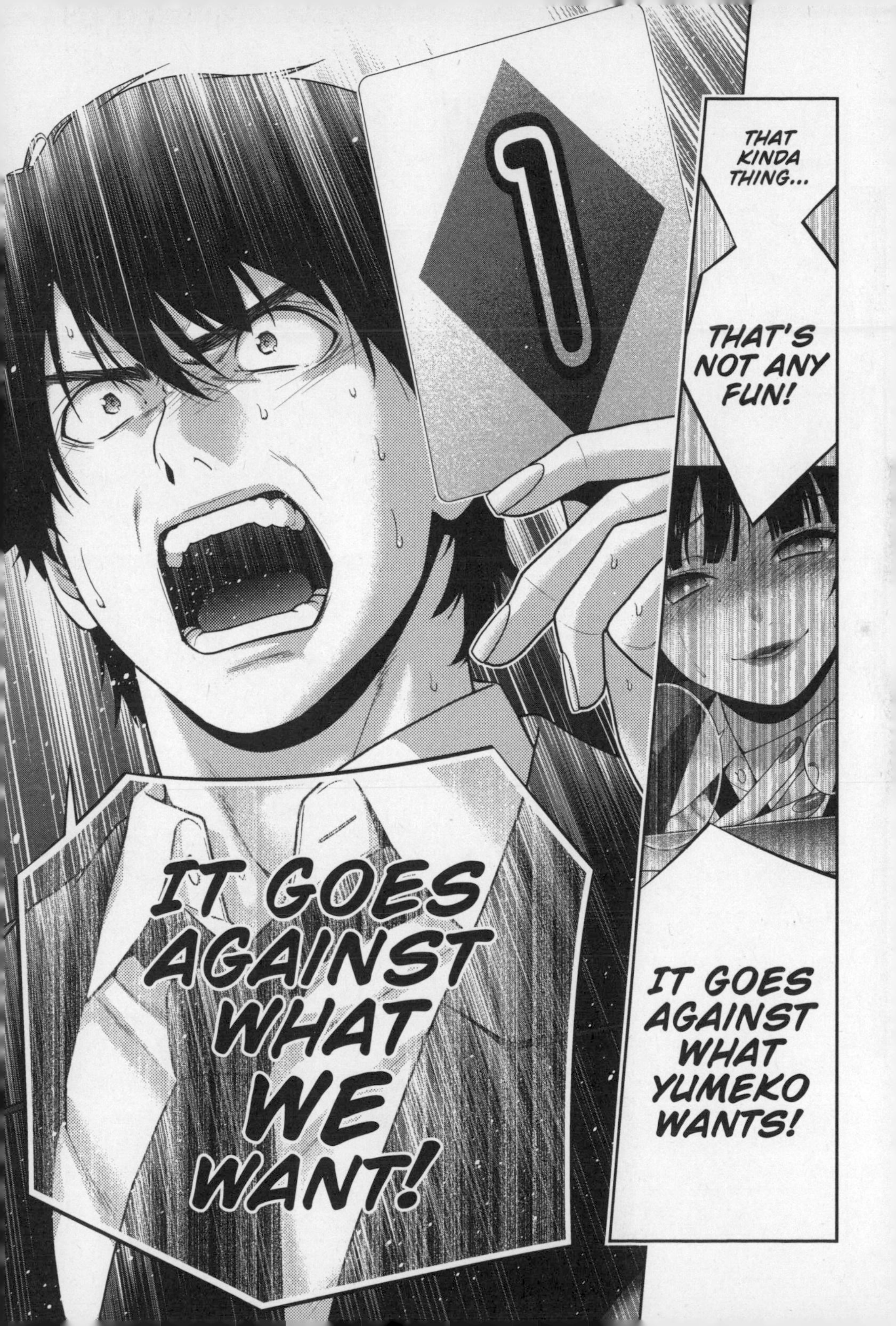
THAT KINDA THING...
THAT'S NOT ANY FUN!
IT GOES AGAINST WHAT YUMEKO WANTS!
IT GOES AGAINST WHAT WE WANT!

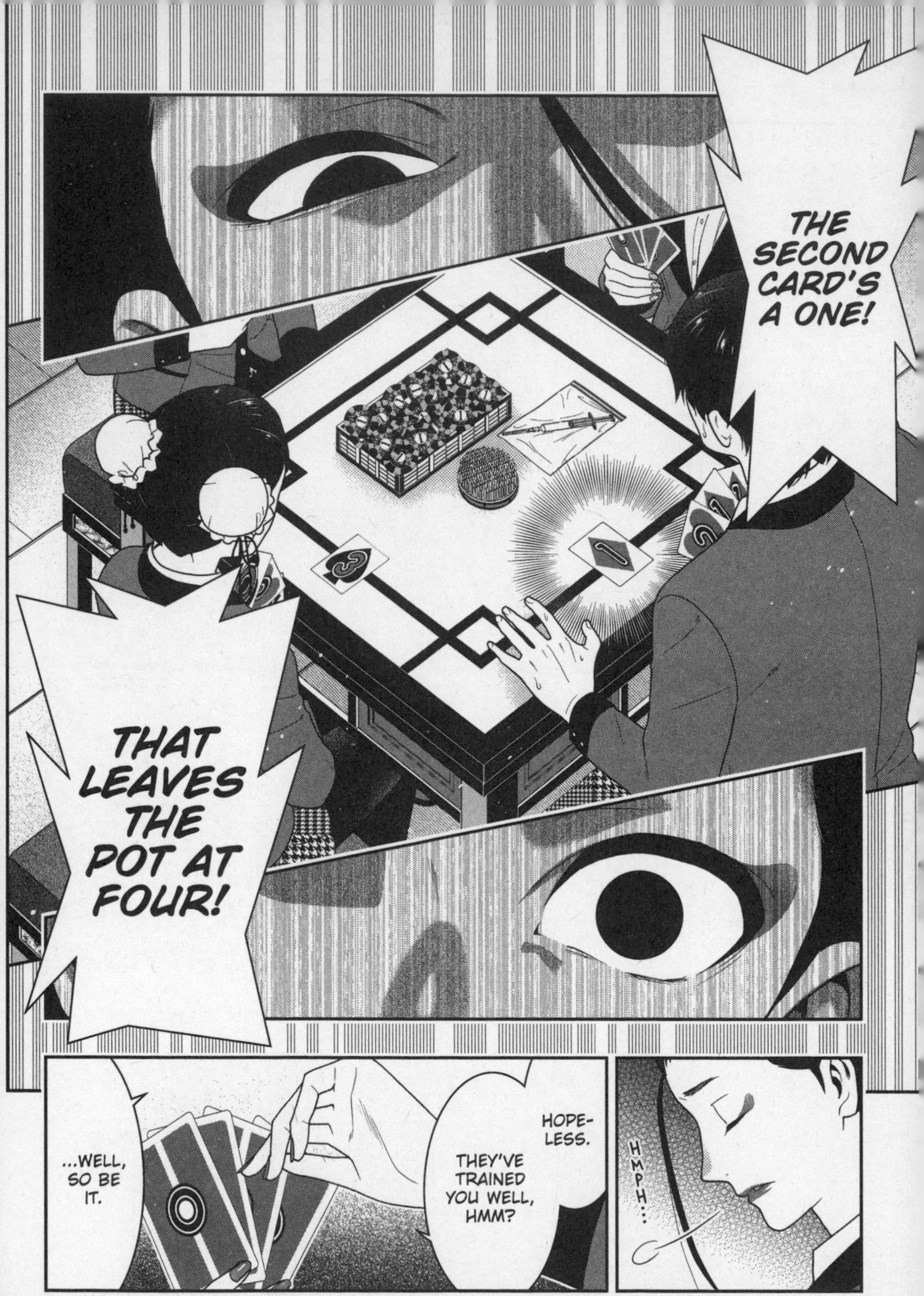
THE SECOND CARD'S A ONE!
THAT LEAVES THE POT AT FOUR!
HMPH...
HOPE-LESS.
THEY'VE TRAINED YOU WELL, HMM?
...WELL, SO BE IT.

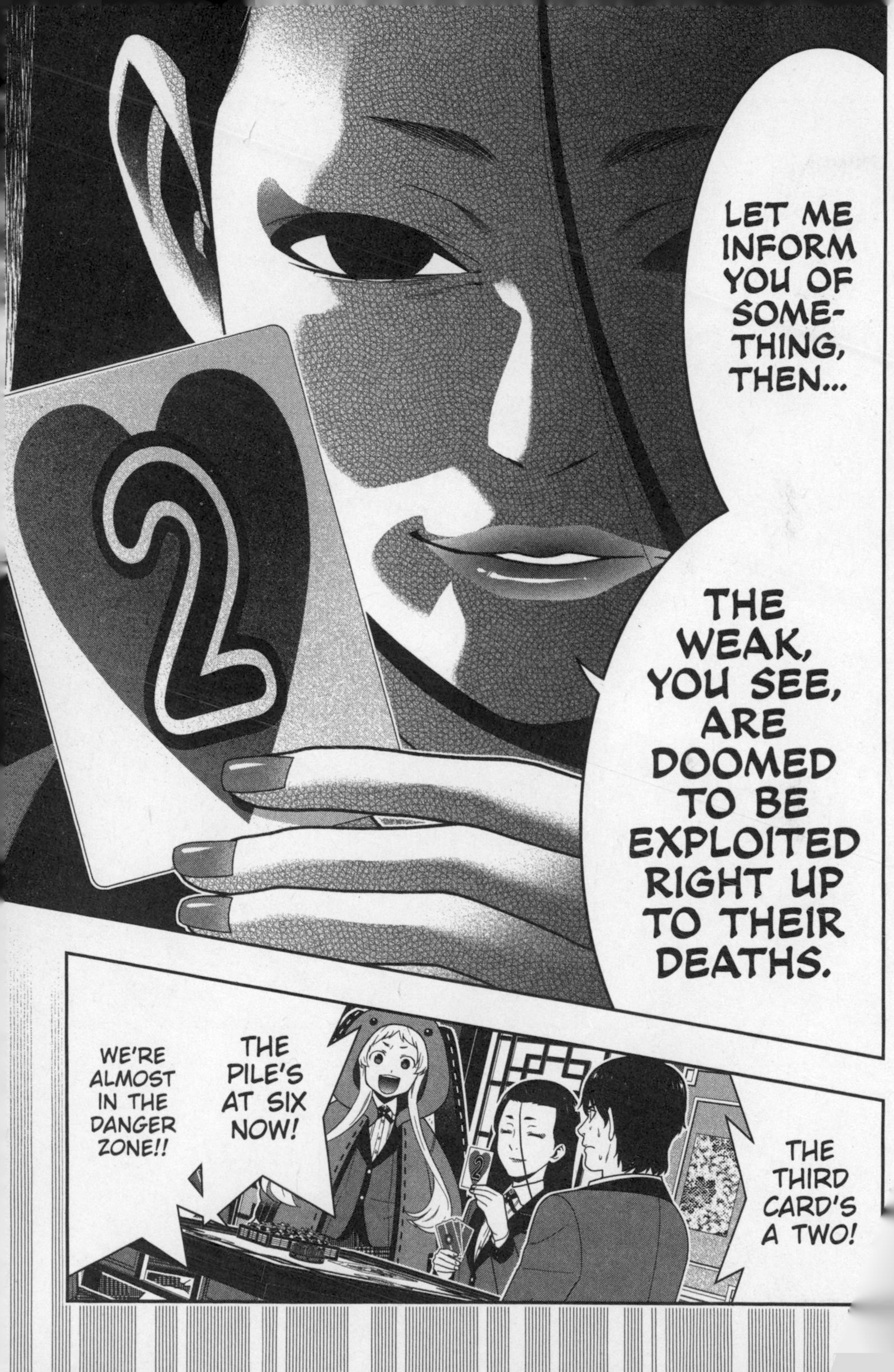
LET ME INFORM YOU OF SOME-THING, THEN...
THE WEAK, YOU SEE, ARE DOOMED TO BE EXPLOITED RIGHT UP TO THEIR DEATHS.
THE THIRD CARD'S A TWO!
THE PILE'S AT SIX NOW!
WE'RE ALMOST IN THE DANGER ZONE!!

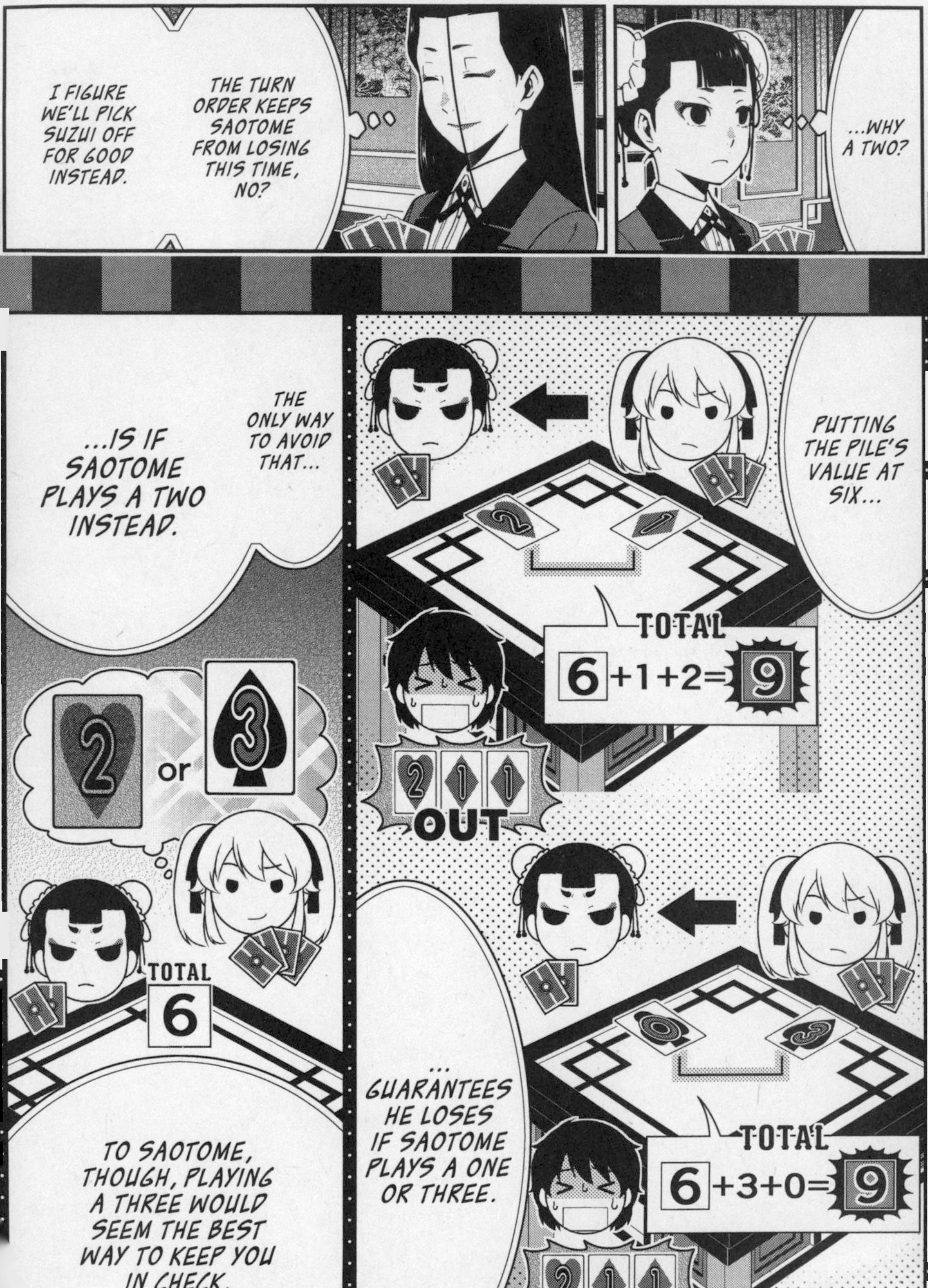
...WHY A TWO?
THE TURN ORDER KEEPS SAOTOME FROM LOSING THIS TIME, NO?
I FIGURE WE'LL PICK SUZUI OFF FOR GOOD INSTEAD.
PUTTING THE PILE'S VALUE AT SIX...
TOTAL
6+1+2=9
2 1 1
OUT
...GUARANTEES HE LOSES IF SAOTOME PLAYS A ONE OR THREE.
TOTAL
6+3+0=9
2 1 1
OUT
THE ONLY WAY TO AVOID THAT...
...IS IF SAOTOME PLAYS A TWO INSTEAD.
2 or 3
TOTAL
6
TO SAOTOME, THOUGH, PLAYING A THREE WOULD SEEM THE BEST WAY TO KEEP YOU IN CHECK.

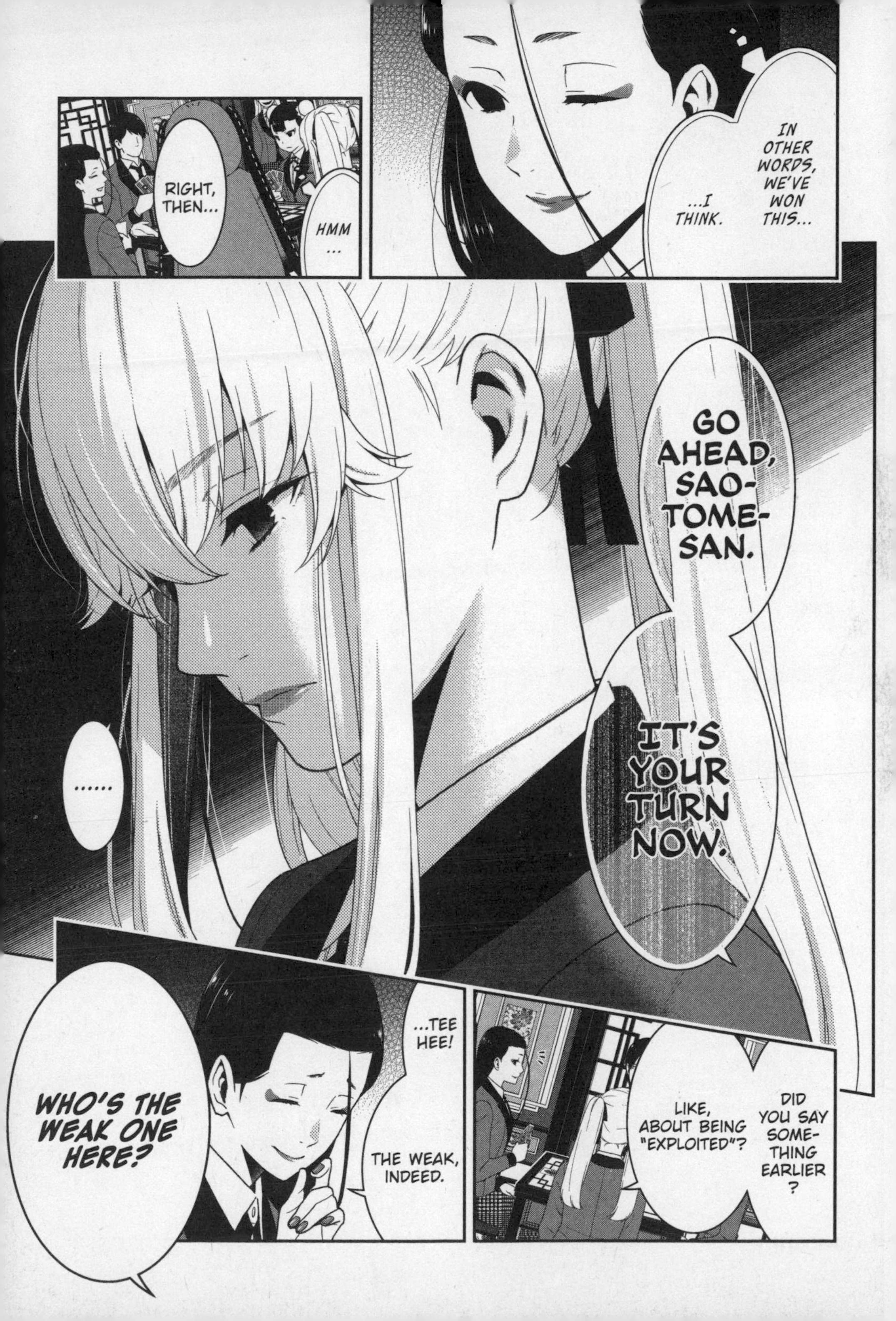
IN OTHER WORDS, WE'VE WON THIS...
...I THINK.
RIGHT, THEN...
HMM...
GO AHEAD, SAO-TOME-SAN.
IT'S YOUR TURN NOW.
......
DID YOU SAY SOMETHING EARLIER?
LIKE, ABOUT BEING "EXPLOITED"?
...TEE HEE!
THE WEAK, INDEED.
WHO'S THE WEAK ONE HERE?

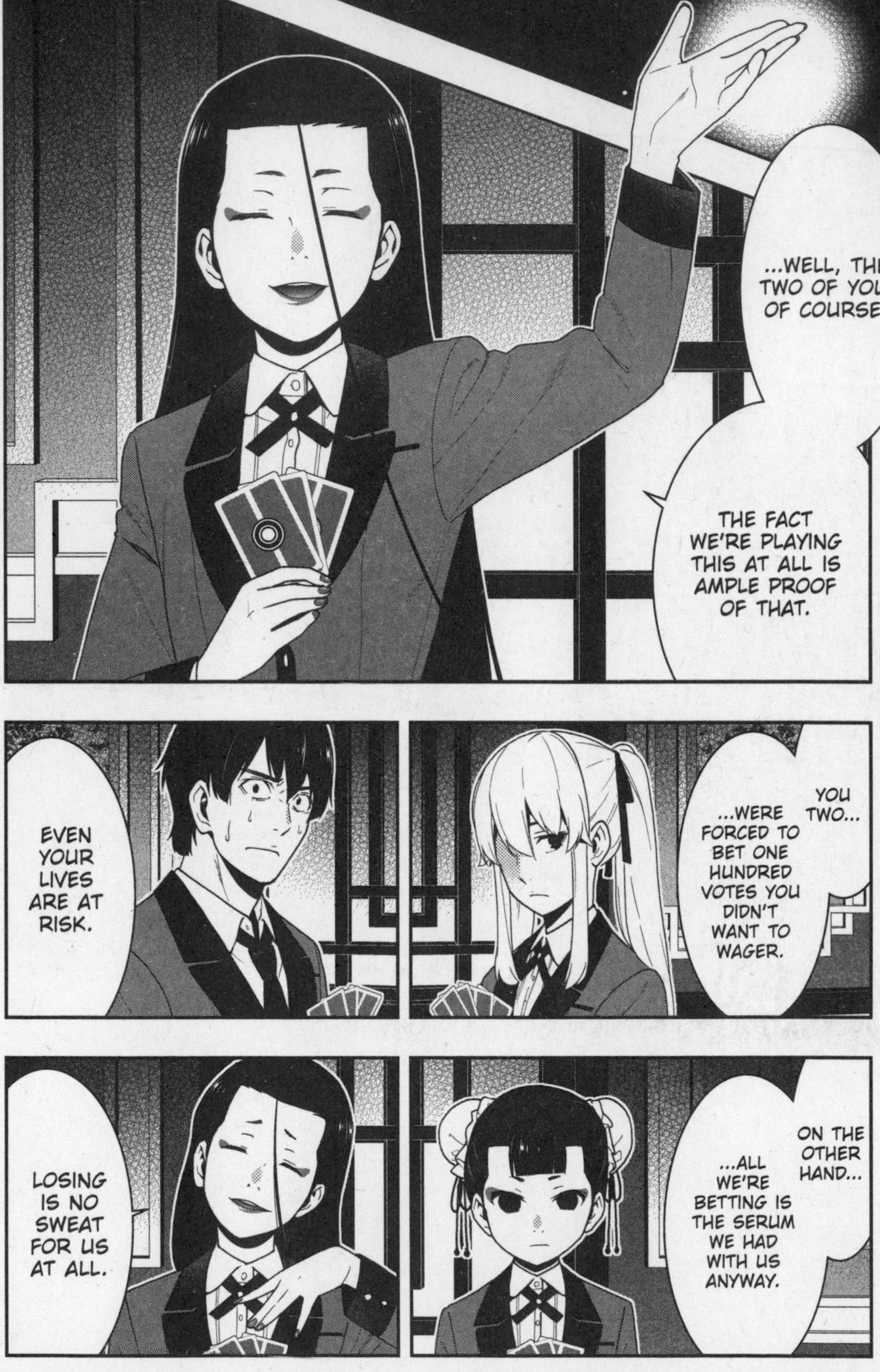
...WELL, THE TWO OF YOU, OF COURSE.
THE FACT WE'RE PLAYING THIS AT ALL IS AMPLE PROOF OF THAT.
YOU TWO...
...WERE FORCED TO BET ONE HUNDRED VOTES YOU DIDN'T WANT TO WAGER.
EVEN YOUR LIVES ARE AT RISK.
ON THE OTHER HAND...
...ALL WE'RE BETTING IS THE SERUM WE HAD WITH US ANYWAY.
LOSING IS NO SWEAT FOR US AT ALL.

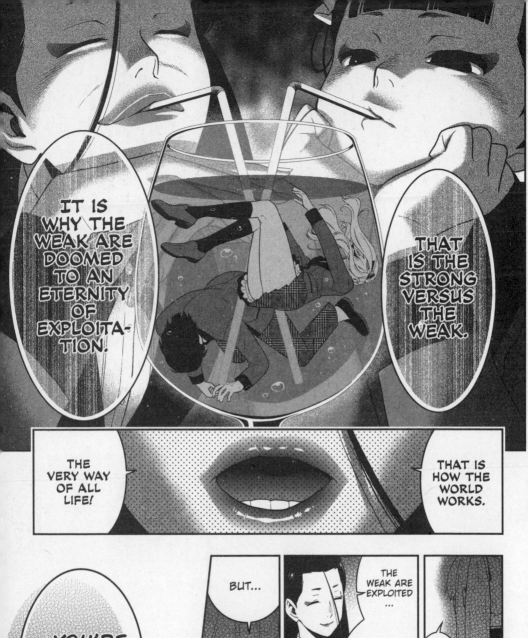

THAT IS THE STRONG VERSUS THE WEAK.
IT IS WHY THE WEAK ARE DOOMED TO AN ETERNITY OF EXPLOITATION!
THAT IS HOW THE WORLD WORKS.
THE VERY WAY OF ALL LIFE!
... MAYBE SO.
THE WEAK ARE EXPLOITED ...
IT'S NOT ABOUT BEING GOOD OR BAD— THE WORLD JUST KEEPS SPINNING.
BUT...
...YOU'RE WRONG ON ONE COUNT.

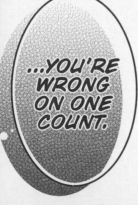

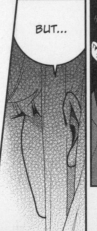

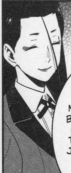

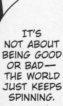

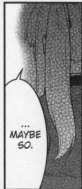

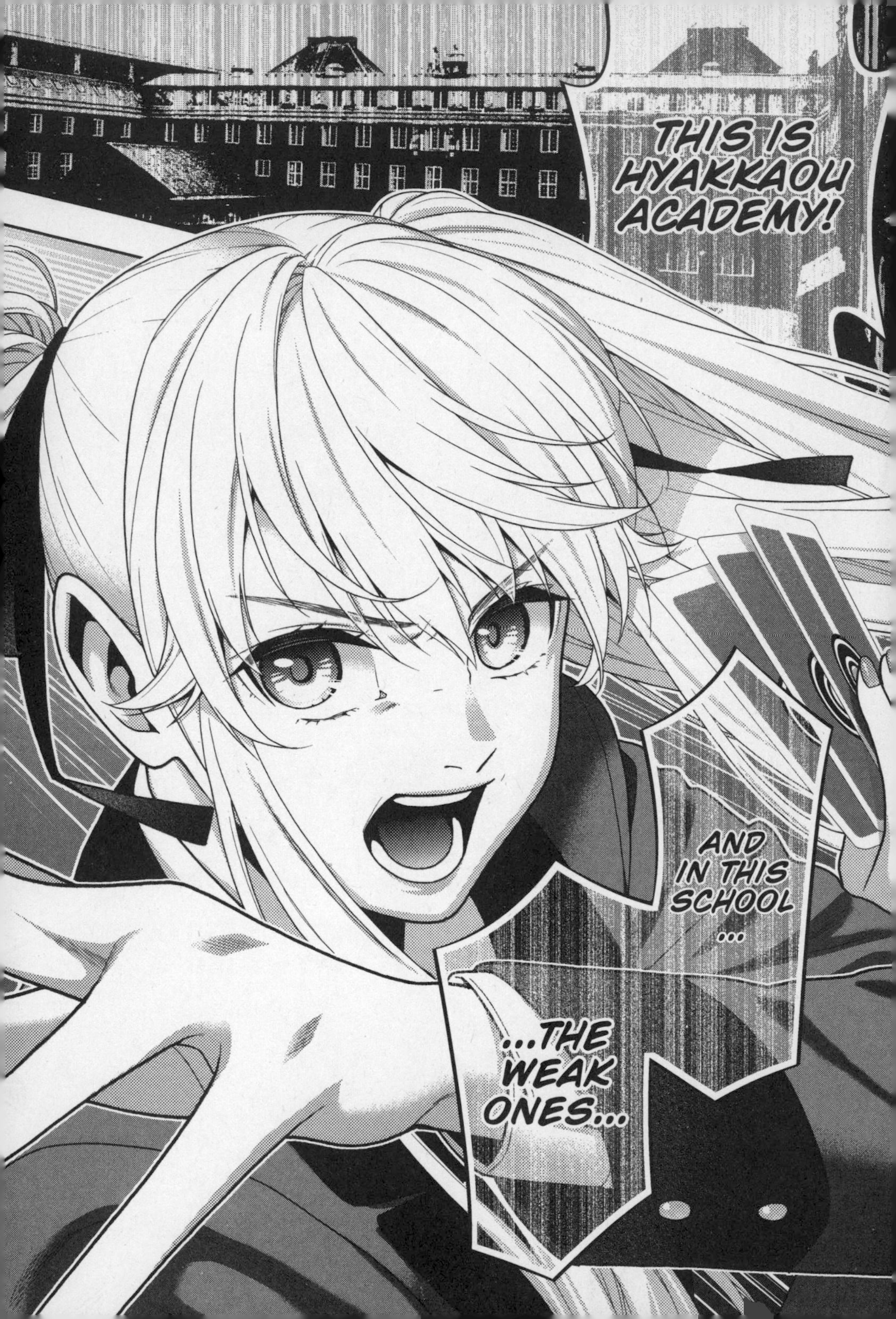
THIS IS HYAKKAOU ACADEMY!
AND IN THIS SCHOOL...
...THE WEAK ONES...

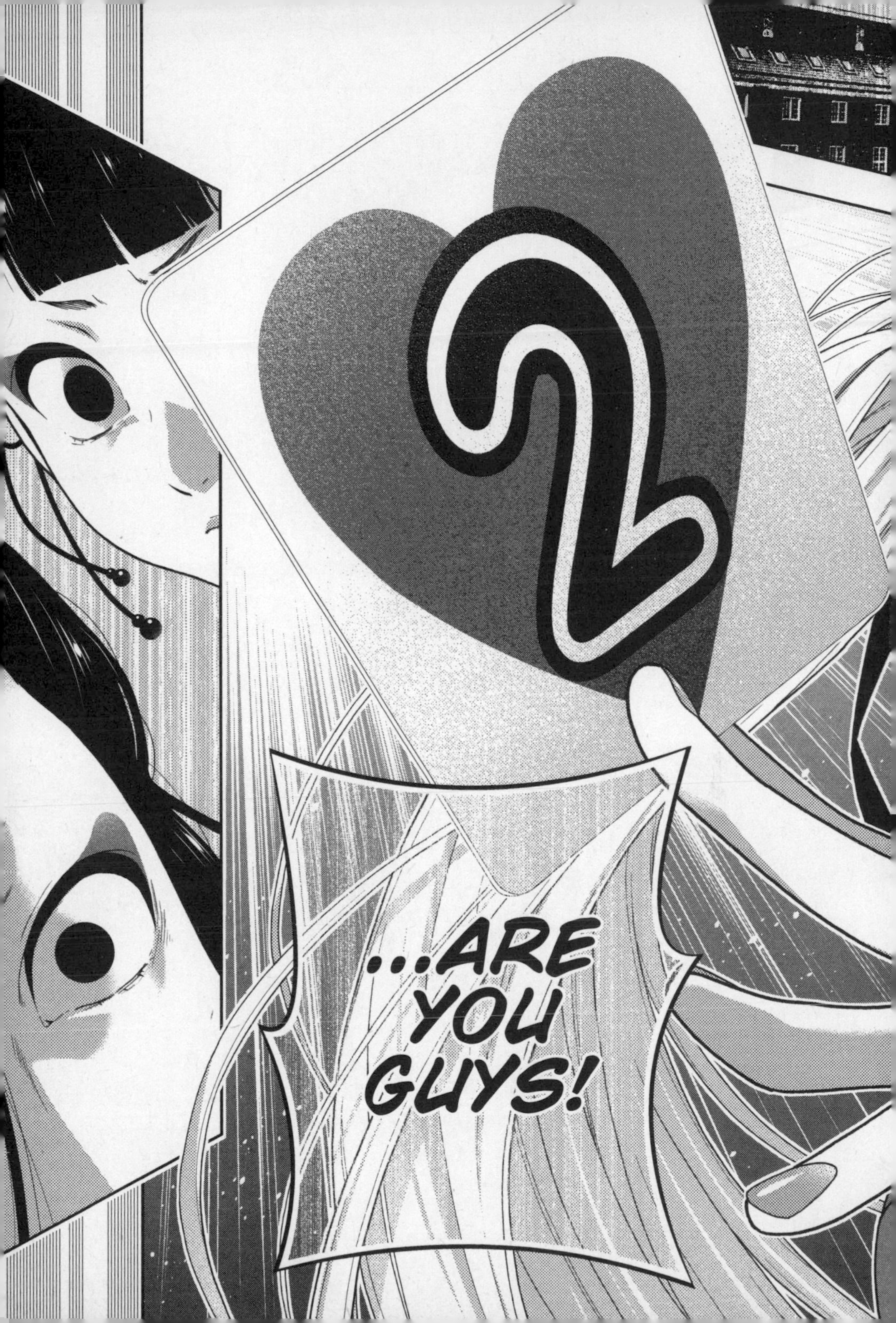
...ARE YOU GUYS!

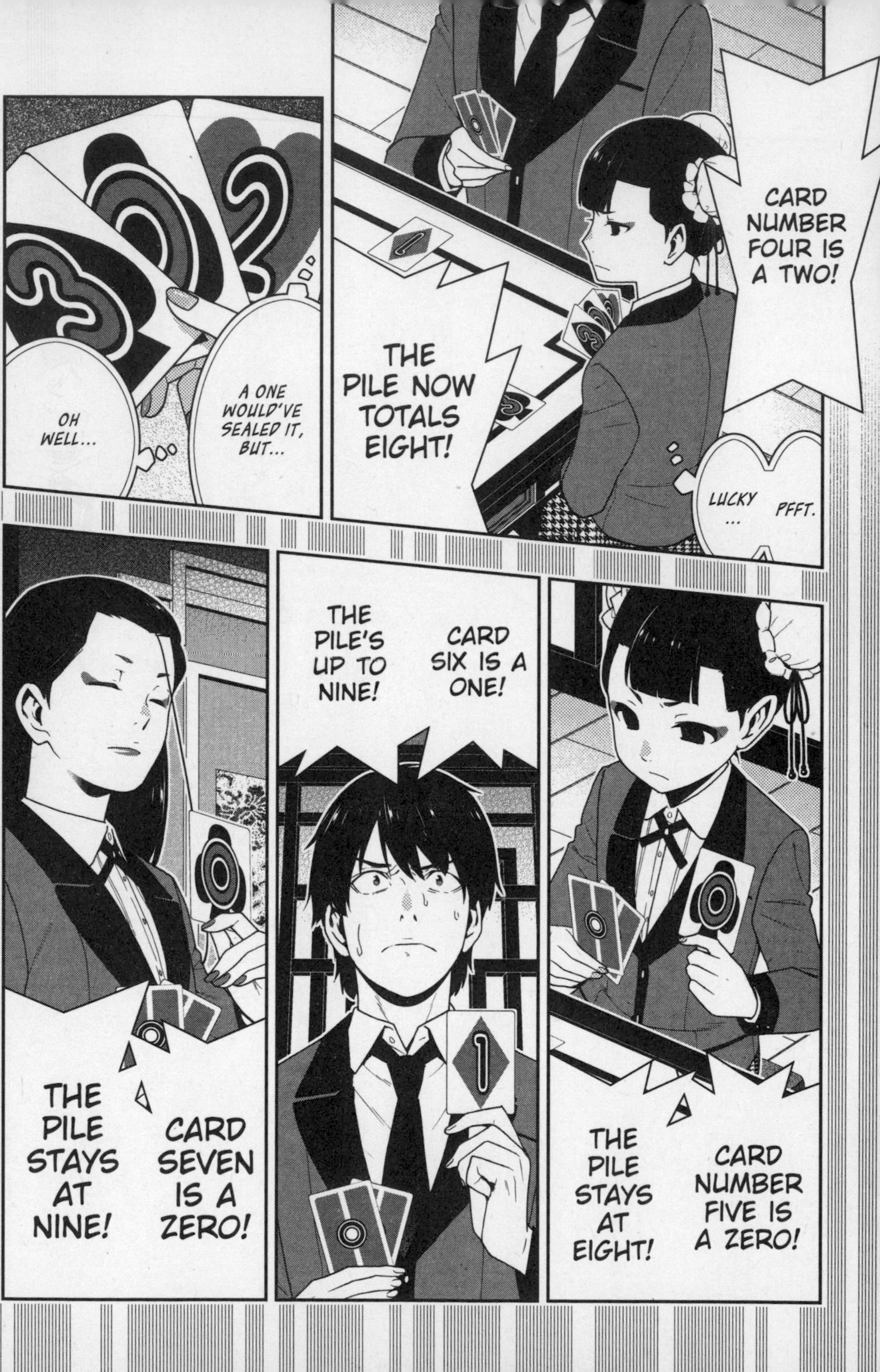
CARD NUMBER FOUR IS A TWO!
THE PILE NOW TOTALS EIGHT!
PFFT.
LUCKY ...
A ONE WOULD'VE SEALED IT, BUT...
OH WELL...
CARD NUMBER FIVE IS A ZERO!
THE PILE STAYS AT EIGHT!
CARD SIX IS A ONE!
THE PILE'S UP TO NINE!
1
CARD SEVEN IS A ZERO!
THE PILE STAYS AT NINE!

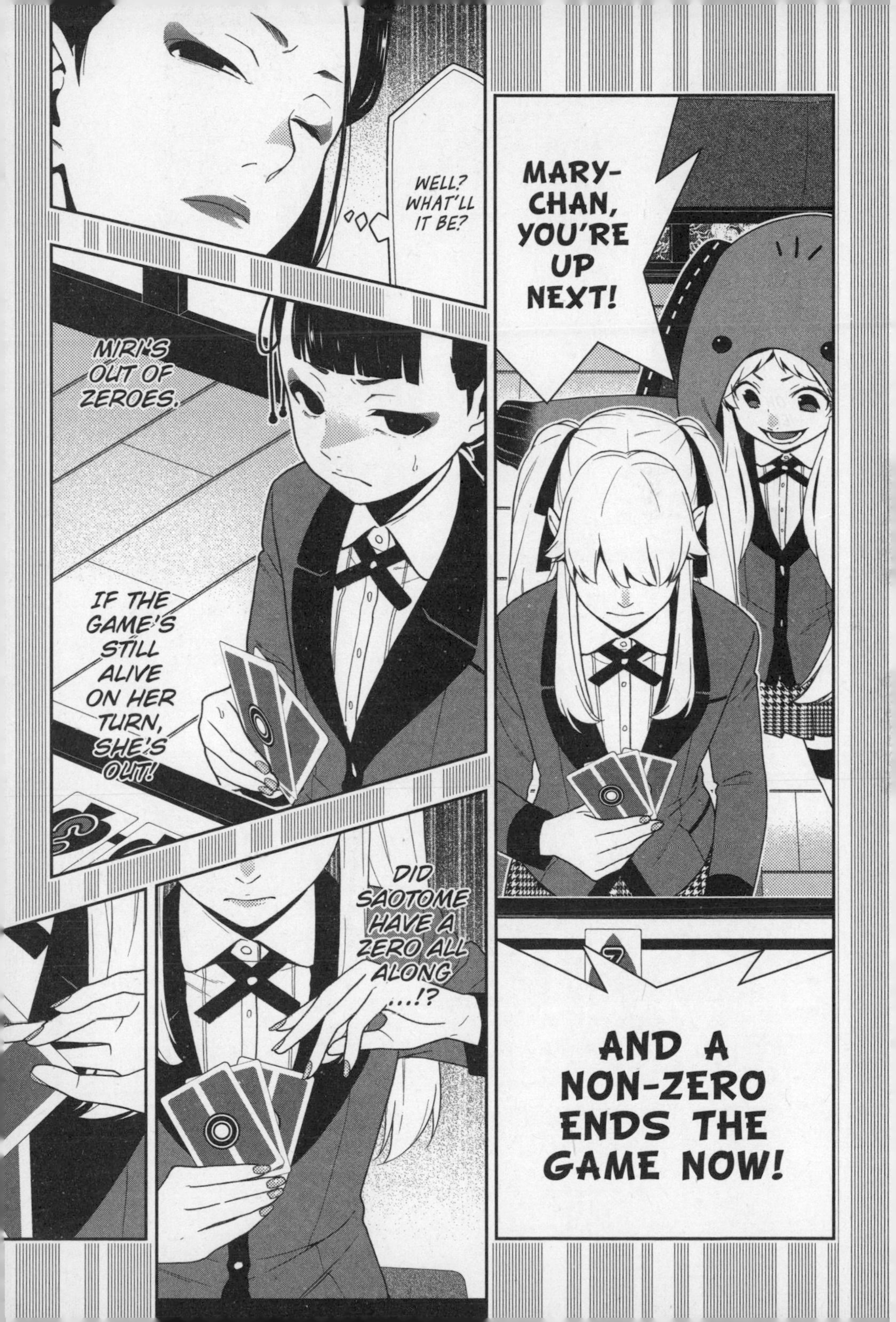
MARY-CHAN, YOU'RE UP NEXT!
AND A NON-ZERO ENDS THE GAME NOW!
WELL? WHAT'LL IT BE?
MIRI'S OUT OF ZEROES.
IF THE GAME'S STILL ALIVE ON HER TURN, SHE'S OUT!
DID SAOTOME HAVE A ZERO ALL ALONG ...!?

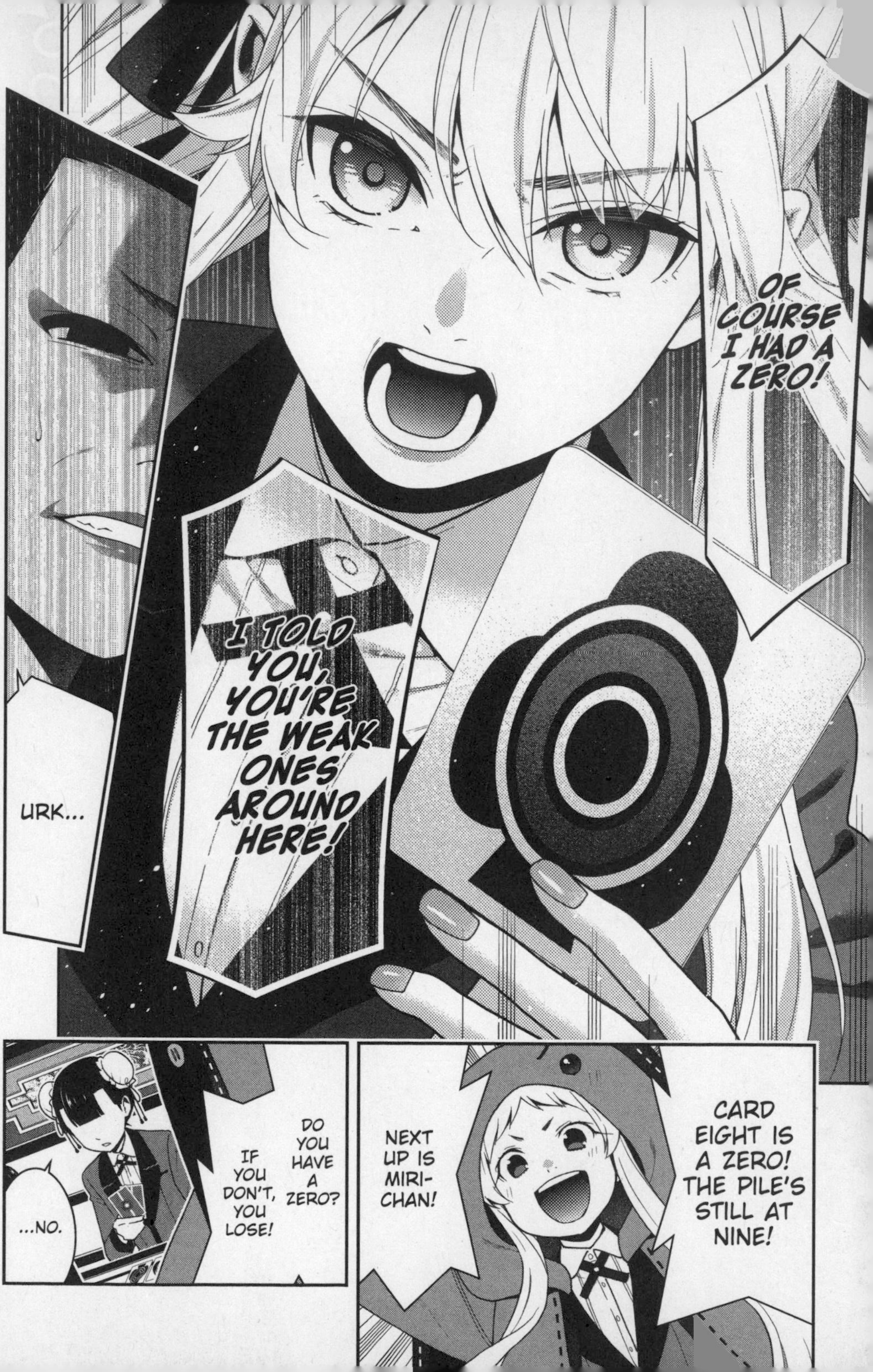
OF COURSE I HAD A ZERO!
I TOLD YOU, YOU'RE THE WEAK ONES AROUND HERE!
URK...
CARD EIGHT IS A ZERO! THE PILE'S STILL AT NINE!
NEXT UP IS MIRI-CHAN!
DO YOU HAVE A ZERO?
IF YOU DON'T, YOU LOSE!
...NO.

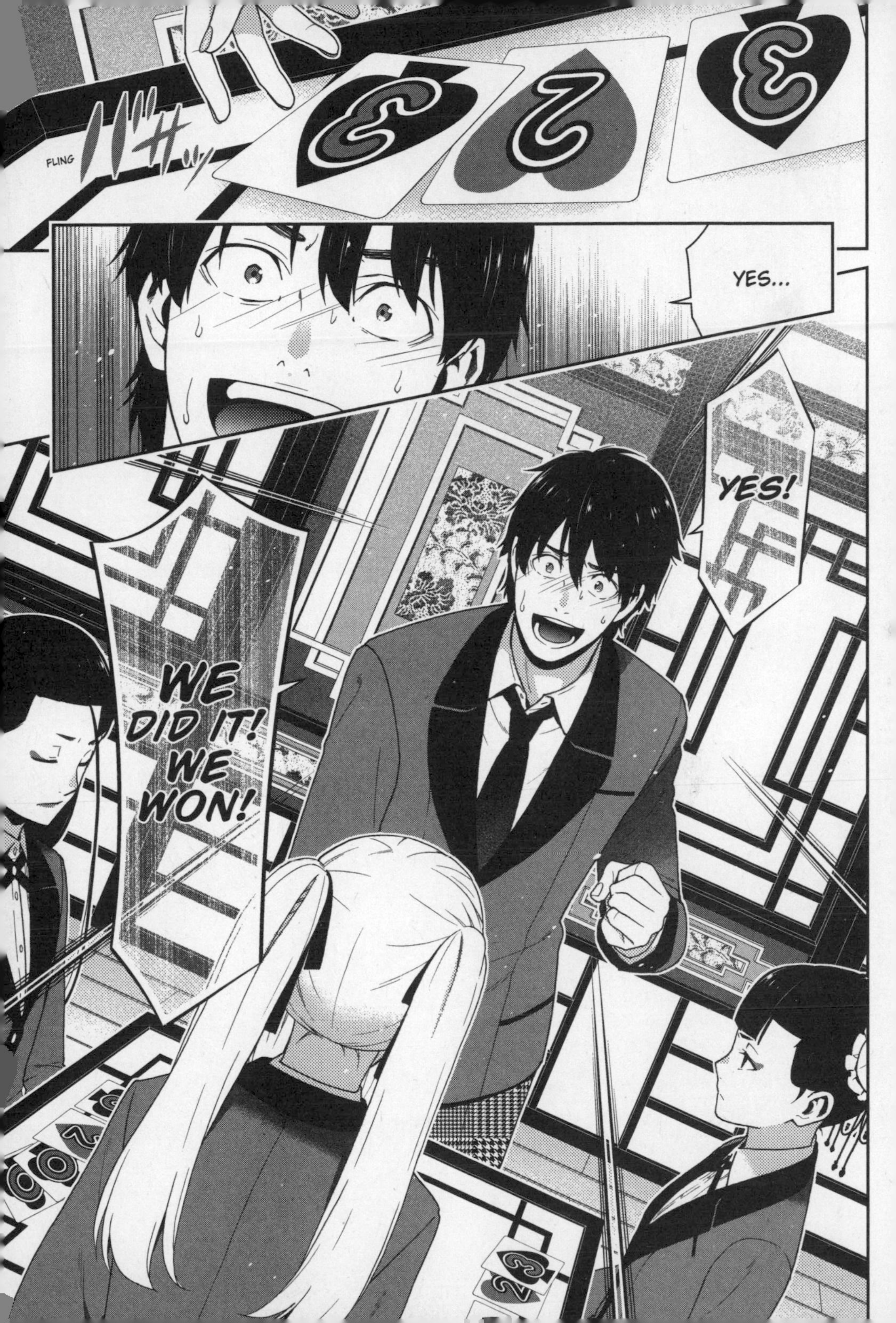

バサッ
FLING
YES...
YES!
WE DID IT! WE WON!

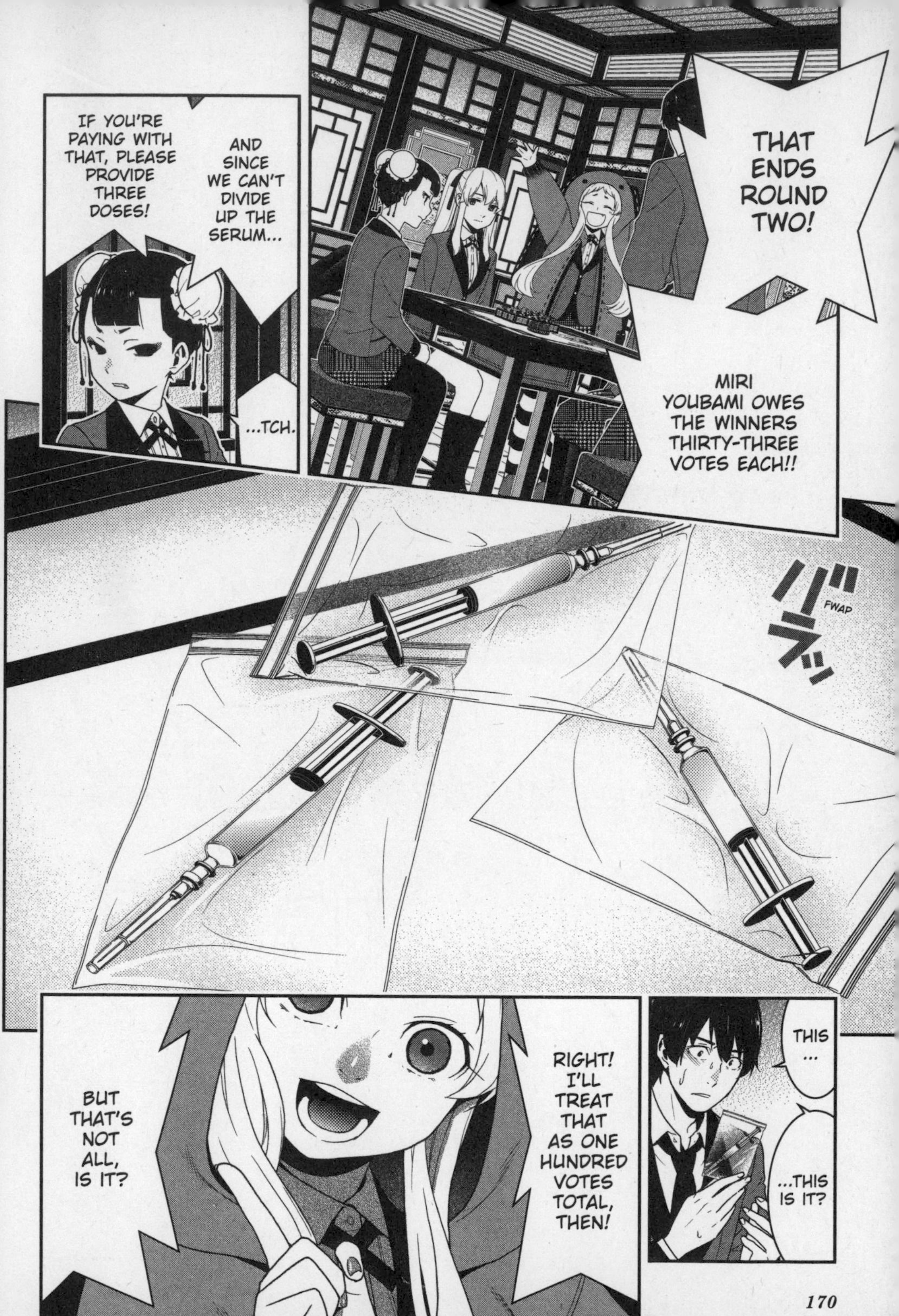
THAT ENDS ROUND TWO!
MIRI YOUBAMI OWES THE WINNERS THIRTY-THREE VOTES EACH!!
AND SINCE WE CAN'T DIVIDE UP THE SERUM...
IF YOU'RE PAYING WITH THAT, PLEASE PROVIDE THREE DOSES!
...TCH.
バラッ
FWAP
THIS...
...THIS IS IT?
RIGHT! I'LL TREAT THAT AS ONE HUNDRED VOTES TOTAL, THEN!
BUT THAT'S NOT ALL, IS IT?

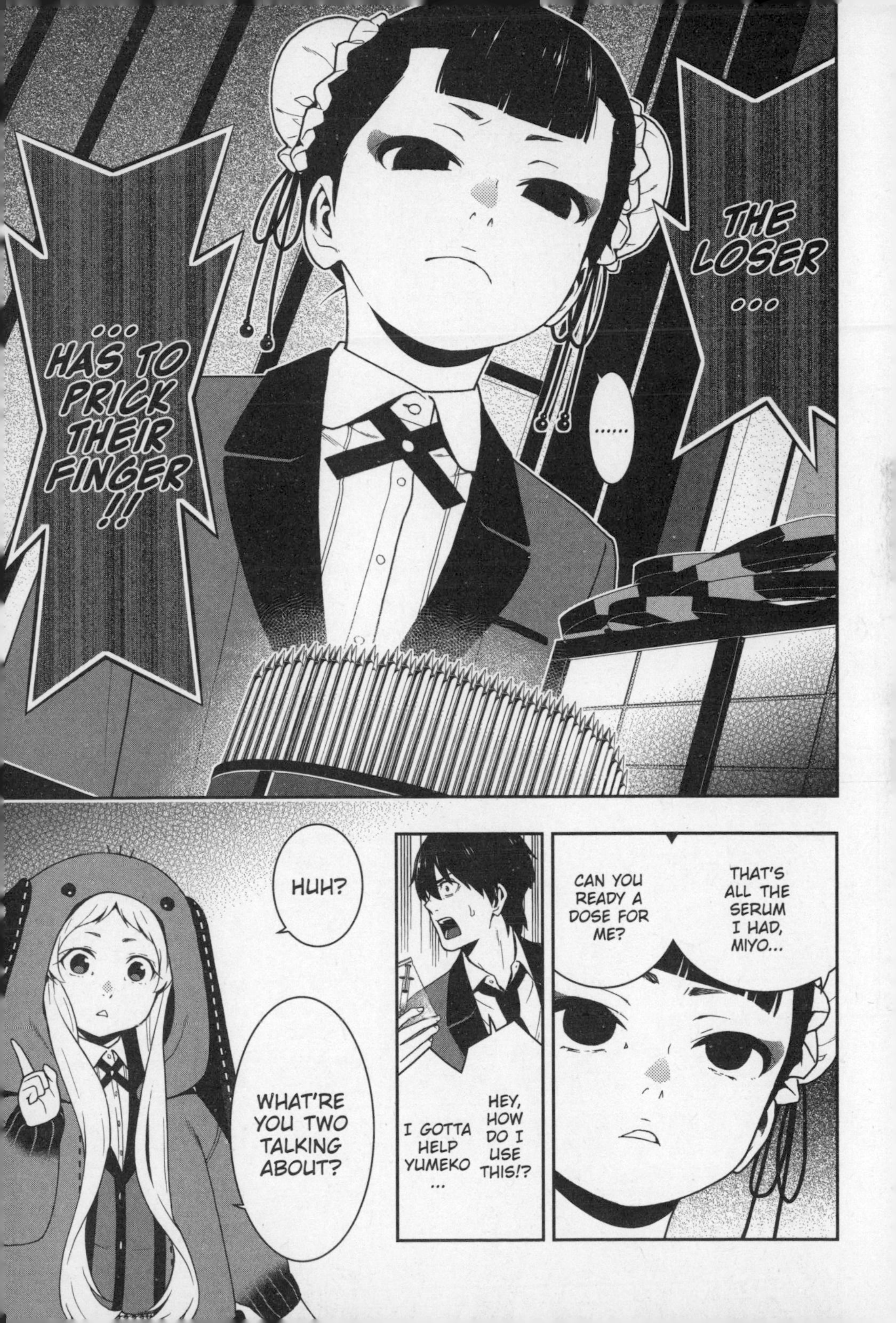
THE LOSER ...
......
... HAS TO PRICK THEIR FINGER !!
THAT'S ALL THE SERUM I HAD, MIYO...
CAN YOU READY A DOSE FOR ME?
HEY, HOW DO I USE THIS!?
I GOTTA HELP YUMEKO ...
HUH?
WHAT'RE YOU TWO TALKING ABOUT?

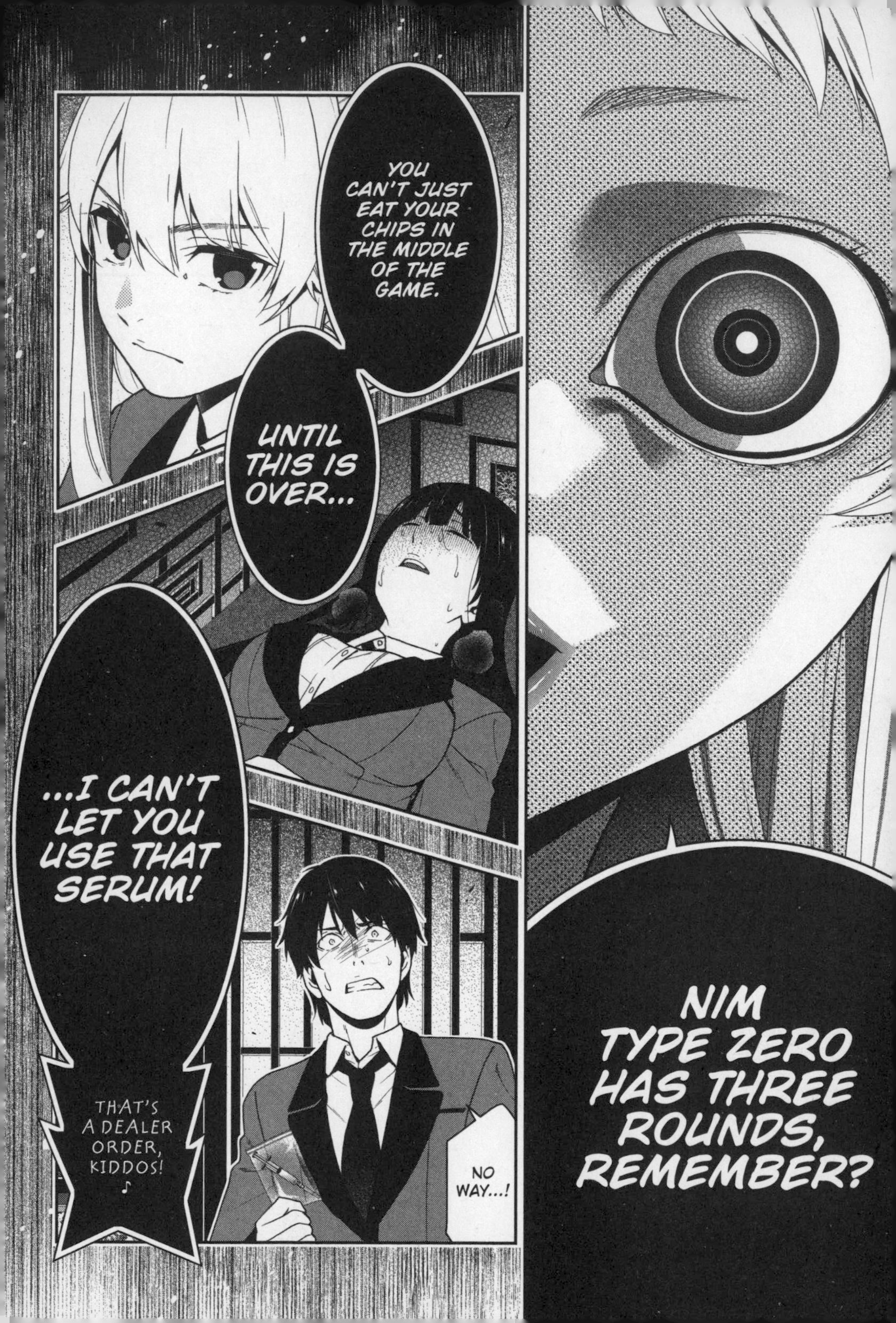
NIM TYPE ZERO HAS THREE ROUNDS, REMEMBER?
YOU CAN'T JUST EAT YOUR CHIPS IN THE MIDDLE OF THE GAME.
UNTIL THIS IS OVER...
...I CAN'T LET YOU USE THAT SERUM!
THAT'S A DEALER ORDER, KIDDOS! ♪
NO WAY...!

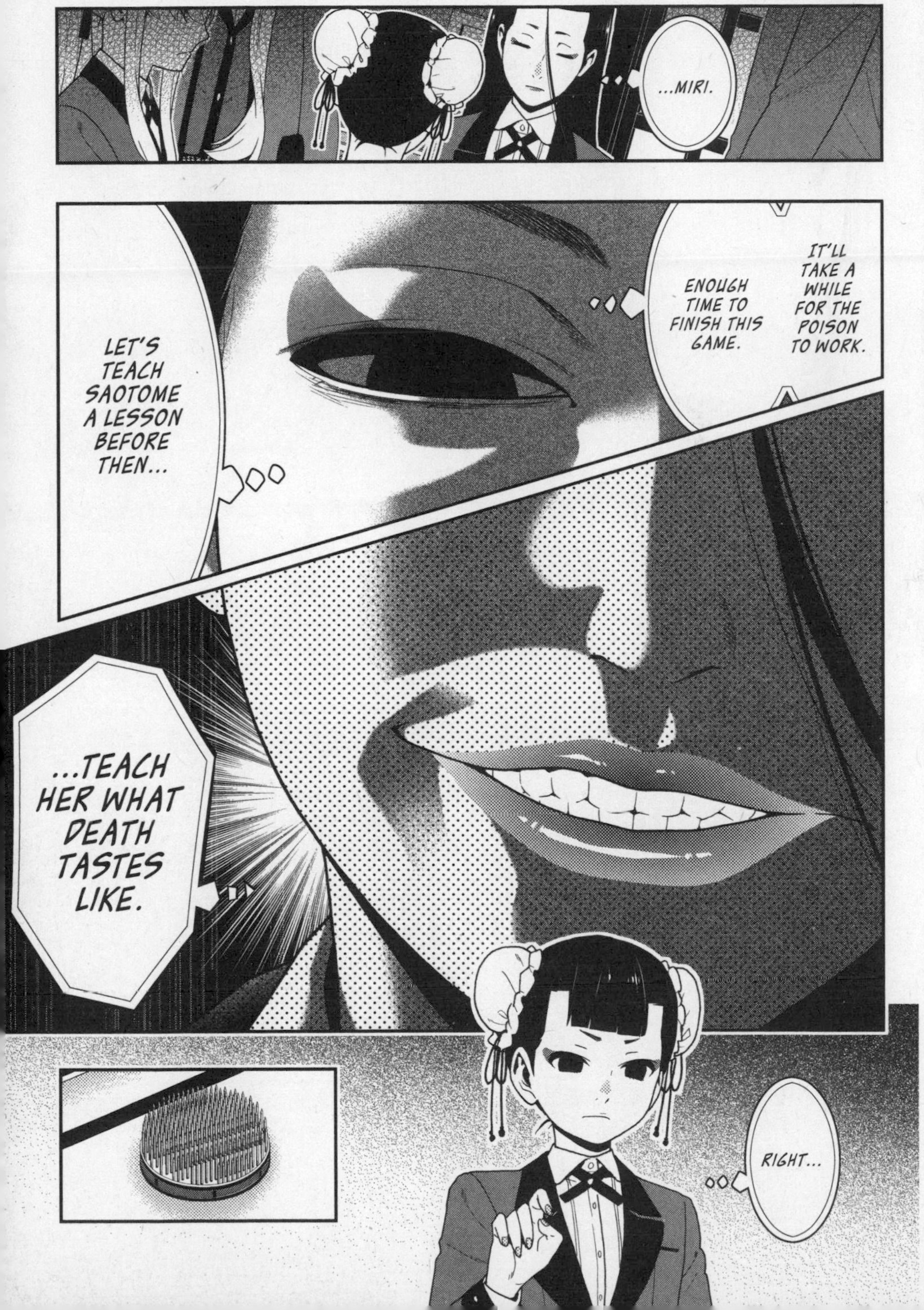
...MIRI.
IT'LL TAKE A WHILE FOR THE POISON TO WORK.
ENOUGH TIME TO FINISH THIS GAME.
LET'S TEACH SAOTOME A LESSON BEFORE THEN...
...TEACH HER WHAT DEATH TASTES LIKE.
RIGHT...

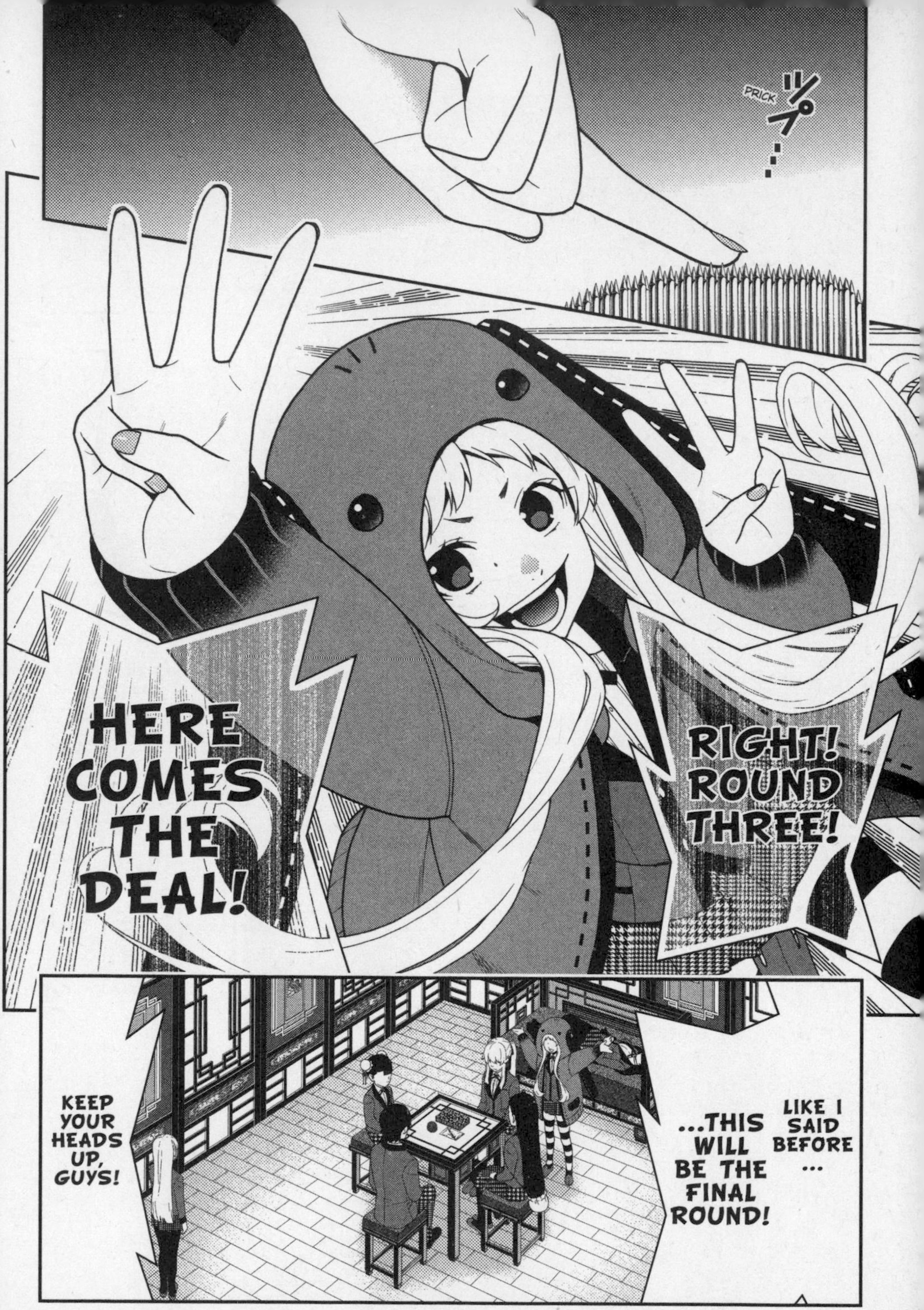
PRICK
RIGHT! ROUND THREE!
HERE COMES THE DEAL!
LIKE I SAID BEFORE...
...THIS WILL BE THE FINAL ROUND!
KEEP YOUR HEADS UP, GUYS!

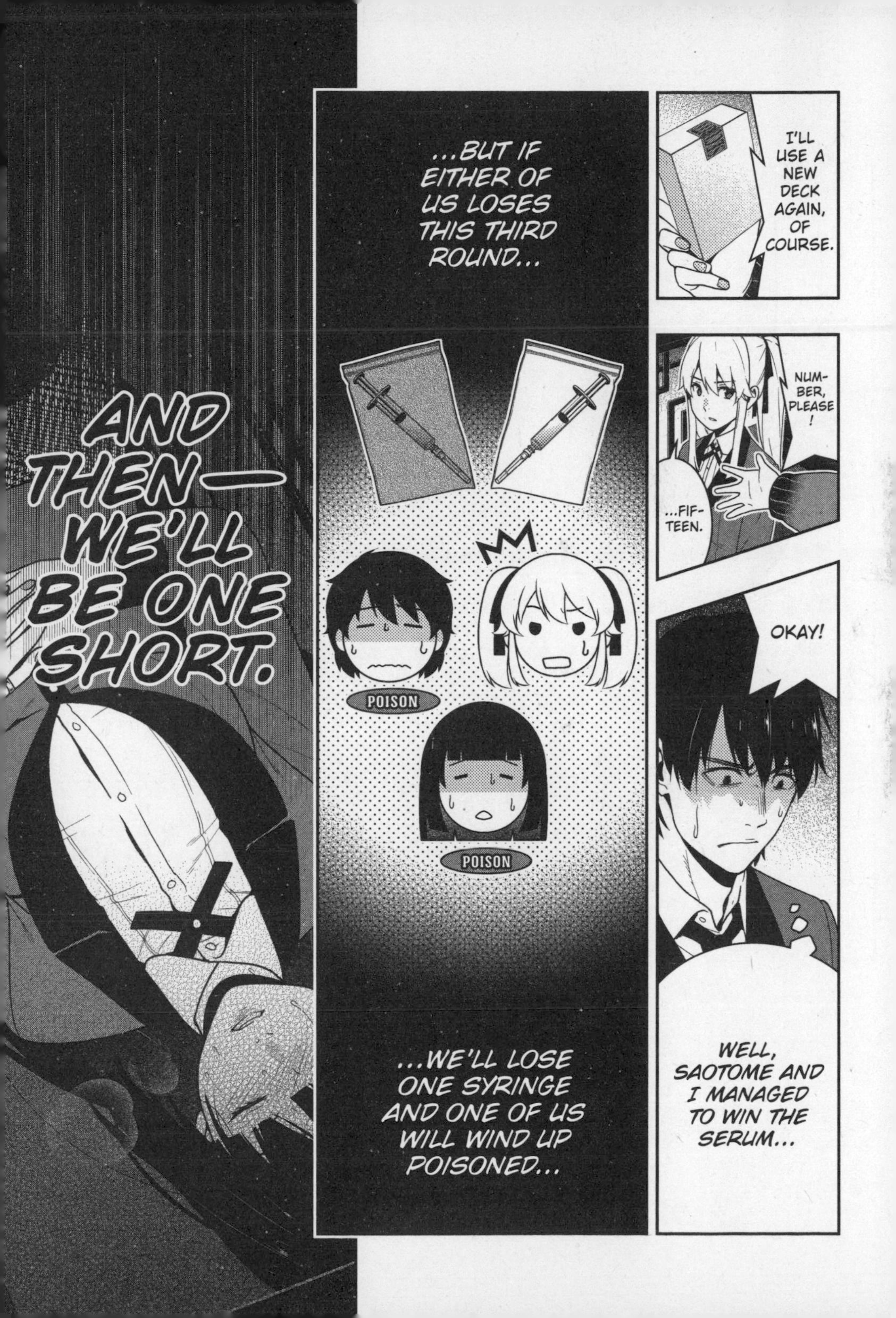
I'LL USE A NEW DECK AGAIN, OF COURSE.
NUMBER, PLEASE!
...FIFTEEN.
OKAY!
WELL, SAOTOME AND I MANAGED TO WIN THE SERUM...
...BUT IF EITHER OF US LOSES THIS THIRD ROUND...
POISON
POISON
...WE'LL LOSE ONE SYRINGE AND ONE OF US WILL WIND UP POISONED...
AND THEN—WE'LL BE ONE SHORT.

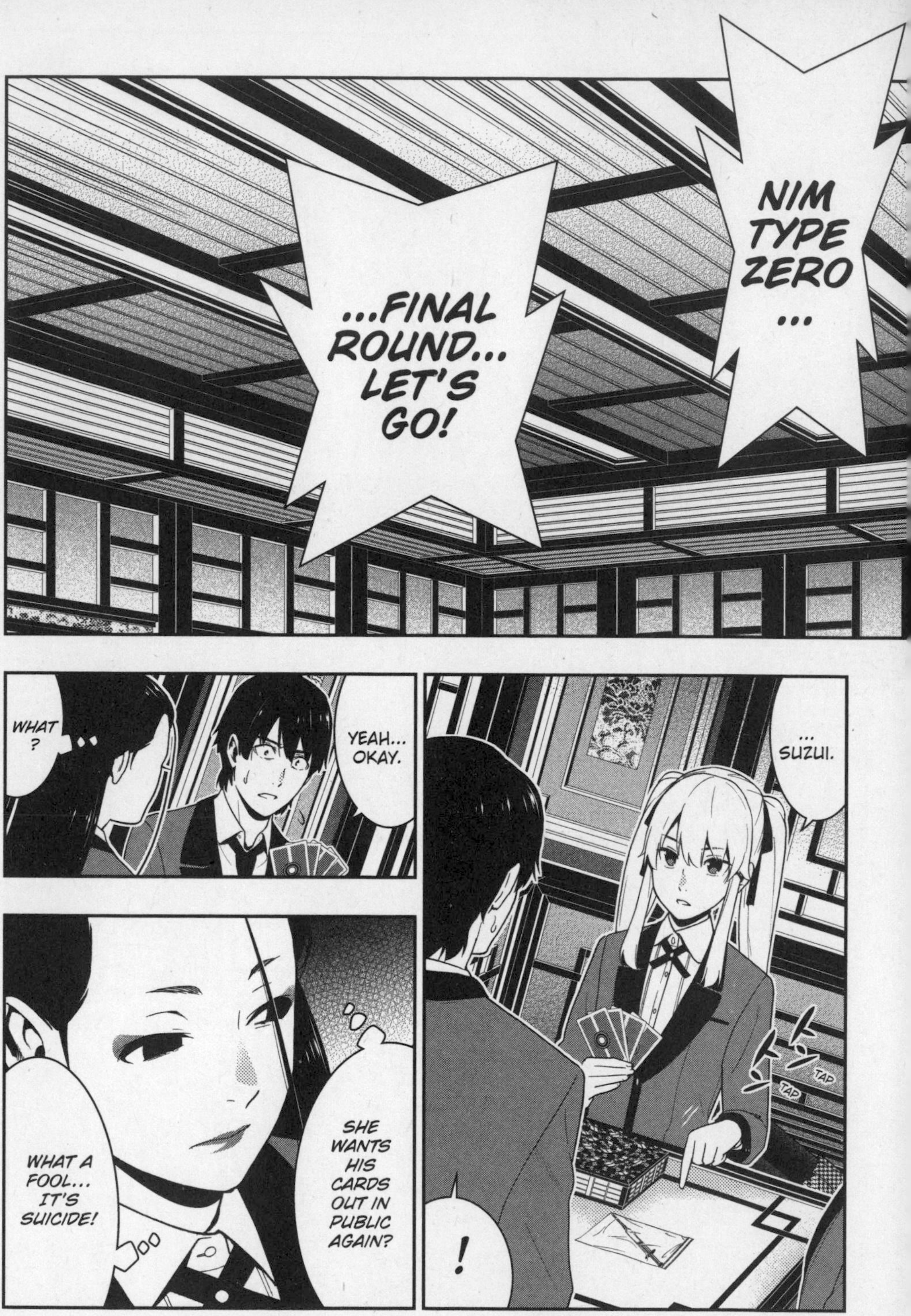
NIM TYPE ZERO...
...FINAL ROUND... LET'S GO!
...SUZUI.
TAP TAP
!
YEAH... OKAY.
WHAT?
SHE WANTS HIS CARDS OUT IN PUBLIC AGAIN?
WHAT A FOOL... IT'S SUICIDE!

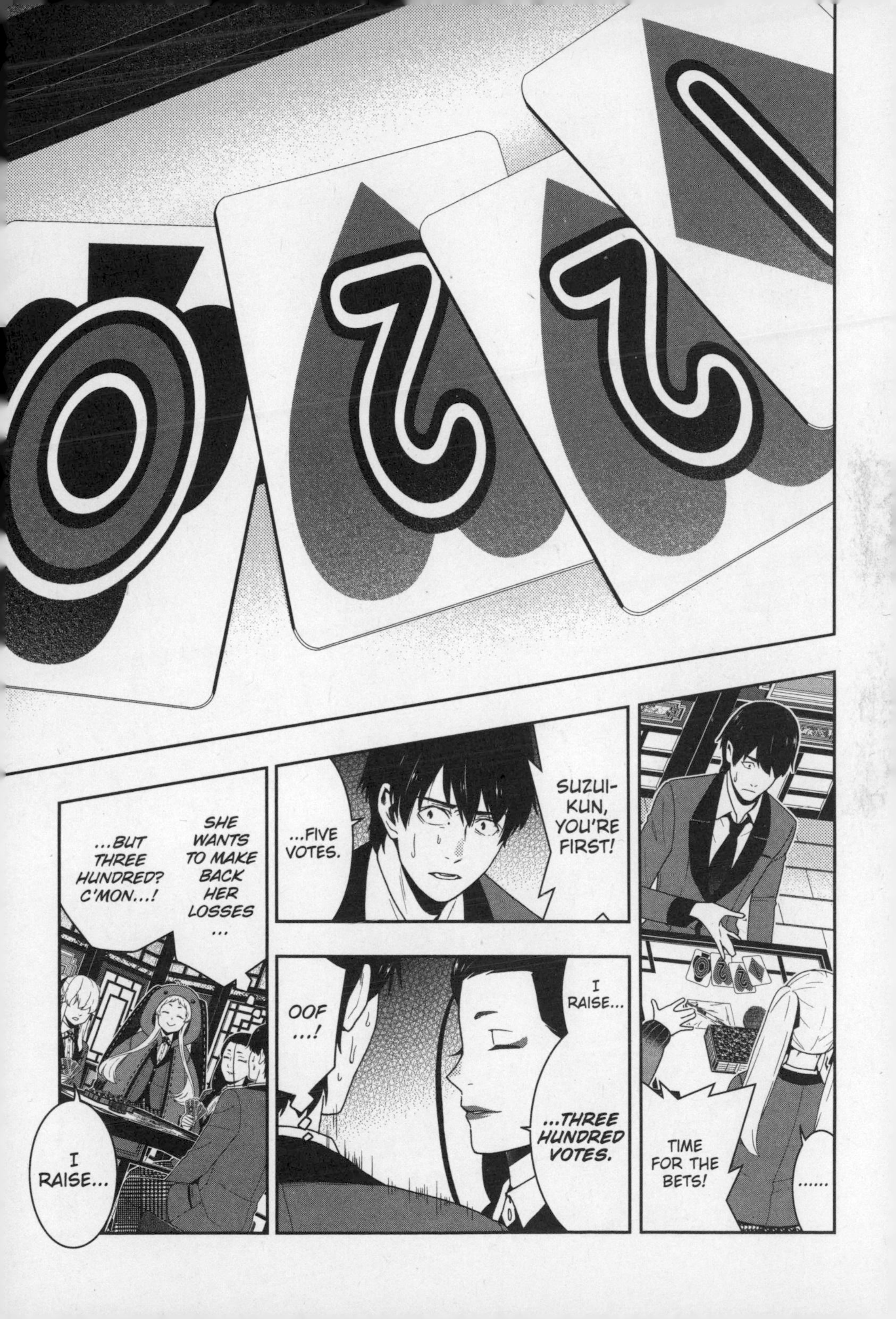
SUZUI-KUN, YOU'RE FIRST!
......
TIME FOR THE BETS!
...FIVE VOTES.
I RAISE...
...THREE HUNDRED VOTES.
OOF...!
SHE WANTS TO MAKE BACK HER LOSSES...
...BUT THREE HUNDRED? C'MON...!
I RAISE...

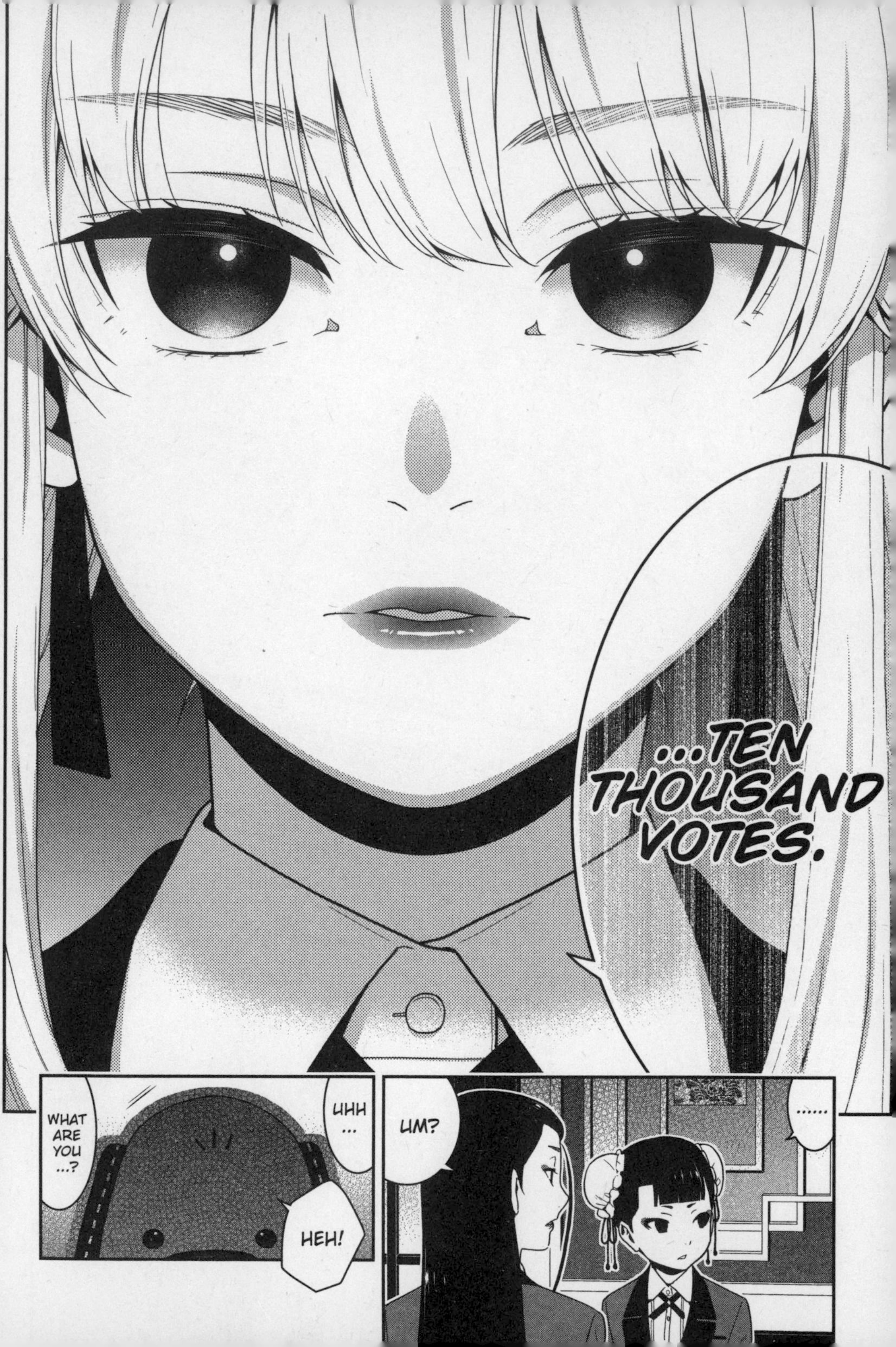
...TEN THOUSAND VOTES.
......
UM?
UHH ...
WHAT ARE YOU ...?
HEH!

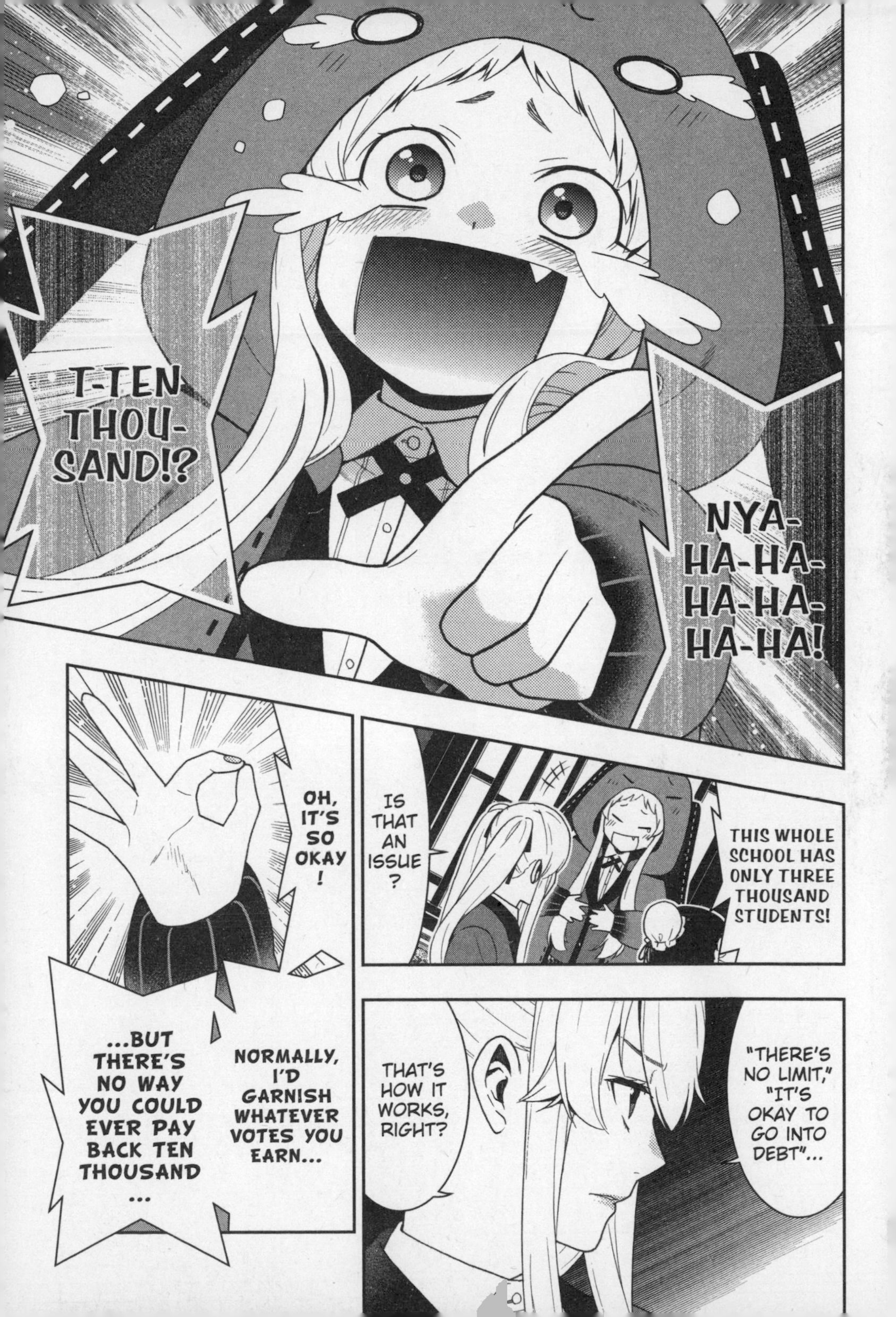
NYA-HA-HA-HA-HA-HA-HA!
T-TEN THOUSAND!?
THIS WHOLE SCHOOL HAS ONLY THREE THOUSAND STUDENTS!
IS THAT AN ISSUE?
OH, IT'S SO OKAY!
"THERE'S NO LIMIT," "IT'S OKAY TO GO INTO DEBT"...
THAT'S HOW IT WORKS, RIGHT?
NORMALLY, I'D GARNISH WHATEVER VOTES YOU EARN...
...BUT THERE'S NO WAY YOU COULD EVER PAY BACK TEN THOUSAND...

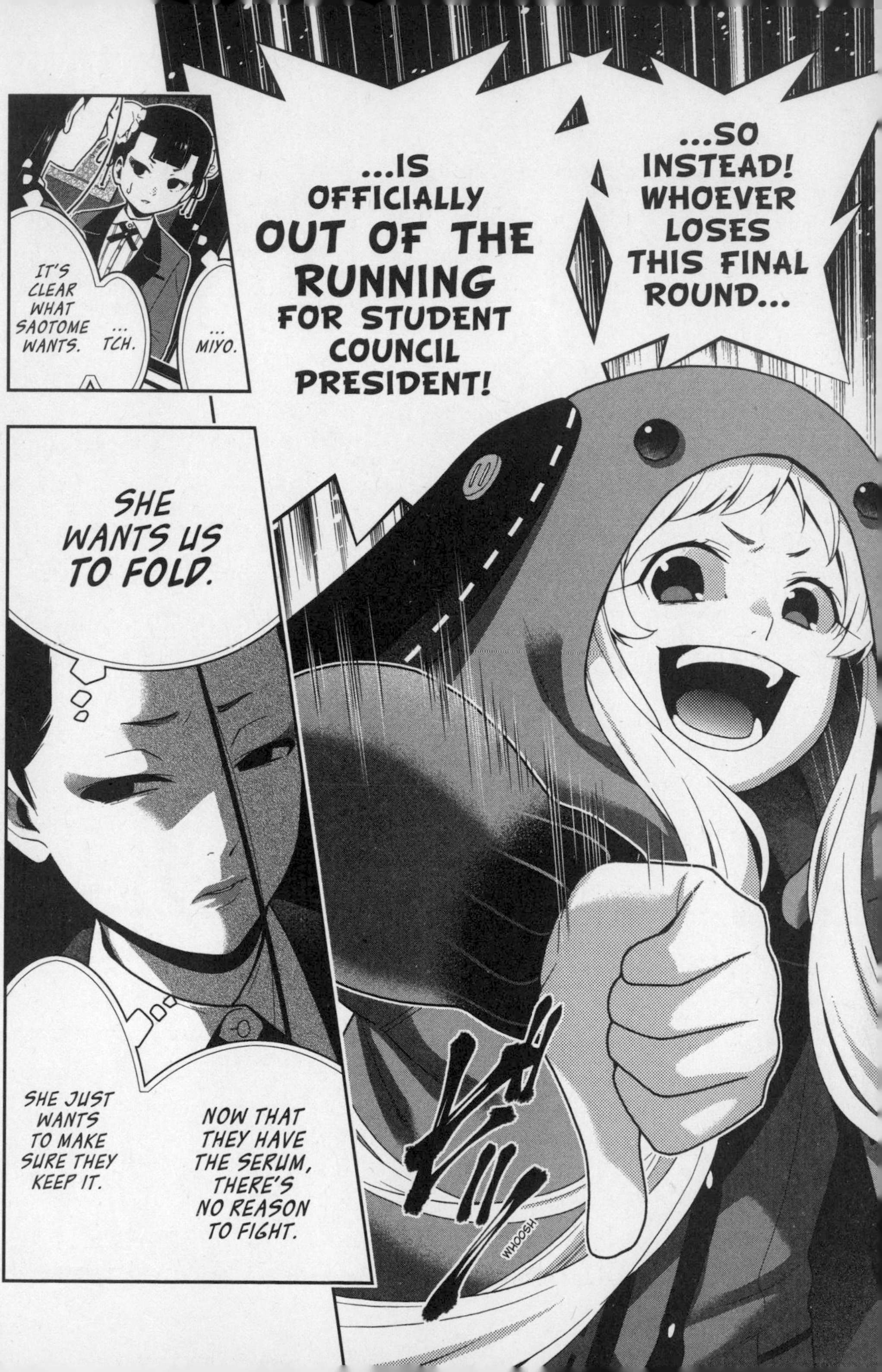
...SO INSTEAD! WHOEVER LOSES THIS FINAL ROUND...
...IS OFFICIALLY OUT OF THE RUNNING FOR STUDENT COUNCIL PRESIDENT!
WHOOSH
...MIYO.
...TCH.
IT'S CLEAR WHAT SAOTOME WANTS.
SHE WANTS US TO FOLD.
NOW THAT THEY HAVE THE SERUM, THERE'S NO REASON TO FIGHT.
SHE JUST WANTS TO MAKE SURE THEY KEEP IT.

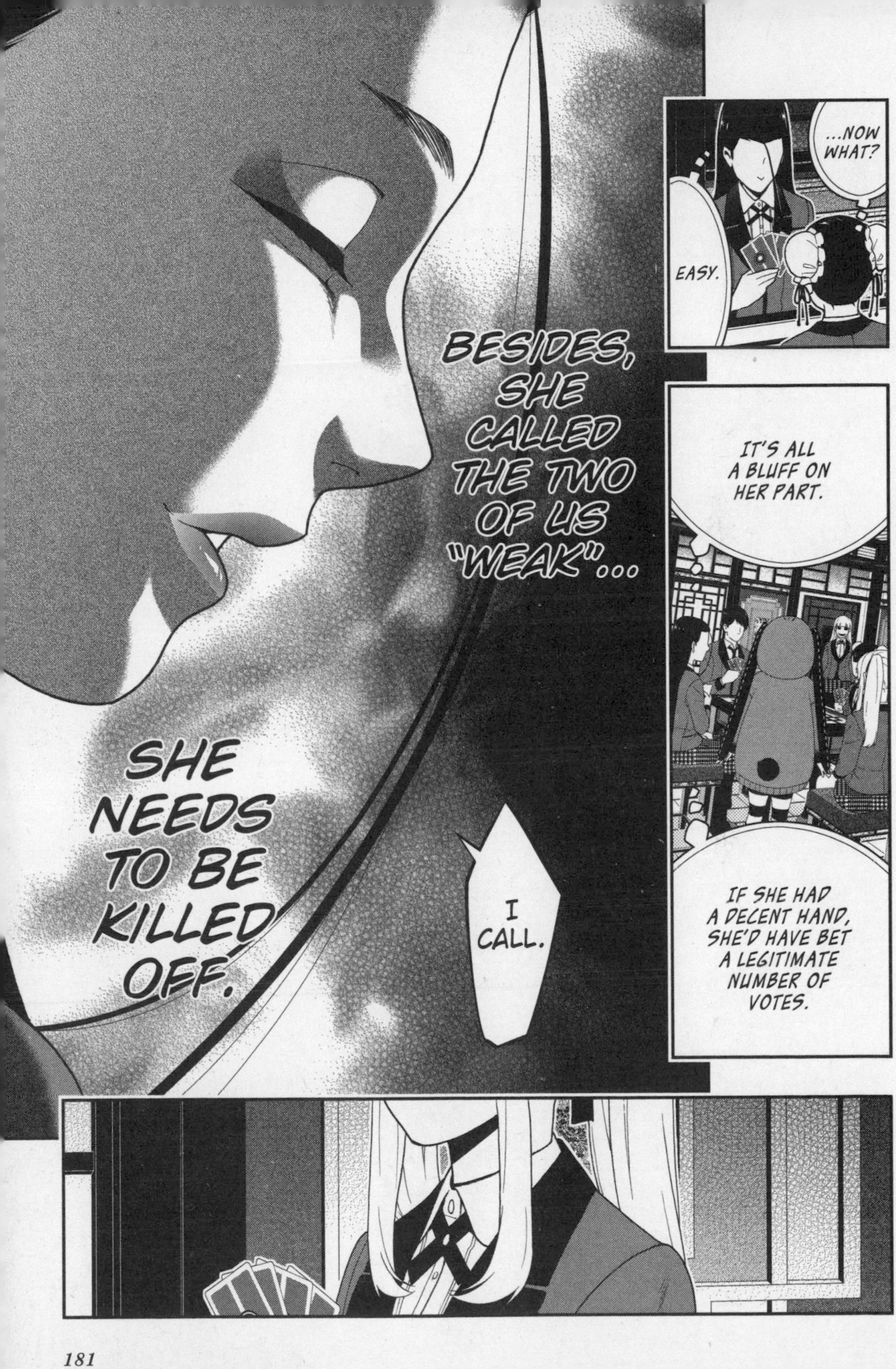
...NOW WHAT?
EASY.
IT'S ALL A BLUFF ON HER PART.
IF SHE HAD A DECENT HAND, SHE'D HAVE BET A LEGITIMATE NUMBER OF VOTES.
BESIDES, SHE CALLED THE TWO OF US "WEAK"...
I CALL.
SHE NEEDS TO BE KILLED OFF.

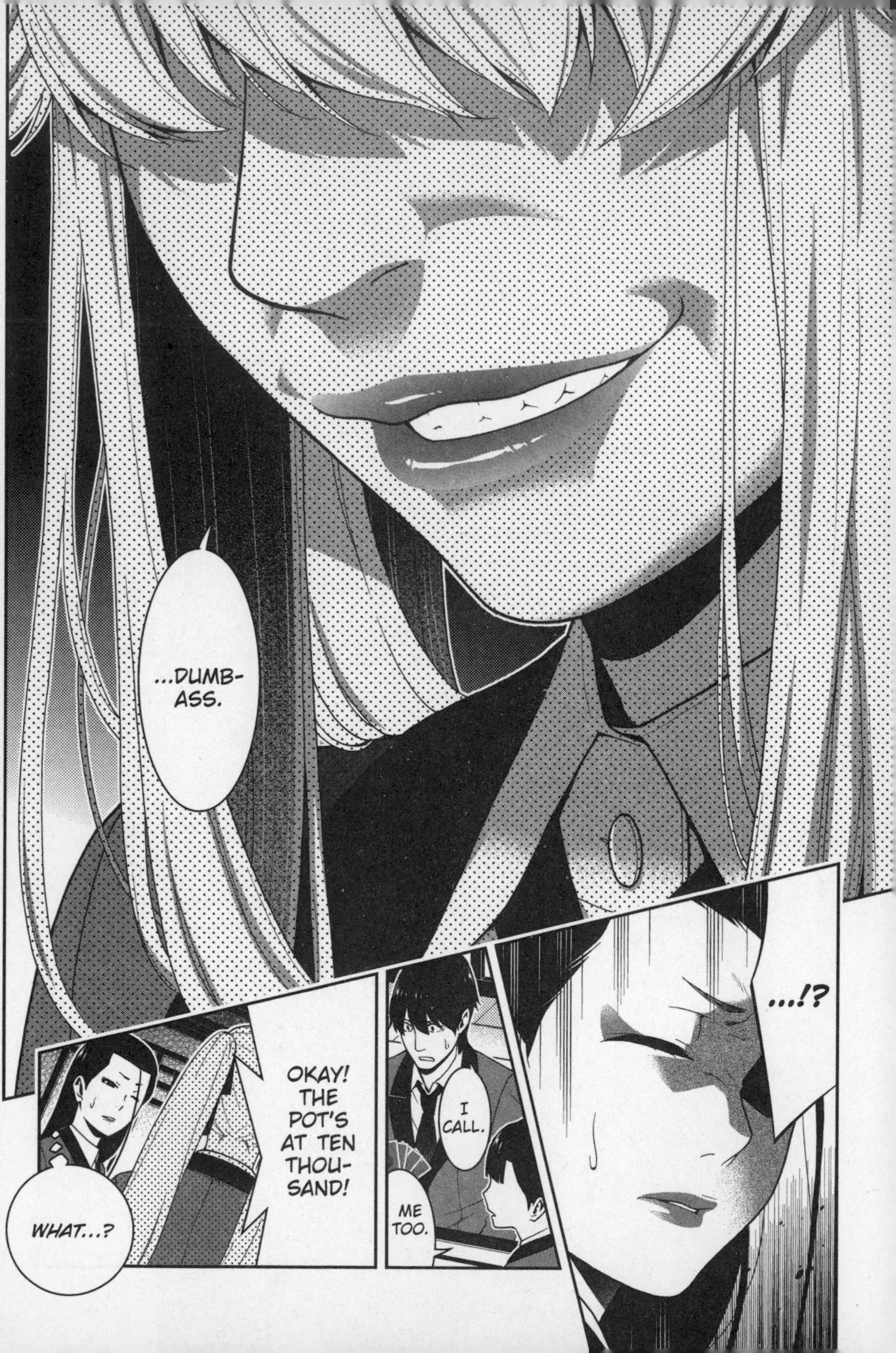
...DUMB-ASS.
...!?
I CALL.
ME TOO.
OKAY! THE POT'S AT TEN THOUSAND!
WHAT...?

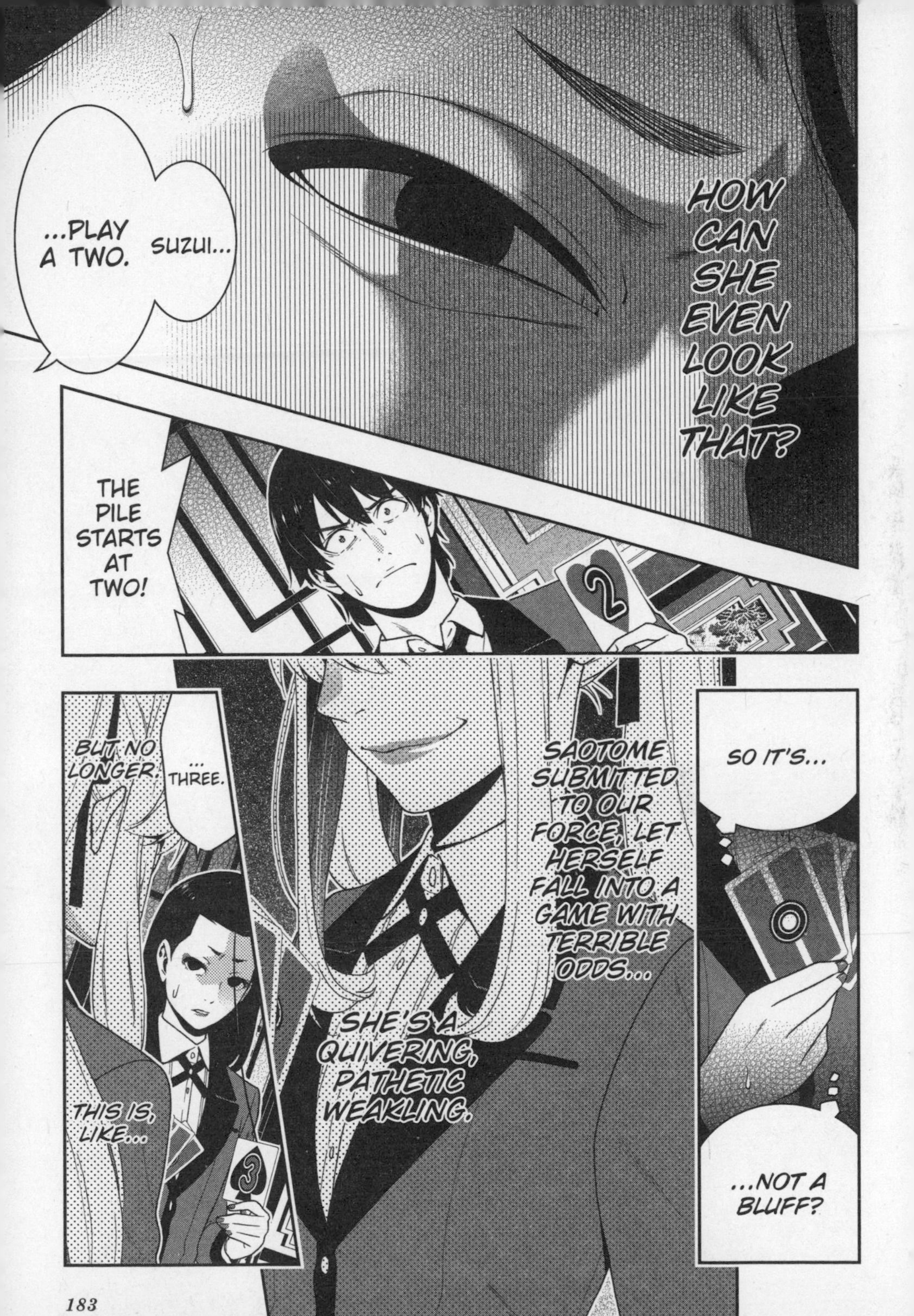
HOW CAN SHE EVEN LOOK LIKE THAT?
SUZUI...
...PLAY A TWO.
THE PILE STARTS AT TWO!
SO IT'S...
...NOT A BLUFF?
SAOTOME SUBMITTED TO OUR FORCE, LET HERSELF FALL INTO A GAME WITH TERRIBLE ODDS...
SHE'S A QUIVERING, PATHETIC WEAKLING.
... THREE.
BUT NO LONGER.
THIS IS, LIKE...

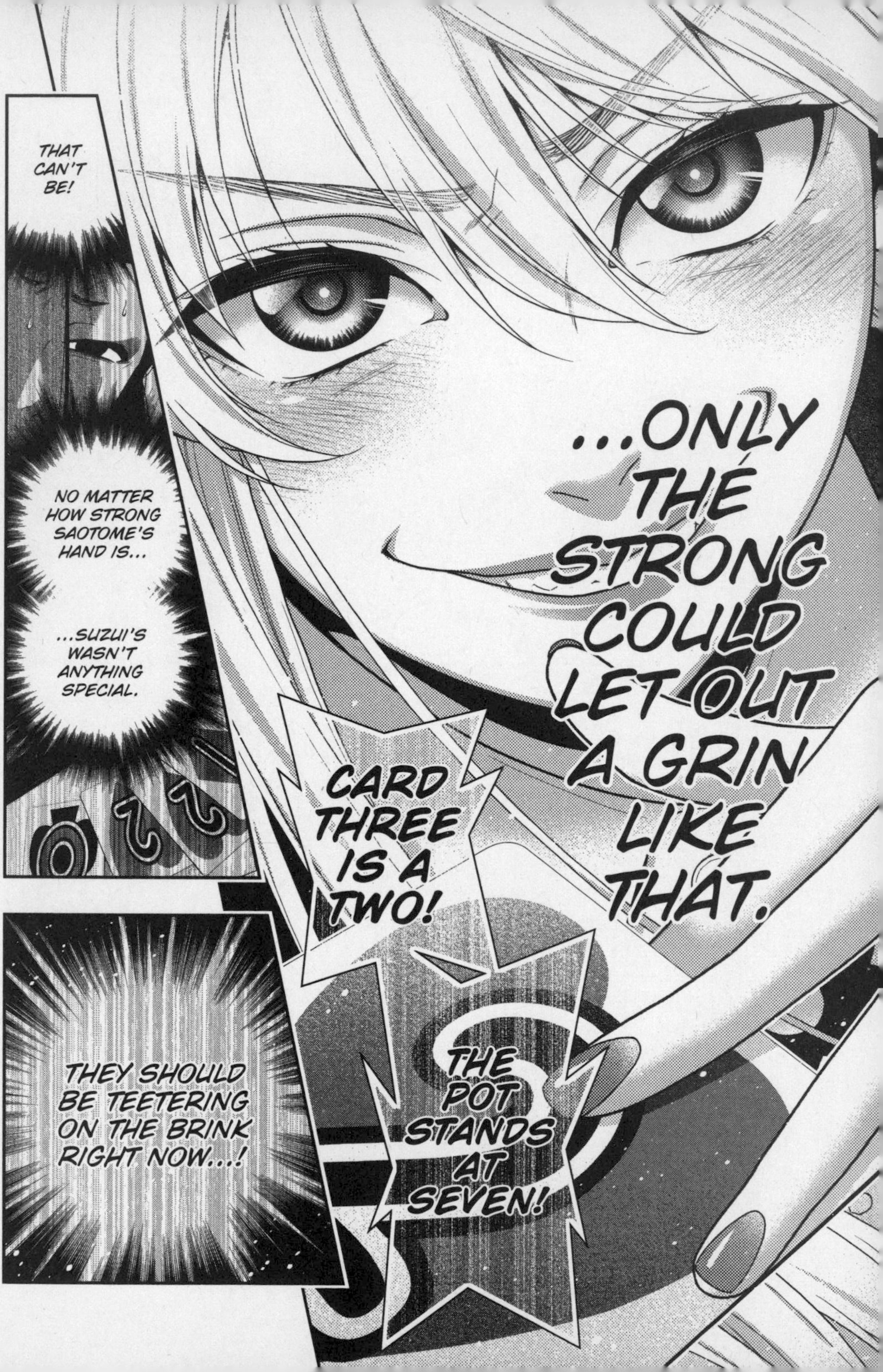
...ONLY THE STRONG COULD LET OUT A GRIN LIKE THAT.
CARD THREE IS A TWO!
THE POT STANDS AT SEVEN!
THAT CAN'T BE!
NO MATTER HOW STRONG SAOTOME'S HAND IS...
...SUZUI'S WASN'T ANYTHING SPECIAL.
THEY SHOULD BE TEETERING ON THE BRINK RIGHT NOW...!

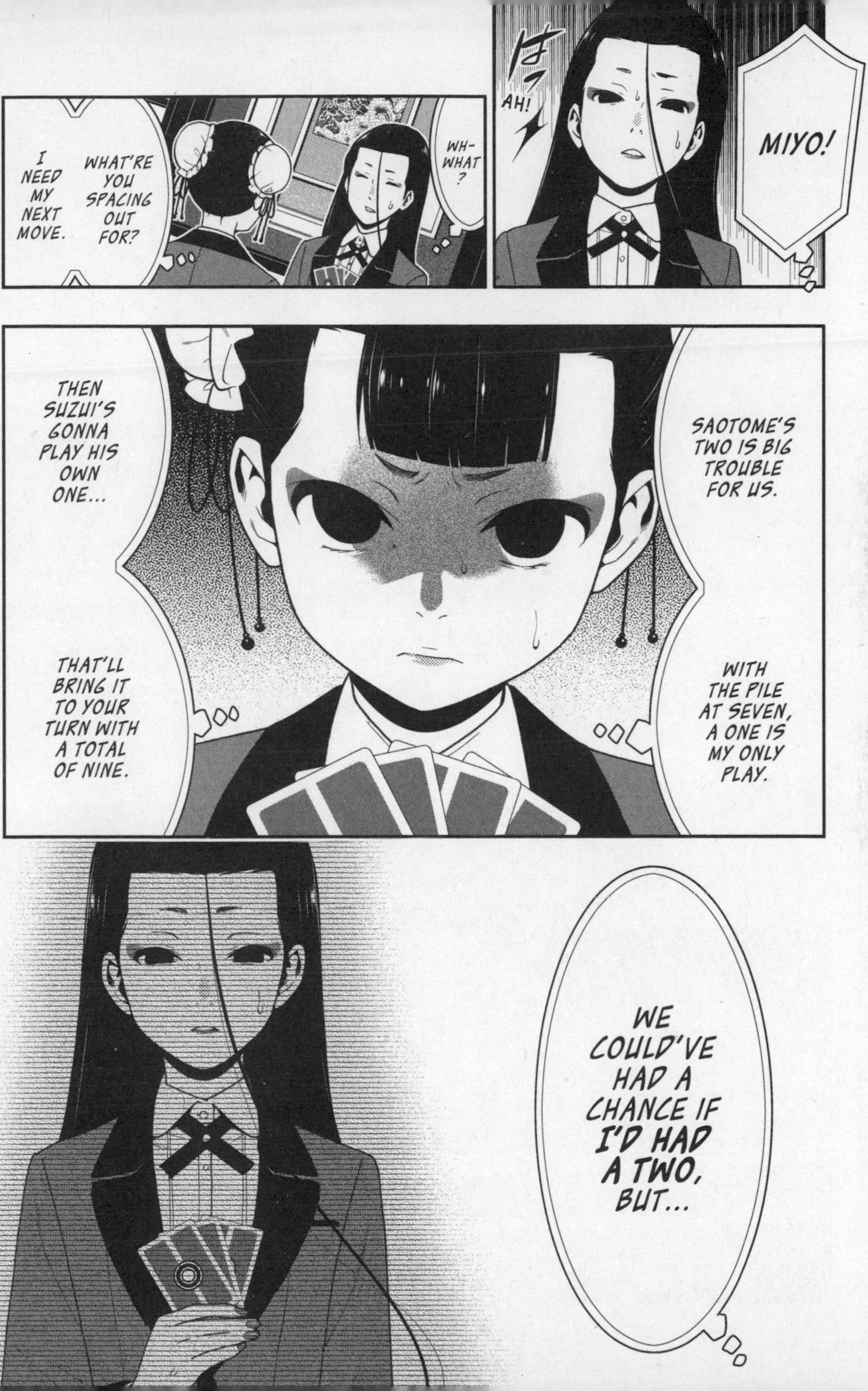
AH!
MIYO!
WH-WHAT?
WHAT'RE YOU SPACING OUT FOR?
I NEED MY NEXT MOVE.
SAOTOME'S TWO IS BIG TROUBLE FOR US.
WITH THE PILE AT SEVEN, A ONE IS MY ONLY PLAY.
THEN SUZUI'S GONNA PLAY HIS OWN ONE...
THAT'LL BRING IT TO YOUR TURN WITH A TOTAL OF NINE.
WE COULD'VE HAD A CHANCE IF I'D HAD A TWO, BUT...

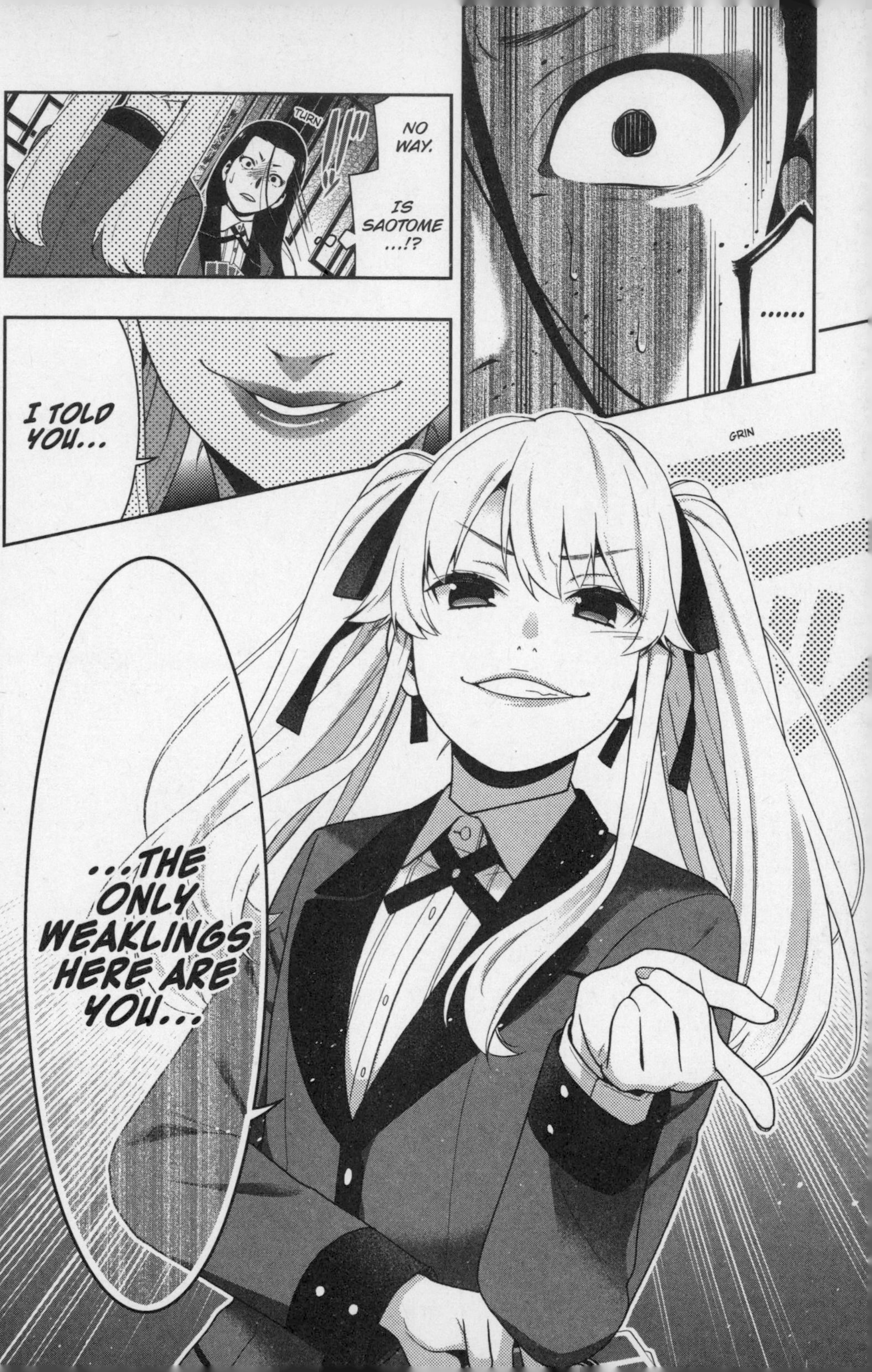
......
TURN
NO WAY.
IS SAOTOME ...!?
I TOLD YOU...
GRIN
...THE ONLY WEAKLINGS HERE ARE YOU...

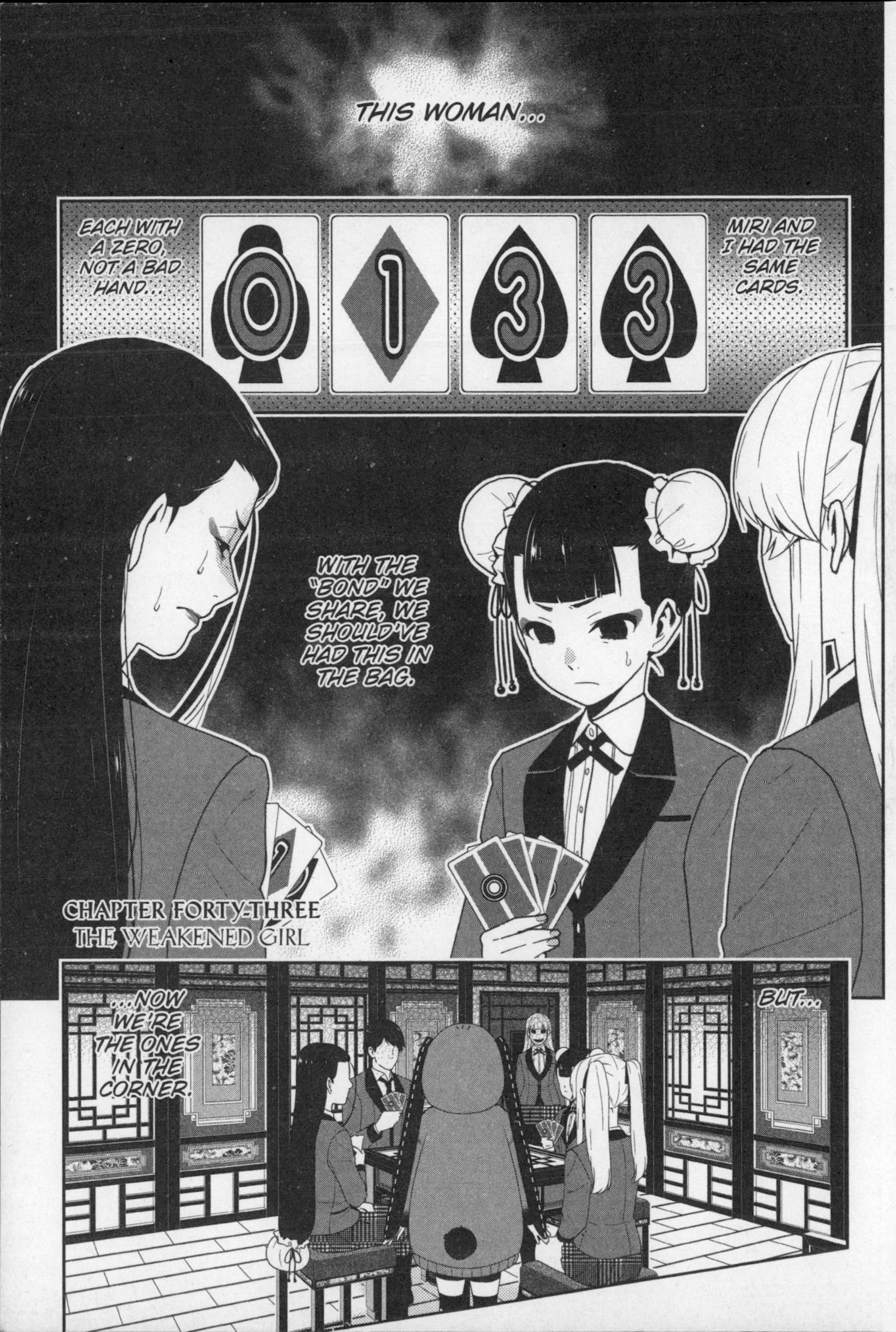
THIS WOMAN...
MIRI AND I HAD THE SAME CARDS.
0
1
3
3
EACH WITH A ZERO, NOT A BAD HAND...
WITH THE "BOND" WE SHARE, WE SHOULD'VE HAD THIS IN THE BAG.
CHAPTER FORTY-THREE
THE WEAKENED GIRL
BUT...
...NOW WE'RE THE ONES IN THE CORNER.

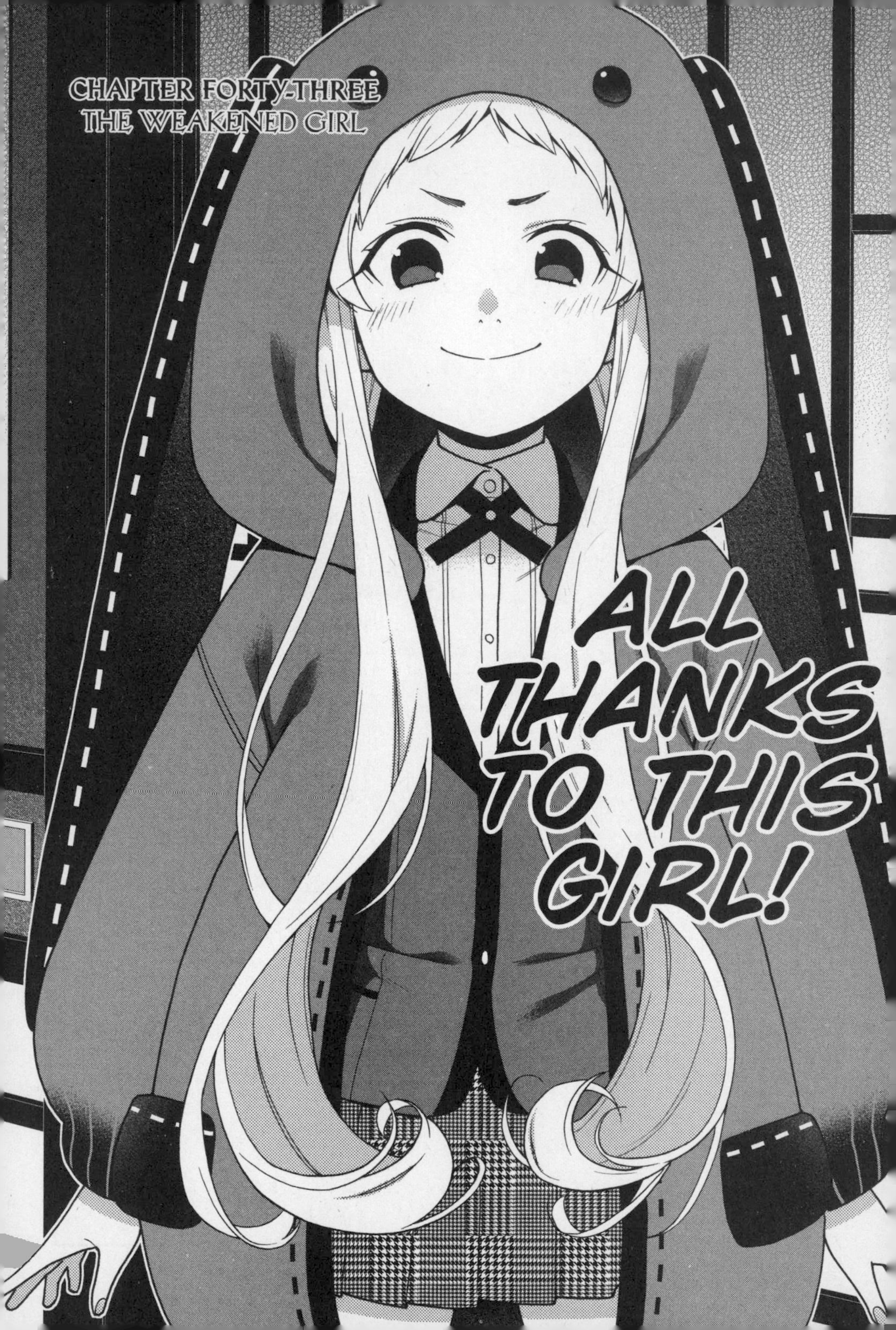
CHAPTER FORTY-THREE
THE WEAKENED GIRL
ALL THANKS TO THIS GIRL!

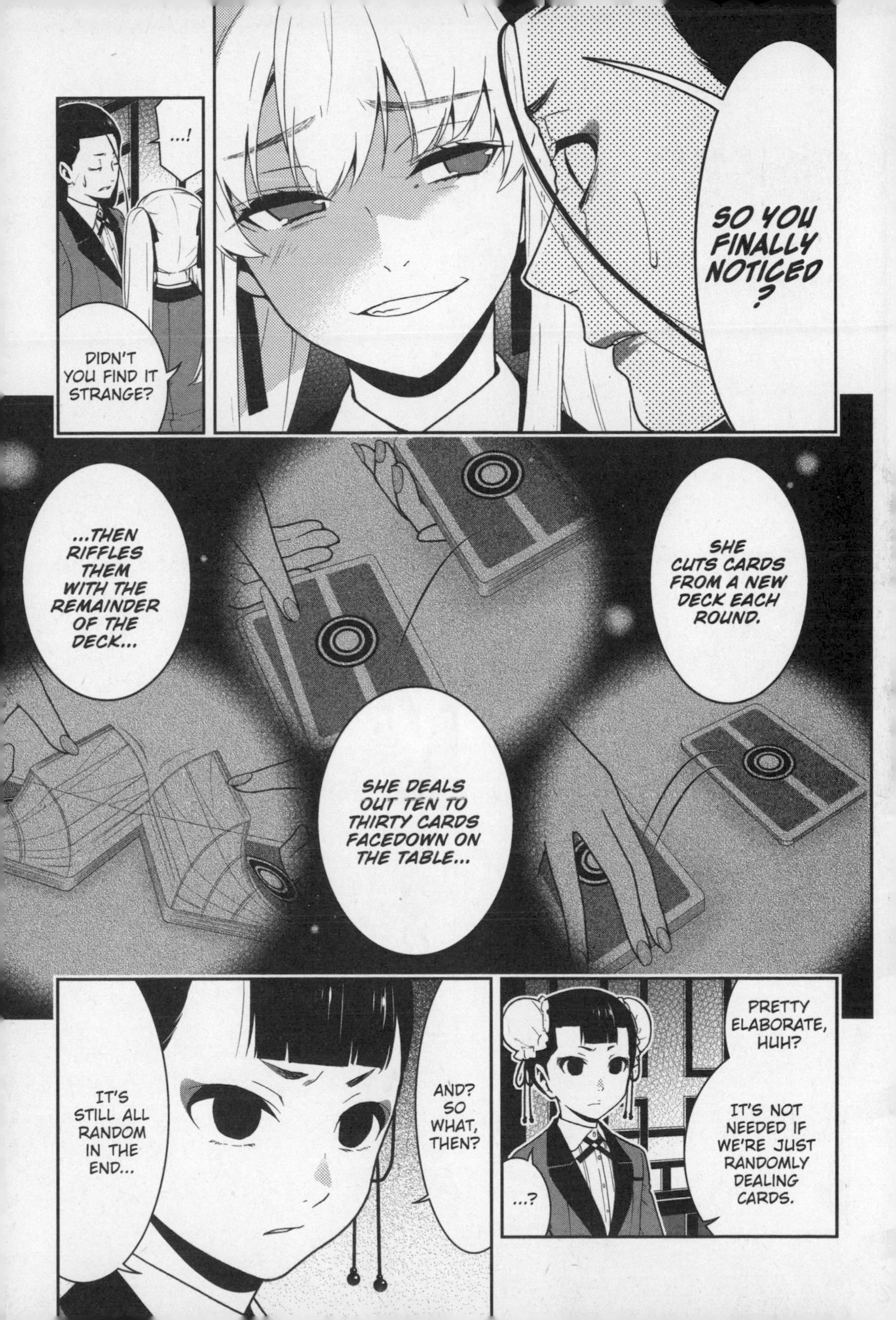
SO YOU FINALLY NOTICED?
...!
DIDN'T YOU FIND IT STRANGE?
SHE CUTS CARDS FROM A NEW DECK EACH ROUND.
...THEN RIFFLES THEM WITH THE REMAINDER OF THE DECK...
SHE DEALS OUT TEN TO THIRTY CARDS FACEDOWN ON THE TABLE...
PRETTY ELABORATE, HUH?
IT'S NOT NEEDED IF WE'RE JUST RANDOMLY DEALING CARDS.
...?
AND? SO WHAT, THEN?
IT'S STILL ALL RANDOM IN THE END...

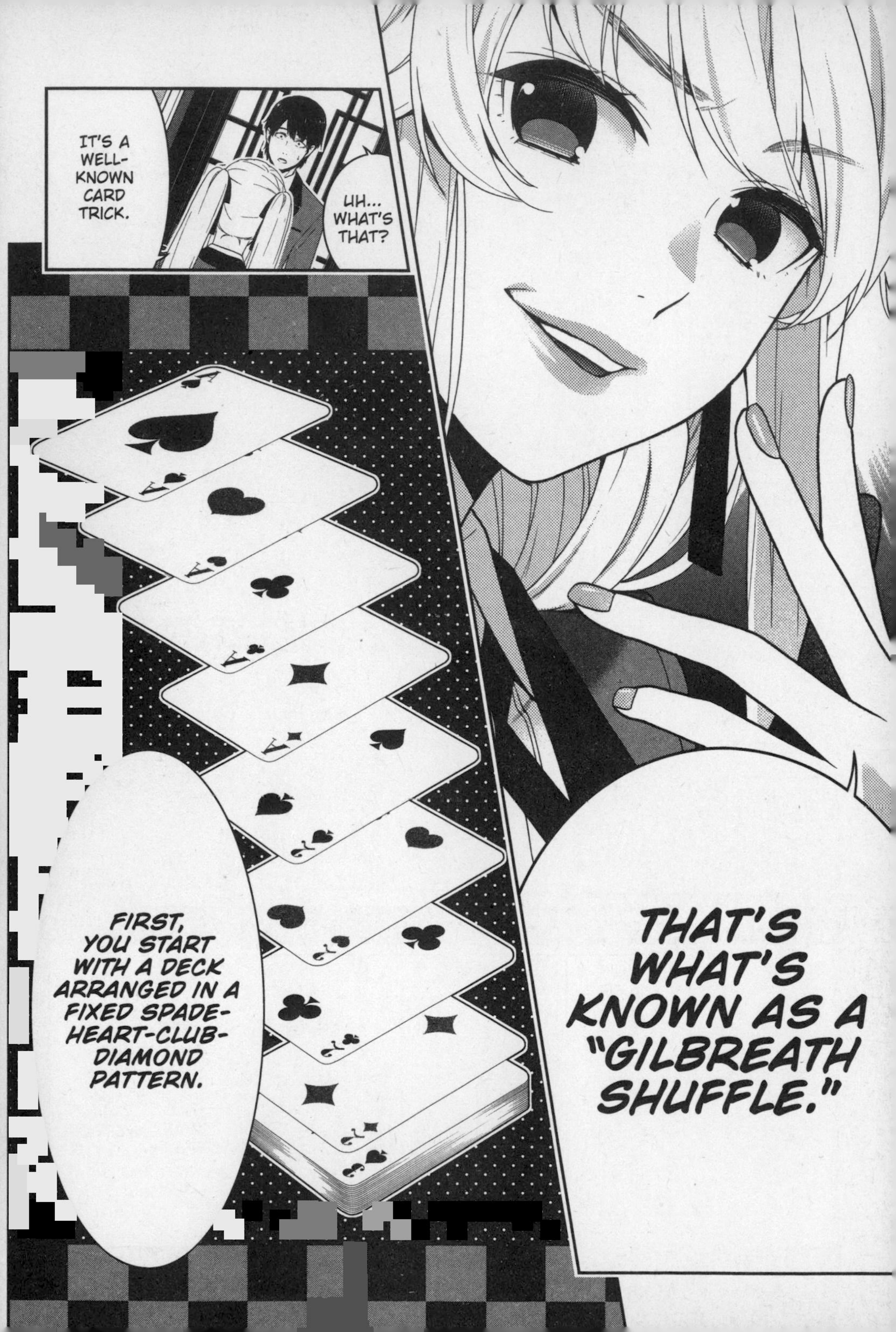
THAT'S WHAT'S KNOWN AS A "GILBREATH SHUFFLE."
UH... WHAT'S THAT?
IT'S A WELL-KNOWN CARD TRICK.
FIRST, YOU START WITH A DECK ARRANGED IN A FIXED SPADE-HEART-CLUB-DIAMOND PATTERN.

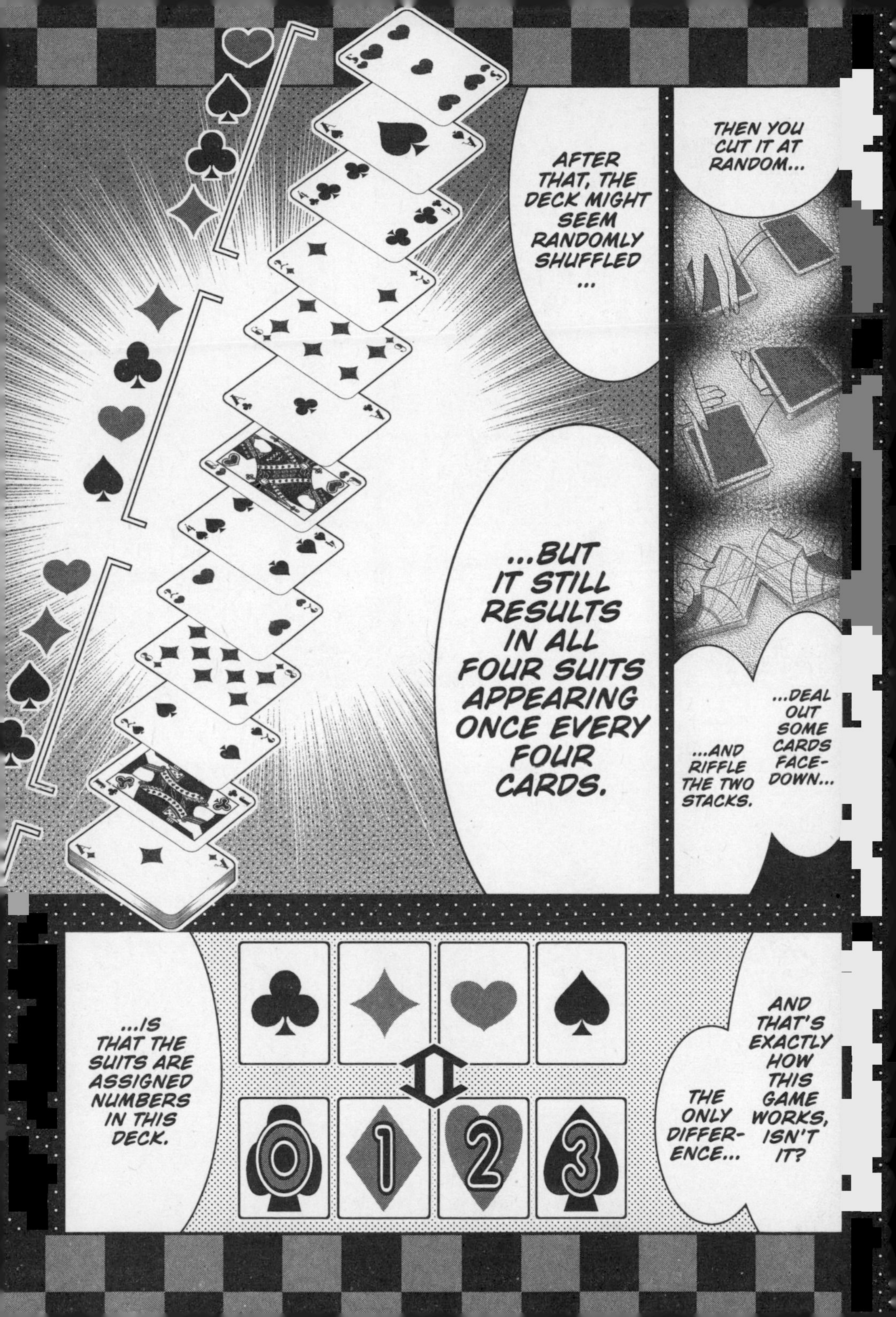

THEN YOU CUT IT AT RANDOM...
...DEAL OUT SOME CARDS FACE-DOWN...
...AND RIFFLE THE TWO STACKS.
AFTER THAT, THE DECK MIGHT SEEM RANDOMLY SHUFFLED...
...BUT IT STILL RESULTS IN ALL FOUR SUITS APPEARING ONCE EVERY FOUR CARDS.
AND THAT'S EXACTLY HOW THIS GAME WORKS, ISN'T IT?
THE ONLY DIFFERENCE...
...IS THAT THE SUITS ARE ASSIGNED NUMBERS IN THIS DECK.
0 1 2 3

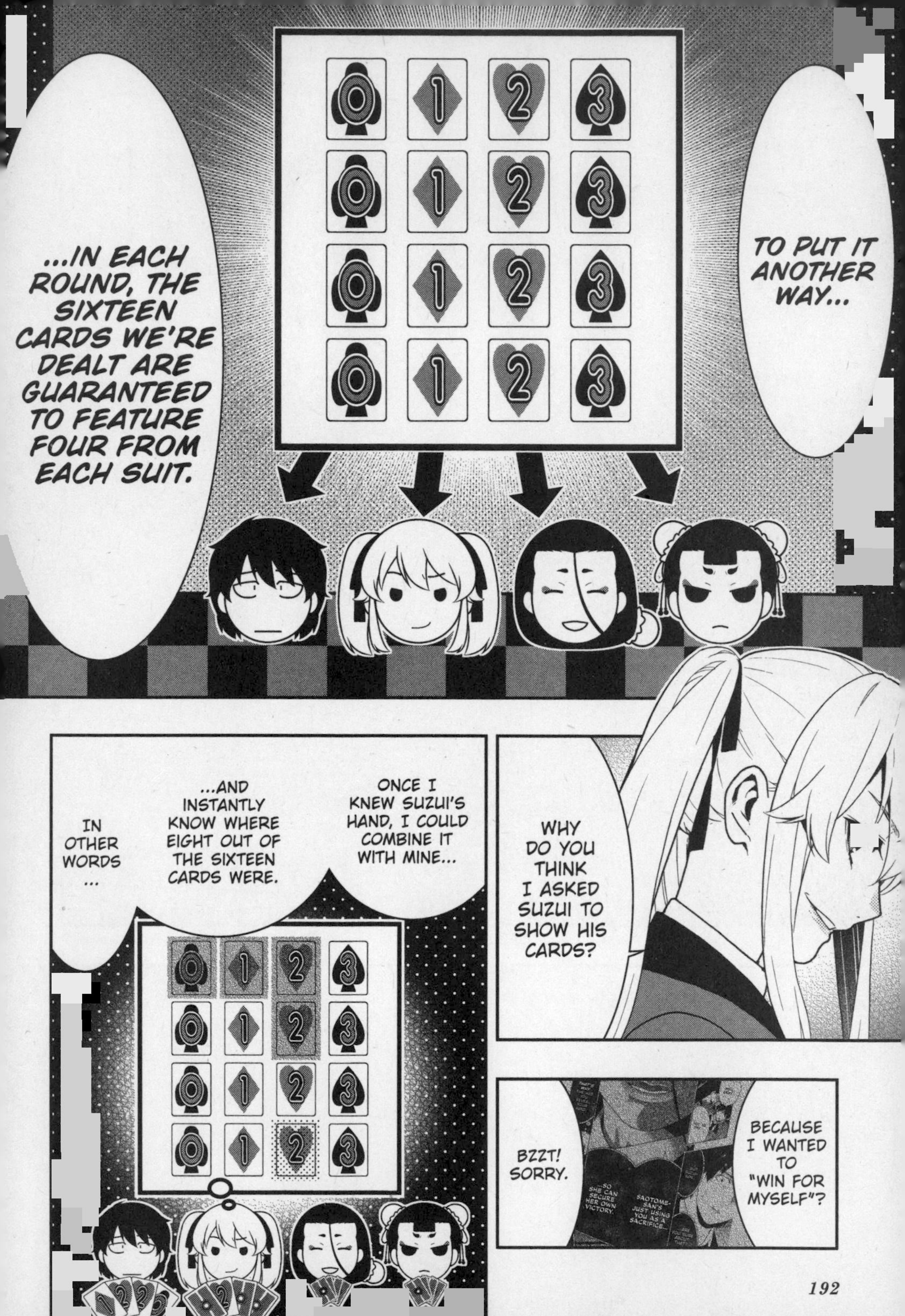
TO PUT IT ANOTHER WAY...
...IN EACH ROUND, THE SIXTEEN CARDS WE'RE DEALT ARE GUARANTEED TO FEATURE FOUR FROM EACH SUIT.
WHY DO YOU THINK I ASKED SUZUI TO SHOW HIS CARDS?
BECAUSE I WANTED TO "WIN FOR MYSELF"?
BZZT! SORRY.
SAOTOME-SAN'S JUST USING YOU AS A SACRIFICE...
...SO SHE CAN SECURE HER OWN VICTORY.
ONCE I KNEW SUZUI'S HAND, I COULD COMBINE IT WITH MINE...
...AND INSTANTLY KNOW WHERE EIGHT OUT OF THE SIXTEEN CARDS WERE.
IN OTHER WORDS ...

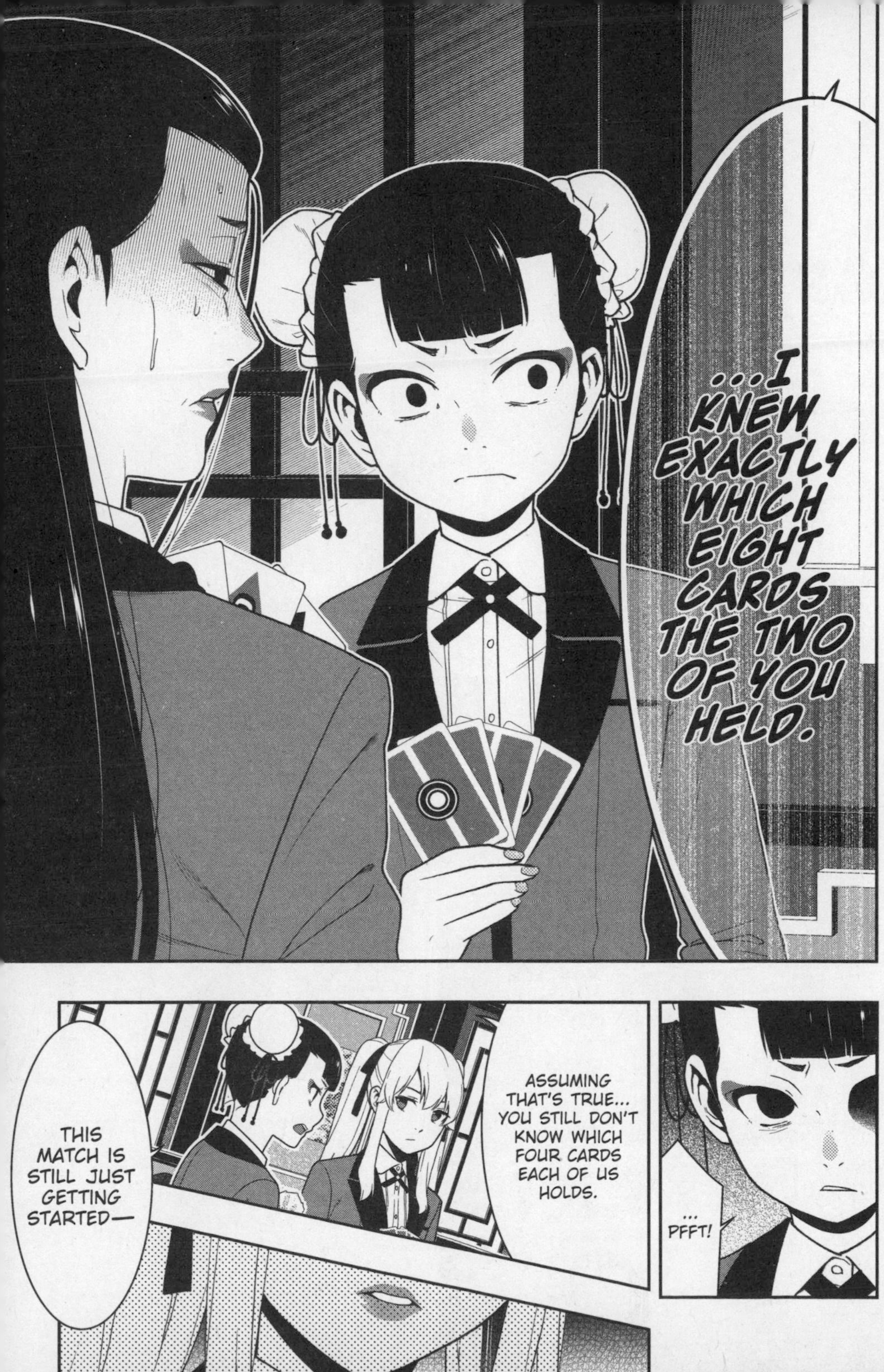
...I KNEW EXACTLY WHICH EIGHT CARDS THE TWO OF YOU HELD.
... PFFT!
ASSUMING THAT'S TRUE... YOU STILL DON'T KNOW WHICH FOUR CARDS EACH OF US HOLDS.
THIS MATCH IS STILL JUST GETTING STARTED—

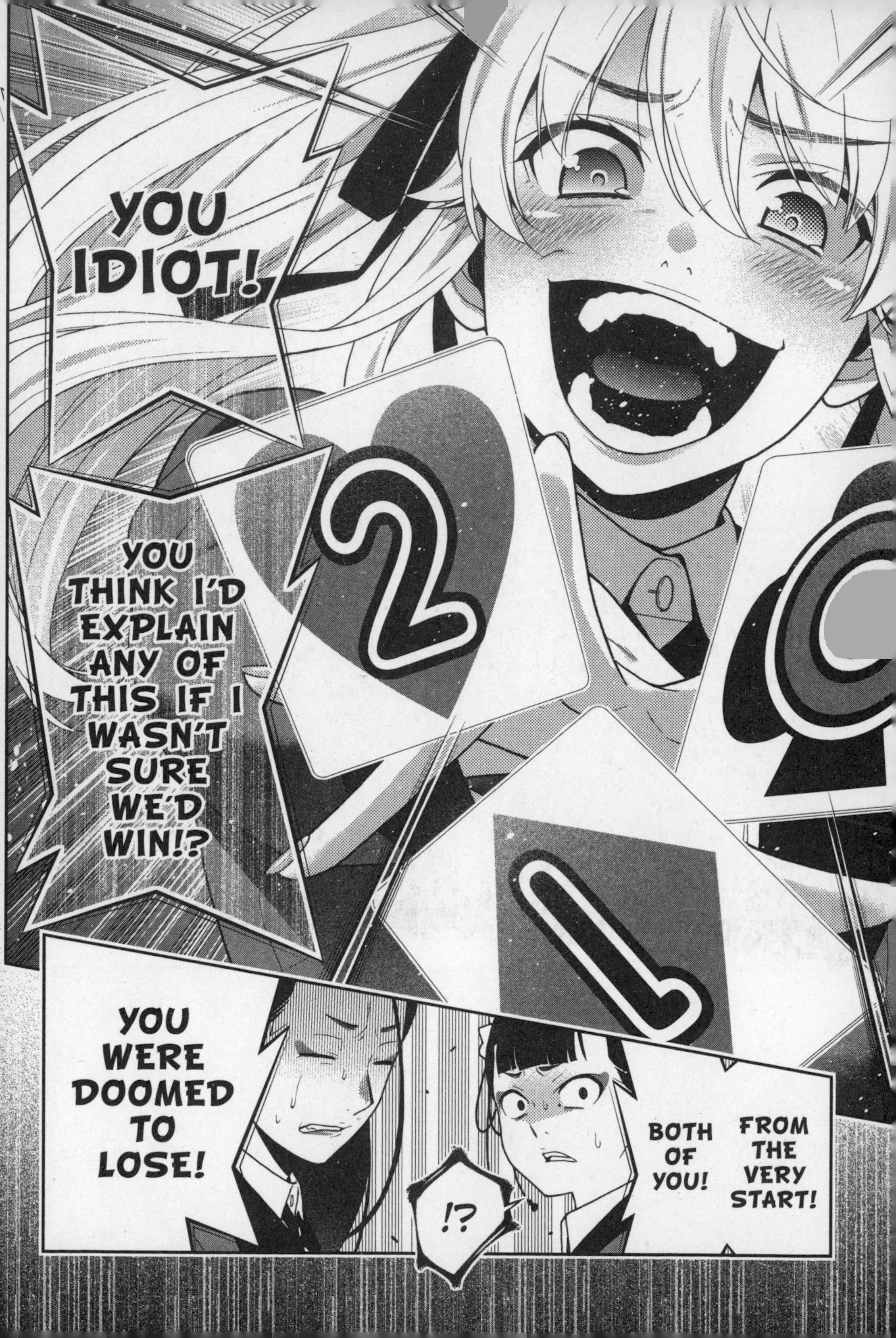
YOU IDIOT!
YOU THINK I'D EXPLAIN ANY OF THIS IF I WASN'T SURE WE'D WIN!?
FROM THE VERY START!
BOTH OF YOU!
!?
YOU WERE DOOMED TO LOSE!

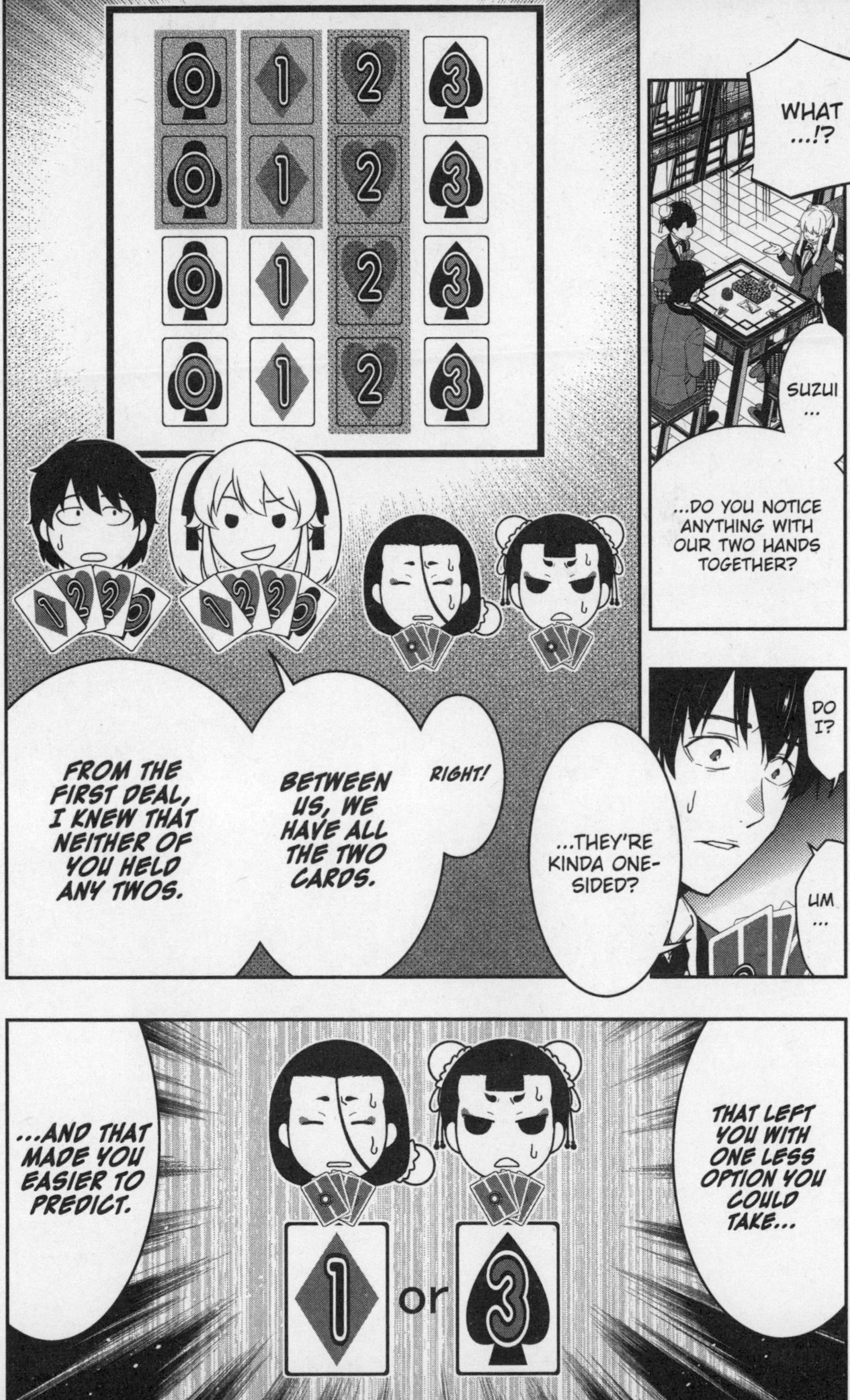
WHAT ...!?
SUZUI ...
...DO YOU NOTICE ANYTHING WITH OUR TWO HANDS TOGETHER?
DO I?
UM ...
...THEY'RE KINDA ONE-SIDED?
RIGHT!
BETWEEN US, WE HAVE ALL THE TWO CARDS.
FROM THE FIRST DEAL, I KNEW THAT NEITHER OF YOU HELD ANY TWOS.
THAT LEFT YOU WITH ONE LESS OPTION YOU COULD TAKE...
1 or 3
...AND THAT MADE YOU EASIER TO PREDICT.

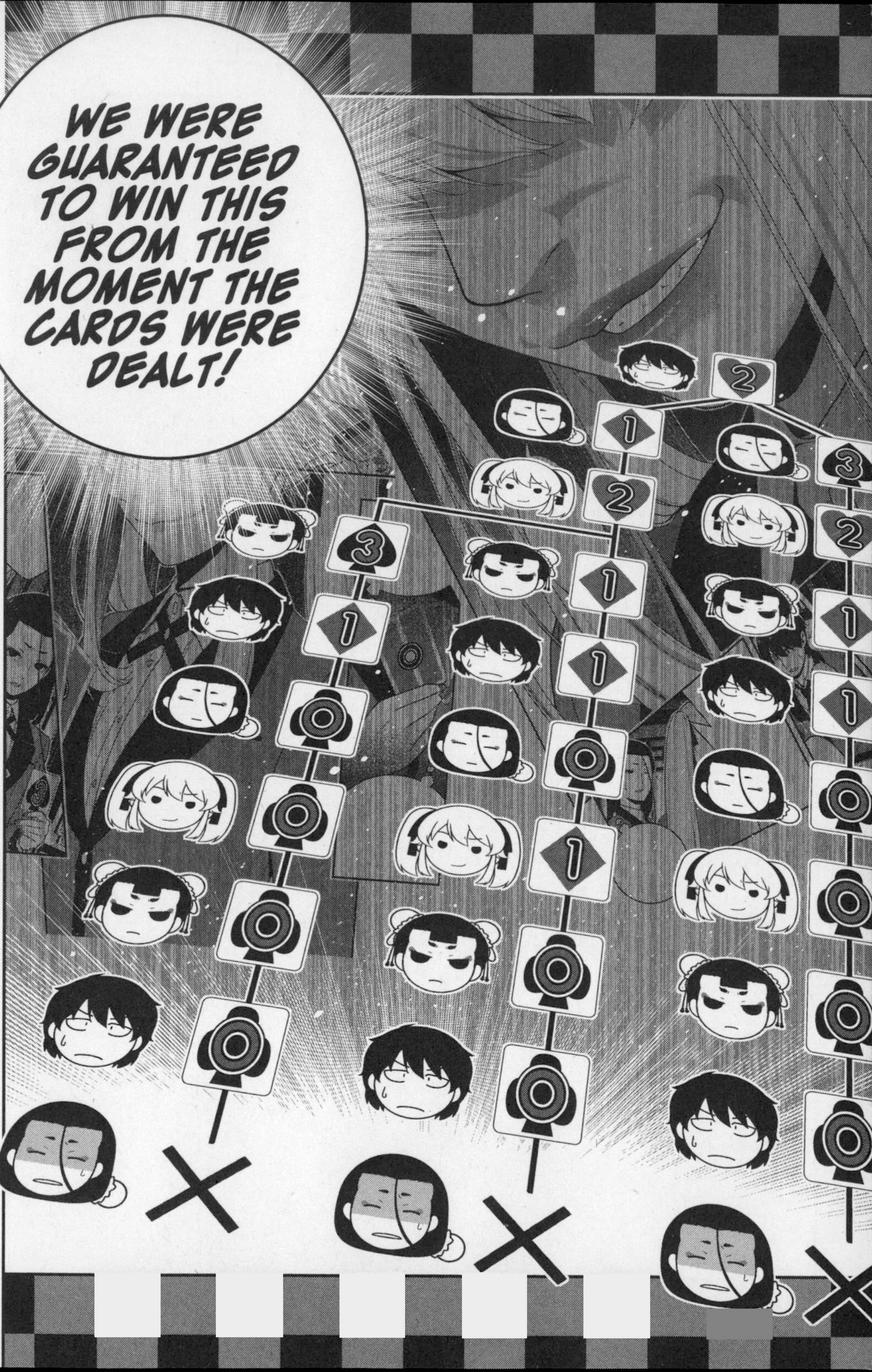
WE WERE GUARANTEED TO WIN THIS FROM THE MOMENT THE CARDS WERE DEALT!

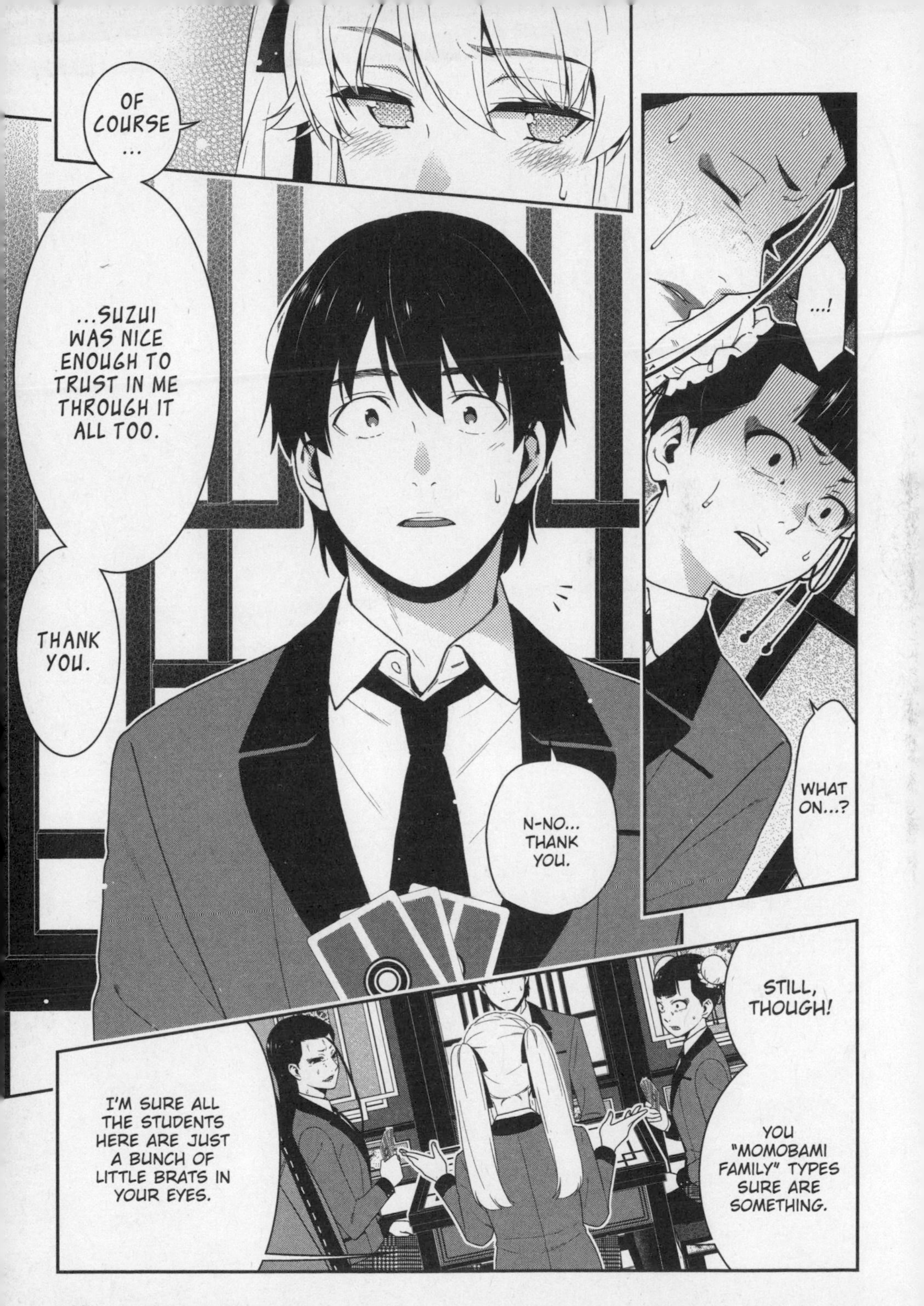
OF COURSE ...
...SUZUI WAS NICE ENOUGH TO TRUST IN ME THROUGH IT ALL TOO.
THANK YOU.
...!
WHAT ON...?
N-NO... THANK YOU.
STILL, THOUGH!
YOU "MOMOBAMI FAMILY" TYPES SURE ARE SOMETHING.
I'M SURE ALL THE STUDENTS HERE ARE JUST A BUNCH OF LITTLE BRATS IN YOUR EYES.

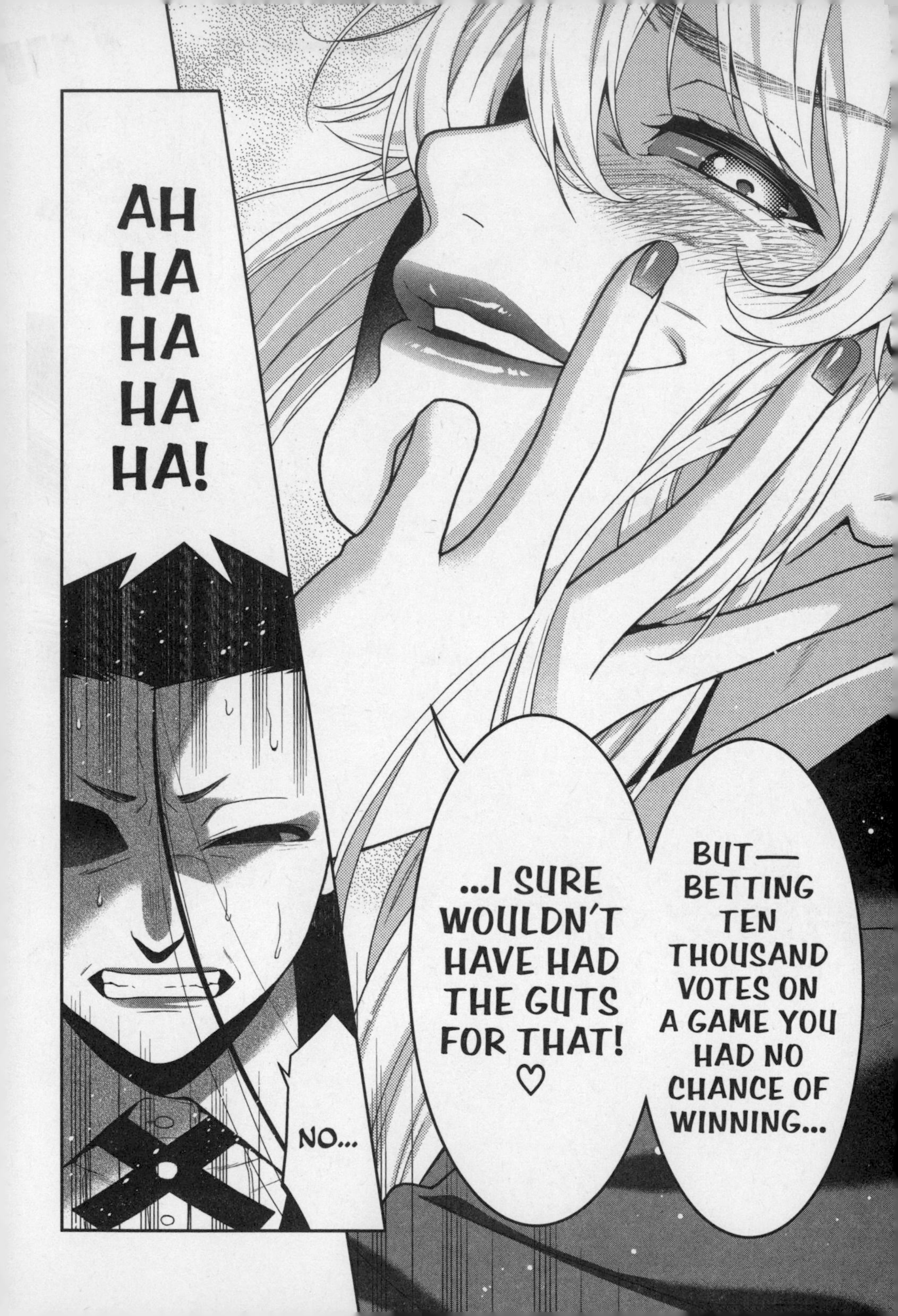
BUT— BETTING TEN THOUSAND VOTES ON A GAME YOU HAD NO CHANCE OF WINNING...
...I SURE WOULDN'T HAVE HAD THE GUTS FOR THAT! ♡
AH HA HA HA HA HA!
NO...

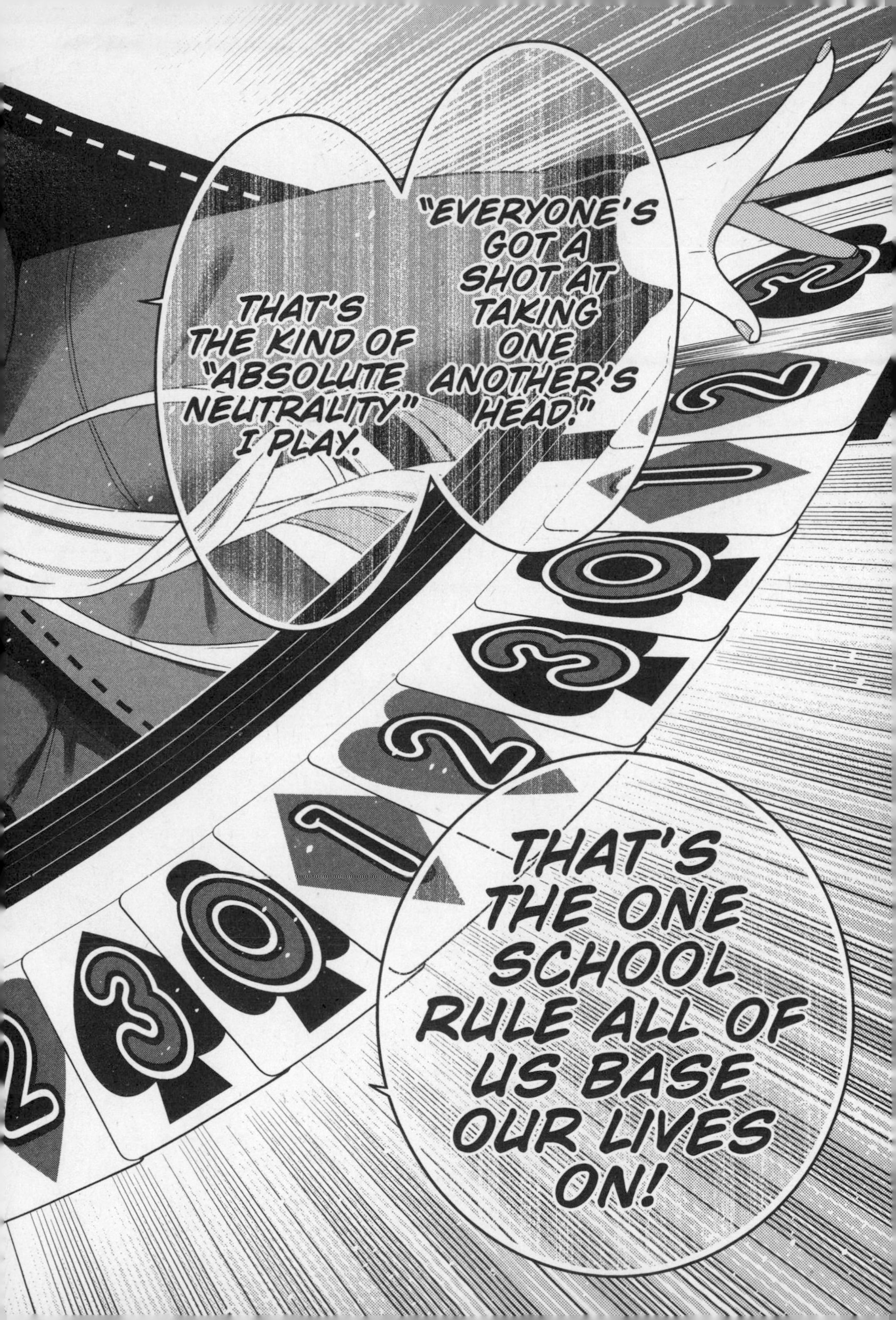
"EVERYONE'S GOT A SHOT AT TAKING ONE ANOTHER'S HEAD."
THAT'S THE KIND OF "ABSOLUTE NEUTRALITY" I PLAY.
THAT'S THE ONE SCHOOL RULE ALL OF US BASE OUR LIVES ON!

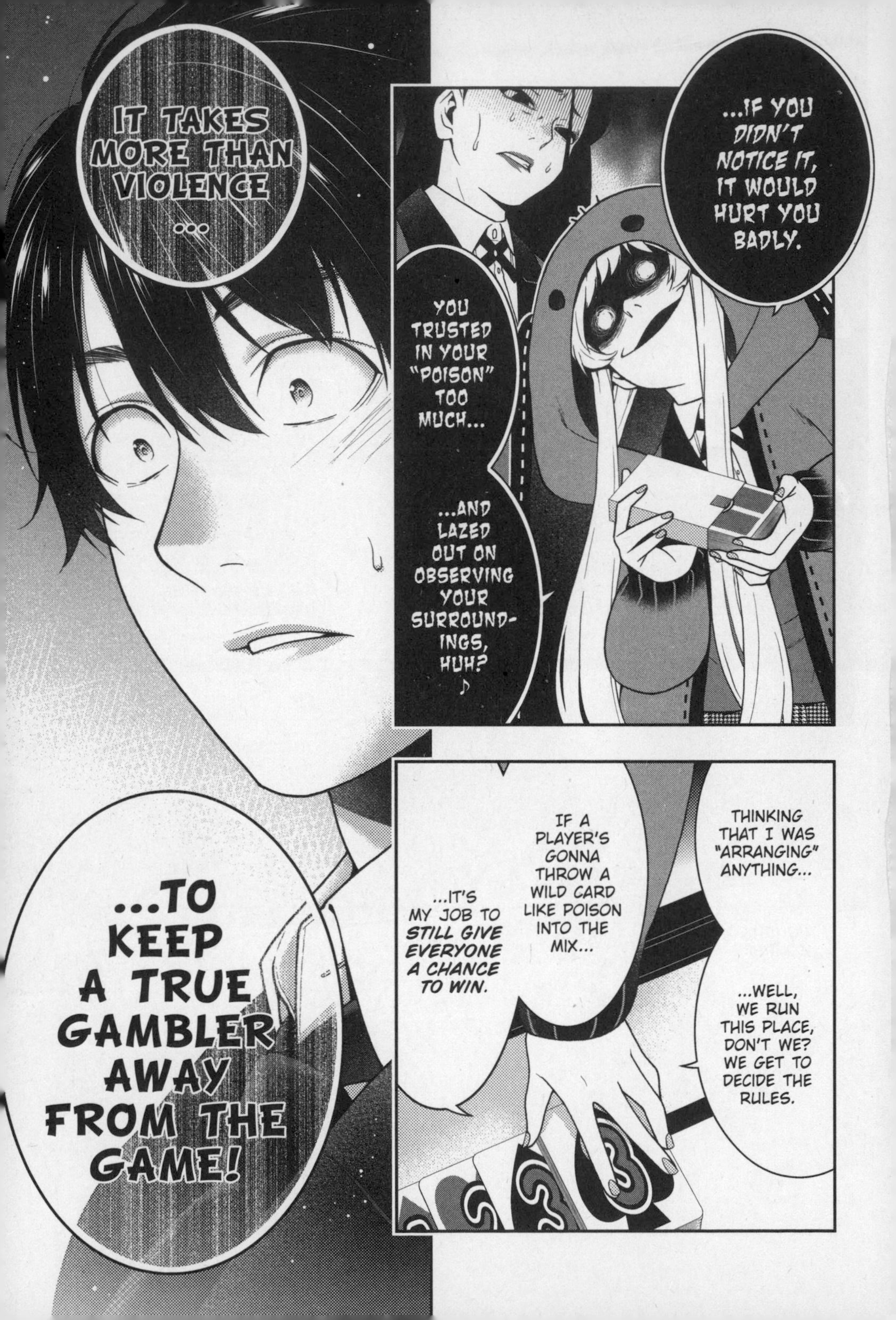
...IF YOU DIDN'T NOTICE IT, IT WOULD HURT YOU BADLY.
YOU TRUSTED IN YOUR "POISON" TOO MUCH...
...AND LAZED OUT ON OBSERVING YOUR SURROUND-INGS, HUH? ♪
THINKING THAT I WAS "ARRANGING" ANYTHING...
...WELL, WE RUN THIS PLACE, DON'T WE? WE GET TO DECIDE THE RULES.
IF A PLAYER'S GONNA THROW A WILD CARD LIKE POISON INTO THE MIX...
...IT'S MY JOB TO *STILL GIVE EVERYONE A CHANCE TO WIN.*
IT TAKES MORE THAN VIOLENCE ...
...TO KEEP A TRUE GAMBLER AWAY FROM THE GAME!

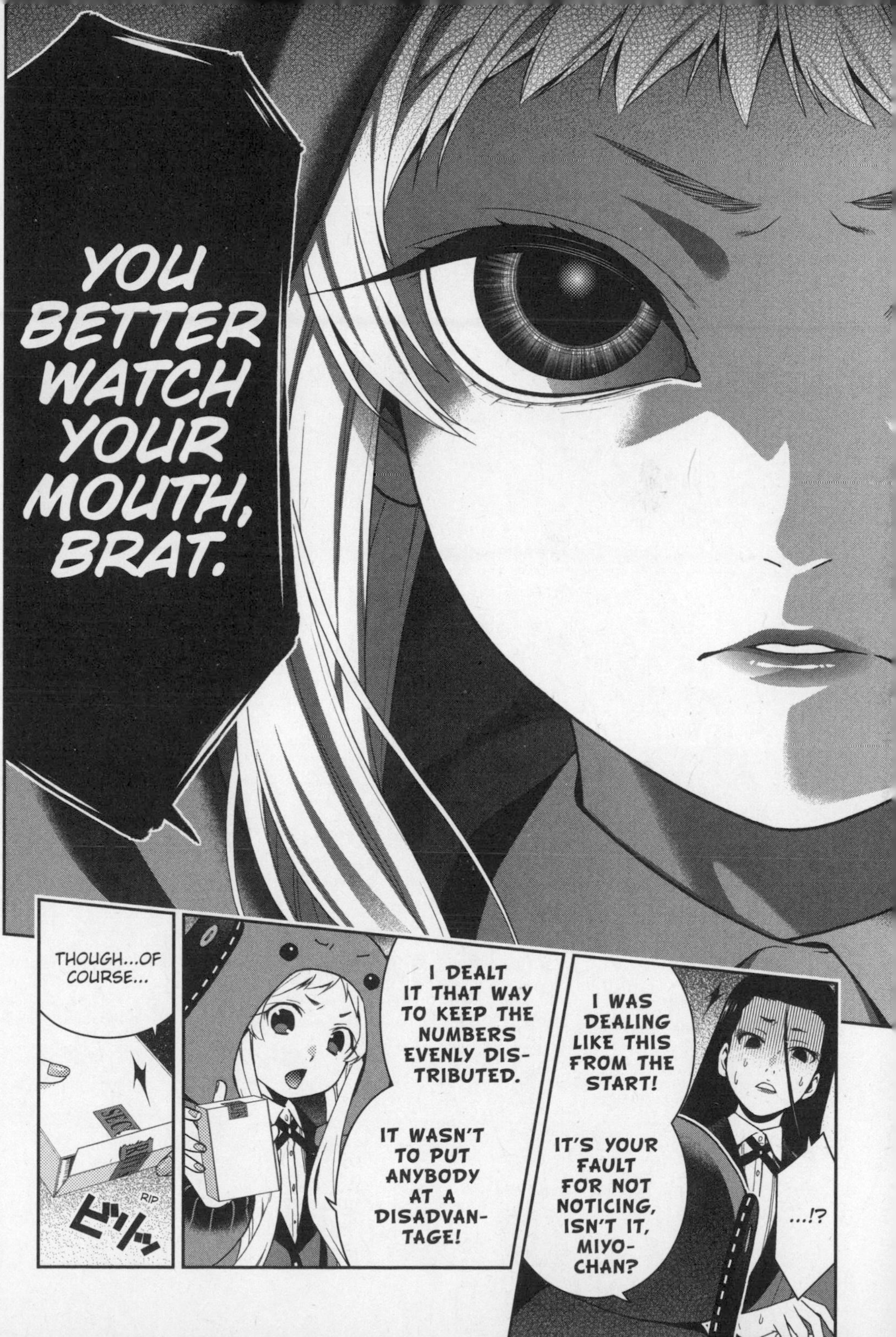
YOU BETTER WATCH YOUR MOUTH, BRAT.
I WAS DEALING LIKE THIS FROM THE START!
IT'S YOUR FAULT FOR NOT NOTICING, ISN'T IT, MIYO-CHAN?
...!?
I DEALT IT THAT WAY TO KEEP THE NUMBERS EVENLY DIS-TRIBUTED.
IT WASN'T TO PUT ANYBODY AT A DISADVAN-TAGE!
THOUGH...OF COURSE...
RIP
ビッッ

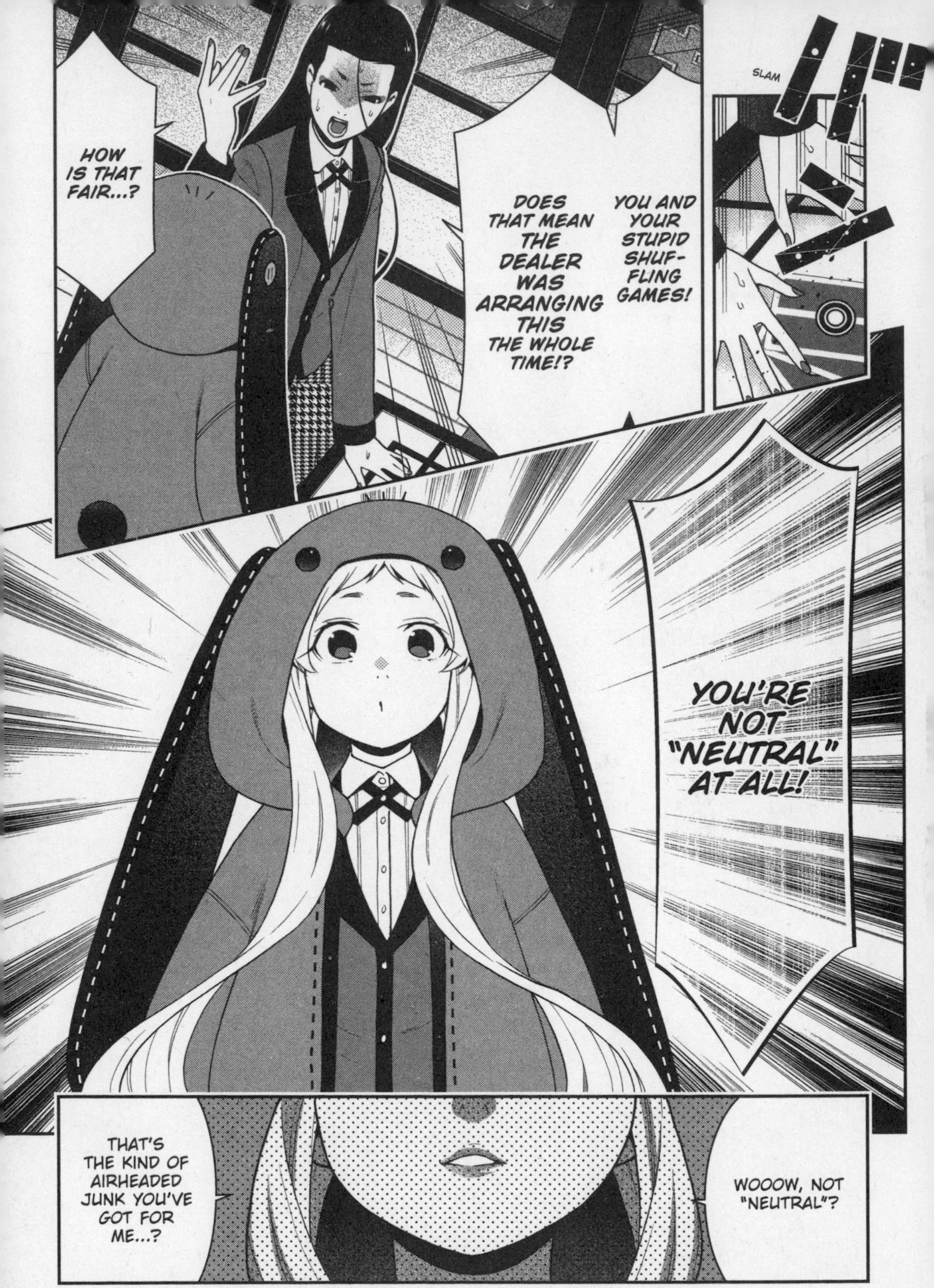
SLAM
YOU AND YOUR STUPID SHUF-FLING GAMES!
DOES THAT MEAN THE DEALER WAS ARRANGING THIS THE WHOLE TIME!?
HOW IS THAT FAIR...?
YOU'RE NOT "NEUTRAL" AT ALL!
WOOOW, NOT "NEUTRAL"?
THAT'S THE KIND OF AIRHEADED JUNK YOU'VE GOT FOR ME...?

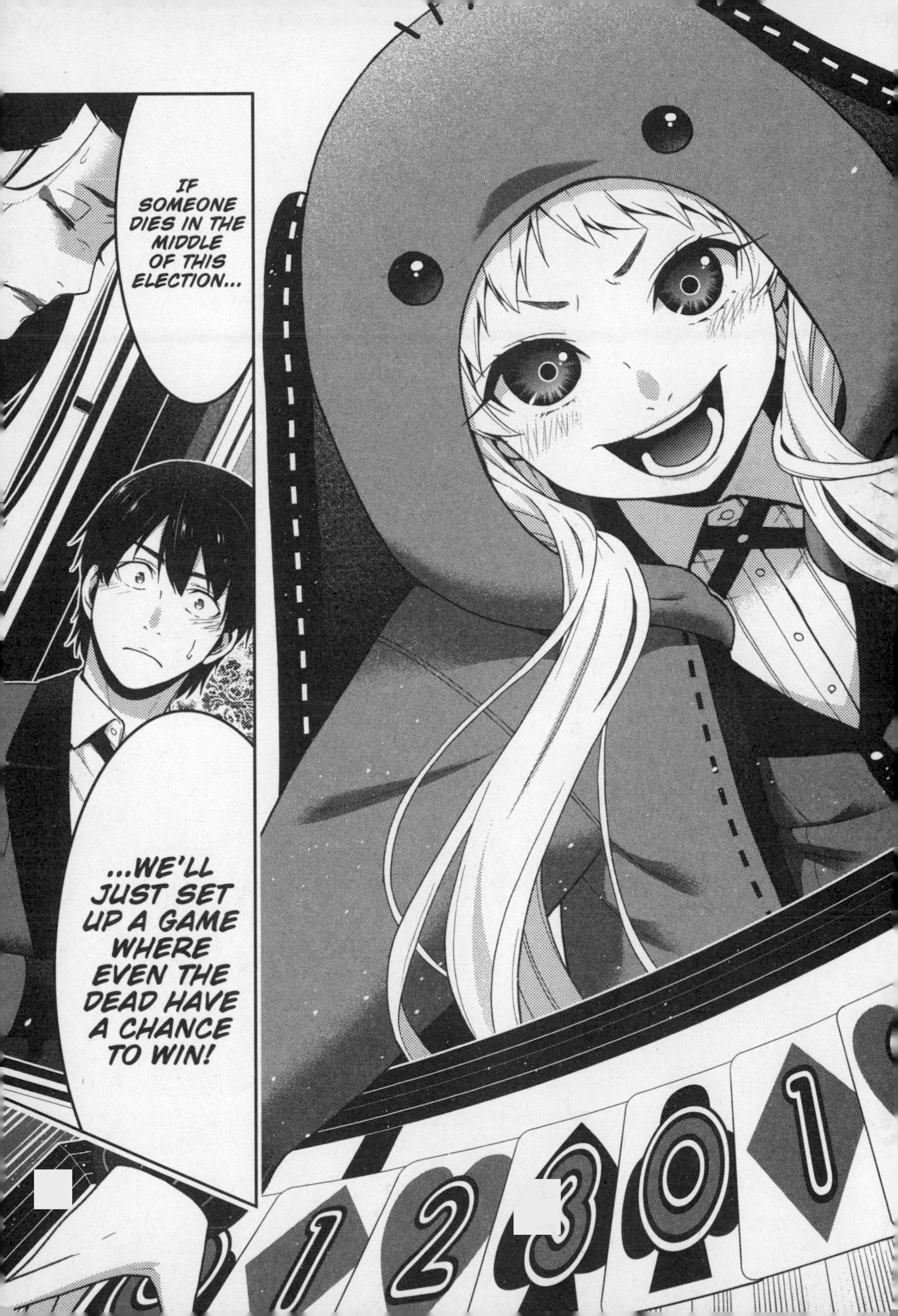
IF SOMEONE DIES IN THE MIDDLE OF THIS ELECTION...
...WE'LL JUST SET UP A GAME WHERE EVEN THE DEAD HAVE A CHANCE TO WIN!

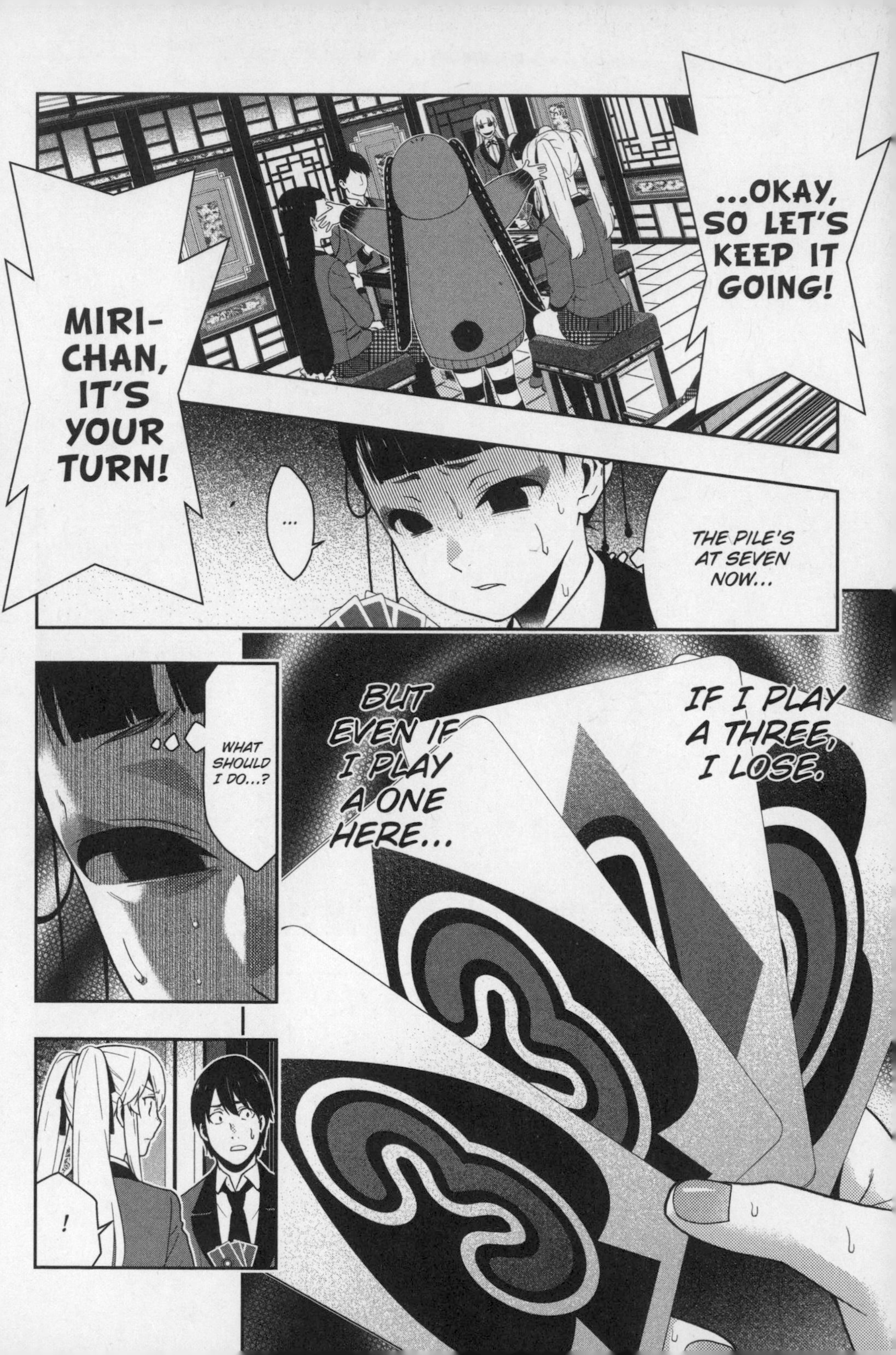
...OKAY, SO LET'S KEEP IT GOING!
MIRI-CHAN, IT'S YOUR TURN!
THE PILE'S AT SEVEN NOW...
...
IF I PLAY A THREE, I LOSE.
BUT EVEN IF I PLAY A ONE HERE...
WHAT SHOULD I DO...?
!

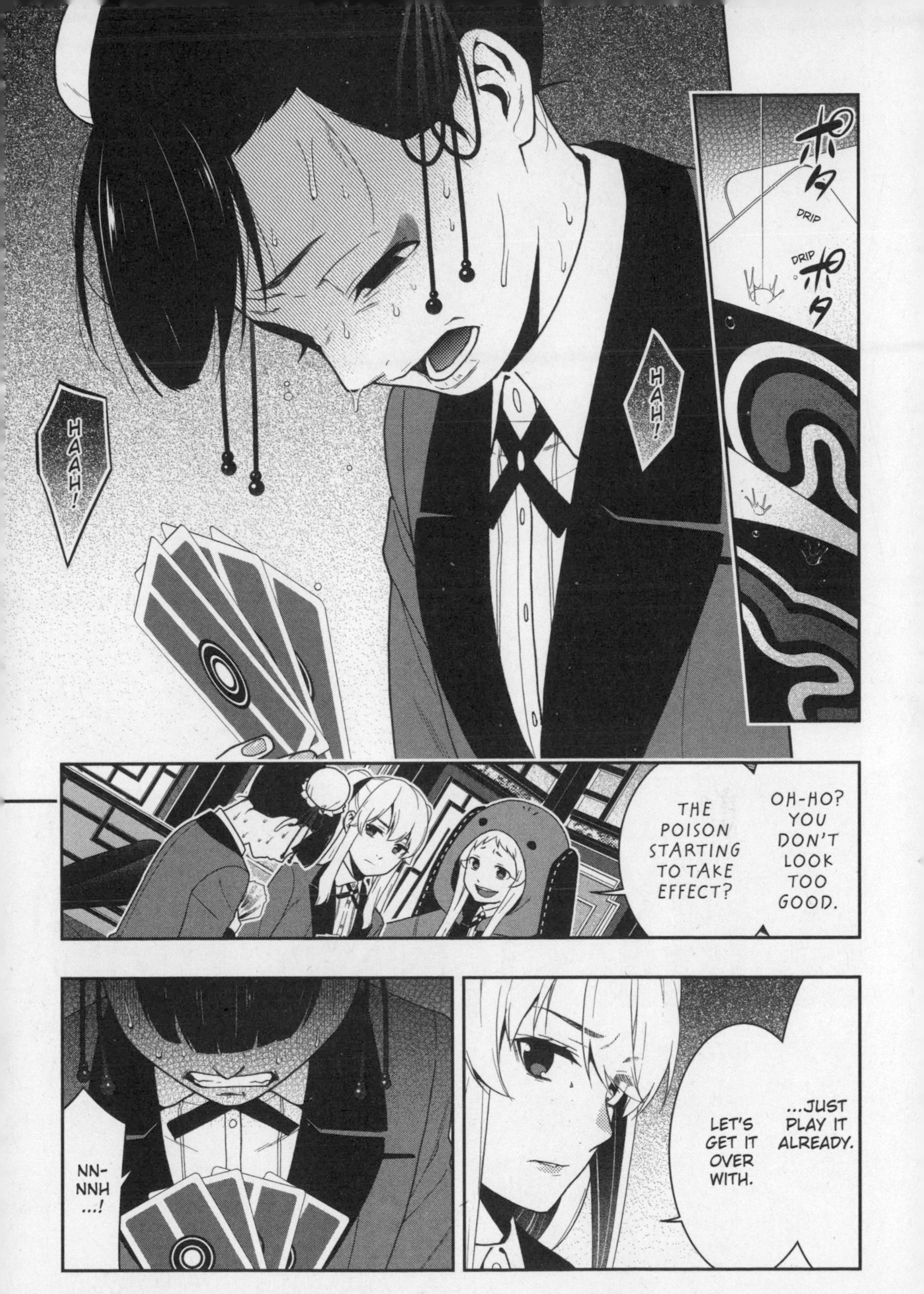
ポタ
DRIP
DRIP
ポタ
HAH!
HAAAH!
OH-HO? YOU DON'T LOOK TOO GOOD.
THE POISON STARTING TO TAKE EFFECT?
...JUST PLAY IT ALREADY.
LET'S GET IT OVER WITH.
NN-NNH ...!

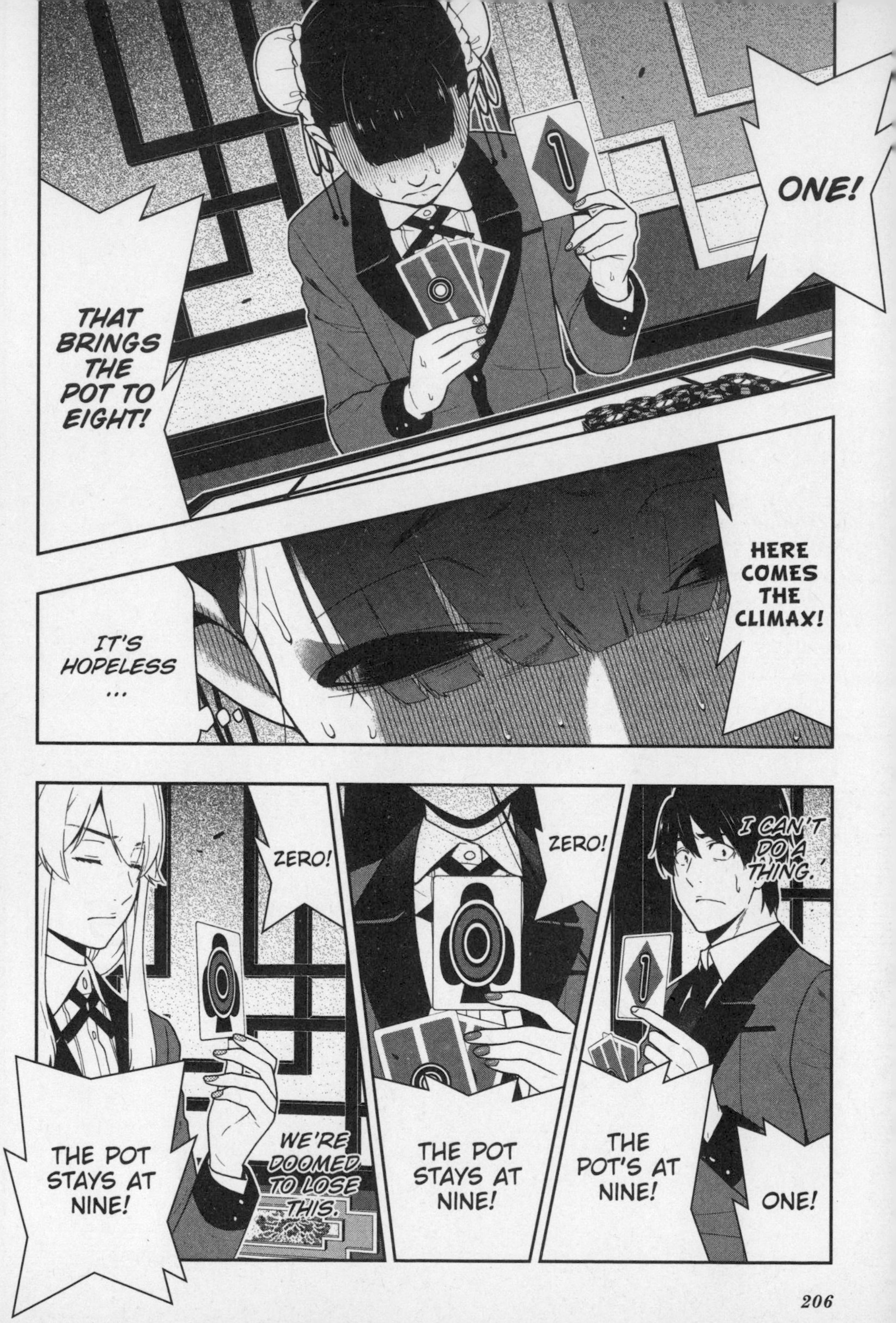
ONE!
THAT BRINGS THE POT TO EIGHT!
HERE COMES THE CLIMAX!
IT'S HOPELESS ...
I CAN'T DO A THING.
ONE!
THE POT'S AT NINE!
ZERO!
THE POT STAYS AT NINE!
ZERO!
WE'RE DOOMED TO LOSE THIS.
THE POT STAYS AT NINE!

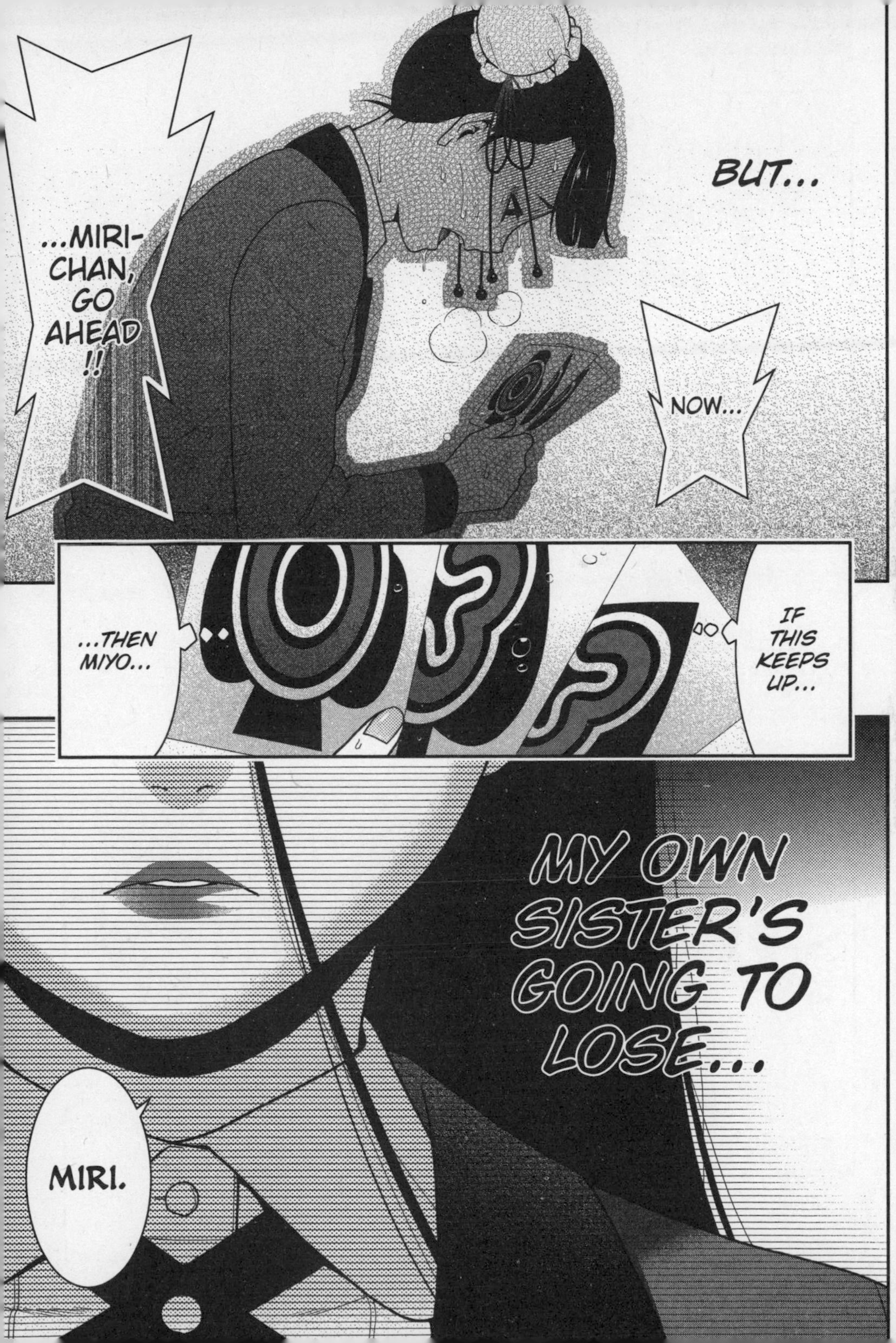
BUT...
NOW...
...MIRI-CHAN, GO AHEAD!!
IF THIS KEEPS UP...
...THEN MIYO...
MY OWN SISTER'S GOING TO LOSE...
MIRI.

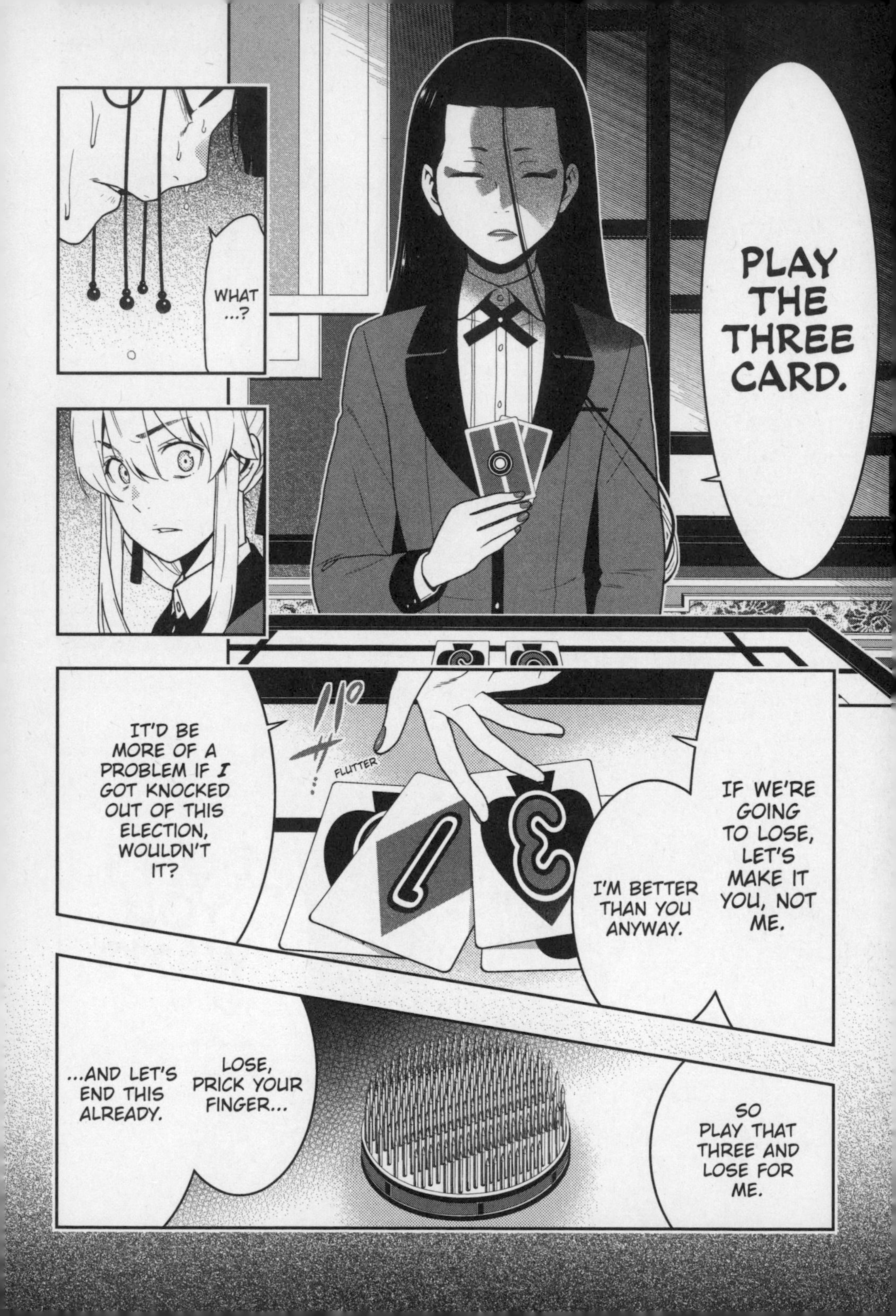
PLAY THE THREE CARD.
WHAT ...?
IF WE'RE GOING TO LOSE, LET'S MAKE IT YOU, NOT ME.
I'M BETTER THAN YOU ANYWAY.
IT'D BE MORE OF A PROBLEM IF *I* GOT KNOCKED OUT OF THIS ELECTION, WOULDN'T IT?
FLUTTER
SO PLAY THAT THREE AND LOSE FOR ME.
LOSE, PRICK YOUR FINGER...
...AND LET'S END THIS ALREADY.

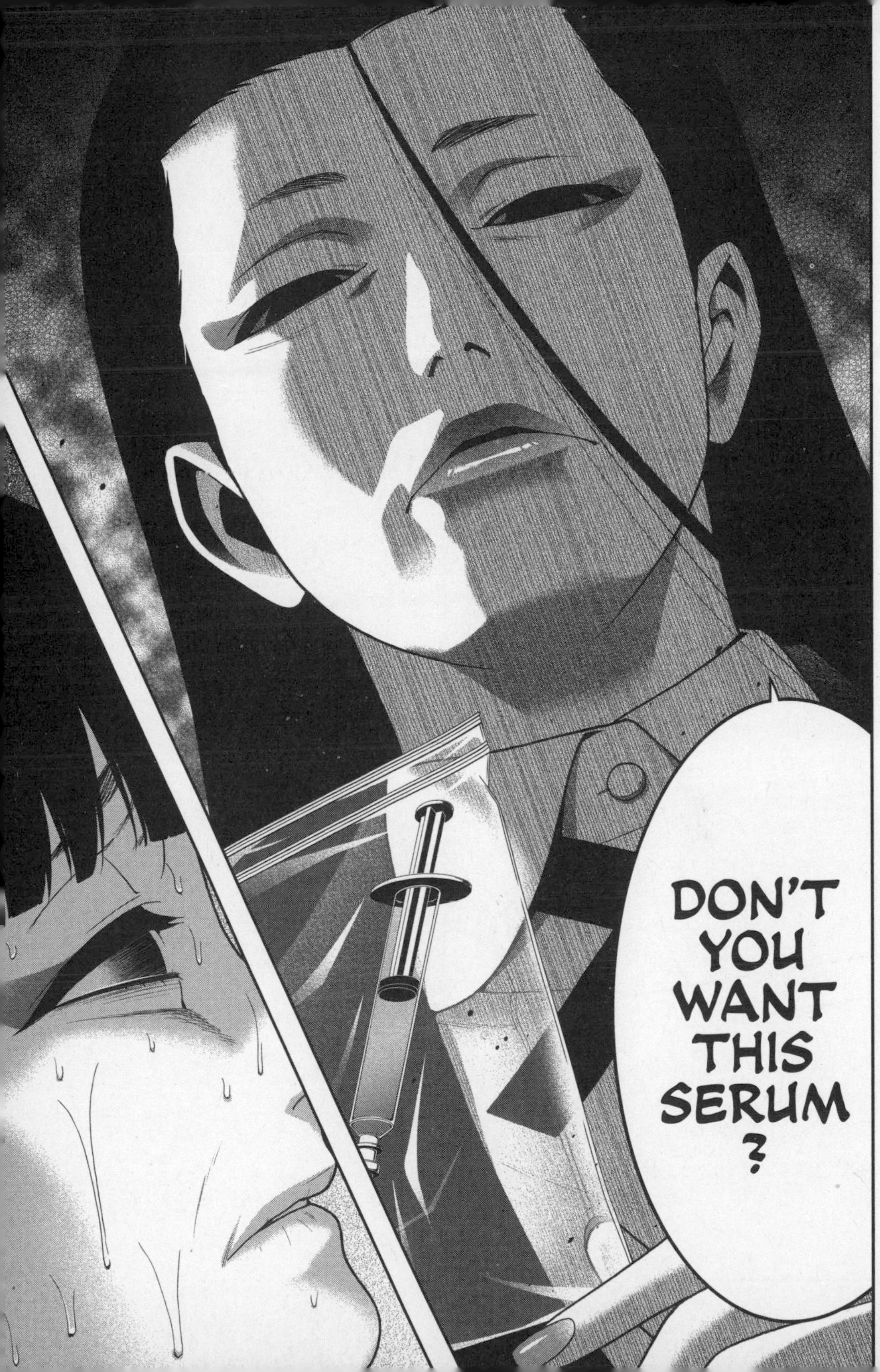
DON'T YOU WANT THIS SERUM?

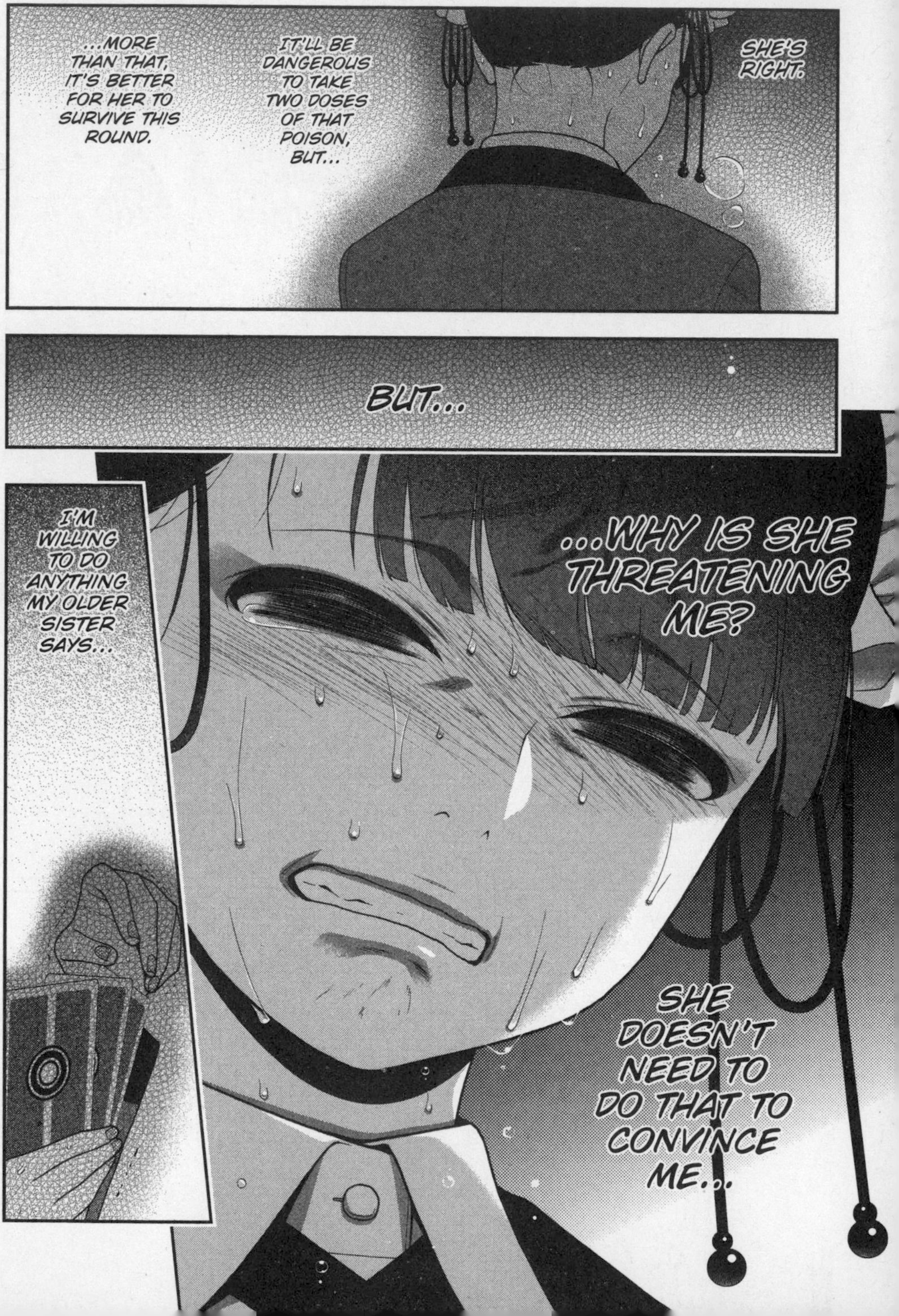
SHE'S RIGHT.
IT'LL BE DANGEROUS TO TAKE TWO DOSES OF THAT POISON, BUT...
...MORE THAN THAT, IT'S BETTER FOR HER TO SURVIVE THIS ROUND.
BUT...
...WHY IS SHE THREATENING ME?
SHE DOESN'T NEED TO DO THAT TO CONVINCE ME...
I'M WILLING TO DO ANYTHING MY OLDER SISTER SAYS...

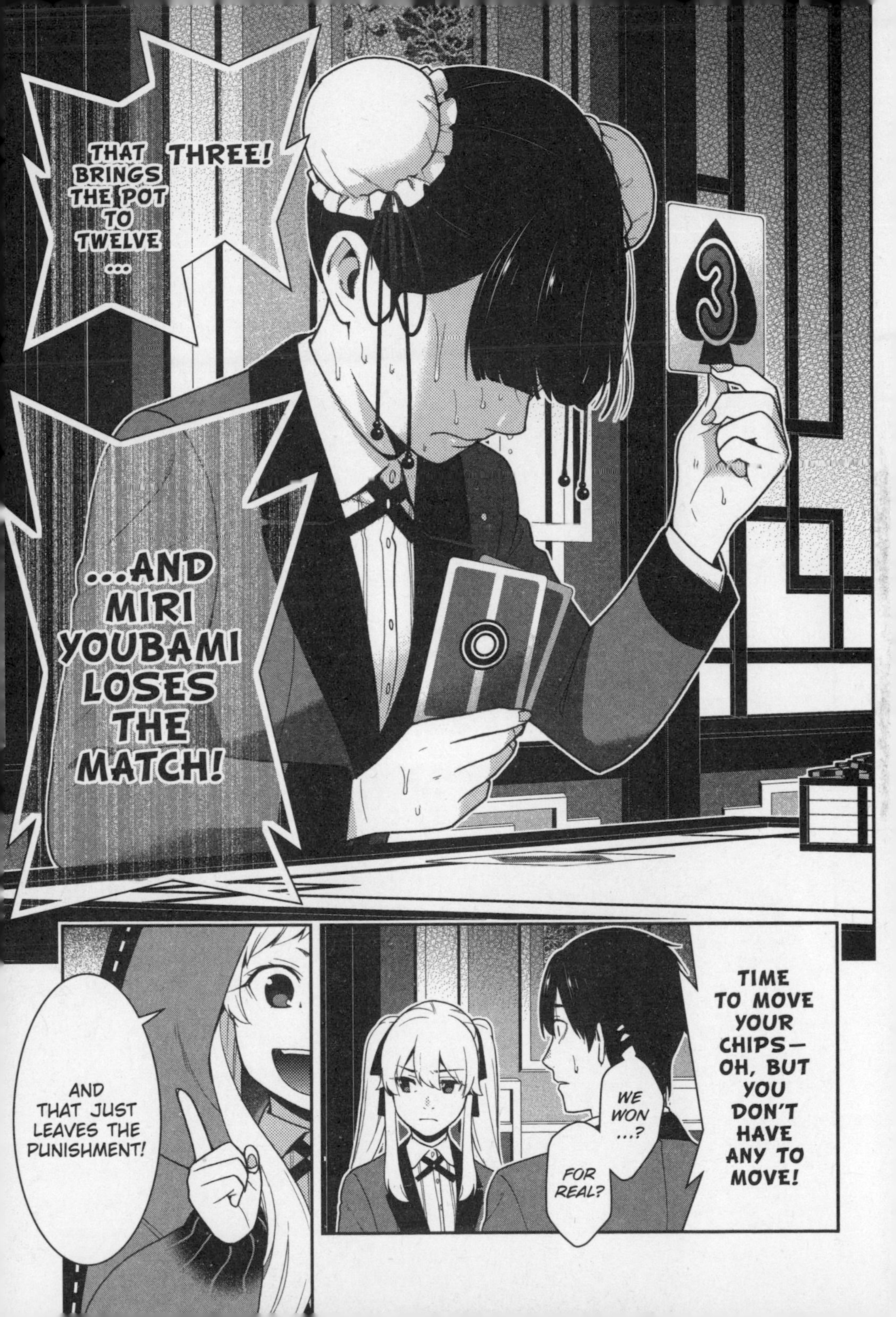
THREE!
THAT BRINGS THE POT TO TWELVE...
...AND MIRI YOUBAMI LOSES THE MATCH!
TIME TO MOVE YOUR CHIPS—OH, BUT YOU DON'T HAVE ANY TO MOVE!
WE WON...?
FOR REAL?
AND THAT JUST LEAVES THE PUNISHMENT!

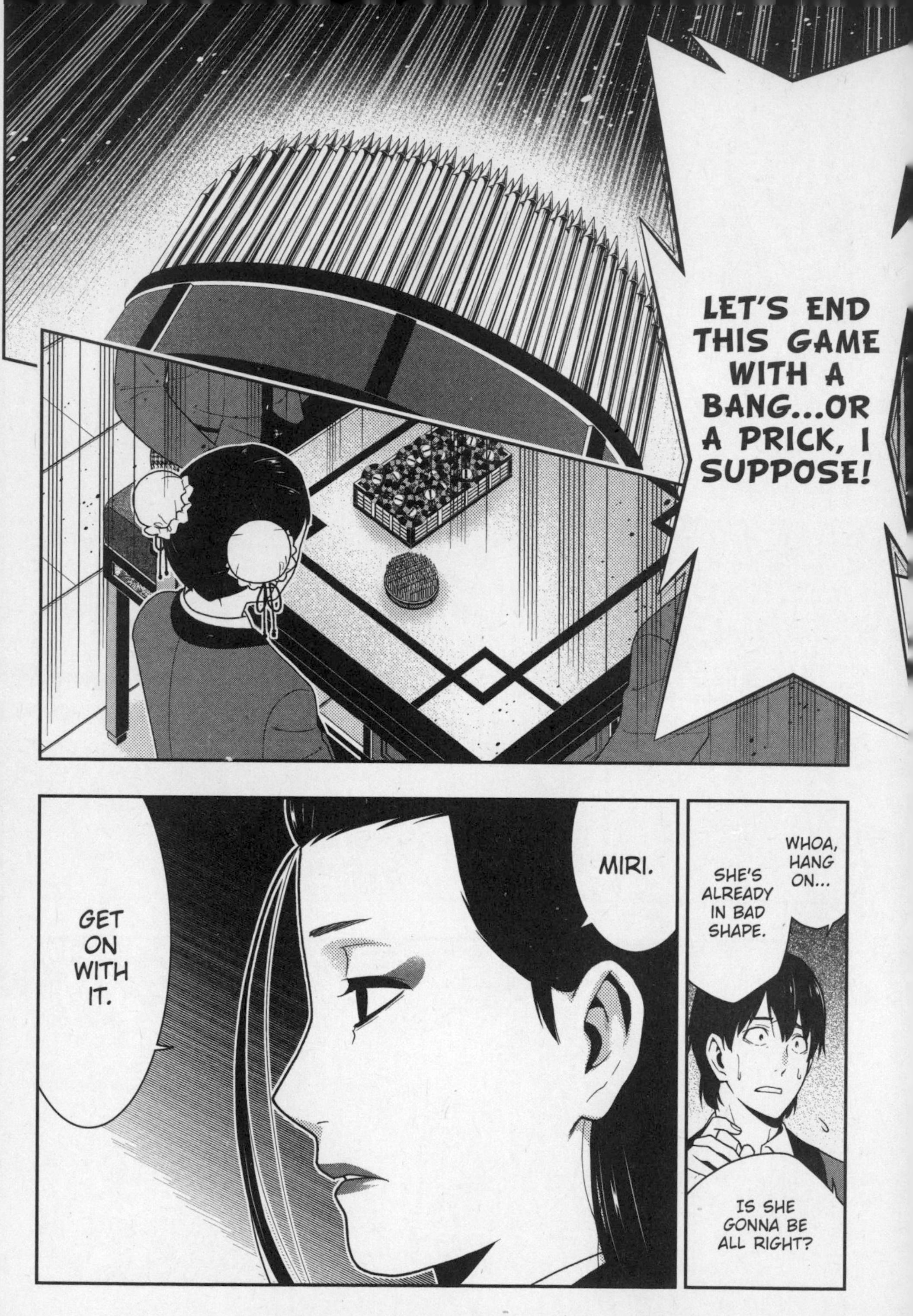
LET'S END THIS GAME WITH A BANG...OR A PRICK, I SUPPOSE!
WHOA, HANG ON...
SHE'S ALREADY IN BAD SHAPE.
IS SHE GONNA BE ALL RIGHT?
MIRI.
GET ON WITH IT.

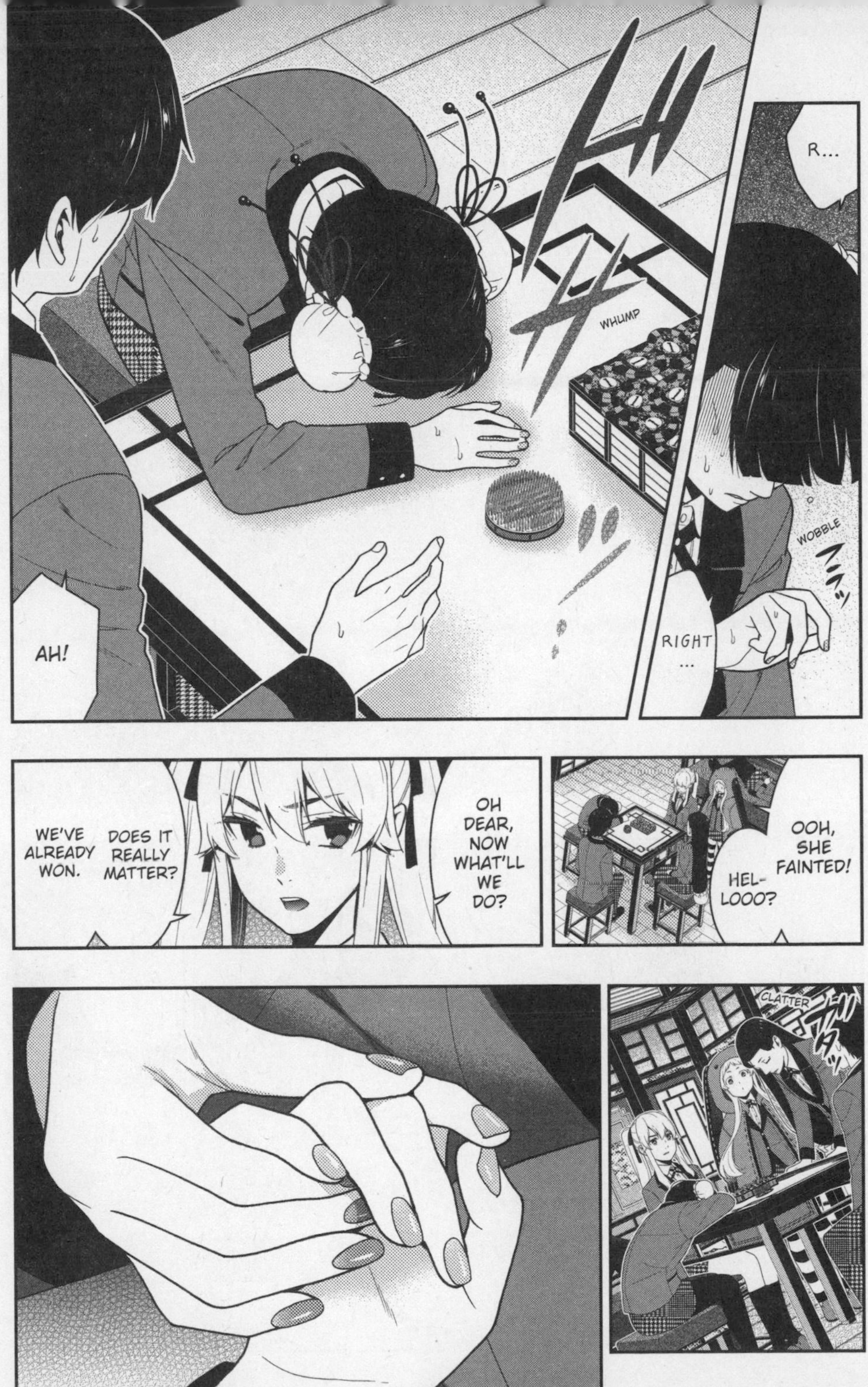
R...
WOBBLE
RIGHT ...
WHUMP
AH!
OOH, SHE FAINTED!
HEL-LOOO?
OH DEAR, NOW WHAT'LL WE DO?
DOES IT REALLY MATTER?
WE'VE ALREADY WON.
CLATTER

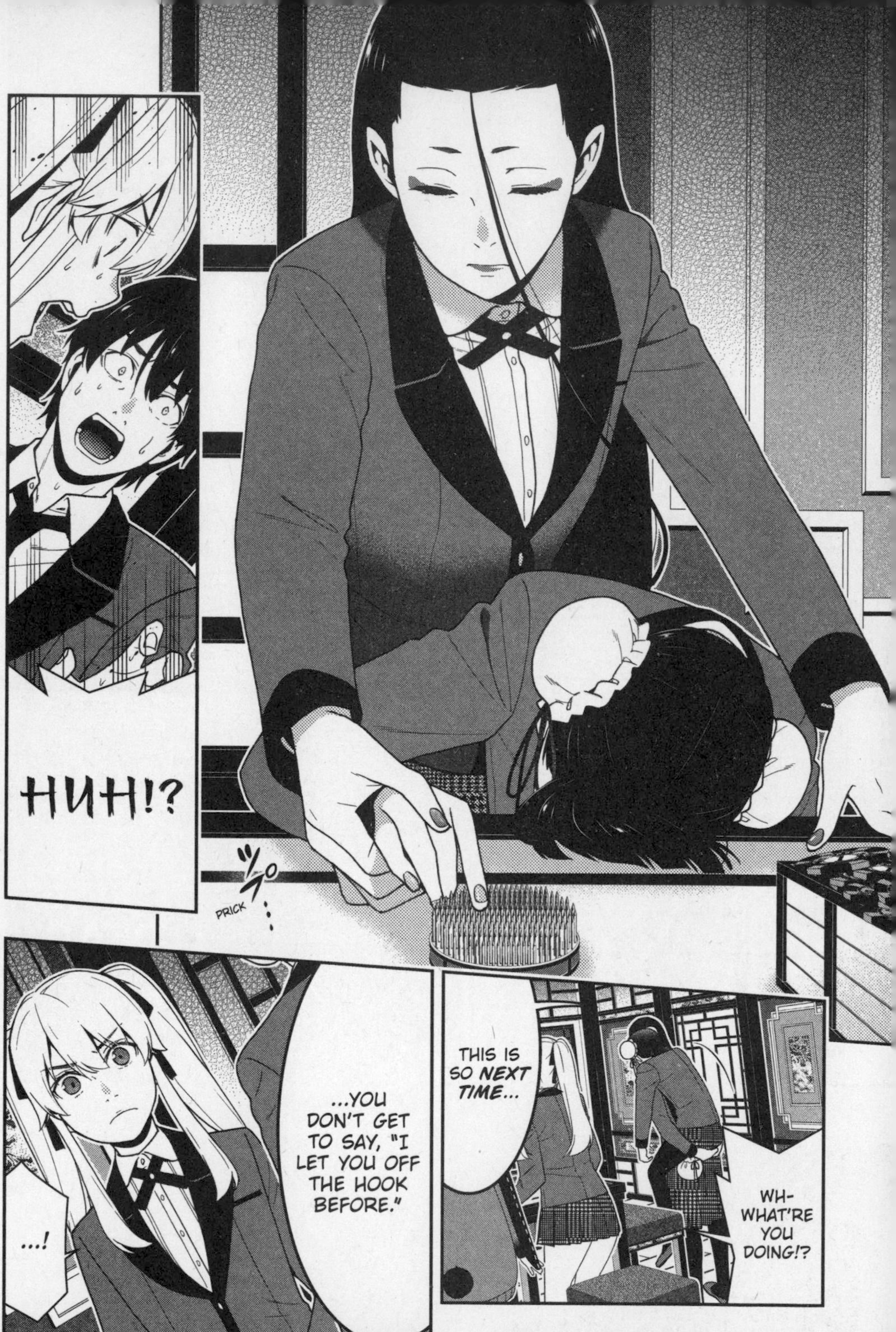
PRICK
HUH!?
THIS IS SO NEXT TIME...
WH-WHAT'RE YOU DOING!?
...YOU DON'T GET TO SAY, "I LET YOU OFF THE HOOK BEFORE."
...!

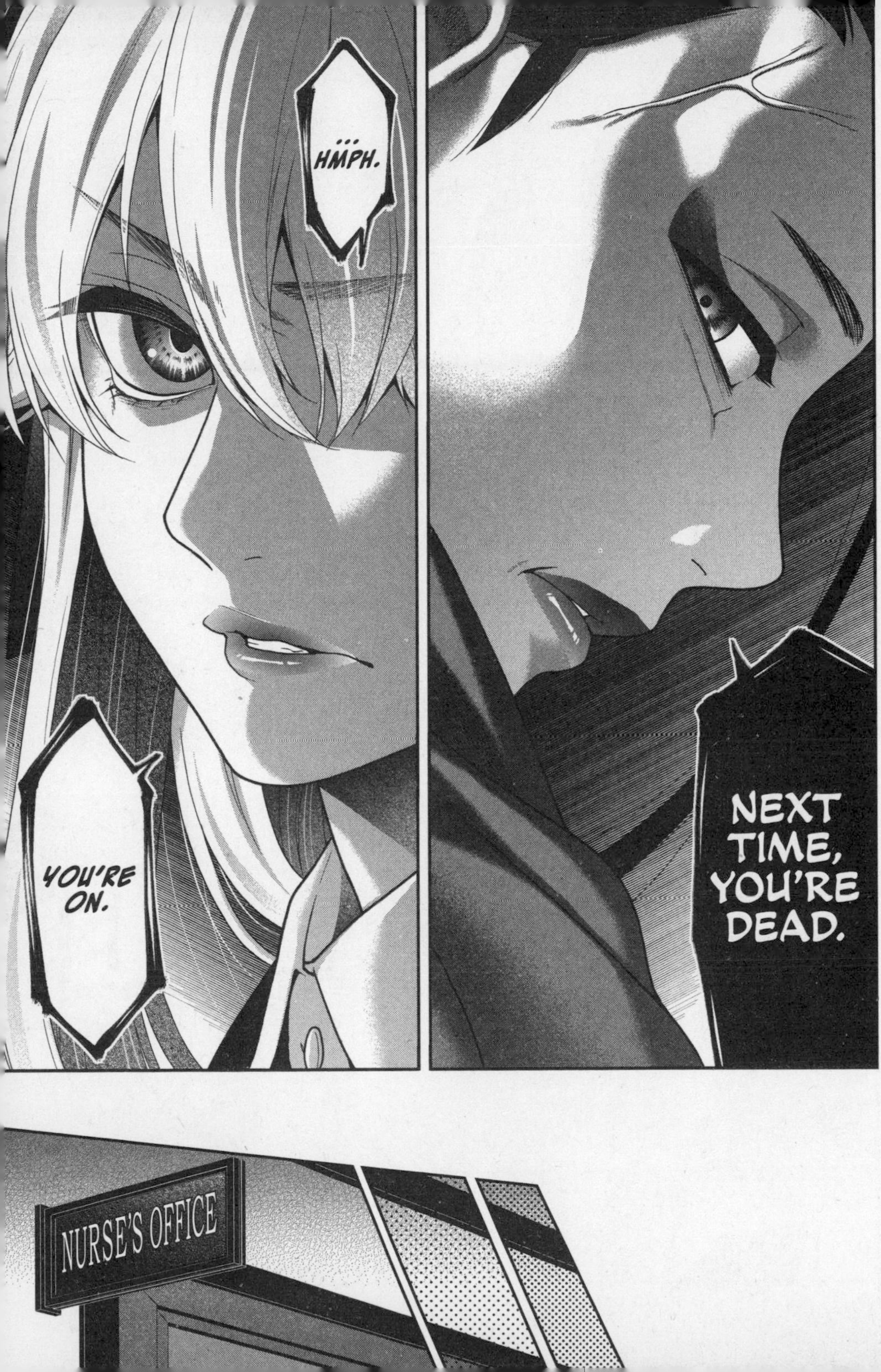
NEXT TIME, YOU'RE DEAD.
...HMPH.
YOU'RE ON.
NURSE'S OFFICE

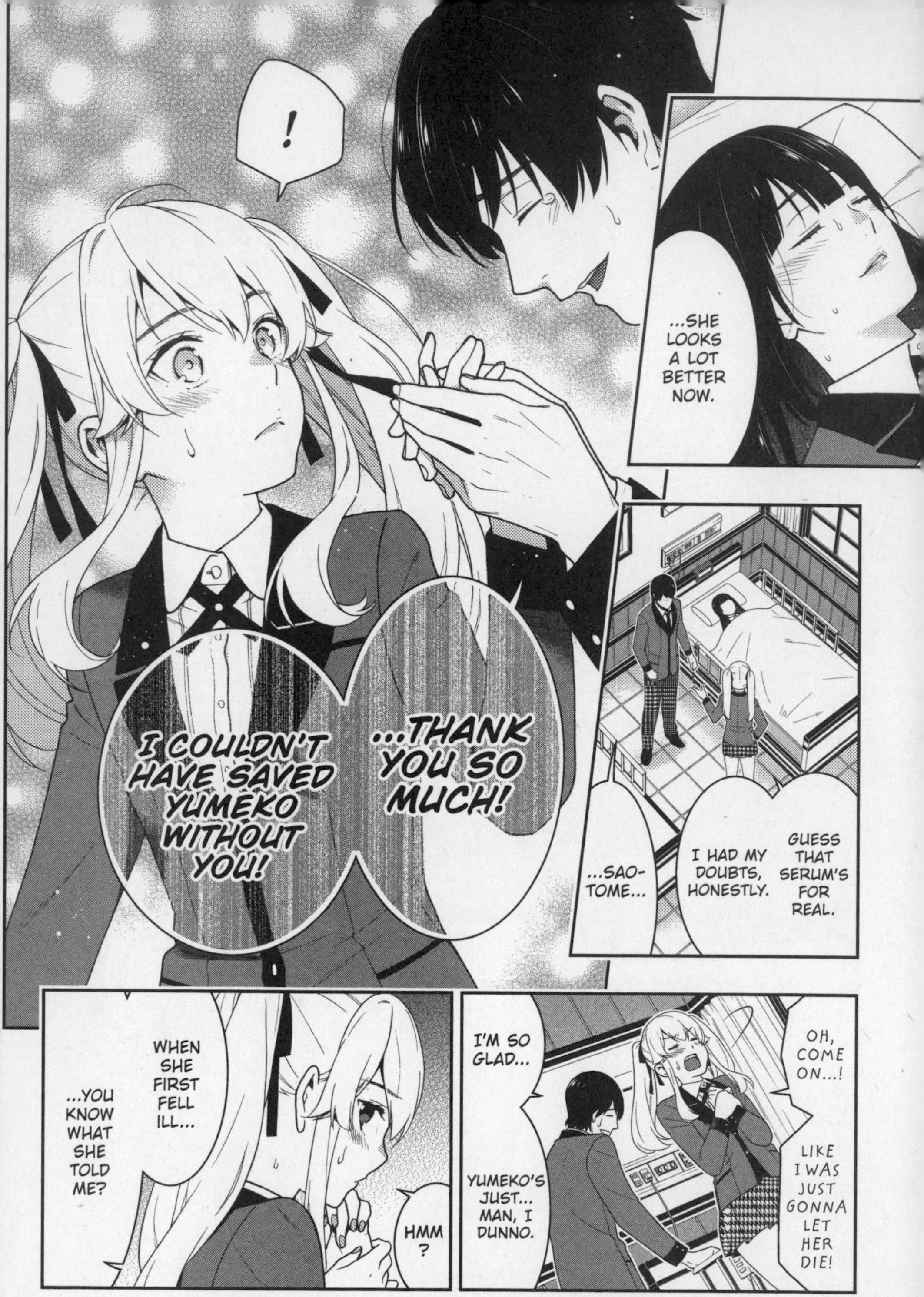
...SHE LOOKS A LOT BETTER NOW.
GUESS THAT SERUM'S FOR REAL.
I HAD MY DOUBTS, HONESTLY.
...SAO-TOME...
!
...THANK YOU SO MUCH!
I COULDN'T HAVE SAVED YUMEKO WITHOUT YOU!
OH, COME ON...!
I'M SO GLAD...
LIKE I WAS JUST GONNA LET HER DIE!
YUMEKO'S JUST... MAN, I DUNNO.
HMM?
WHEN SHE FIRST FELL ILL...
...YOU KNOW WHAT SHE TOLD ME?

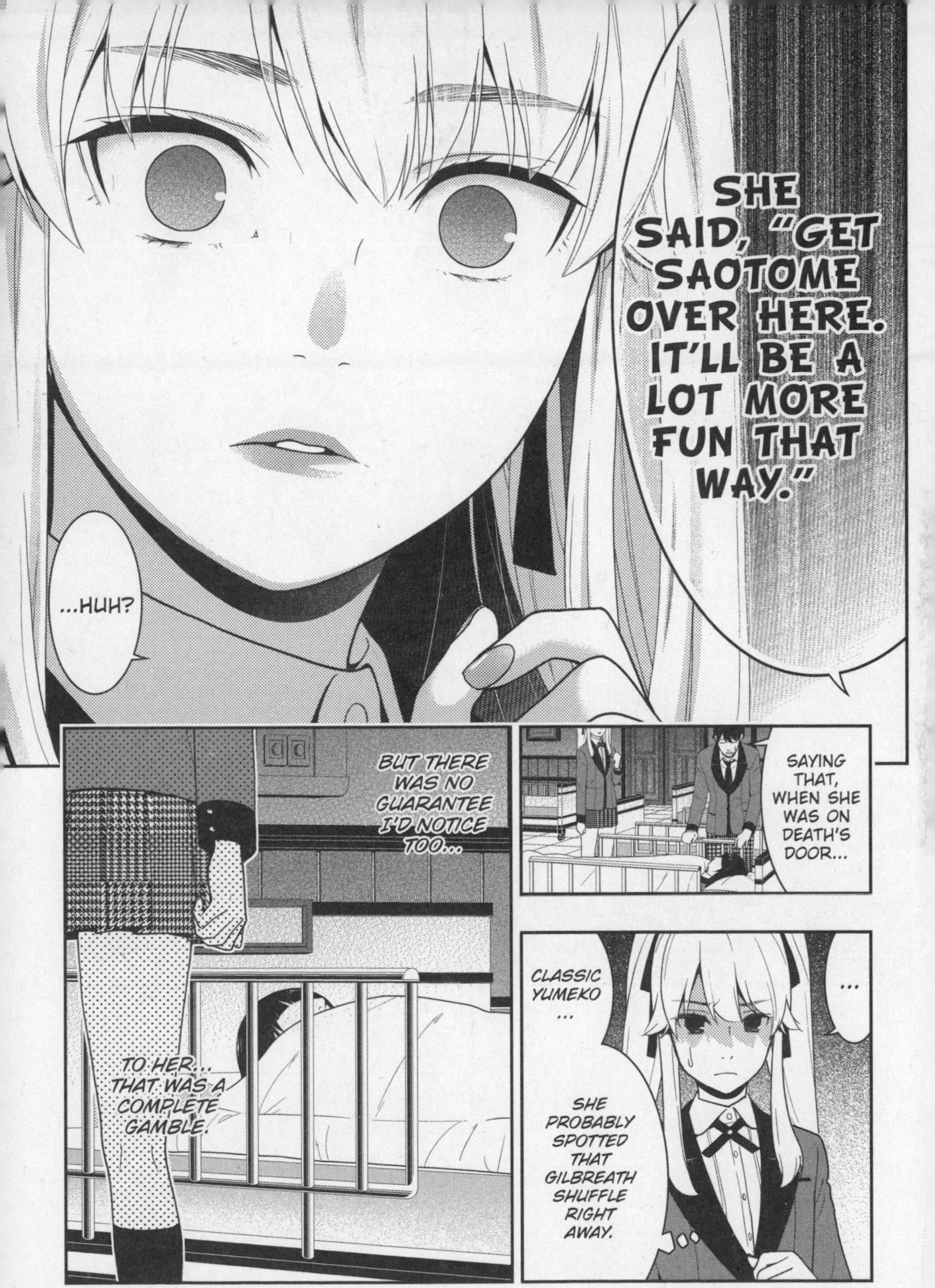
SHE SAID, "GET SAOTOME OVER HERE. IT'LL BE A LOT MORE FUN THAT WAY."
...HUH?
SAYING THAT, WHEN SHE WAS ON DEATH'S DOOR...
...
CLASSIC YUMEKO ...
SHE PROBABLY SPOTTED THAT GILBREATH SHUFFLE RIGHT AWAY.
BUT THERE WAS NO GUARANTEE I'D NOTICE TOO...
TO HER... THAT WAS A COMPLETE GAMBLE.

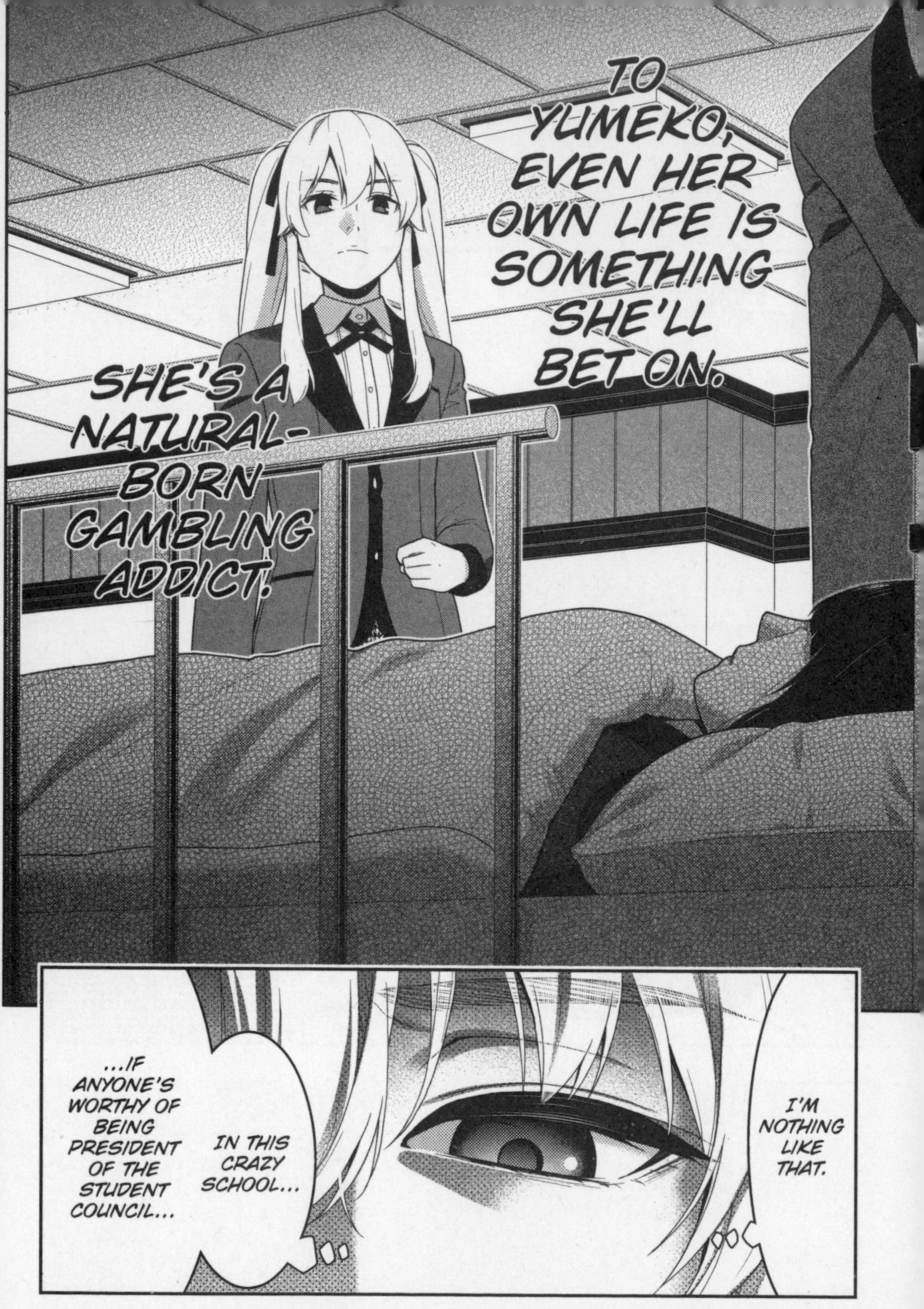
TO YUMEKO, EVEN HER OWN LIFE IS SOMETHING SHE'LL BET ON.
SHE'S A NATURAL-BORN GAMBLING ADDICT.
I'M NOTHING LIKE THAT.
...IF ANYONE'S WORTHY OF BEING PRESIDENT OF THE STUDENT COUNCIL... IN THIS CRAZY SCHOOL...

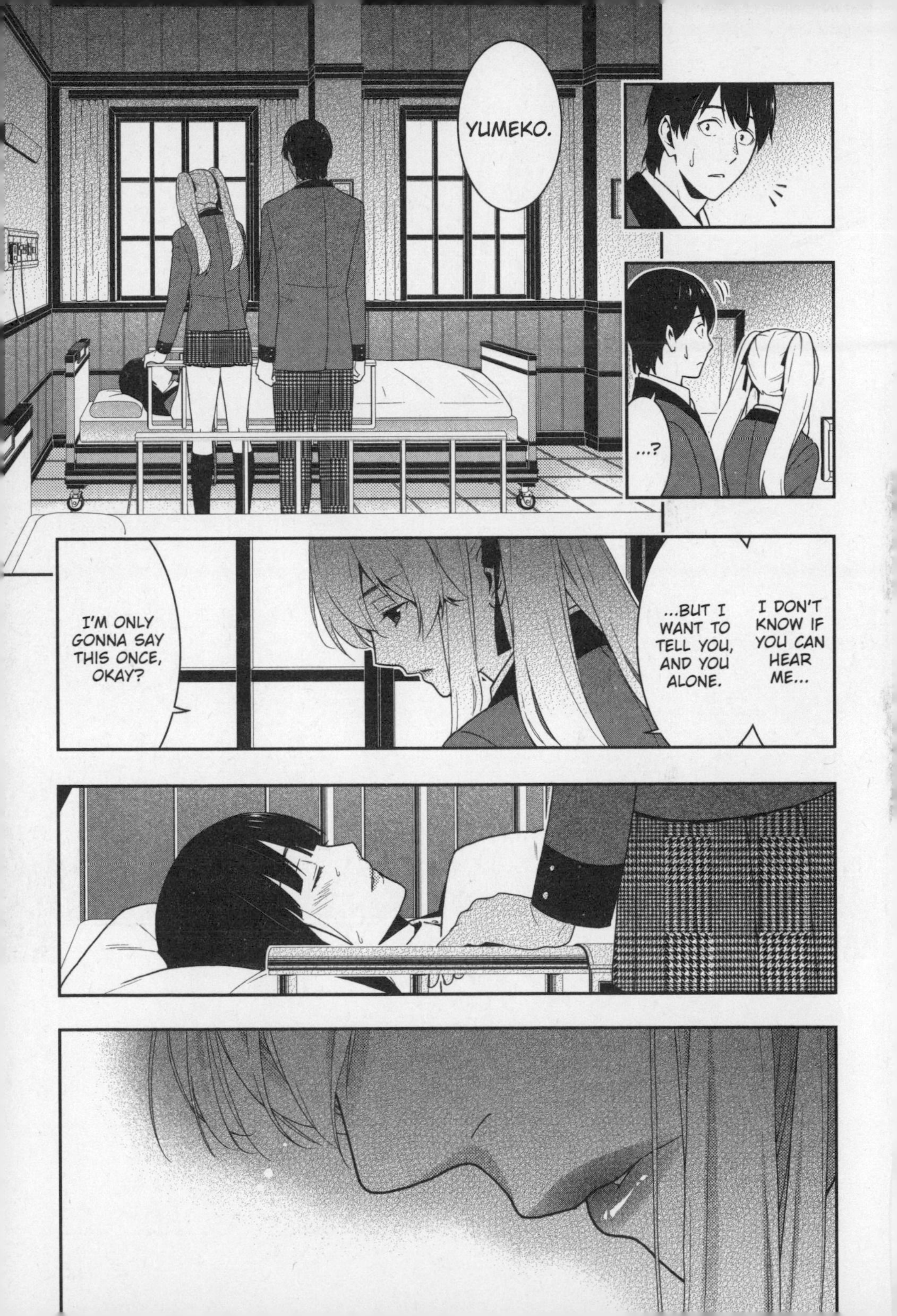
...?
YUMEKO.
I DON'T KNOW IF YOU CAN HEAR ME...
...BUT I WANT TO TELL YOU, AND YOU ALONE.
I'M ONLY GONNA SAY THIS ONCE, OKAY?

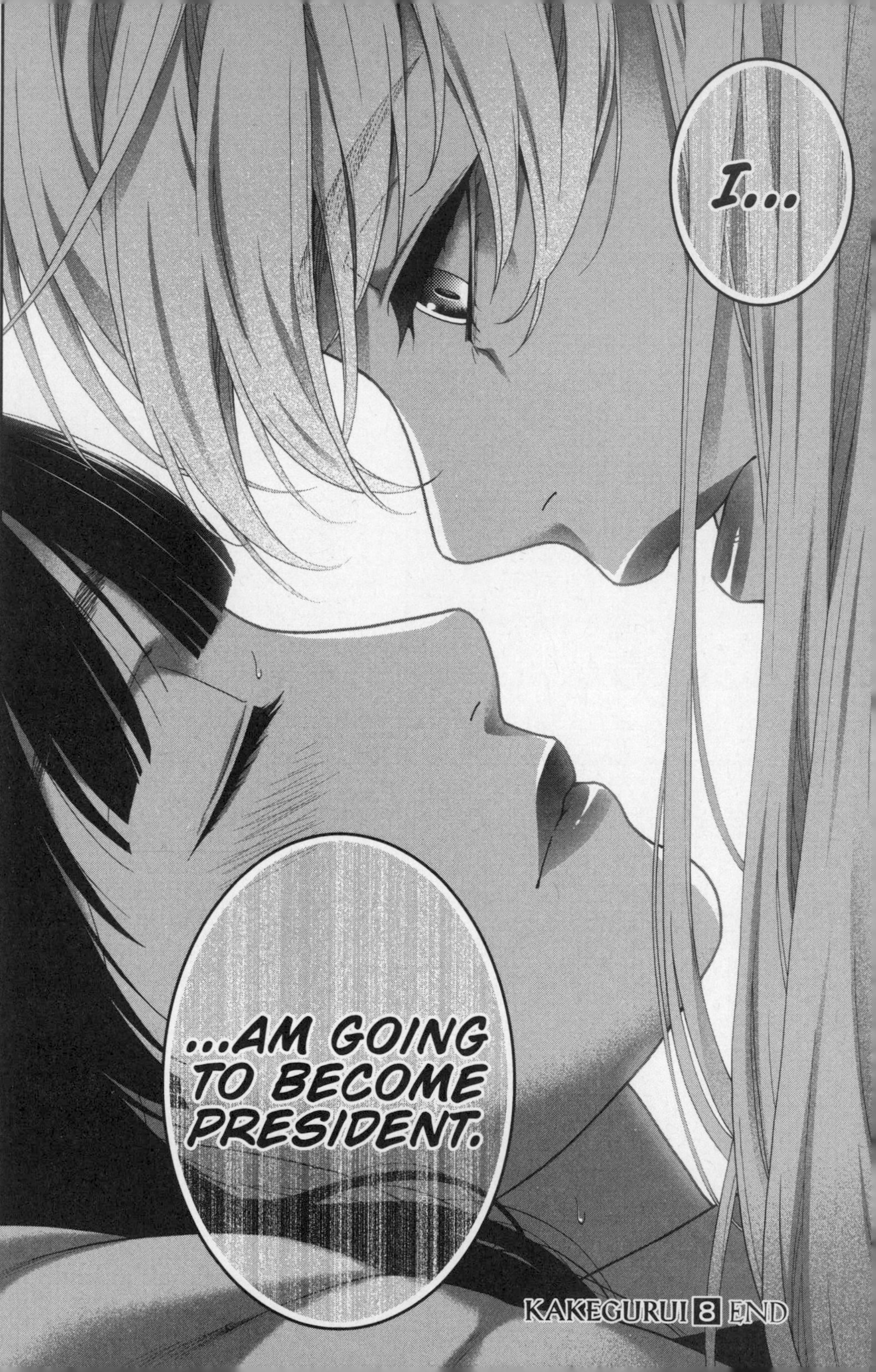
I...
...AM GOING TO BECOME PRESIDENT.
KAKEGURUI 8 END

TIME FOR SOME END-OF-THE-VOLUME BONUS COMICS!

WE REVEAL IT ALL!

ELECTION DOCUMENTARY

※THIS HAS NO RELATION TO THE ACTUAL STORY.

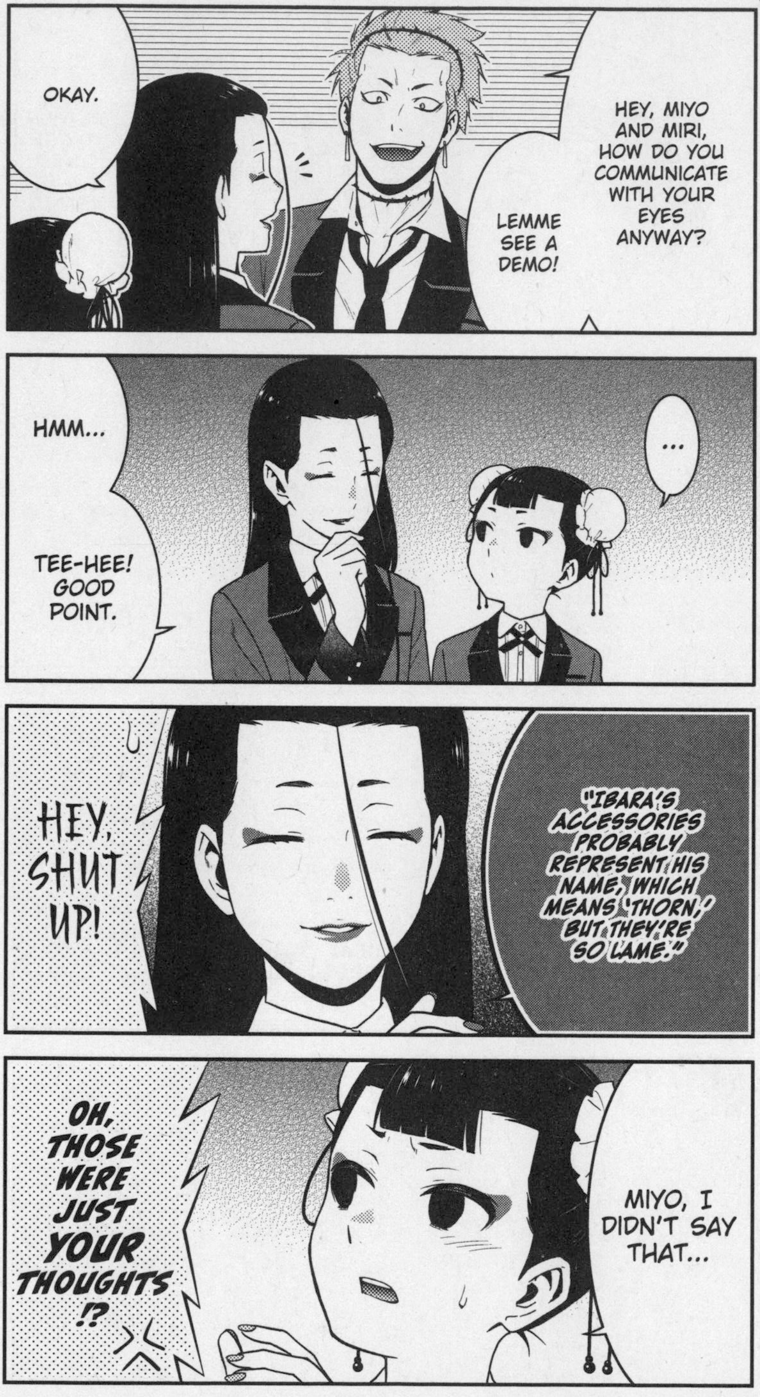
HEY, MIYO AND MIRI, HOW DO YOU COMMUNICATE WITH YOUR EYES ANYWAY?
LEMME SEE A DEMO!
OKAY.
...
HMM...
TEE-HEE! GOOD POINT.
"IBARA'S ACCESSORIES PROBABLY REPRESENT HIS NAME, WHICH MEANS 'THORN,' BUT THEY'RE SO LAME."
HEY, SHUT UP!
MIYO, I DIDN'T SAY THAT...
OH, THOSE WERE JUST YOUR THOUGHTS!?

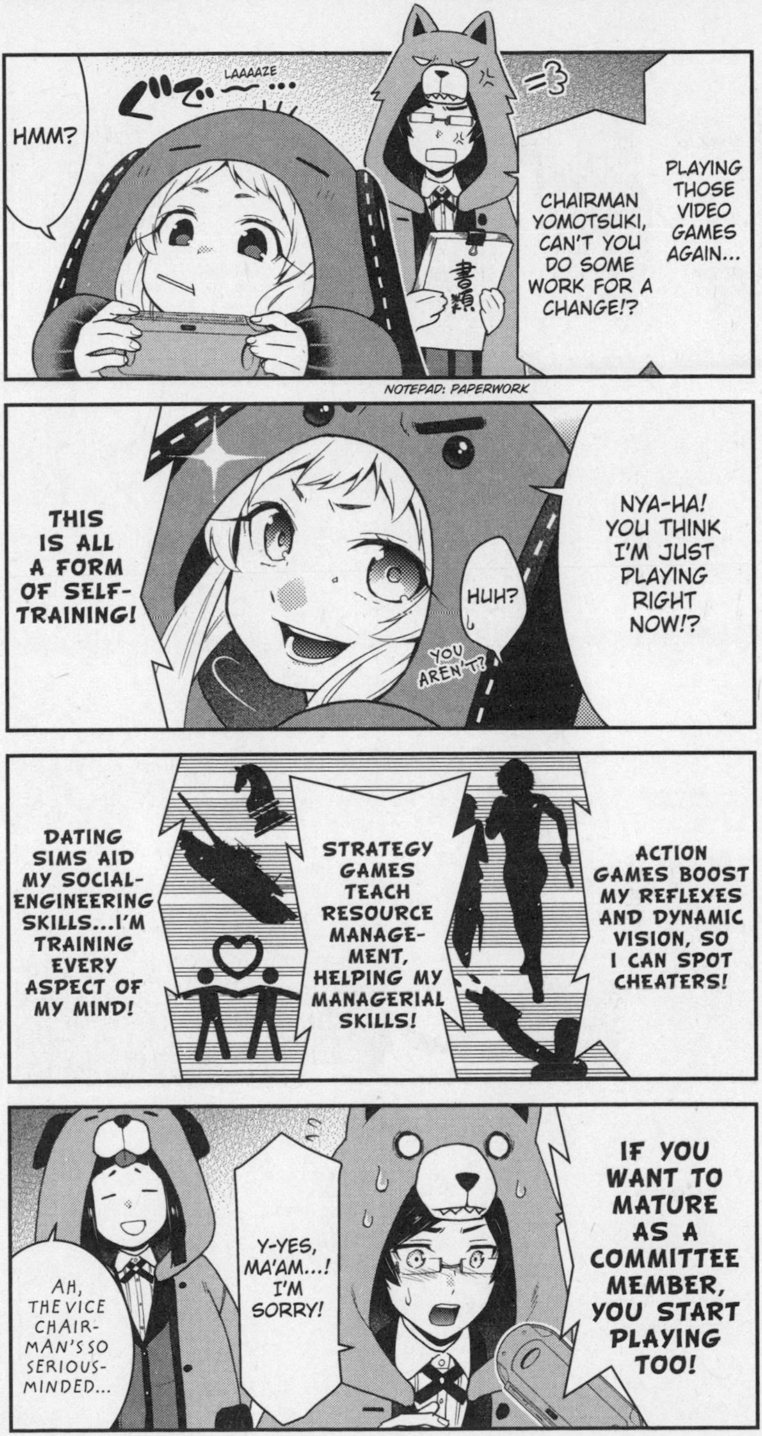
PLAYING THOSE VIDEO GAMES AGAIN...
CHAIRMAN YOMOTSUKI, CAN'T YOU DO SOME WORK FOR A CHANGE!?
書類
ぐでー…
LAAAAZE
HMM?
NOTEPAD: PAPERWORK
NYA-HA! YOU THINK I'M JUST PLAYING RIGHT NOW!?
HUH?
YOU AREN'T?
THIS IS ALL A FORM OF SELF-TRAINING!
ACTION GAMES BOOST MY REFLEXES AND DYNAMIC VISION, SO I CAN SPOT CHEATERS!
STRATEGY GAMES TEACH RESOURCE MANAGEMENT, HELPING MY MANAGERIAL SKILLS!
DATING SIMS AID MY SOCIAL-ENGINEERING SKILLS...I'M TRAINING EVERY ASPECT OF MY MIND!
IF YOU WANT TO MATURE AS A COMMITTEE MEMBER, YOU START PLAYING TOO!
Y-YES, MA'AM...! I'M SORRY!
AH, THE VICE CHAIRMAN'S SO SERIOUS-MINDED...

GAMBLING, THAT IS MY RAISON D'ÊTRE.

This takes the game of Nim, where you can spot the winning strategy pretty readily in normal play, and adds card restrictions and the number zero into the mix, making the results less certain. For ease of understanding, the "out" number was set to ten in the story, but adjusting this number and the amount of cards dealt could allow any number of players to join in. I wouldn't bet real money on it, though, to say nothing of my own life.

Nim Type Zero

Gilbreath Shuffle

Runa's choice of shuffling in the story is called the Gilbreath shuffle, named after its inventor, Norman L. Gilbreath. This technique is unique in its approach to riffling, or mixing two piles of cards together. To an amateur, riffling looks like it randomly mixes up the cards—but perform it as described in this manga, and anybody can pull off this type of trick. Try it out with a deck of your own cards; I bet you'll be surprised.

Thank you for picking up Volume 8 of *Kakegurui*. The story this time revolves around the idea of having someone in Hyakkaou Academy, this world where gambling decides everything, try to attain a goal through something very far removed from gambling. I hope you liked it. The relationships among people in and out of the school are growing more complex—how will the election turn out? I'm looking forward to it too. Sorry I can't say more. Naomura-sensei and his assistants are churning out art that keeps improving beyond all limits for each chapter while also pointing out the flaws in my story details. My editors, Sasaki-sama and Yumoto-sama, stick with me as I have continual trouble sticking to a schedule. T-kun provided some medical advice for this one. Also, you too, Tanaka. Oh, and my readers too. Thanks to all of them and many others, Volume 8 is finally here. Thank you all so much! P.S. This volume comes out in Japan on the same day as *Kakegurui Trip*, a novel written by my younger brother! He wrote it before my eyes, really, and I've checked up on it throughout, so I suppose you could say I've supervised the entire project. Make sure to check that out too!

Homura Kawamoto

STORY: **Homura Kawamoto**
ART: **Toru Naomura**

Translation: Kevin Gifford
Lettering: Anthony Quintessenza

KAKEGURUI Vol. 8 ©2017 Homura Kawamoto, Toru Naomura/SQUARE ENIX CO., LTD. First published in Japan in 2017 by SQUARE ENIX CO., LTD. English translation rights arranged with SQUARE ENIX CO., LTD. and Yen Press, LLC through Tuttle-Mori Agency, Inc.

English translation ©2019 by SQUARE ENIX CO., LTD.

Yen Press
1290 Avenue of the Americas
New York, NY 10104

Visit us at yenpress.com
facebook.com/yenpress
twitter.com/yenpress
yenpress.tumblr.com
instagram.com/yenpress

First Yen Press Edition: January 2019
The chapters in this volume were originally published as ebooks by Yen Press.

Yen Press is an imprint of Yen Press, LLC.
The Yen Press name and logo are trademarks of Yen Press, LLC.

The publisher is not responsible for websites (or their content) that are not owned by the publisher.

Library of Congress Control Number: 2017939211

ISBNs: 978-1-9753-0262-7 (paperback)
         978-1-9753-0263-4 (ebook)

10 9 8 7 6 5 4 3 2 1

WOR

Printed in the United States of America

Afterword

Thank you for picking up Volume 8 of *Kakegurui*.

Miyo and Miri are such a nice pair of sisters...I can hardly withstand their charms.
Miri-chan in particular, who acts so cool and prim but just loves her big sister deep down...
I sincerely hope she'll appear again. I also love Ririka-chan, the vice president, a scary amount.
That kind of nervously obedient type is just the best. I wish Mary could've knocked
her down on the sofa at the end of Chapter 40.

And don't forget the anime version! I may be a tad biased, but this is turning
into something really fascinating! Please take a look! It's just...totally awesome!!,
(Sorry for my lack of vocabulary skills...^_^;)

Here's hoping you enjoy both the anime and the next volume of *Kakegurui*.

SPECIAL THANKS:
My editors / Kawamoto-sama / Imoutoko / Hα-sama / AO-sama
Toru Naomura (artist), August 2017